The Siberian Intervention

The
Siberian Intervention

By John Albert White

GREENWOOD PRESS, PUBLISHERS
NEW YORK

TO
DOROTHEA WHITE

Preface

IN the Soviet Far East October 25, 1947 was observed as a day of historical importance. The Moscow organ *Izvestiia* took note of the developments there since the arrival on the Amur River three hundred years before of the adventurer, Erofei Khabarov, who gave his name to one of the two most important cities and territorial divisions of the area. In the course of the intervening centuries and particularly since the rise of the Soviet regime, the article continued, the cultural, industrial, and agricultural progress of the Khabarovsk and Maritime regions has taken place at an increasingly accelerated rate. The writer emphasized especially the achievements of the period of the Second World War and the current Five Year Plan. It was with this optimistic note that the Soviet Government marked the twenty-fifth anniversary of the departure, after more than four years of military occupation, of the Japanese troops from Vladivostok and therewith the end of the intervention.

For many months after the revolution of November 1917, foreign intervention in Siberia was considered an imminent danger. Then in the spring of 1918 it became a reality and for nearly two years the representatives of a number of Allied nations participated in a military intervention. By early April 1920, all but the Japanese troops had been withdrawn and for the next two and a half years Soviet Russia and Japan were the principals in a duel for possession of the Far Eastern areas of the former Russian Empire. Finally, in October 1922, with the departure of the Japanese, the Soviet Government entered for the first time into full possession of the Russian Pacific coast. Not until May 1925, however, did Japan relinquish to the Soviets the northern half of Sakhalin Island.

It is this struggle for the Russian Far East, especially the phase which preceded the departure of all but the Japanese interventionist forces in the spring of 1920, which forms the theme and subject matter of this book. The theme was selected as an introductory study of the Soviet Union in the Far East for a number of reasons. The most obvious of these is of course the fact that the struggle is the period of transition from the Imperial to the Soviet regime and therefore forms chronologically a natural introduction to the general subject. In addition, this transitional period exemplifies to an unusual degree the significance of the Russian Far East in the international and especially the Far Eastern arena of power politics. Finally, the importance of the intervention period, so well illustrated by the recent observance of the anniversary of its termination, is such that it has left its mark on the subsequent history of the relationships both of the Soviet Union and of other powers having East Asiatic or Pacific possessions and interests.

The significance of this period of Soviet Far Eastern history was first pointed out to me by Dr. Harold Fisher of Stanford University and the Hoover Library. Dr. Fisher had for many years directed the work of a number of competent scholars in a study of the revolution, civil war, and intervention in Russia. He was, therefore, not only aware of the tremendous significance of these events but, during the years of studying them, had made the Hoover Library a repository for a unique collection of personal correspondence, manuscript memoires and specialized accounts, periodicals, newspapers, and books dealing with the subject. Many of these materials will be found in the bibliography appended to the documentary collection, *The Testimony of Kolchak and Other Siberian Materials,* translated and edited by Elena Varneck and Harold H. Fisher. Others appear in the bibliography of the present book. Among the manuscript materials at Hoover Library I found the picture which appears facing page 1 and which is one of the finest available views of Admiral Kolchak and General Horvath, two of the anti-Bolshevik leaders in Siberia. It is used here by the kind permission of Dr. Fisher.

It has been my aim in carrying out this study to make a contribution to the scholarly and objective investigation of a period and an area which has heretofore either been totally neglected or described either in purely partisan or specialized

PREFACE

accounts. As in the case of any period of revolution or civil war, important issues were at stake and, as a result, personal and group conflicts were bitter, suffering was great, and emotional stresses were sharp and prolonged. These facts have colored both the contemporary and subsequent literature on the subject and have left controversies over some of the events of the struggle so bitter that almost any definite statement will seem biased to the participants and their sympathizers. It is too much, therefore, to expect that the facts as stated here will meet with anything like universal approval. Nevertheless, the importance of the Soviet Union in contemporary international life makes it imperative to obtain all possible light upon this formative period of its development.

I wish to express here a much deserved word of appreciation to all those who have helped me in important ways. Miss Nina Almond, Mr. Philip McLean, Mrs. Ruth Perry, Mrs. Jirina Frisbie, Mr. Dimitry Krassovsky, Dr. Fritz Epstein, and Mr. Kihei Matsuo have made the task of using a large and highly specialized library collection a pleasant and relatively simple undertaking. Dr. Anatole Mazour, Mrs. Xenia Eudin, Mr. Dimitry Krassovsky, and Mr. N. I. Rokitiansky have made many important suggestions which, though difficult to acknowledge fully, have been invaluable in writing this account. In addition, the materials which Mrs. Xenia Eudin and Mrs. Elena Varneck have for a number of years been engaged in selecting and translating at the Hoover Library have been of special value to me. Finally, the cartography is the work of Mrs. Dorothea White.

The opportunity to carry on this study uninterruptedly for many months was made possible by a grant from the Rockefeller Foundation. I wish to express here my deepest appreciation to the directors of this Foundation for their generous and farseeing policy.

J. A. W.

Honolulu, T. H.
December 1948

Contents

A GROUP OF PROMINENT RUSSIANS AT HARBIN, APRIL 1918.

Seated, second from left, Admiral Aleksander Vasilevich Kolchak; seated, third from left, General Dmitrii Leonidovich Horvath.

CHAPTER 1

Defeat and Civil War in Russia

IN 1914 the leaders of the Russian Empire had reason to be acutely aware of the fact that their country lay between Germany and Japan. These two nations had in the course of the late nineteenth century risen to the position of world powers with the result that Russia not only was thereby limited in her expansive possibilities but, in addition, was confronted with the threat and danger of a war on two widely separated fronts. Thus, in spite of the fact that she had grown to national stature in the West and that her capital city as well as the major portion of her population and wealth were concentrated there, Russia was both a European and an Asiatic power, sharing with these areas both local and international problems. Russia had, moreover, participated to the limit of her capacity in the imperialistic struggle which was waged during the nineteenth and early twentieth centuries in both the East and the West. Furthermore, both Germany and Japan, although officially members of opposing alliances, remained essentially rivals to Russian ambitions in their respective sectors of the Eurasian continent. The First World War was thus only the military phase of an actual or potential struggle which had long been in progress and which the legalities of the alliance systems were powerless to alter. In the long run these prewar agreements were found valid only insofar as they conformed to existing local requirements or served to clothe with formal consent the real or acquired ambitions of the members of the alliance systems.

It was in this historical and geographical perspective that the Russian Revolution of 1917 and the political and military collapse which went hand in hand with it created for the time being a vast power vacuum reaching from the Baltic

1

Sea to the Pacific Ocean. The Eastern Front ceased to support the Allies or to oppose the Central Powers. In view of their obligations to the Allied nations and the formidable and imminent threat of the Central Powers, there were two courses of action open to the Russian leaders. The first, a revival of the fighting strength of the Russian army and a reconstitution of the Eastern Front, was tried without any success by the Provisional Government, which assumed the nominal headship of the Russian state in March 1917. The second choice, a separate peace with Germany, was made by the Soviet Government which assumed power in November 1917 under increasingly strong Bolshevik leadership and control. In doing this, the Bolshevik leaders assumed that a peace agreement with Germany would be only temporary and would in time be more than counterbalanced by the conspiratorial activities of the Bolsheviks in Germany, where all efforts were directed toward the complete undermining of the Imperial Government and the achievement of a workers' government sympathetic to Russia and therefore willing to annul the Treaty of Brest-Litovsk and all the benefits it conferred upon the Central Powers.

The German revolution, however, failed to mature as expected. Instead, the armies of the Central Powers occupied the Ukraine and the Germans proceeded to make arrangements to replenish their depleted stocks of food, petroleum, and other necessities. The Allies, on their part, countered by carrying out an intervention in the peripheral areas of North and South Russia as well as in Siberia. The collapse of the Central Powers in the fall of 1918 found the Allies and the cooperating Russian anti-Bolshevik forces engaged in a struggle with the Soviet Government and the Red Army. Finally, the realization that the task of overthrowing the Soviet regime was not possible under postwar conditions resulted in the withdrawal of all Allied forces from Russian soil and of support from the Russian anti-Bolshevik armies. This ended the effort to punish the Soviet Government by military force for its share in causing Russia's failure to fulfill her prewar and wartime obligations to the Allied nations.

2

The intervention, as carried out in Russia, consisted of a number of separate and distinct elements, all of which, however, were called into being by the defection of Russia from the ranks of the Entente Powers. Internally, for example, the intervention was based upon the cooperation with the interventionary powers of those who, for one reason or another, actively opposed the Bolshevik program. There were some who opposed the Bolsheviks in principle and were willing either to see Russia revert to the old Imperial regime or to suspend the revolution pending the overthrow of the Bolsheviks and the convocation of a Constituent Assembly. Others, stressing the Bolshevik willingness to sign a separate peace with Germany, quite frankly feared the consequences of the inevitable subjection to the Central Powers and of placing themselves, by virtue of refusal to continue the struggle against Germany and Austria, both morally and legally beyond any claim to Allied help or sympathy. Neither of these shared the apparent Bolshevik optimism with respect to the anticipated role of a German revolution in undoing the work of the Treaty of Brest-Litovsk. It was from the ranks of those who held such views as well as a number whose opposition arose from somewhat less laudable objections that the internal support for the interventionary powers was drawn. It should be emphasized that many of these White Russians, as they came to be called, were prompted to cooperate with the foreign powers by the best of motives and intentions. Among their fatal weaknesses, however, were their apparent inability to place a workable progressive program in immediate operation, their failure to achieve general cooperation among themselves, and their dependence on foreign assistance for the realization of their objectives. Each of these deficiencies contributed to the ultimate collapse of the whole anti-Bolshevik movement.

This internal opposition to the Bolsheviks was first called upon to reckon with a foreign intervention when the forces of the Central Powers began their occupation of the Ukraine. A measure of cooperation was available to the Central Powers, first from the anti-Bolshevik Central Rada at Kiev

3

and later from the government of General Skoropadsky which replaced it. Simutlaneously, in the Far East the Japanese were actively pressing for a general intervention in Siberia. While the Treaty of Brest-Litovsk, signed March 3, 1918, provided Germany with the legal basis for her intervention, the same treaty, for the very same reason, provided Japan with the excuse for demanding an intervention to prevent the spread of German power through Siberia to the Pacific Ocean. The Allies, on their part, understood well enough the implications of these two sources of pressure upon the Russian territory. In the West the German intervention threatened to provide the Central Powers with an inexhaustible supply of food and fuel which would enormously enhance their military strength during the war. In the Far East the long history of Japanese pressure against both China and Russia was well known. The relatively even balance between Japan and Russia before the war was upset by the concentration of Russian strength in the West after the outbreak of war in 1914. This change was already registered in the Russo-Japanese treaty of 1916 which, as will be seen in succeeding chapters, signified the beginning of the Russian retreat before Japan. The Japanese pressure for an intervention which developed in the course of 1917 was thus closely related both to the opening moves of Germany in the West and to the long-standing Russo-Japanese rivalry in the Far East and the incentive this provided Japan for the acquisition of the Pacific coastal possessions of Russia.

It was in response to these conditions that the Allied nations carried out an intervention both in European Russia and in Siberia. Their first efforts to promote internal support for an intervention in their own behalf, it is true, predated the actual occupation of Russian soil by German and Austrian armies and both France and Great Britain shared with Japan the early efforts in introducing anti-Bolshevik forces to the Far East. But these Allied efforts to carry out an intervention of their own were to a very large extent aimed at preserving an existing relationship with Russia rather than at bringing about any radical change in that relation-

4

ship. The close prewar economic ties between the Western Allied Powers and Russia as well as the balance of power which had been achieved by the establishment of the Triple Entente were both endangered by the ambitions of Germany and Japan with respect to Russia. Realizing the tremendous strategic advantage which these two nations enjoyed by reason of their proximity to Russia, the Allies saw the necessity of acting to combat this danger. The menace from the side of Germany was overcome by the defeat which the Central Powers suffered on the Western Front in the autumn of 1918. The threat from the East was not overcome until the Washington Conference brought enough international pressure to bear upon Japan to dislodge her from the Russian Far East four years later.

The international order out of which the First World War developed was characterized by a division of the major powers into three systems of alliances. The first of these to take shape was the Triple Alliance, consisting basically of the Dual Alliance formed by Germany and Austria-Hungary in 1879. Three years later these two powers were joined by Italy to form the Triple Alliance. The strength and growing menace of this central bloc of powers was the chief factor in bringing together Great Britian, France, and Russia to form the second of these power systems, the Triple Entente. This was based on the Franco-Russian Alliance of 1894, the Anglo-French Entente Cordiale of 1904, and the Anglo-Russian Convention of 1907. This last was in a sense a continuation of the Anglo-Russian agreement to cooperate in China concluded in 1899 and was itself concerned with Asiatic problems.

A third set of agreements was concerned with the problems of the Far East, particularly Japan. The first of this group was the Anglo-Japanese Alliance of 1902, afterward renewed in 1905 and 1911. The second group consisted of treaties signed by Russia and Japan, the first of which was the Treaty of Portsmouth of 1905. This was followed by Russo-Japanese treaties, both public and secret, concluded in 1907, 1910, and 1912. The third of these pacts consisted of the

5

Root-Takahira notes exchanged by the United States and Japan in 1908. This agreement, it should be noted, was signed at a time when Germany, fearing isolation in the Far East, was hoping to build an American-German-Chinese Alliance.[1] Finally, there was the Franco-Japanese Alliance of 1907. This group of mutual alliances not only drew Japan close to the Entente Powers but formed the diplomatic background against which the activities of Japan during the world war and the intervention must be understood. Japan used the unusual opportunity provided by the war in Europe to enhance her Far Eastern position by the acquisition of the German islands of the Pacific Ocean as well as the German possessions on the Asiatic mainland. The same policy was continued with the presentation of the Twenty-One Demands to China in 1915. Furthermore, building upon these prewar alliances, Japan continued to seek general approval for her growing power by means not merely of aggressive acts but also by continuing the system of mutual guarantees by additional treaties. The Russo-Japanese treaty of 1916 and the Lansing-Ishii agreement of 1917 were guarantees of this kind. Even the Siberian intervention, by which she hoped to quell once and for all the troublesome opposition of Russia to her plans for continental expansion, was carried out by the express invitation of the United States and with the formal approval of the other Allied powers.

The First World War opened the military phase of the long-standing rivalry represented by the Triple Alliance and the Triple Entente. The formal beginning of hostilities may be dated from the presentation of the Austro-Hungarian ultimatum to Serbia on July 23, 1914. On July 25 Russia took a direct hand in the increasingly tense situation by warning Austria not to cross the Serbian frontier. Three days later, on July 28, Austria-Hungary declared war on Serbia and the bombardment of Belgrade, the capital of Serbia, began the following day. On this same day, the 29th,

[1] L. J. Hall, "The Abortive German-American-Chinese Entente of 1907–08," *The Journal of Modern History* (Chicago), i, No. 2, June 1929, pp. 227–228.

Russia declared a general mobilization against the Austro-Hungarian Empire.

Thus far the conflict might have appeared to be a purely local one, confined like the recent Balkan Wars to Eastern Europe. And, in fact, both Great Britain and Germany expressed themselves in favor of trying to localize and mediate the whole affair. Even Russia, on the very day of her mobilization, seemed favorable to mediation. But it turned out that neither localization nor mediation was feasible. Instead, the various nations concerned in the competing alliances began to align themselves according to their respective interests or the demands of their traditional animosities. On August 1 Germany declared war on Russia and on August 2 German troops crossed the border into Luxembourg. The following day Germany declared war on France. Then on August 5, after sending an ultimatum to Germany regarding nonviolation of Belgian territory, Great Britain declared war against Germany.

The decision of the remaining participants in the war was based either upon the necessities of their geographical locations or on a calculation of the relative advantages offered by each side. Thus, on August 3, Italy, although nominally a member of the Triple Alliance, announced her neutrality, a status she retained until she eventually declared war on her former ally, Austria-Hungary, on May 23, 1915. Turkey, on the other hand, took her stand with the Central Powers by a secret treaty hastily signed with Germany on August 2, 1914.[2] The existence of this agreement did not long remain unknown. On August 10, two German warships passed the Straits and anchored at Constantinople. In the end, Turkey purchased these ships although they remained under German command. On September 27, 1914 Turkey closed the Straits and shut off the supply line to the West so badly needed by Russia. Finally, on October 28, 1914 the Turkish fleet, acting under German command, carried out an attack against units of the Russian Black Sea Fleet as well as against

[2] J. T. Shotwell and F. Deak, *Turkey at the Straits, A Short History,* New York, 1940, p. 95.

7

various Russian coastal cities there. This attack evoked a Russian declaration of war against Turkey on November 4. The stage was thereby set for a prolongation of the war and for the undermining of Russian fighting strength. With respect to this troublesome problem, it must be added that in March and April 1915 Russia received the assurances of Great Britain and France respectively that, after the conclusion of hostilities, she would be permitted to have what amounted to exclusive control of the Straits.[3] This realization of the historic ambitions of the Russian state was lost by the Soviet renunciation of the secret treaties and agreements of Imperial Russia, of which this Allied understanding was one. In the Far East, Japan chose to reap the full benefits of opposing Germany in that area. She declared war on Germany on August 23, 1914 and by November 10 was in possession of Kiaochow in Shantung. By 1916, while Russia was still engaged in the desparate struggle in the West, Japan was making frank demands for economic and other concessions in the Far Eastern possessions of Russia. Thus, the secondary participants were ranged in what they hoped would be the most congenial and profitable associations with the major contestants.

Russia, though ill-prepared for a full-scale war against the Central Powers and badly in need of the supplies that might have come through the Straits from her Allies, nevertheless played a large and important part in the early stages of the war. The war on the Eastern Front was opened by Russia in August with an offensive into East Prussia. This thrust was stopped by the end of August by a German force under General von Hindenburg. To the south, however, the Russian advance against the armies of Austria-Hungary in Galicia continued until, by the end of the year, that entire province had been occupied by Russian forces. During September the Germans moved 52 additional divisions into the Eastern Theater. But the Russian forces held their lines

[3] *Ibid.,* pp. 100–102.

8

and by October 27 the German armies were again in retreat. In November, with the aid of 14 additional divisions drawn from the Western Front, Germany succeeded in preventing the development of an anticipated Russian offensive. Thus, in the first months of the war and during the critical battle of the Marne between September 6–12, the growing Russian threat in the East prevented the German armies from concentrating sufficient force on the Western Front to produce the knockout blow as expected. Instead, Germany was impelled to send re-enforcements eastward to prevent the mounting danger not only directly from Russia but also that caused by the inability of the armies of Austria-Hungary to withstand Russian pressure.

By the spring of 1915 the initial driving force of the Russian armies was spent and the real weakness of the Russian preparation for sustained warfare began to become apparent. Germany, having decided to concentrate a larger proportion of her efforts in the East, moved additional divisions in that direction and placed General von Mackensen in command of the Eastern Front. The Russian armies, fighting with nearly a third of the troops filling up the ranks but carrying no rifles, were not prepared for this concentration of force against them. The Allies having failed to open up the Dardanelles in their campaign of April 1915, this source of renewed supplies and of encouragement to Russian morale was thereby closed off, at least for the time being. Meanwhile, a combined Austro-German force of about two million men was preparing a vast offensive and by May 1 the Russians were being pushed eastward. By autumn the Russian armies had been forced out of most of Poland and Galicia.

In June 1916 Russia again assumed the offensive against the Austro-Hungarian armies. This move helped to bring Rumania into the Allied camp and on August 27, 1916 Rumania declared war against Austria-Hungary. But by early December Bucharest was captured by Austro-German armies and the grain fields and oil wells of Rumania were

9

at the disposal of the Central Powers. In the south the Allied position had been further weakened by the collapse of Serbia during the previous summer.

A general Allied offensive was planned for the spring of 1917. In the West these plans were carried out, but with very slight gains and at such a cost in men and material that mutiny broke out in several divisions of the French Army. In Russia the results were even more disastrous. In March 1917 the lowered morale and the internal economic weakness resulted in the first stage of the political revolution. While at the front the armies began the long process of disintegration which helped to bring about the complete and official withdrawal of Russia from the war as registered in the Treaty of Brest-Litovsk twelve months later, at Petrograd the Imperial Government was officially replaced by the Provisional Government headed by Prince George Lvov. Simultaneously, the Petrograd Soviet of Workers' and Soldiers' Deputies began to conduct itself as an unofficial government. It was in this capacity that on March 14 it issued the order known as "Order Number One" which gave the final impetus to the collapse of the Russian armies. This famous document made the Petrograd Soviet the supreme source of authority in all military matters. The will of the Soviet was to be effectuated, not by the officers and non-commissioned officers of the army and navy, but by soldiers' and sailors' committees which were to be organized in all military and naval units. The effect of this order was to undermine and finally wipe out the authority of the officer corps and thus render the army and navy useless as fighting forces. Compliance with it would in itself have rendered anything short of defeat a sheer miracle. Those in Russia who foresaw this result and sought to take action to prevent the growth of Soviet power by this means came in time to constitute the political and military anti-Bolshevik forces. The foundation for the civil war was laid.

By the end of November 1917 there had developed all the elements which led to the outbreak of the five-year period of civil war and intervention. In the first place, on November 7, the Petrograd Soviet of Workers' and Soldiers' Deputies officially assumed power. From the very start its position with respect both to domestic and foreign policy was clear. By a series of decrees it placed all industrial, commercial, and agricultural enterprises under the control of the workers.[4] Its international problems were to be settled by "an immediate peace without annexations and without indemnities." It need scarcely be added that these and succeeding decrees raised in the minds of Allied business and political leaders both the question of the security of foreign investments under such a regime and the immediate future of the Eastern Front. It was partly in response to these events at Petrograd that the liberal Ukrainian Government of the Central Rada was proclaimed at Kiev on November 20. It was around this political center that the Allies tried to rally the Russian people to a renewal of the war with the Central Powers. But the latter, attracted by the prospects of a division of Russia and of obtaining access to the food and fuel of South Russia, represented an immediate force too strong for the Rada to resist. The result was an incompatible and short-lived partnership between the Central Powers and the Rada Government providing for the supply of provisions and fuel for the former and survival for the latter.

Meanwhile the Allies had, during November, taken the first steps toward an intervention. The first of these was a collective Allied note which was dispatched on November 23, 1917 to General Dukhonin, the Commander-in-Chief of the Russian Armies, warning him of the severe consequences that might be expected as a result of the peace proposals then being made by the Soviets.[5] More active steps were undertaken by the Allies, both in their efforts to reach an understanding with the Central Rada and in their proposals to General Kornilov, a former Commander-in-Chief of the Russian Armies, with the hope of re-establishing the Russian fighting strength. In the Orenburg region, it should be added,

[4] J. Bunyan and H. H. Fisher, *The Bolshevik Revolution, 1917–1918,* Stanford, 1934, pp. 277–279.
[5] *Ibid.,* p. 245.

11

the military struggle against the Soviets began at this time under the leadership of the Cossack Ataman Dutov. This was the front into which the Czechoslovak Legion and later the armies of Admiral Kolchak were introduced. In the Far East, the Japanese had been moving troops in Korea and Manchuria since the previous summer and by November, as will be seen in succeeding chapters, the Western European Allies were actively anticipating the beginning of an intervention in Siberia.

Although the stage was thus set for one or more of a number of different acts of intervention against Russia, the first of these to develop was from the side of the Central Powers. As contrasted with the Western European Allies, the armies of Germany and Austria-Hungary were already on the very border of Russia, prepared to move in. With the establishment of the Soviet and Rada regimes, there now remained only the problem of embodying all the advantages of their victory in some legal instrument. Insofar as the Ukraine was concerned, this was accomplished by the treaty which Germany signed with the Central Rada on February 9, 1918.[6] This treaty provided for "a reciprocal exchange of the surplus of their [i.e., the Ukraine] more important agricultural and industrial products, for the purpose of meeting current requirements." A succeeding agreement defined these requirements more minutely and stipulated the precise quantities of grain and grain products, eggs, livestock, bacon, textiles, iron ore, manganese, and other products which the Rada was to deliver to the Central Powers in exchange for agricultural implements, chemical and other manufactured products. During the following month, March 1918, the Central Powers partitioned the Ukraine.[7] The German sphere consisted of the provinces of Kiev, Chernigov, Poltava, Kharkov, Taurida, and eastern Volynia: that of Austria-Hungary consisted of the provinces of Podolia,

---

[6] X. Eudin, "The German Occupation of the Ukraine in 1918," *The Russian Review* (New York), i, No. 1, November 1941, pp. 92–93.

[7] "Interventsiia," *Bolshaia Sovetskaia Entsiklopediia*, Moscow, 1937, xxviii, p. 643.

Kherson, Ekaterinoslav, and western Volynia. It has also been asserted that Germany, with the object of tapping the cotton and other products of Central Asia and, undoubtedly as part of a plan either for a more permanent occupation or for closer future economic cooperation, projected a Berlin to Bukhara railway.[8]

Meanwhile, in order to prevent the resurgence of a hostile Russian power, and to insure Ukrainian compliance with the demands for food and other products so necessary for German prosecution of the war against the Allies, the Central Powers proceeded to carry out a military occupation of the Ukraine and to assert military control of a part of the Caucasus. From a line running approximately from Riga southward through Tarnopol and Chernowitz to the mouth of the Danube River, the armies of Germany and Austria-Hungary began their advance into Russia on February 18, 1918. They occupied Kiev on March 1, Odessa on March 13, Kharkov on April 8, Kerch on May 2, and Rostov-on-the-Don on May 8. By the end of May the Central Powers were in full control of the Ukraine and their military occupation had taken place up to a line running from Narva southward through Pskov, Polotsk, Kursk, Belgorod, and Millerovo, in addition to their occupation of a part of the Caucasus in the South and of Finland in the North. The total initial occupation force in the Ukraine was between 200,000 and 220,000 men.

On the basis of their unquestionably victorious position and of their tremendous advantage in being able to deal separately with the strategically and economically important Ukraine, the Central Powers proceeded to exact the full price of defeat from the Soviet Government. It must be added that the attitude of the Soviet negotiators did nothing to improve the conditions of the peace which was finally concluded. Discussions were opened between the representatives of Soviet Russia and the Central Powers at Brest-Litovsk on December 3, 1918 which resulted in an armistice, signed

[8] S. Kotliarevsky, "Pravovye Dostizheniia Rossii v Azii," *Novyi Vostok* (Moscow), No. 1, 1922, p. 36.

on December 15. The negotiation of peace terms began on December 22 and continued for over two months. The refusal of the Soviet representatives to accept the German terms resulted in the advance of the armies of the Central Powers into Russia as already explained and, finally, in the Soviet acceptance of the German terms on March 3, 1918.[9] This Treaty of Brest-Litovsk was disastrous for Russia. The Baltic states, Eastern Poland, the Ukraine, and part of the Caucasus came under either German or Turkish control. In addition, Russia was to pay a large war indemnity. The treaty brought Russia to another of the periods of crisis that occurred so frequently after the March Revolution. It will be seen presently that the month of March was fraught with possibilities for the future development of Russia. In the Far East the developments of this period culminated in the landing of a small Japanese naval force at Vladivostok in early April 1918.

Having thus occupied strategic areas of Russia, established relations with Russian governments which they felt could be controlled, and legalized their victory by the signing of treaties, the Central Powers furnished not only an incentive but an excuse as well as a model for an Allied intervention. As already noted, well before the signing of the Treaty of Brest-Litovsk the Allies had started formulating plans for an intervention. Due to the advantageous position of Germany, the Allies were forced to plan their own interventionary strategy exclusively with reference to the peripheral areas. The first and most menacing moves were those of Japan in the Far East. Her military preparations, evident since the summer of 1917, began to become more obvious by December of that year. It was in December that the Chinese, acting under the threat of Japanese and other Allied activity in the Chinese Eastern Railway zone, dispatched a military force to the area, ejected the Russian guard there, and themselves assumed the duty of patrolling the railway zone. Then in the following month the Japanese moved ships into the harbor

[9] Bunyan and Fisher, *op. cit.*, pp. 523–525.

at Vladivostok, thereby serving notice on the Allies that if consent were not soon forthcoming, they might take the responsibility of carrying out an intervention alone instead of leaving Russia to be appropriated by the Central Powers whose armies were even then poised for an expected march into Russia. It was in this way that Japan, though formally a member of the Allied group, became, along with Germany, one of the primary centers of pressure against Russia. The monopolistic activities and plans of Germany and Japan with respect to Russia were, in fact, the basic forces which give meaning and purpose to the plans formulated by the Western Allies and the United States for the intervention as it took shape after the Bolshevik Revolution.

In European Russia, also, the opening moves of the Allied intervention were being made in the early months of 1918. In January 1918 the British dispatched a force from Bagdad under General Dunsterville. On February 17, this detachment reached Enzeli on the Persian coast of the Caspian Sea. By the following summer the British were at Baku. On March 7, 1918 the British cruiser *Cochrane* arrived at Murmansk and two days later the landing of troops began. By the end of March there were about one thousand Allied troops at Murmansk with landings continuing throughout the summer.

Along with the arrival of external support, there were developing within Russia a number of anti-Soviet political and military groups whose members saw more and more that their own advantage, and indeed their only hope of survival in this new stage of revolutionary development, lay in cooperation with the Allies. The military activities in the West centered in the Cossack regions of the lower Don River.[10] Here on November 7, 1917 General Kaledin assumed the leadership of the Cossack Voisko Government of the Don region. One week later, General Alekseev, a former commander-in-chief of the Russian army, arrived there to undertake the organization of the anti-Bolshevik Volunteer Army, with which also General Kornilov was presently to become associated.

[10] *Ibid.,* pp. 404ff.

15

Meanwhile, at Moscow a number of political groups with pro-Entente and anti-Bolshevik orientation began to be formed almost immediately after the Bolshevik Revolution. One of these, the Union for the Regeneration of Russia, was formed in April from members of various political parties. Its aim was the overthrow of the Bolsheviks, the renewal of the war with Germany, and the convocation of another Constituent Assembly, the first having been dismissed by the Bolsheviks three months previously. Another of these organizations was the Union to Defend the Country and Liberty. This was formed during the spring of 1918 under the leadership of Boris Savinkov with headquarters at Moscow and associated organizations in some thirty-four other cities. Savinkov had established a wide network of relationships including the military leaders of the lower Don as well as the Allied representatives from whom he received financial assistance. The entire success of his organization depended upon its coordination with an Allied miltary advance into Russia. Since this cooperation was not forthcoming, the revolts which he stirred up in July in Iaroslavl and elsewhere served only to expose his plans and intentions insofar as the Soviet Government was not already aware of them. Generally speaking, it may be said that these White movements failed because they lacked unity and because their program lacked popular appeal since among them the crucial land question was considered too important to be decided by anyone but the members of a future Constitutent Assembly. In general, also, these organizations looked abroad for support and their failure to receive it in time, in adequate amounts, and under favorable conditions constitutes an important element in bringing about the failure of the anti-Bolshevik movement.

By the spring of 1919 the Allied and White Russian forces were ready for the first major attempt to unseat the Soviet regime. By this time the Armistice had already been signed some months before and, with the German threat eliminated, the issues of the struggle in Russia were clear to both sides. The White armies had meanwhile been reenforced from the

16

large military surpluses of the Allied powers. The general strategy of the anti-Bolshevik campaign was a march on Moscow from four different directions. From the North, the British-Russian force would move southward, joining hands with the forces of Admiral Kolchak moving westward from the Ural-Volga region; from the West the Baltic army of General Iudenich and from the South that of General Denikin would move toward Moscow. The campaign was a failure in a number of important ways. In the first place, it failed in its main objective, the overthrow of the Bolsheviks. Furthermore, it demonstrated the strength of the new Red armies and, at the same time, the weakness of the White armies. Another result even more foreboding for the White forces was that the Allies, whose plans called for assisting the White armies only until they could establish their hold upon affairs in Russia, decided after the failure of this campaign to withdraw their active assistance from all but the Siberian theater of operations. Thus, by the end of March 1919 the Allied withdrawal from the Ukraine had begun, followed in April by the commencement of a British withdrawal from Central Asia and in June from Transcaucasia. In August the British began to evacuate Baku while the withdrawal from North Russia began at the same time. In November 1919 the last ship sailed from North Russia, leaving Allied troops only in Siberia.

The second anti-Bolshevik campaign was launched in the autumn of 1919. With the Anglo-Russian force of North Russia in the process of withdrawal and the armies of Admiral Kolchak having been beaten in the previous campaign and now in retreat through Siberia, the major effort in this campaign was in the South. Here General Denikin was leading a powerful drive which reached Orel on the road to Moscow while General Iudenich cooperated with a drive against Petrograd from Esthonia. But in October the Red army counteroffensive began and the White armies were rapidly pushed back. With the failure of this campaign, the command of the southern army passed to General Wrangel. The campaign which he launched from the South, carried out in apparent cooperation with the Polish offensive against Soviet Russia from the West, constituted the third and last of the major anti-Soviet campaigns in European Russia. The Soviets were aided in this case by the fact that the Polish participation in the struggle had the effect of arousing considerable patriotic sentiment in Russia. By October and November 1920, the Polish and White Russian drives respectively were beaten and the civil war in the main theater of Russia was over. Meanwhile, the Allied blockade against Russia, declared in the autumn of 1918, was lifted in January 1920 and some economic connections with the outer world were established. In the Far East the struggle continued for more than two and a half years.

In Siberia, although the desires and hopes of a number of other parties were vigorously represented, the intervention was from first to last conditioned by the objectives and activities of Japan. The intervention here can be conveniently divided into three periods. The first was the preparatory period which lasted from about the summer of 1917 to the Czechoslovak rising against the Soviets in May 1918. This period was characterized by the consolidation of Bolshevik rule in Siberia and the growing tension in Allied circles over the question of an Eastern Front and of the Japanese aims in the Russian Far East. The Czech rising in May introduced the period of Allied intervention which lasted until the departure of the American forces in April 1920. During this time Japan, the United States, Great Britain, France, and several other nations sent forces into Siberia. In November 1918 Admiral Kolchak was made the commander-in-chief of all the Russian forces operating in Siberia and in the Ural-Volga region as well as supreme political and military head of all anti-Bolshevik forces then operating in Russia. His defeat in the spring of 1919 meant the beginning of the end of Allied intervention in Siberia. Kolchak's long retreat through Siberia ended with his official surrender of power in January 1920 and his death in the following month. By April 1, the Allied intervention had ended. It was followed by the third and last period, that of

18

the Japanese intervention which lasted until the withdrawal of the Japanese forces from Vladivostok in October 1922, although, strictly speaking, the withdrawal of the Japanese from North Sakhalin in May 1925 would be a more accurate date for the end of the intervention.

Among the Allies, the Japanese role in intervention, while unique in the availability of her armies for duty in Siberia and the propinquity of the Russian area in which she was interested, had a historical background which distinguished it from that of all the other Allies. France and Britain, to be sure, had investments and commercial interests which made them anxious to promote their claims to specific areas in Russia while the United States had very important commercial interests in Siberia. But none of these necessitated any specific kind of direct control there. Japan, however, financially weaker than these other nations and therefore less able to compete with them in a free market, had interests which did contemplate close control and monopoly of rights. These interests were the same as those which grew out of her general concern with the Asiatic mainland areas which were adjacent to her own home islands and rich in economic possibilities. The policies regarding these areas were formulated during the particular phase of prewar imperialism which concerns the development of the Far Eastern Question. The policies, to be sure, were formulated in the competitive drive for rights and interests in China. But they were possible in China only because the weakness of the Central Government, economic system, and military establishments of that nation prevented her from resisting the encroachment of foreigners upon her territory.

In 1917 the collapse of the general government in Russia produced a similar situation in the valuable areas north of China. The occasion thus arose for the application in Siberia of the policies which had already been formulated by Japan with reference to China. The significance of railway control, the exercise of special rights and interests based upon territorial contiguity, and the need for room for expansion were arguments and policies which characterized

19

the Japanese share in the Siberian intervention as they had long been evident in her conduct with respect to China. It was in this manner that the position of Japan in relation to the Siberian intervention became of such vast import not only from a military but from a geographical as well as a historical standpoint. Indeed, it is not too much to say that the Siberian intervention as it will presently be described not only grew out of the relationships of Japan to the adjacent continental areas but that it was an integral part of that relationship and all its implications for the development of the Far East.

This purely local history of the Siberian intervention is thus the most decisive aspect of it. With the military dominance of the Russian Far East which the Japanese achieved during the Allied phase of the Siberian intervention they were able to control to a very large extent the traffic over the Trans-Siberian Railway and, therefore, the supply line to Admiral Kolchak in Western Siberia. Therefore, if the Allied and Russian plans which centered around the leadership of Admiral Kolchak in the great offensive of the spring of 1919 ever had any hopes of realization, their dependence upon the supply line through Siberia rendered success almost impossible. For these plans anticipated the unity of Russia after the victory of Kolchak and this would have deprived Japan of her long-standing desire to dominate the territory of Siberia east of Lake Baikal.

CHAPTER 2

The Russian Empire in the Far East

THE southeastern corner of Siberia is the natural base for Russian communications with the Pacific world. As long as the Russian Empire retained the power to do so, she used this region as a springboard for imperialistic adventures in Manchuria and Mongolia. While under the Empire it was part of the so-called Far Eastern Region, it comprised, during the Japanese phase of the intervention, the buffer state known as the Far Eastern Republic. On the continent the Far Eastern Region consisted of the Transbaikal, Amur, and Maritime provinces. In addition, it included the northern half of the island of Sakhalin and the peninsula of Kamchatka. At the outbreak of the First World War these provinces were economically weak and strategically vulnerable to external attack. The reason for this was in part the vast distances which separated them from European Russia as well as the undeveloped regions which lay between. But the Far Eastern Region, though rich in forest, mineral, and other natural resources, was itself poorly developed and lacked the strong local economic and military base required to support the aggressive Far Eastern policy which had in past years emanated from St. Petersburg. Furthermore, the fine river system which opened the area up to the Pacific seaboard as well as the easy access the region enjoyed with respect to the Chinese frontier–factors that might have served as means of establishing a dominant position for Russia in the Northwestern Pacific–proved of negative value in that they served only to incite Japan to use every opportunity to strike down a potential though weak competitor.

Many of the inhabitants of the Far Eastern Region were acutely aware of the economic and military weakness of their position. Even after the stern warnings of the Russo-Japanese

21

War, the Trans-Siberian and Chinese Eastern railways still constituted the thin and vulnerable economic life-line of these distant provinces at the time of the outbreak of the First World War. The industrial developments of the intervening years had hardly been more than the auxiliary activities necessary to maintain terminal and coaling facilities for the railways. The other light industries, such as there were, did not supply all the essentials even of a predominantly agrarian community. Imports were necessary to make up deficiencies, not only in manufactured articles but even in some basic items of food supply. Under these circumstances, the presence of the nearby densely populated Far Eastern countries, and especially the menace of the Japanese advance on the Asiatic continent, gave rise to considerable foreboding on the part of the people of the Region. These and a number of other sources of resentment against the Imperial Russian Government were crystallized into political movements which represented not only demands for reform but even separatist tendencies. It was in the face of this precarious balance of power in the Far East that Russia entered the war in the West in 1914 and almost lost its standing as a Pacific power.

The Far Eastern Region of Russian Siberia had common frontiers with the three major national states of Northeastern Asia. It faced Japan across the Japan Sea and had a common frontier with that nation along the fiftieth parallel of latitude on the island of Sakhalin. Its frontier with China ran from its own western limits south of Lake Baikal, along the northern border of Manchuria. Near the city of Khabarovsk the boundary turned southward and here the borders of the Maritime Province and Chinese Manchuria ran together until they reached Korea. In its southernmost limits, just beyond Poset Bay, the Maritime Province bordered on Korea. Several aspects of these geographical relationships contained elements of possible danger for Russia. One of these was the long and militarily vulnerable frontier. Under a passive regime in China, this was not a matter for any particular concern. But with the increase of Japanese power after the Russo-Japanese War in both Korea and Manchuria,

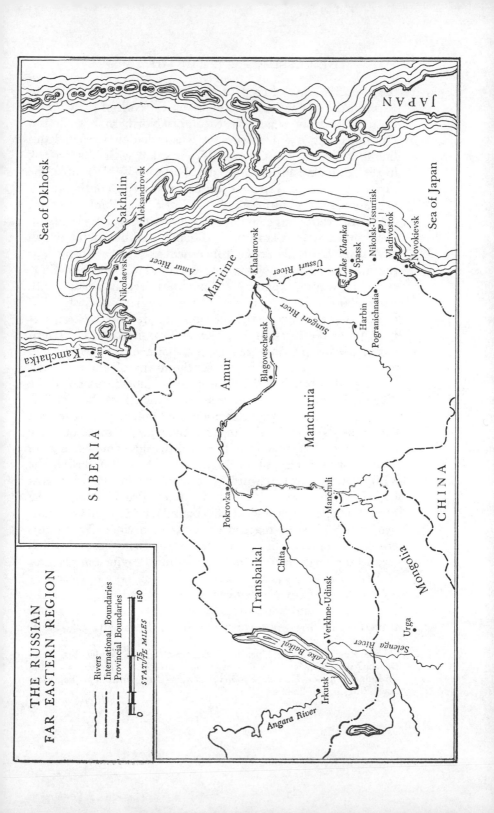

THE RUSSIAN
FAR EASTERN REGION

Rivers
International Boundaries
Provincial Boundaries

STATUTE MILES
0   75   150

SIBERIA

Sea of Okhotsk

Sakhalin
Aleksandrovsk

Nikolaevsk

Amur River

Kamchatka

Alan

Maritime

Khabarovsk

JAPAN

Sea of Japan

Lake Khanka
Spassk
Nikolsk-Ussuriisk
Vladivostok
Novokievsk

Ussuri River

Amur

Blagoveschensk

Sungari River

Harbin
Pogranichnaia

Manchuria

Pokrovka

Manchuli

CHINA

Transbaikal

Chita

Mongolia

Urga

Verkhne-Udinsk

Selenga River

Lake Baikal

Irkutsk

Angara River

the situation was altered to the increasing disadvantage of Russia. Another source of danger was the zone of the Chinese Eastern Railway which passed across Northern Manchuria. During its more aggressive days Russia had constructed this line in order to join Chita in Transbaikal with Vladivostok in the Maritime Province by the shortest possible route. The rapid increase of Japanese influence on the continent, especially after the outbreak of the World War, had, however, made this route appear more like a source of danger than a mere shortcut to Vladivostok. Finally, a third factor which gave Russia reason to be concerned about the future was the presence nearby of the densely populated states of Eastern Asia whose expansive propensities were observed with particular alarm by publicists of the Russian Far East.

The westernmost of the provinces of the Far Eastern Region under the Russian Empire was Transbaikal.[1] The boundaries of this province ran from a point on the Mongolian border just across from the southern tip of Lake Baikal, northward through the lake itself to the northern end of the lake at the city of Nichevsky, near the mouth of the Verkhnaia Angara River. From this point the boundary followed the course of the Verkhnaia Angara River but at some distance to the north, then looped northward and came back to a point near the city of Korolon. From here it followed the Vitim River southeastward. The northern border of Transbaikal Province ran with that of Iakutsk Province and in the eastern part of the province this boundary followed the Stanovoi Range until it reached the Amur Province. The southern border of Transbaikal was the Amur River beyond which was Manchuria. Here it touched Amur Province at the city of Pokrovka.

The Amur Province lay east of Transbaikal and was, like the latter, a land-bound region. Its northern boundary continued along the Stanovoi range from the border of Trans-

---

[1] See Russia. Glavnoe Upravlenie Zemlenstroistva i Zemledeliia. Pereslencheskoe Upravlenie, *Atlas Aziatskoi Rossii,* St. Petersburg, 1914; "Administrativnoe Delenie," *Sibirskaia Sovetskaia Entsiklopediia,* Moscow, 1931, II, pp. 23–26.

baikal to a point about halfway between there and the Pacific Ocean. From here its northeastern boundary ran in a jagged line southeastward to the Amur River near the city of Khabarovsk. Its southern boundary was the Amur River and Manchuria. Finally, as the name implies, the Maritime Province constituted the coastal area of the Far Eastern Region. Its northern boundary continued along the Stanovoi Range from Amur to Kamchatka Province, then southward along the Pacific coast from Aian past the mouth of the Amur River and then the city of Vladivostok to the Korean border just south of Poset Bay and the city of Novokievsk. From this point it turned northward along the border of Manchuria to the boundary of the Amur Province on the Amur River. The northernmost of these provinces was Kamchatka, which included the peninsula of that name as well as the coastal area of the mainland between a line running from Aian to Chaun Bay on the Arctic Ocean and the Pacific Ocean. Finally, the Region included also the northern half of the island of Sakhalin which lay strategically athwart the mouth of the Amur River, across the Straits of Tartary.

The dominant topographical characteristics of what then comprised the Far Eastern Region are its mountainous terrain and the excellent and strategically arranged river systems. The Stanovoi range, which then formed most of the northern boundary, cuts through the former Transbaikal Province near the city of Chita. Between this point and Lake Baikal the country is prevailingly mountainous while to the east it is hilly. Amur Province is also to a great extent hilly, though it becomes more mountainous as it approaches the Stanavoi Range. Within this area there is a spur of the Lesser Khingan Range, important for the iron is contains. The Sikhota-Alin Mountains dominate the zone of the old Maritime Province south of the Amur River. But in spite of this generally high relief the Region contains important lowlands suitable for agriculture. One of the largest of these lies along the Amur River between the Zeia and Bureia Rivers. Another is located in the upper Ussuri region around Lake Khanka.

The river systems of the Far Eastern Region are dominated

by the Amur River itself. This great river is formed by the confluence at the city of Pokrovka of the Argun River running out of Mongolia and the Shilka, which runs through the city of Chita in Transbaikal. From Pokrovka the Amur passes on until it receives the waters of the southward-flowing Zeia River at the city of Blagoveshchensk and is then joined by the Bureia River at the city of Innokentevsk. After the Amur has turned northward it is joined by the Sungari River from northern Manchuria and then by the Ussuri River flowing from the Lake Khanka area of the southern Maritime Province. This latter confluence takes place near Khabarovsk from which point the Amur flows northward past the city of Nikolaevsk near its mouth and into the Straits of Tartary across from Sakhalin Island. The total length of the Amur River from the point of the confluence of the Argun and Shilka Rivers is 1,485 miles. The Amur system provides a total of 3,000 miles of navigable waters while the Amur itself is accessible to ocean-going ships up to the city of Khabarovsk. Another river system of importance in the Region is that which forms the Selenga River. Like the Sungari River, which drains northern Manchuria, the Selenga runs out of northern Mongolia. It passes the Mongolian frontier at the city of Kiakhta and runs northwards past Troitskosavsk and Verkhne-Udinsk to Lake Baikal. The significance of the Sungari and Selenga rivers is a consideration which cannot be forgotten in a study of the international relations of the Far Eastern Region.

Two other characteristics of the rivers of this area must be mentioned. One is the fact that, due to the high relief of the terrain and the torrential summer rains, the rivers frequently overflow their banks and cause disastrous floods. Heavy floods were recorded, for example, in thirty-three of the years between 1861 and 1931, the one in 1872 being particularly bad, since it was responsible for the destruction of twenty-seven villages.[2] But these river valleys also

[2] J. Harrison, *Peace or War East of Baikal?* Yokohama, 1910, p. 55.

provide the extensive fertile areas that for many decades gave the Far East its chief attraction for colonization both from European Russia and from other countries of the Far East. Passing north through the Ussuri Valley in 1918, General Graves noted a striking similarity to parts of Nebraska or Kansas.[3] He found it unexpectedly fertile with fine stands of oats, wheat, buckwheat, and hay. As already noted, such fertile areas are found most extensively in the Amur and upper Ussuri basins. But they exist to a lesser degree along the many other rivers of the Region.

Both the rainfall and climate of the area are strongly influenced by the monsoons.[4] This is of course most generally true of the Vladivostok area. It is so to a lesser extent in the Ussuri-Lower Amur Lowland which lies beyond the Sikhota-Alin range, and is true to a far lesser degree in the Zeia and Bureia River areas, which are far more continental climatically than the Ussuri-Lower Amur River region. The mean annual precipitation is not great, being about 19.8 inches at Blagoveshchensk and 14.7 inches at Vladivostok. The torrential rainfall characteristic of the Region is shown by the fact that at Blagoveshchensk about one quarter of the total annual precipitation falls during July. In general, about eighty-five to ninety percent of the entire annual rainfall occurs between the months of April and November. The winters, therefore, have very little precipitation and considerable sunshine while the summers are quite cool with many cloudy or foggy days on the coast. At Vladivostok between May and August one-third to one-half of the days are foggy while the temperature remains mostly in the sixties.[5] The coastal area is thus a far more pleasant place than the name "Siberia" generally connotes to the reader of Russian

[3] W. S. Graves, *America's Siberian Adventure, 1918–1920,* New York, 1931, pp. 87–88.
[4] J. S. Gregory and D. W. Shave, *The U.S.S.R.; A Geographical Survey,* New York, 1944, pp. 89–90.
[5] A. Darinsky, *Nature and Nature Resources of the Soviet Far East,* Moscow, 1936, p. 2.

literature dealing with political exiles. The inland areas, on the other hand, approach the general conception more closely.

Among the natural resources of Siberia, fur-bearing animals and fish have been of special importance. The former attracted the Russians into Siberia, the latter have constituted one of their major Pacific problems. During the two decades after 1889 the fishing industry was developed by the Japanese. But after the building of the Trans-Siberian Railway, and particularly after 1907, a Russian fishing industry developed more rapidly because of the increase of population in Siberia and because the railway made European markets available. By 1914 a well-developed Russian industry was using twenty-two steamers of the Volunteer Fleet with a registered tonnage of 41,000 tons and supplying fish to Japan, Siberia, European Russia, Western Europe, and British markets.[6]

Another natural resource of great significance is the extensive growth of forest found in the Region. The forests along the Zeia, Bureia, and Amur Rivers are particularly rich in available and commercially profitable stands of timber.[7] But the most valuable of all are the forest reserves of the Ussuri Basin, which for diversity and richness are unequaled in all of Siberia. Many forest areas, such as those of the lower Amur, were scarcely touched by the Soviet Union even in its Second Five Year Plan.

Before the Revolution the chief users of timber were the War Office, the railways, and the towns. Not only was the large potential timber market of China, Japan, Australia, and other countries entirely ignored but for certain purposes, such as the fishing industry in Kamchatka, wood or wood products were imported from Japan.[8] Moreover, the forests were worked from the railways back, without any

[6] The Special Delegation of the Far Eastern Republic to the United States of America, *Fisheries of the Far Eastern Republic,* Washington, 1922, p. 13.

[7] A. Tsymek, *The Forest Wealth of the Soviet Far East and Its Exploitation,* Moscow, 1936, pp. 10–11.

[8] *Ibid.,* p. 16.

efforts at reforestation. They were thus receding rapidly from the railway lines, leaving large areas, such as that about Vladivostok, almost treeless.

The largest and most easily available sources of coal at the time of the intervention were the fields of Sakhalin, where the reserves were estimated at 2,070,000,000 tons.[9] Poor harbor facilities, however, prevented full exploitation. Therefore, the deposits most exploited at the time of the Russian Revolution were those of the Maritime Province where the Suchan mines became famous for the dependence of the railroad on them as well as for the revolutionary activities which centered there. The reserves here are very large as are those of the Suifun or Pogranichnaya area near Nikolsk-Ussuriisk or present Voroshilov.[10] There are also considerable coal reserves in the Amur and Transbaikal provinces, but they were less explored and exploited than those of the Maritime Province.

Oil had been known to exist in North Sakhalin since 1880. Only in 1910, however, were any serious efforts made at drilling.[11] During the intervention the Japanese extracted some quantities of oil there. Bad port facilities continued to prevent anything like complete exploitation of these fields and not until 1928 did the Soviet Government commence real operations.[12] Reserves there were, at about the time of the Second Five Year Plan, estimated at 300,000,000 barrels.

Before the First World War the metal industries were developed chiefly by government enterprises.[13] The shipbuilding yards of Vladivostok and Blagoveshchensk, the railway shops of Nikolsk-Ussuriisk, and the arsenal at Khabarovsk were the most important of these enterprises. Mineral reserves were poorly explored and only slightly worked. The

[9] P. P. Goudkoff, "The Economic Geography of the Coal Resources of Asiatic Russia," *The Geographical Review* (New York), XIII, 1923, p. 292.
[10] Darinsky, *op. cit.*, pp. 10–11.
[11] B. Kireev, *The Economic Development of the Soviet Far East*, Moscow, 1936, pp. 17–18.
[12] V. Conolly, *Soviet Trade from the Pacific to the Levant; with an Economic Study of the Soviet Far Eastern Region*, London, 1935, p. 13.
[13] Kireev, *op. cit.*, p. 13.

chief known iron reserves were those of the Lesser Khingan Range, west of Khabarovsk and the Sikhota-Alin Range of the Maritime Province.[14] Lead, zinc, and silver deposits were also worked, the best known being those at Tetiukhe and Olga Bays in the Maritime Province. Gold mining was developed to the detriment of other minerals. The extensive gold deposits of the Zeia-Bureia area and of the Maritime Province have been mined since the 1880's, those of Transbaikal even earlier.

With the meager development of industrial life before the Revolution the chief natural resource of the Russian Far East was by all odds agriculture. Although the most available lands had been occupied by 1914, transportation and use of subsidies or loans could have opened millions of additional acres to the land-hungry Russian peasant. Estimates made by the Far Eastern Republic in 1921 place the land then in cultivation in the Region at 3,598,356 acres, land fit for cultivation at 54,000,-000 acres.[15] According to these figures, the three continental provinces had approximately the same acreage in cultivation, the Amur Province being the highest and the Maritime Province the lowest. Cereals were the chief crops in all three provinces.[16] Among these, wheat led in planted acreage while oats stood first in quantity of yield. Vegetables were grown both in Transbaikal and the Maritime Province. The latter province also grew beets, soya beans, tobacco, opium, potatoes, hemp, and other crops. Land under cultivation had increased in Siberia as a whole by 122 percent between 1897 and 1917.[17] In the latter years, the marketable surpluses of Siberia as a

[14] Darinsky, op. cit., pp. 17–18.

[15] The Special Delegation of the Far Eastern Republic to the United States of America, Trade and Industries of the Far Eastern Republic, Washington, 1922, pp. 42–43.

[16] Great Britain. Foreign Office, Eastern Siberia (handbook prepared under the direction of the Historical Section at the Foreign Office, No. 55), London, 1920, pp. 57–58; United States. Department of Commerce, Bureau of Foreign and Domestic Commerce, Daily Consular and Trade Reports, March 25, 1913, Washington, 1913, p. 1465. (Hereafter cited as Daily Consular and Trade Reports.)

[17] A. B. Baikalov, "Siberia Since 1894," The Slavonic and East European Review (London), xi, No. 33, January 1933, pp. 333.

whole were far above those of European Russia, the respective figures being 336 cwt. per one hundred persons as against 130 in European Russia.

Cattle breeding was confined largely to Transbaikal Province, which adjoins Mongolia, also a cattle-breeding area. Yet the Transbaikal was unable to produce enough meat to supply the Region and the meat shortages were made up by shipments from Mongolia just as grain shortages were made up by shipments from Northern Manchuria.[18] The dairy industry of the Region was far less developed than that of Western Siberia.[19] Consequently, quantities of butter were shipped in from Western Siberia. At the time of the outbreak of the war the government was trying to stimulate cattle-raising in the Region in order to reduce the dependence for meat and butter on Mongolia and Western Siberia respectively. These efforts were continued by the cooperatives during the war with some success. Horses were far more commonly used by the peasants of all three provinces than in European Russia. Pigs, sheep, and goats were raised principally in Transbaikal which, in 1911, also had 11,000 camels.

It has been mentioned above that the agricultural production of the Far Eastern Region was insufficient to fill the needs of the people, the difference being made up by shipments from Manchuria. The period of the intervention saw the level of production drop as the region was plundered and many of the able-bodied men joined the guerrilla and partisan bands.[20] Yet, until the revolution came, the peasant here was more prosperous than in European Russia and used far more agricultural machinery. Throughout Siberia the Colonization Department of the Ministry of Agriculture maintained between 250 and 300 agricultural stations which tested machinery of various kinds and supplied it to poor settlers on a time-payment basis.[21] Machinery could also be obtained directly through the

[18] P. I. Derber and M. L. Sher, *Ocherki Khoziaistvennoi Zhizni Dalnego Vostoka*, Moscow, 1927, pp. 91, 113.
[19] Great Britain. Foreign Office, *op. cit.*, pp. 59–60; *Daily Consular and Trade Reports*, May 23, 1914, p. 1071.
[20] Kireev, *op. cit.*, p. 31.
[21] N. Peacock, *The Russian Year-Book, 1916*, London, 1916, p. 535.

credit facilities of the International Harvester Company, which carried on a prosperous business before 1914, particularly in Western Siberia.[22] But the distance to world markets and the high railway rates kept wheat from being an economically profitable crop. Stock and animal breeding were more profitable since they could stand the high transportation rates better than the bulkier grain. The latter continued largely to be imported from an area of lower production costs. i.e., from Heilungkiang Province in Northern Manchuria.[23]

The provinces of the Region were divided between two separate governor-generalships.[24] Transbaikal in the West was part of the Irkutsk governor-generalship centered in the city of Irkutsk west of Lake Baikal. From this center the neighboring provinces of Irkutsk, Iakutsk, and Eniseisk, as well as Transbaikal, were administered. The other provinces of the Region, the Kamchatka, Sakhalin, Amur, and Maritime provinces, constituted the Priamur governor-generalship which had its center at the city of Khabarovsk. For a two-year period, between 1903 and 1905, the Far Eastern Region was part of an even larger unit, a viceroyalty headed by Admiral Alekseev which also had jurisdiction over Kuantung in southern Manchuria, the regions covered by the Russian railway rights throughout Manchuria, as well as all Russian subjects living near the areas covered by these rights.[25] In addition to these duties, the viceroy of the Far East was charged with all foreign relations that concerned his special province. The rule pertaining to the conduct of his office were modeled after those established for the viceroy or Imperial Lieutenant in the Caucasus. The effect of establishing this powerful and largely independ-

[22] Baikalov, *op. cit.*, p. 332.
[23] Chinese Eastern Railway Company, *Northern Manchuria and the Chinese Eastern Railway*, Harbin, 1924, p. 4.
[24] Russia Pereselencheskoe Upravlenie Glavnago Upravleniia Zemleustroistva i Zemledeliia, *Aziatskaia Rossia*, St. Petersburg, 1914, I, p. 44 (hereafter cited as *Aziatskaia Rossiia*); "Administrativnoe Delenie," *op. cit.*, pp. 23–26.
[25] J. V. A. MacMurray, *Treaties and Agreements with and Concerning China, 1894–1919*, New York, 1921, I, p. 122; V. I. Gurko, *Features and Figures of the Past; Government and Opinion in the Reign of Nicholas II*, Stanford, 1939, p. 281.

ent administrative unit was to create the impression, especially in Japan, that a foundation was being laid for even greater expansion in the Far East.

The provinces of the Region had military governors who were also atamans or commanders-in-chief of the Cossacks of their respective provinces.[26] The administrative centers were Vladivostok for the Maritime Province, Blagoveshchensk for Amur, Chita for Transbaikal, and Aleksandrovsk for Sakhalin. The provinces were divided into districts (uezd), cantons (volost) and villages. Cossacks managed their own affairs, but a special committee presided over by the deputy governor and including one representative each of the Ministries of Finance and Agriculture existed in each province for regular peasant affairs.[27] The peasant and his village organization were somewhat stronger in Siberia than in European Russia.

In addition to these secular divisions, the Far Eastern Region was also divided for purposes of ecclesiastical administration.[28] There were three eparchies or bishoprics in the area, the Transbaikal, the Blagoveshchensk, and the Vladivostok. The provinces of Kamchatka and Sakhalin were included within the jurisdiction of the last. The black or regular clergy numbered four hundred and sixty nine, the secular priests about four hundred and thirty eight, in addition to sacristans, deacons, and other members of the white or secular clergy. The church maintained here over six hundred churches and about an equal number of chapels, in addition to several monasteries and convents as well as religious libraries and schools.

The church performed both a spiritual and a political role in that it aimed not only at conversion to Orthodox Christianity but also at helping to produce a unified state through a program of Russification. The importance attached to this work in an area of such diverse ethnic groups and in such close proximity to older Far Eastern civilizations is not difficult to imagine. The work of the church in this and other respects

---

[26] *Aziatskaia Rossiia,* i, pp. 49–52.
[27] *Ibid.,* i, p. 51.
[28] B. Kandidov, *Iaponskaia Interventsiia v Sibiri i Tserkov,* Moscow, 1932, pp. 13–15.

was carried out in close coordination with the secular organs of government and under the same difficult internal and international conditions.

Most of the larger cities of the Region were founded shortly after the middle of the nineteenth century, though the most rapid growth came during the twenty years immediately preceding the revolution. Thus, Vladivostok, chartered as a city in 1876, had a population of 28,933 in 1897 which grew to 84,578 in 1911.[29] Blagoveshchensk, founded in 1856, grew from a population of 32,834 in 1897 to 64,383 in 1911. Other cities of importance were: Nikolsk-Ussuriisk, where the Chinese Eastern Railway branched off from the Ussuri line; Chita, which was a railway center in Transbaikàl; Khabarovsk, the administrative center of the Priamur governor-generalship; and Nikolaevsk, a fishing center at the mouth of the Amur. Outside the borders of Siberia proper the cities of Harbin, the center for the administration of the Chinese Eastern Railway in North Manchuria, and Urga in northern Outer Mongolia, a commercial center closely associated with Russia, are of special significance in the life of the Russian Far East.

Vladivostok was the largest city, the chief port of the Russian Far East, the terminus for the Trans-Siberian Railway, as well as the only Russian naval base on the Pacific. As a city it illustrates many of the weaknesses of the Russian Imperial Administration in Siberia. The lack of organizational unity for these distant territories in St. Petersburg was reflected in the divided administration of the city. The municipal administration, the Navy Department, the War Department, the Chinese Eastern Railway, and the Volunteer Fleet all had, up to 1909, a hand in its administration. In that year the Ministry of Commerce and Industry took it over with somewhat better results. But as a commercial port it remained poorly equipped to compete with the newer Japanese port of Dairen. It had poor equipment for loading and warehousing. Vessels in need of repairs or water and coal stores had to go to Japan for these services since Vladivostok lacked workshops as well as water and coaling facilities.

[29] *Aziatskaia Rossiia,* I, pp. 292, 346.

Yet the main street, the Svetlanskaia, and some others were among the few paved streets of Eastern Siberia.[30] The city had an Oriental Institute, the only school above secondary rank east to Tomsk. It had also a number of large department stores, among them the one owned by the German firm of Kunst and Albers. It had four daily newspapers. One of them, the *Dalekaia Okraina,* had been established by a Mr. Garfield, a nephew of the American President.[31]

Another city of considerable interest was Blagoveshchensk. Originally a military post and a Cossack stanitsa under the name of Ust-Zeisky, it received its present name from Count Muraviev-Amursky who came there in May 1858 to celebrate the signing of the new treaty with China. It also had a branch of Kunst and Albers as well as thirty mills and factories including iron foundries, breweries, tanneries, and rope factories. It stood at the confluence of the Amur and Zeia Rivers and therefore received the benefit of the gold mining and lumbering industries of that region. Blagoveshchensk gained additional importance as the civil and military administrative center of Amur Province. Culturally, it could offer twenty educational establishments, a library of 10,000 volumes, and four daily newspapers.[32]

The economy of this valuable and promising area has been characterized as colonial. Considering the wealth of the Region and the international pressures to which it was subject, there was certainly a waste of resources, both material and human. The indiscriminate use of forest and animal wealth has been mentioned. Moreover, the Russian people of the area lacked the capital for large-scale enterprise. As a result, even internal trade, such as was not handled from European Russia, was conducted largely by foreigners. The small commerce was largely in the hands of Chinese. Most of the larger business was handled by three groups of interests.[33] There was the local

[30] Harrison, *op. cit.,* pp. 143–145.
[31] *Ibid.,* p. 148.
[32] *Ibid.,* p. 100.
[33] V. Komarov, "Problemy Razvitiia Dalnevostochnogo Krai," *Planovoe Khoziaistvo* (Moscow) No. 2, 1936, p. 169, *Daily Consular and Trade Reports,* December 19, 1914, p. 1226.

branch of the Moscow firm of Chorin and Samsonov. German interests were represented by Kunst and Albers, already mentioned. Finally, there was considerable American business, especially in agricultural machinery. This was handled by the International Harvester Company. It was common for foreign firms not only to import the articles required but also to provide facilities for their distribution through local branches. The stores of Kunst and Albers and the local stations used for distribution purposes by the International Harvester Company were examples of this practice. Foreign participation in the economic life of the area extended even to the management of industrial enterprises. Skilled labor for these industries was quite commonly drawn from among the Chinese, the unskilled from the Koreans. It is evident that the people of the area were alarmingly dependent upon external sources both for skill in conducting their business and industrial life and for the manufactured goods which their primitive industries failed to supply.

Some improvement in the situation was being made before and during the war by the cooperatives. For Siberia as a whole, the cooperatives promoted the dairy industry, carried on credit and loan facilities, and even promoted such cultural activities as publishing journals, maintaining elementary and secondary schools, and arranging popular lectures.[34] They had more than two million members by 1916 and a joint yearly turnover of four hundred million rubles.

There were in these Far Eastern provinces forty different types of peoples.[35] Seventy-four percent of these were Russians; eighteen percent were Japanese, Chinese, or Korean; about six percent were natives. The native population was at the time of the war in a state of decline. It decreased from 54,466 in 1897 to 45,842 in 1911.[36] The other non-Russians such as Chinese, Japanese, and Koreans, on the other hand, increased in those same years from 82,104 to 176,588. The Russian increases will be noted below.

---

[34] Baikalov, *op. cit.*, p. 336.

[35] P. Derber, "Demografiia i Kolonizatsiia Sovetskogo Dalnego Vostoka," *Novyi Vostok* (Moscow), No. 7, 1925, p. 5.

[36] *Aziatskaia Rossiia*, I, p. 70.

The most numerous and most significant of the native people are the Buriats. They live to the west, east, and south of Lake Baikal and therefore in a very strategic location so far as communications between Central and Eastern Siberia are concerned. They are closely related to the Khalkas of Eastern Mongolia and the Barga people of northwestern Manchuria.[37] At the time of the intervention they numbered about 200,000 persons. It was they who detained the Russians in the early years of Russian advance into the Transbaikal area. They came to hold a favorable social position among the Russians and were free to share the benefits of Russian citizenship. This was due to their strength and the fact that a national movement had been vigorous among them for some time.[38] Resentment against the confiscation of their lands in times past and the building of the Trans-Siberian Railway through their territory had given the movement a broad popular base. During the period of the Provisional Government in 1917 they held three separate congresses, two at Irkutsk and one at Verkhne-Udinsk, the purpose of which was to plan for eventual autonomy.[39] This comparatively high degree of political consciousness which had developed among the Buriats was the basis for a separatist movement sponsored by the Japanese during the intervention with the idea of making use of their strategic location at Lake Baikal to sever Russia from the Pacific.[40] Their demand for a separate political status was recognized by the Far Eastern Republic set up in the Region in 1920 by the creation of the "Autonomous Buriat-Mongol Territory" and later the Soviet Government in the present "Buriat-Mongol Autonomous Soviet Socialist Republic."[41]

[37] Waldemar Jochelson, *Peoples of Asiatic Russia*, New York, 1928, p. 33; *Aziatskaia Rossiia*, I, pp. 82–85.
[38] G. D. D. Phillips, *Dawn in Siberia; the Mongols of Lake Baikal*, London, 1943, pp. 113ff.
[39] Maksakov and Turunov, *Khronika Grazhdanskoi Voiny v Sibiri, 1917–1918*, Moscow, 1926, pp. 34, 42, 45.
[40] B. Z. Shumiatsky, *Borba za Russkii Dalnii Vostok*, Irkutsk, 1922, p. 191; A. F. Speransky, "Materialy k Istorii Interventsii," *Novyi Vostok* (Moscow), No. 2, 1922, p. 593.
[41] H. K. Norton, *The Far Eastern Republic of Siberia*, London, 1923, p. 299.

It was among these and other native peoples that the Russian Cossack adventurers came in the first half of the seventeenth century. One of the earliest was Maksim Perfilev, who came in 1636.[42] He was followed by Poiarkov in 1643 and Khabarov in 1649. They spread terror among the people, plundered villages, and annihilated the native population. All this has left a vivid impression upon the legends of these peaceful natives. Legends grew about the people who came in large boats and had long red beards and blue eyes.[43] "Their noses are so large that the right eye can see nothing when looking to the left and the left sees nothing when looking to the right," ran one of their stories. The Russians found these Amur people cultivating fields and keeping cattle. Ten years later many of the fields were deserted and the region that had exported grain failed to support its own reduced population.[44] Since these initial cruelties, however, the government as a general rule interfered little with the people and even encouraged the strengthening of the clan system among them.

Statistics regarding the number of East Asiatic peoples in the Region are undependable. The Chinese, however, formed the largest group, their numbers estimated as high as 120,000 and as low as 49,000 about the time of the Revolution.[45] They began to enter in the 1870's at about the same time that serious colonization of Manchuria itself began.[46] The Chinese never became really assimilated and as a rule did not learn the Russian language or understand the Russian laws. Some were shopkeepers and tradesmen. But many others were small farmers and laborers who worked for lower wages. This was partly because of their social sep-

[42] A. Zolotarev, "Iz Istorii Narodov Amura," *Istoricheskii Zhurnal* (Moscow), July 1937, pp. 31–33; F. A. Golder, *Russian Expansion on the Pacific, 1641–1850,* Cleveland, 1914, pp. 33ff.
[43] Zolotarev, *loc. cit.,* p. 33.
[44] Great Britain, Foreign Office, *op. cit.,* p. 12.
[45] *Trade and Industry of the Far Eastern Republic,* p. 13; Harrison, *op. cit.,* p. 238. See also P. Derber and M. L. Sher, *op. cit.,* p. 10.
[46] C. W Young, *Japan's Special Position in Manchuria; Its Assertion, Legal Interpretation and Present Meaning,* Baltimore, 1931, pp. 14–17.

arateness and partly because they tended to look upon their residence as temporary and expected to return to China.

The Koreans, happy to escape the Japanese administration in their homeland, adapted themselves much better to their new surroundings. They learned the Russian language, joined the Orthodox Church, and adopted Russian dress. They were excellent farmers and most of them lived in the rural areas of the Maritime Province. There were more than 40,000 at the time of the Revolution. Regarding the number of Japanese settlers who also lived mostly in the Maritime Province there is wide difference of opinion. Official Russian statistics for 1911 set their number at 3,545 while estimates by American representatives there during the intervention set the figure at ten to twelve thousand.[47]

Long before the great period of expansion inaugurated in the sixteenth century, Russian fur traders had become acquainted with Siberia.[48] The growth of the city-state of Novgorod and its dependence on furs for its rich share in the trade of the Hanseatic League made an eastward movement of its fur trappers through the forest areas of Russia almost inevitable. As time went on the forest wealth of Siberia, known in an early period as Ugria, was tapped more and more. Although Russian military forces had operated in Siberia as early as 1483, it was apparently not until after the conquest of Kazan under Ivan IV in the middle of the sixteenth century that relations with Siberia became close and that anything like the complete submission of the area to Russian power was contemplated.[49] It was the refusal of the Siberian Khan to submit to Russian authority and his interference with the valuable enterprises of the powerful

[47] *Asiatskaia Rossiia*, I, p. 80; F. F. Moore, *The Far Eastern Republic of Siberia and Japan; Together with a Discussion of their Relations to the United States*, New York, 1922, p. 6.

[48] A. V. Baikalov, "The Conquest and Colonization of Siberia," *The Slavonic and East European Review* (London), xv, No. 30, April 1932, p. 550; R. J. Kerner, *The Urge to the Sea: The Course of Russian History; the Role of Rivers, Portages, Ostrogs, Monasteries, and Fairs*, Berkeley, 1942, pp. 67–68.

[49] V. V. Barthold, *La Decouverte de L'Asie; Histoire de L'Orientalisme en Europe et en Russie*, Paris, 1947, p. 215.

Stroganov family which presently resulted in stern Russian reprisals. Thus it came about that Vasilii Timofevich Alemin-Povolsky, better known as Ermak, set out for Siberia under the banners of the Stroganov family in 1581 and, two years later, on October 25, 1583, defeated Khan Kuchum at his capital, Isker or Sibir. The purpose of this and succeeding expeditions was, as already indicated, to achieve unobstructed access to the furs of Siberia. The significance of the movement can be appreciated from the fact that the revenues from furs rose at times to ten percent of the total income of the state.[50] In addition, the search for metals and the desire to open trade with the East may have been other incentives for this eastward expansion.[51] The almost simultaneous expansion of the seaboard states of Western Europe toward the centers of trade and easy wealth were well known to the Russian ruler. Since Ivan IV was directly interested in England and her commercial growth, it is not impossible that a sense of competition for these desirable objectives was a part of this eastward expansion. A silver smeltery was in fact not established at Nerchinsk Zavod in Transbaikal until 1704.[52] But furs were themselves of tremendous value as North American experience shows and were paid for in gold by the merchants on the European market.

Although the Russians reached the Pacific during the seventeenth century, the new Manchu Dynasty in China took vigorous steps to hold them back from the whole Amur region and by the Treaty of Nerchinsk, signed September 6, 1689, Russia recognized Chinese sovereignty in what later became the three continental provinces of the Region.[53] The first treaty between China and a Western power thus ended in a triumph for China.

[50] Raymond H. Fisher, *The Russian Fur Trade, 1550–1700*, Berkeley, 1943, p. 119.

[51] See V. A. Ulianitsky, *Snosheniia Rossii s Sredneiu Azieiu i Indieiu v XVI–XVII vv.*, Moscow, 1889, pp. 4–5.

[52] N. Iliukhov, "Dalnevostochnyi Krai," *Bolshaia Sovetskaia Entsiklopediia* (Moscow), 1931, III, 278.

[53] China. The Maritime Customs, *Treaties, Conventions, Etc., Between China and Foreign States*, Shanghai, 1917, I, pp. 3–13.

Not until China had been weakened by the external attacks of other Western nations and the internal revolt against a government so weak as to be incapable of resisting these blows, not until this situation arose in the middle of the nineteenth century was the Chinese relationship to Russia, established by the Nerchinsk Treaty, reversed. While externally Russia was, to be sure, acting in a competitive Far Eastern situation, internally she had ample reason for wishing to distract the attention of her people. It was a time when the pressures of population growth and land hunger were increasing to a point which in the long run resulted in the disappointing peasant emancipation.[54] It was against this background and in the same decade as the Crimean War that a series of rapid moves on the Pacific transformed the Far Eastern Region into a possession of the Russian Empire.

Russian aggression against China in the Amur region developed rapidly after 1850. In 1850 Nikolaevsk at the mouth of the Amur was founded. In 1852 the island of Sakhalin was seized against rather weak Japanese opposition, the first open clash of these two nations. This was followed by the occupation of key points along the coast of the Maritime Province. In May 1854, Muraviev moved in force down the Amur, founded Khabarovsk, and moved on to the coast, where he repelled an Anglo-French attack on Kamchatka. An Allied landing party of 700 to 1,000 men was driven off from the vicinity of Petropavlovsk. By the treaties of Aigun in 1858 and Peking in 1860, the whole continental portion of the Far Eastern Region came into Russian hands.[55] China, weakened by the T'ai P'ing Rebellion and the renewed attacks of the Western nations, was thus forced to recognize by these legal instruments the loss of the strong position she had held against Russia since 1689. The work of Erofei Pavlovich Khabarov, the first adventurer in the Amur Valley, was thus completed by another adventurer and parts of his name have been commemorated in two cities along

[54] M. S. Miller, *The Economic Development of Russia, 1905–1914,* London, 1926, p. 93.
[55] China. The Maritime Customs, *op. cit.,* I, pp. 81–84, 101–120.

the Amur Railway, Erofei Pavlovich, the first station after entering Amur Province from the West and Khabarovsk, the last station before entering the Maritime Province.[56]

The settlement of this distant area proceeded slowly until means of transportation were provided. The trip across Siberia by foot or around Africa by ship was so arduous as to cause the opportunities of a new land to be regarded with indifference even by the land-hungry peasants of Russia. However, the opening of the Suez Canal in 1869 and the establishment by Russia of the Volunteer Fleet in 1870 made the region somewhat more accessible. The main run of the Volunteer Fleet was from Odessa to Vladivostok and since many of the early settlers came from the overpopulated farms of the Ukraine, a means of transportation became available for these early non-Cossack settlers.[57] But the movement was slow. A law of 1861 offered land to prospective settlers in large quantities and on a long-term payment basis with such additional benefits as exemptions from military service and from imperial taxation for periods of ten and twenty years respectively and from rural taxes for three years.[58]

The results were not encouraging if the purpose was to relieve the situation in the Ukraine and, at the same time, populate the Far East against future days of trouble. To the 20,000 settlers in the Amur and Maritime provinces in 1858 there was added a meager 90,000 by 1900.[59] Transbaikal, which remained the most populous province before the Revolution, was somewhat better off, having over 350,000 persons in 1858 and 672,000 in 1897.[60] A law of 1881, giving active aid to peasant settlement, was somewhat more effective since the settlements between 1883 and 1899 in the Amur and the Maritime Provinces were seven times what they had been in the preceding twenty-three years.[61] In this same

---

[56] *Aziatskaia Rossiia,* I, p. 513.
[57] Miller, *op. cit.,* p. 5; Conolly, *op. cit.,* p. 18.
[58] *Aziatskaia Rossiia,* I, p. 520.
[59] *Ibid.;* Great Britain, Foreign Office, *op. cit.,* p. 17.
[60] Iliukhov, *op. cit.,* p. 279.
[61] Derber, *op. cit.,* p. 111.

period the Maritime Province grew to have almost twice the population of Amur. But the Settlement Bureau, established in 1896, probably helped to produce this result. This provided free land to settlers, information as to available sites, the maintenance of feeding stations and hospitals along the way, and the establishment throughout Siberia of depots for the supply of agricultural implements and machinery.[62] By 1914 the assistance being given to these settlers had increased its scope considerably.[63] Before the building of the Trans-Siberian Railway the arrivals coming by sea from Odessa were cared for by facilities at Vladivostok. After the completion of the railway similar provisions were made at Khabarovsk, Harbin, Pogranichnaia, Nikolsk-Ussuriisk, and other localities. Not only were barracks and hospitals available for the new arrivals, but milk and warm food were provided for children and others in need of special treatment.

The greatest aid to settlement was of course the building of the Trans-Siberian Railway, the significance of which will be dealt with presently. Due to the fact that it was completed during the progress of hostilities, the full effect of the railway was not really felt until after the Russo-Japanese war. In 1907, however, came the greatest year of all in the colonization of the Amur and Maritime provinces. In this year the number exceeded the last prewar year, 1903, by more than five times and the second greatest year, 1910, by almost two times.[64] By 1916 the total population of the three continental provinces of the Far East was 1,709,400, of which Transbaikal had over 830,000, Amur over 300,000, and the Maritime Province more than 560,000.[65]

Among the settlers there were certain special groups which have influenced the life of Siberia in varying degrees. The political and criminal exiles had brought some of the best and some of the worst to Siberia. The really criminal elements who were thrust into the life of Siberia (as they have

[62] Baikalov, "Siberia since 1894," *op. cit.*, pp. 328–329.
[63] *Daily Consular and Trade Reports,* May 21, 1914, p. 1023.
[64] *Aziatskaia Rossiia,* I, p. 524.
[65] Iliukhov, *op. cit.*, p. 279.

been in many other colonial areas) were a source of resentment to the serious and self-respecting Siberian peasants. It was estimated that there was, before the war, a floating population in Siberia of roughly 100,000 persons who begged and stole and made the problem of maintaining public order difficult and expensive for the Siberians.[66] On the other hand, there was also the political transgressor who, in many cases, contributed much to his new home. Revolutionary upheavals of the past had resulted in several additions to the population. There were the Decembrists who came to Chita after the uprising of 1825. There were also the Polish patriots who had taken part in the revolt of 1863 and the Russian revolutionaries of 1905 and 1906. After 1914 there came thousands of war prisoners. It is of course the war prisoners who are of special importance during the intervention period. But the exiles are also of great importance because of their share in giving expression to discontent with the old order and the formulation of specific demands for revolutionary change.

The Cossacks were of particular significance in the settlement of Eastern Siberia. Their stanitsas were established along the Amur and the Ussuri on the Manchurian border and in Transbaikal. They received the best lands in the largest quantities and constituted the real privileged caste against which–rather than the landlord as in European Russia–the peasant could be aroused. Their attitude toward the rest of the farmers will be seen in the succeeding pages.

While the population of Eastern Siberia grew steadily up to the Revolution, the rate of growth decreased after 1908,[67] partly because of the decrease in the supply of the most available land and partly because of some unfavorable farming years in Siberia. Also, there was the constant flux in the population. It is estimated that in 1913 only thirty-five percent of those who went to the Far Eastern Region remained there.[68] The increase in population, moreover, was higher

---

[66] Great Britain. Foreign Office, op. cit., p. 34.
[67] Ibid., p. 18.
[68] Conolly, op. cit., p. 19.

among the Slavic then among the other stocks, the increase in these years being fifteen and seven percent respectively.[69] This was aided of course by the Russification and consequent loss of racial identity by some of the natives. Whatever the reason, the Russian stock who had constituted sixty-six percent of the population in 1897 amounted to eighty percent twenty years later. Another change that took place during these same twenty years was the increased urbanization, the urban population of Siberia as a whole increasing by one hundred and eighteen percent.[70]

More than seventy-five percent of the people in the Eastern Siberia region were village dwellers.[71] Between 1897 and 1917, the urban growth, although great, was not as large as the rural so that the rural population, which equaled seventy-three percent of the population in 1897, rose to seventy-seven in 1917. Occupational changes also show the effects of the railways with a larger number of residents entering the transportation and commercial occupations. Between 1914 and 1920 the ravages of civil war registered a radically different proportion of men and women.[72] In the former year there were 67 women for every 100 men while in the latter there were 104 women for every 100 men.

It has already been noted that among this predominantly rural population the Cossacks rather than the traditional landlords as in European Russia were the privileged group. Among the non-Cossacks there was another conservative group, the old settlers who had come when land was distributed in larger quantities and in more accessible locations.[73] But the absence, generally speaking, of landlordism and of the big estates gave a much more harmonious tone

[69] Baikalov, "Siberia Since 1894," *op. cit.,* p. 331.
[70] *Ibid.*
[71] Derber, *loc. cit.,* p. 107; also F. Lorimer, *The Population of the Soviet Union: History and Prospects,* Geneva, 1946, p. 70.
[72] Derber, *op. cit.,* pp. 104–105.
[73] B. Pares, *My Russian Memoirs,* p. 518; W. H. Chamberlain, *The Russian Revolution, 1917–1921,* II, p. 194; U.S. Dept. of State, *Papers Relating to the Foreign Relations of the United States, 1919, The Paris Peace Conference,* v, pp. 545–547 (cited hereafter as *Peace Conference Papers*).

to the population as compared to the situation in European Russia. As a result of this, land reforms were less pressing and discontent was directed chiefly against the Cossacks and to a lesser extent against the old settlers.

The privileged Cossack land tenure made this difference considerable in many cases. In Siberia ninety-six percent of the land was owned by the State.[74] It was allotted to settlers on the basis, as of 1917, of from 20–40 acres for each male in the family among regular settlers and 100 acres for each Cossack male. The land was conveyed by letters of allotment and held for the perpetual benefit of the settler, who had no right either to sell or mortgage it. The land remained the possession of the State and sales were made only in Amur Province. Both the common and individual holdings existed, the latter being much more frequent than in European Russia. There was a higher level of prosperity among the peasants of Siberia. Only the Cossack had a distinctly separate status since by virtue of military service he held and occupied some of the most desirable lands. The Cossack stanitsas were noted by all travelers on the Amur. Here and on the Ussuri as well as in southern Transbaikal their duty was to guard the frontier.

The protective functions of the Cossacks were not too well performed. The area was very disturbed, not only by the unattached exiles but by the Chinese robber bands.[75] Some of these latter, known as Hung Hu Tze, came out of the Chinese settlements in Siberia itself while others crossed the border from Manchuria. These disorderly bands particularly afflicted the Maritime Province and the Ussuri Valley. Their terroristic activities affected the Chinese as well as the Russians, and robbery and murder threatened wherever these bands appeared. When conditions were unsafe for the bands they disappeared into the villages or recrossed the frontier into Manchuria.

Racial issues made labor conditions unsettled. The largest

[74] Great Britain. Foreign Office, *op. cit.*, pp. 67–68.
[75] V. K. Arsenev, *Russen und Chinesen in Ostsibirien*, Berlin, 1926, p. 149.

number of the workers of the Region not engaged in agriculture, forestry, or fishing were employed in transportation or some other form of public service, with a considerably lesser number occupied in mining and small manufacturing.[76] Since the natives, with the exception of the Buriats, did not usually engage in industrial occupations, the free colonists were farmers by preference, the Cossacks seldom hired themselves out for anything, and the number of exiles coming to Eastern Siberia grew increasingly smaller, the growth of these essential enterprises seemed to depend on the increasing influx of Chinese. Yet the political situation in the Far East in the years before the war aroused a fear of the surrounding Oriental peoples, both Japanese and Chinese, and led to an attempt to exclude them from labor markets. The hiring of Japanese in the fishing industry was forbidden in 1900 and a law of June 21, 1910 placed limitations on the employment of Chinese.[77] The Chinese also worked cheaply and kept wages down, thus making the industrial occupations still less attractive to the land-bound Russian peasant. The Chinese, however, continued to come.

The economic life of Siberia was dependent to an extraordinary degree upon the thin line of railway track that bridged the distance between Petrograd and Vladivostok. The rise and development of anything more than a natural economy can hardly be imagined apart from the railway.

The whole line, known as the Trans-Siberian Railroad, was financed, built, and managed by the Imperial Government.[78] Administratively the Trans-Siberian Railway, exclusive of the Chinese Eastern, consisted of five separate railways. The westernmost of these links was the Omsk line, which ran from Cheliabinsk to Novonikolaevsk. The second was the Tomsk line, which ran from the latter city to Innokentevsk with a

[76] G. Reikhberg, "Dalnevostochnyi Proletariat v Borbe s Iaponskoi Interventsiei," *Istoriia Proletariata S.S.S.R.* (Moscow), No. 2, 1934, p.153; Lorimer, *op. cit.*, p. 71.

[77] Z. Karpenko, *Grazhdanskaia Voina v Dalnevostochnom Krae (1918– 1922)*, Khabarovsk, 1934, p. 14; Peacock, *op. cit.*, p. 478.

[78] I. Tsakni, "Zheleznye Dorogi," *Sibirskaia Sovetskaia Entsiklopediia,* Moscow, 1931, I, pp. 912–913.

47

branch line to Tomsk. From here the Transbaikal line went on to Sretensk with a branch line to Manchuli, the western link with the Chinese Eastern Railway. The Amur line from Kuenga to Khabarovsk and the Ussuri line from there to Vladivostok with a branch line to Pogranichnaia, the eastern link with the Chinese Eastern, completed the Trans-Siberian line. While the management was thus subdivided, it was, nevertheless, concentrated in faraway Petrograd.[79] Much of the local management was equally inefficient. Trains were not dispatched but were handled on a station-to-station basis by the station masters. Timetables and printed train rules were non-existent while even watches were rare among the trainmen. Fueling was slow and handled in a primitive fashion. A given locomotive was driven exclusively by one engineer and went back and forth with him as he made his round-trip runs. This fact alone cut down the efficiency of the road to a considerable extent. All in all, the management was poor and the result was almost to be expected—the railway ran at a loss. In 1909 the Chinese Eastern Railway alone was said to be running at a loss of twenty million rubles per year.[80]

The reasons for building the Trans-Siberian Railway were various. The chronic peasant overpopulation, especially in the South, was one of the chief reasons. Along with this must also be considered the famine of 1891 as well as the conditions which helped to produce it.[81] The pressure of the increasingly influential Russian capitalists was a factor of considerable significance in forcing the government to find this outlet for pent-up discontent and ambitions.[82] Externally, the Anglo-Russian competition, particularly for the markets of the Far East as well as the determined rise of Japan, were additional factors.[83] The question as to whether the line was intended primarily for economic or strategic purposes is not too reward-

[79] J. E. Greiner, *The Russian Railway Situation and Some Personal Observations,* Baltimore, 1918, pp. 14–15.

[80] Harrison, *op. cit.,* p. 182.

[81] Tsakni, *op. cit.,* p. 910.

[82] M. Pavlovich, "Iaponskii Imperialism na Dalnem Vostoke," *Novyi Vostok* (Moscow), No. 2, 1922, p. 7.

[83] Tsakni, *op. cit.,* p. 909.

ing a speculation. One writer maintains that the building of the railway in sections indicates an attempt to open up successive areas for economic ends rather than a consistent plan having a strategic purpose.[84] Whatever the reason, a special committee of four ministers recommended the immediate building of a railway to establish more rapid communications with cities to the East and the work began.

Building began on the Ussuri line at Vladivostok on May 31, 1891 (N.S.), and on the Omsk line at Cheliabinsk on July 29, 1892 (N.S.).[85] The problem raised by the difficult terrain over which the Amur section of the railway would pass was seriously considered as early as 1894. A number of factors, however, pointed to the use of the Manchurian route even before the opportunity arose for acquiring it. Both the climate and the rugged terrain of the Amur region in addition to the fact that the Manchuria route was shorter by four hundred miles caused Witte and others to favor the latter. Fortunately for the planners, the Sino-Japanese War and the Triple Intervention were so timely as to make possible the building of the Chinese Eastern Railway before any work had begun on the Amur line. Meanwhile, the Omsk line to Novonikolaevsk was completed and opened in 1896.[86] In the following year the Ussuri line from Vladivostok to Khabarovsk was opened. By 1903 the whole line through Siberia and Manchuria to Vladivostok was completed except for the section around Lake Baikal between Baikal and Mysovaia which was finally finished in 1905. The new political situation which arose in the Far East after 1905, however, made the shortcut through Manchuria look far less dependable as a route to Vladivostok and the Pacific. In 1908, therefore, the building of the alternate Amur Railroad began.[87] This was finally opened for traffic in 1914 though not completed until two years

[84] J. Mavor, *An Economic History of Russia,* London, Toronto, New York, 1925, II, p. 228.

[85] Mavor, *op. cit.,* II, p. 226; E. D. Grimm, "Kitaiskii Vopros ot Simonosekskogo Mira do Mirovoi Voiny (1895–1914)," *Novyi Vostok* (Moscow), No. 6, 1924, p. 50.

[86] Tsakni, *op. cit.,* pp. 910–912.

[87] Kireev, *op. cit.,* pp. 25–26.

later. Most of the line east of Omsk and around Khabarovsk was double-tracked. The 2,261 miles eastward from Omsk was at that time the longest stretch of double-tracked railway in the world.[88]

The significance of the railway to the economic life of Siberia and Northern Manchuria has probably become apparent already. The loosely associated, primitive economies of both these regions were given a lifeline which tied them together and connected them for the first time with the outside world.[89] The growth of population, the rise of cities, the opening of markets, the beginning of industry all followed from the building of the railway. Interference with the railway could also break down and wreck this economic structure.

It was the railway that created the first demand for coal.[90] The Suchan mines of the Maritime Province, the Kvidinsk of Amur, and others were opened under railway demands. Likewise, the fishing industry of Eastern Siberia and the dairy industry of Western Siberia both began and thrived because of the new transportation system.[91] The railway also remained one of the chief users of mineral and forest products, thus contributing also in this sense to the rise of industry. Above all, the railroad was a means of increasing and supporting a growing population. A journey which had once taken from two to four years even if made by horse was now reduced to a matter of days. Travelers often noted the peculiar relationship of the railway to the cities of Siberia.[92] Many of them were at some distance from the railroad so that when a new town" was built nearer that railway, a branch line became necessary to establish a connection between the railway and the towns which were already established. The cities of Cheliabinsk, Omsk, Tomsk, and Khabarovsk are notable examples of the latter.

[88] Greiner, op. cit., p. 5.
[89] Tsakni, op. cit., p. 915; Chinese Eastern Railway Company, op. cit., p.14.
[90] Goudkoff, op. cit., p. 285.
[91] Baikalov, "Siberia Since 1894," op. cit., pp. 334–335.
[92] C. W. Ackerman, Trailing the Bolsheviki; Twelve Thousand Miles with the Allies in Siberia, New York, 1919, p. 50.

Aside from the railways there were a number of other means of transportation. There was the Volunteer Fleet, a public company organized in 1870.[93] Its main line was from Odessa to Vladivostok, though it sent ships to Siberian ports to the north and to ports of Japan and China to the south, as well as to the United States and Western Europe. There were also river fleets such as the Amur and Sungari River Fleet, the latter a subsidiary of the Chinese Eastern Railway.

The great expansive movement of Russia just described had made her a Far Eastern nation, sharing from this time on in the historical development of the Pacific area. A writer in the *Edinburgh Review* in January 1896, thinking perhaps of how the pressure on India was being relieved by these developments, wrote: "A vast landlocked empire with only two issues to the open sea, upon waters that are for many months frozen, may be pardoned for vigorous, if not violent efforts to break through her barriers."[94] Cooperation with England, however, was some time in the future. With France the situation was somewhat different. Her investments in the railroad were well repaid by her advance in South China, too far away to feel the threat of the Russian movement toward a warm-water port. Outside of China, the nation that reacted most vigorously to this movement was Japan. For, in her advance to Vladivostok and Port Arthur, Russia seemed about to absorb the very areas that Japan considered vital to her existence. Moreover, once in possession of these key points, Russia would undoubtedly come to look upon Korea as a natural prize. The same geographical circumstance which brought about Triple Intervention against Japan in 1895 was therefore also a basic cause of the Russo-Japanese War of 1904–1905, this time aimed at Russian expansion.

The fundamental international incentive which gave rise to the advance of Russia into this hazardous position was the new relationship she established between herself and China by the treaties of 1858 and 1860, according to which she had

---

[93] "Dobrovolnyi Flot," *Bolshaia Sovetskaia Entsiklopediia*, xxii, p. 793.
[94] W. L. Langer, *The Diplomacy of Imperialism*, 1890–1902, New York, 1935, i, p. 400.

acquired the whole Amur and Maritime territories. In the first place, Russia was the only nation which actually took territory at that time, thus committing the first large territorial grab at the expense of China. By the same action, moreover, she cut off China from access to the sea along the eastern coast of Manchuria and, at the same time, acquired the valuable port of Vladivostok.[95] Geographically, this left Russia facing her major antagonist, Japan, across the narrow stretches of the Japan Sea. Unhappily for China, it established the new principle that encroachment upon the rights and even the territory of China required only the acquiesence of other potential aggressors. By this stroke of misfortune for the Far East and for the world, China became a negligible factor, a land to be exploited. She was, in fact, removed from this time on as a determining factor in the further developments in Northeastern Asia.

With China eliminated as an active factor in Far Eastern affairs, there remained now the question of how freely Russia could move her boundary southward. The chief conflict over this issue developed with Japan, the new and wholly Far Eastern power. Historically, this conflict first arose in Sakhalin, which Japan claimed by virtue of certain explorations there in the eighteenth century.[96] But Russia was the first to arrive there in force. The Japanese retreat in this issue was given legal sanction by the treaty of 1875, which recognized Russian sovereignty in almost all of the island.[97] Aniva Bay in the south and the Kurile Islands were to become Japanese possessions. As the crisis of the late nineteenth century developed, hints of future troubles, if the Russian pressure against Korea were continued, were given by the governor of Amur Province in a report to the Russian Foreign Office.[98] He suggested that it would be unwise to take Korea since its distance made it hard to defend and occupation would almost certainly result in a conflict with Japan or with China, backed by Britain. It

[95] E. B. Price, *The Russo-Japanese Treaties of 1907–1916 Concerning Manchuria and Mongolia,* Baltimore, 1933, p. 13.
[96] Ishii, *Gaiko Yoroku,* Tokyo, 1931, p. 91.
[97] A. Lobanov-Rostovsky, *Russia and Asia,* New York, 1933, p. 146.
[98] Langer, *op. cit.,* I, p. 169.

was better, he felt, to work with Japan and the United States against Chinese pretensions in Korea. Thus the working arrangements of the future were quite clearly foreseen, even before the beginning of any hostilities.

After the Sino-Japanese War and the Triple Intervention of 1895, Russian eagerness to move southward was stimulated by fears and forebodings of a possible English or Japanese advance into regions she had herself planned to occupy. Fortunately for her ambitions, the developments in the Far East provided Russia with the excuse to carry out a program of encroachment on China which might have resulted in her control of Manchuria had not Japan been interested in forestalling the Russian advance. The Russian thrust southward was made in three separate moves. The first of these was a Russian plan to aid China against possible Japanese encroachment by the building of a railway across Manchuria between the Transbaikal and Maritime provinces.[99] The first step toward implementing this plan was taken with the organization in December 1895 of the Russo-Chinese Bank, an institution financed by French interests and empowered to secure railway concessions. The second step was the signing of the Russo-Chinese Treaty in May 1896 permitting the construction of the railway. Finally the actual terms under which the Russo-Chinese Bank was to carry out the construction were defined in an instrument called the "Contract for the Construction and Operation of the Chinese Eastern Railway," signed on September 8, 1896.

The second of the major Russian moves toward a monopoly position in Manchuria took place during 1897 and 1898. The excuse for this was the German occupation in 1897 of Kiao Chow followed by the acquisition of other valuable rights in the province of Shantung. Since Russia knew in advance of the German intention to carry out this attack, ways and means of counter balancing it by another Russian acquisition were discussed in St. Petersburg. The most obvious point for a Russian base on the Yellow Sea was of course Port

[99] Chinese Eastern Railway Company, *op. cit.*, p. 35; Conolly, *op. cit.*, pp. 165–168; MacMurray, *op. cit.*, I, pp. 74–77, 81–82.

Arthur. Count Witte, as though repeating the advice given nine years before by the Amur governor, counseled against taking this step on the grounds that the taking of Port Arthur would be a betrayal of Japan and the undertakings which led to the retrocession of Liaotung in 1895, and would certainly end disastrously.[100] Moreover, the treaty with China, he urged, was based on the territorial integrity of that nation and an occupation of Port Arthur would in this respect be nothing less than treachery, and might, in addition, endanger the safety of the railway already projected in Manchuria. But in November 1897, the Council of Ministers, meeting under the presidency of the Tsar, decided otherwise and Port Arthur was occupied the following month. With the aid of a large bribe paid over to the key Chinese officials concerned, Li Hung-chang and Chang Yin-huang, the desired lease to Port Arthur was signed on March 27, 1898.[101]

The Boxer Rebellion provided the next opening for a Russian advance into Manchuria. When he heard of this event, War Minister Kuropatkin is said to have remarked, "I am very glad. This will give us an excuse for seizing Manchuria."[102] And Russia proceeded to do just this. By October 1900, she had sent over 50,000 troops into Manchuria and established control. These moves helped to solidify the opposition to Russia on the part of Japan, Britain, and the United States, and gave the policies of these nations a somewhat false appearance of unity. The Anglo-Japanese Alliance was, however, one of the results of this. Yet even these developments failed to change Russian policy. She not only remained in possession of all her Manchurian gains but actually went on to enhance her position. The establishment in 1903 of a Russian viceroyalty in the Far East was taken by Japan to mean that Russia was preparing for permanent occupation.[103]

[100] Pavlovich, *op. cit.*, pp. 5–6.
[101] MacMurray, *op. cit.*, pp. 119–121.
[102] E. H. Zabriskie, *American-Russian Rivalry in the Far East; A Study in Diplomacy and Power Politics, 1895–1914*, Philadelphia, 1946, p. 95.
[103] H. Kobayashi, *Shosetsu Nippon Rekishi*, Tokyo, 1929, III, p. 494; Gurko, *op. cit.*, p. 281.

The Russo-Japanese War followed. This was a significant event for Russia. It meant that an Asiatic power had taken the offensive against her for the first time since pre-Muscovite days.[104] With such a reversal the Asiatic revolt might spread and the counterattack grow more effective in the future. In treaties signed during 1907 Russia therefore came to an understanding with both Japan and Great Britain. The growing disturbances in the Near and Middle East and the American ambitions in Manchuria helped to give these new treaty relationships a more solid basis than might otherwise have been expected.

But the treaties did not alter the new relationship which the war had brought about between Russia and Japan. This new relationship bred fear and a loss of self-confidence among the people of the poorly defended Russian frontier. Mr. Harrison, traveling through there in 1909, found that, "The question uppermost in the minds of East Siberian publicists at the present time would therefore seem to be the ability of Russia to retain possession of her vast Asiatic heritage."[105]

There was the feeling among the people of the Far Eastern Region that Russia was friendless in the Far East and that, even though her Chinese Eastern Railway represented a yearly loss of millions, she could not with safety sell it either to Japan or China since it would only increase their strength against her. One newspaper expressed the fear, not entirely unjustified as diplomatic observers well knew, that Japan was increasing her military forces as rapidly as possible and that Korea would surely be used as a base of operations against Vladivostok. Japan, it was appreciated, did not have to disperse her strength all over Asia as did Russia. She could concentrate her forces in Korea and South Manchuria at her leisure, and strike when the moment was propitious. There was, in short, a mixture of a sense of guilt about the past and well-founded fear of the future.

Roosevelt had seen this threat during the Russo-Japanese War and felt that, should Japan drive Russia out of the Far

[104] Lobanov-Rostovsky, *op. cit.,* pp. 235–236.
[105] Harrison, *op. cit.,* p. 2.

East and annex Siberia up to Lake Baikal, the balance of power in the Far East would be upset.[106] He saw clearly that this would be against the interests of the United States. Moreover, within Russia there was considerable sympathy for some type of arrangement which would make use of this American interest. The *Novoe Vremia,* a St. Petersburg daily, frankly advocated a Russo-American entente.[107] Kokovtsev, Russian Minister of Finance, strongly favored the sale of the Chinese Eastern to the American financial group. But other counsels prevailed and, in the end, a bargain was struck with the most immediate competitor in the new Russo-Japanese treaty signed in 1910. Meanwhile the progress of the Amur Railway was kept a deep secret even though all knew that the site was visited openly by Japanese agents.[108] But the railway was to be the means of salvation when the Japanese struck from the south. That might happen, predicted the Harbin journal, the *Kharbinskii Vestnik,* by the spring of 1912.

At the outbreak of the First World War, the last governor-general of the Priamur governor-generalship, Nikolai Lvovich Gondatti, was actively trying to alter this precarious balance to Russian advantage. He had been the leader of the so-called Amur Expedition of 1910, an investigating commission sent out by Stolypin to find out what could be done.[109] The following year he succeeded General Unterberger as governor-general of Priamur and proceeded immediately to take active measures. He tried to block the growth of Japanese commercial and fishing interests and to shut out all alien labor, whether Chinese, Japanese, or Korean.[110] In these and other enterprises he had little success. Russian weakness in the direct line of Japanese advance was hard to overcome in so short a time. The undeveloped areas north of Kuan Cheng-tze station on the South Manchuria Railway remained an invitation and a challenge to Japanese ambitions.

The Far Eastern situation which Russia faced with such

[106] Zabriskie, *op. cit.,* p. 116.
[107] *Ibid.,* p. 152.
[108] Harrison, *op. cit.,* p. 127.
[109] *Aziatskaia Rossiia,* I, p. 467.
[110] F. A. Ogg, "Siberia and the Japanese," *The New York Times Current History* (New York), XIV, No. 3, June 1921, p. 467.

misgivings, and to which she reacted so aggressively, was one which in the long run would amount to a revolution in international power relationships. While in the Pacific, Japan and the United States were bringing new forces to bear upon the political balance, in Europe the development of the German Empire and naval power was drawing the attention of Britain and France away from the Far East. These developments would presently force France and Great Britain to adjust themselves to these new naval powers.

The year 1894 was in many respects a turning point in this development. This was the year in which Japan, already remodeled domestically along Western, aggressive lines, launched a war against China and became an open competitor for power in the Far East. As the Sino-Japanese War came to an end in 1895 and the Treaty of Shimonoseki registered the results, it became obvious that at least three new factors had forced themselves upon the attention of the world. The first was the rise of Japan to the status of a world power and the realization that her voice would have to be heard in future imperialist developments in China. The second was that, if allowed to stand, the Treaty of Shimonoseki, which demanded the cession to Japan of the Liaotung Peninsula, would raise a threat not only to the Chinese capital at Peking but to the very sovereignty of the Chinese Empire itself. Finally, it was obvious even then that the center of attention in imperialistic developments in China was shifting to the regions contiguous to Japan, the area of Manchuria and North China.

On April 23, 1895, six days after the signing of the Treaty of Shimonoseki, Russia, France, and Germany sent notes to the Japanese Government "advising" her not to retain the Liaotung Peninsula.[111] Before accepting this advice Japan tried to find a way out. She found, however, that a refusal to accept the terms of the European Powers could expect no support from Britain, the United States, or Italy.[112] She tried to bargain with the interventionist powers by suggesting that

[111] Zabriskie, *op. cit.,* p. 29.
[112] T. Takeuchi, *War and Diplomacy in the Japanese Empire,* New York, 1935, pp. 116–119.

they accept compensation for themselves in China while allowing Japan to keep Liaotung.[113] Failing this she tried to forestall any territorial gain by the interventionists by having a clause inserted into the new agreement to the effect that the retroceded territory could not be given by China to any other power. But this also failed. Finally, in the face of naval demonstrations carried out by the interested powers so close to the shores of Japan as to leave little doubt of their meaning, Japan yielded and an Imperial Rescript of May 10 announced the retrocession.[114]

The significance of the Sino-Japanese War and the Triple Intervention in Far Eastern developments of the next quarter century was tremendous, to state the case mildly. In Japan there was an outburst of indignation in the press, not against the victorious Japanese army, but against the interventionist powers that had snatched the prize of victory.[115] Formulas were found to explain away the loss and, what is more important plans were proposed in the press for the building of an "Asia for the Asiatics" and a "Greater Japan" including, according to Palovich, not only the Philippines to the South, but Korea, Manchuria, and the Amur and Maritime provinces as well as Kamchatka to the West and North. Here were the makings of a definite expansionist program which promised to make the Japan Sea truly a Japanese Sea. In this compensatory and hopeful dreaming lay the pattern of future events. But no doubt the wildest dreamers hardly hoped for such an opportunity as the World War to effectuate these plans.

Not only Japan, but Britain as well, keenly felt the effect of the retrocession. The great Japanese objective in Asia, the stemming of Russian progress southward, appeared to have been defeated. The way was now clear for Russia to move even farther southward. It soon became evident that China, hitherto so largely oriented toward Britain, might be forced

[113] Shuhsi Hsü, *China and Her Political Entity*, New York, 1926, pp. 187ff.
[114] MacMurray, *op. cit.*, I, pp. 52–53.
[115] Pavlovich, *op. cit.*, p. 8; Takeuchi, *op. cit.*, pp. 119–120.

into a Franco-Russian orientation.[116] In June, the very next month after the retrocession, a Sino-French treaty was signed giving such large mutual concessions as to create the impression of complete Russo-French dominance in China. A four million franc loan was made to cover the first indemnity payments to Japan. The treaty also conferred rights to the exploitation of mines in Yunnan, Kwangsi, and Kwangtung, adjusted the China-Annam border, and, even more, it granted to France the first railway concession ever given to a European power. "The international relations of China between 1895–1900," writes Remer, "were dominated by the politics of railway concessions."[117]

In the following year, 1896, the wild scramble for concessions, thus started by France in 1895, was eagerly continued by Russia when she wrested from China the right to construct the Chinese Eastern Railway across northern Manchuria and down to Port Arthur. In 1898 came the lease of Kiaochow to Germany, and of the Liaotung Peninsula to Russia in March, of Kwangchowan to France in May, of Kowloon to Britain in June, and Weihaiwei to Britain in July. In connection with these events it is important to remember two others. In China the first anti-foreign outbreaks which grew into the important event known as the Boxer Rebellion were under way by 1897 and continued to increase through 1898 during which the "hundred days of reform" were tried in a vain attempt to stem the increasing breakdown of Chinese resistance.

To Japan the new circumstances appeared to be nothing less than a menace to her national safety.[118] For at Port Arthur and Weihaiwei there were now located two of the strongest European powers—or so it was feared. Within a day or two by sea, all the forces these nations cared to muster in the Yellow Sea could move toward the Japanese Islands. The Russo-Japanese War, concludes Viscount Ishii, was the

[116] G. E. Sokolsky, *The Story of the Chinese Eastern Railway*, Shanghai, 1929, p. 12.
[117] C. F. Remer, *Foreign Investments in China*, New York, 1933, p. 143.
[118] Ishii, *op. cit.*, p. 13.

answer to this threat. In the scramble for concessions Japan had managed only a nonalienation treaty with China concerning the Fukien coast, opposite Formosa.[119] The Boxer Rebellion, on the other hand, had opened up new possibilities for Russian aggression in Manchuria and from there into Korea. Russia poured in her troops and conducted herself as a permanent occupant, making plans for improving her position by adventures in Korea. She was thus trespassing on ground Japan desired badly or had given up on the plea that these were rights which must not be held by any nation except China. Furthermore, Russian progress southward was also against the interests of Britain. Under these circumstances there was a real basis for an understanding between these two nations. This community of interest led to the Anglo-Japanese Alliance of 1902. This document was the first to recognize the special interests of Japan in China.[120] In this sense it gave international sanction to the future expansion of Japan. In exchange, Britain received a similar guarantee in China and, in effect, a diminution of the Russian menace in India.[121] It was also Britain's initial success in ending her isolation and, at the same time, the first of the Far Eastern treaties which came to form a system opposed to Germany and the Triple Alliance.

Thus fortified, Japan proceeded to reexamine the full significance of the Russian threat. There were troop movements into Manchuria, Russian military and financial advisors in Korea, large and lucrative Russian timber concessions in the Yalu River valley, a viceroyalty which gave Russian activities in the Far East the appearance of permanency, and, lastly, but still of primary importance, the obviously unfavorable strategic position of Korea between Vladivostok and Port Arthur which seemed to make her almost a natural appanage of the new viceroyalty. Since Russia refused to commit herself to any definite and satisfying statements re-

[119] MacMurray, *op. cit.*, I, p. 126.
[120] Ishii, *op. cit.*, p. 134; MacMurray, *op. cit.*, I, pp. 324–325.
[121] A. W. Griswold, *The Far Eastern Policy of the United States*, New York, 1938, pp. 88ff.

garding her activities, there appeared now for Japan another happy coincidence of a foreign war which served to avoid once more the long-overdue internal political and economic readjustments demanded by certain elements of the Japanese population.

It is significant that the United States at that time saw the problem as Japan did. It was Russia that was seen by many as the major threat. As late as January 1905, Paul Reinsch, later ambassador to China, wrote in the *North American Review*, "Japan is fighting our battle . . . ."[122] Although his opinions had undergone some changes in the meantime, President Roosevelt had expressed a similar view only a year before. Some American bankers also hoped for a Japanese victory and had expressed this by joining in Anglo-American loans to Japan. Jacob Schiff, influenced perhaps by the notorious Jewish pogroms such as that of Kishinev in 1903, joined in the effort to help the Japanese cause.[123] The American attitude was known in Russia where *Novoe Vremia* asserted on April 5, 1905 that America was the real enemy and was responsible for hounding Japan into the war while herself conducting an economic invasion of Eastern Siberia.[124]

It was under these circumstances that Japan severed diplomatic relations with Russia on February 6, 1904, landed troops on the eighth, and declared war on the tenth.[125] That the Japanese were victorious is well known. A brilliant naval victory early in the war gave them command of the approaches to Port Arthur and made possible the landing of Japanese forces. Led by inferior commanders, the Russian army suffered defeats at Port Arthur and Mukden. The Baltic Fleet under Admiral Rozhestvensky was destroyed by Admiral Togo at Tsushima. Yet appearances were deceiving. The victories were apparently due more to Russian lack of preparation and inferiority in command than to ac-

[122] Zabriskie, *op. cit.*, p. 112.
[123] Griswold, *op. cit.*, pp. 104–105.
[124] Zabriskie, *op. cit.*, p. 112.
[125] H. Kobayashi, *op. cit.*, III, p. 494.

tual Japanese strength. After the battle of Mukden in March 1905, General Kodama returned to Tokyo and demanded that the war be stopped.[126] Even while the conference was in session at Portsmouth, General Kodama was joined by Admiral Yamamoto in demanding an early end to the war, stressing the military impossibility of continuing it. In fact, it required some urging on the part of the Japanese government to persuade the army to take the island of Sakhalin as a diplomatic advantage at the conference.

The significance of the Treaty of Portsmouth, signed on September 5, 1905, is the new balance of power or, from another viewpoint, the stalemate which resulted. Had either contestant been in a position to obtain for itself all the territory north of the Great Wall and east of Lake Baikal, there would have occurred the serious disruption of the balance of power which Roosevelt began to fear as soon as the relative superiority of the Japanese forces became apparent. But besides the political considerations of balance of power, the United States had more specific interests in Manchuria, those of trade and industry for which, though they were small in 1905, a future was believed promising in this undeveloped area. In this respect Japan, whose objectives were the same as those of Russia, was as great a rival as Russia. Thus the real gainers from the comparatively mild settlements agreed upon at the Portsmouth Conference were neither Russia nor the United States but Japan and Great Britain.[127]

On the other hand, Japan, though firmly established now at Port Arthur, had by no means obtained all she felt entitled to. The Portsmouth settlements, therefore, appeared to Japan as another species of Triple Intervention for which in this instance she held the United States responsible.[128] The violent demonstrations which occurred in Tokyo upon receipt of the full news of the treaty were kept in check only by heavy police guards and at the cost of 1,100 casualties. Between September 7 and November 28, 1905, Tokyo was under

[126] Takeuchi, *op. cit.,* p. 149ff.
[127] Griswold. *op. cit.,* p. 120.
[128] Pavlovich, *op. cit.,* p. 10; H. Kobayashi, *op. cit.,* III, p. 501.

martial law for the first time since 1868. Moreover, the danger of a war between the United States and Japan was very grave during the succeeding two years. Rumors were rife of a Japanese attack on the Philippine Islands or even on the mainland of the United States, the racial issue in the schools of San Francisco became intense, and it was not until the possibility of an American financial threat in Manchuria drew Russia and Japan together that the question achieved any real equilibrium.[129]

The effects of the Japanese victory upon the Far Eastern position of the United States were very quickly evident. The secret Taft-Katsura Agreement signed in Tokyo on July 29, 1905 exemplified the new dispensation. In this agreement, signed two weeks before the renewal of the Anglo-Japanese Alliance, the United States gave her blessing to the Japanese activities in Korea in exchange for assurances that Japan would look benevolently upon the American occupation of the Philippines.[130] This unratified treaty, more than any other single event, brings into proper focus the new relationship in the Pacific. In 1898 Germany and Russia had both objected to American occupation of the Philippines. But up to this time the United States had not been forced to give ground because of her occupation there, as she now did with reference to Japan in Korea. The situation is further emphasized by another incident of the same year. Relying upon the guarantees of the Schufeldt treaty of 1882, the Emperor of Korea sent a delegation to Washington to ask for assistance.[131] The delegation was never received. In later years Roosevelt explained the reason. " . . . It was out of the question," he said, "to suppose that any other nation, with no interest of its own at stake, would do for the Koreans what they were utterly unable to do for themselves." Here was a measure of the changes in the Far East since 1882. Our com-

[129] H. Kobayashi, op. cit., III, p. 506.
[130] Zabriskie, op. cit., p. 121.
[131] F. M. Nelson, Korea and the Old Orders in Eastern Asia, Baton Rouge, 1946, pp. 141ff., 258; L. O. Battle, "Japan's Policy of Expansion," The New York Times Current History (New York), XIV, No. 3, June 1921, p. 462.

mitments of that year were beyond our power to fulfill by 1905. A gunboat alongside the dock was no longer sufficient.

The "open door" notes, associated with the name of John Hay, had been formulated under the circumstances of the Russian pressure on China in 1899 and 1900.[132] Their cause was therefore the same as that which provoked the outbreak of the Russo-Japanese War. This is why the United States found herself in sympathy with Japan in 1904. It is also the reason the United States found her relations with Japan growing steadily worse after 1905. Japan had not only succeeded to the menacing position held by Russia before the war but as a growing naval power she appeared as an even more imminent threat. She could challenge even more strongly than had Russia the freedom of trade and the territorial integrity of the Chinese Empire, the two key contentions of the "open door" doctrine. In addition, she menaced in a more active sense the American territory in the Philippines and, potentially, as a naval power, her new power raised considerable foreboding with respect to the freedom of access to significant parts of the Asiatic continent. Nothing could thus be more contrary to American policy than the exclusive position asserted by Japan under the "special interest" doctrine.

The "open door" notes of John Hay have been pronounced a failure.[133] Hay himself tells us the reason. "I take it for granted," he wrote, "that Russia knows as we do that we will not fight over Manchuria, for the simple reason that we cannot. . . . We could never get a treaty through the senate, the object of which was to check Russian aggression."[134] The doctrine, in fact, did not receive any adequate military support until the American troops under General Graves were sent to counterbalance the masses of troops poured into the Russian Far East by Japan during the Allied intervention there.

[132] M. Pavlovich, "Tikho-Okeanskaia Problema" in *Novyi Vostok* (Moscow), No. 1, 1922, p. 24.
[133] Griswold, *op. cit.*, pp. 77ff.
[134] Hay to Roosevelt, April 28, 1903, *ibid.*, p. 84.

Thus the events of 1904–1905 and the ambitions and objectives of the new Pacific power which they revealed drew the United States and Japan further and further apart. After the victory in 1905, the Japanese troops in Manchuria, duplicating the Russian performance of 1900, were rapidly creating a special position for Japan.[135] Under the pretense of an emergency, they were actively engaged in preventing the entrance of American commerce into Manchuria, meanwhile solidifying their own position in order to make any other foreign trade unnecessary. These actions brought a protest from the United States in 1906. On the other hand, Britain, heretofore the only partner of Japan, was becoming less reliable due to the growth of German imperialism and naval power. A situation was thus arising which would eventually bring Britain and Russia more closely together in self-defense.[136] A whole new alignment of powers resulted from this growth of German power in the West and Japanese power in the East. One aspect of the realignment became evident when Japan and Russia, building on the basic understandings of 1905, began to draw closer together. The rapprochment was in a sense initiated by the treaty signed by France and Japan in June 1907.[137] France, a financial partner of Russia in 1904–1905, was thus reassured against a Japanese threat to Indo-China. In July 1907, the Russo-Japanese Treaty was signed and was followed in September by the Anglo-Russian Treaty.[138] Japan thus became the center of a new system of alliances to which the United States was presently added by virtue of the Root-Takahira agreements already described.

Between 1905 and 1914 the United States was engaged in the building of the Panama Canal, a project which sought among other things to give her a great advantage in the Far

[135] M. J. Bau, *The Open Door Doctrine in Relation to China*, New York, 1923, p. 52.
[136] P. Krainov, "Iaponskaia Agressia v Kitae vo Vremia Mirovoi Imperialistricheskoi Voiny," *Istoricheskii Zhurnal* (Moscow), IV, September 1938, p. 73.
[137] MacMurray, *op. cit.*, I, p. 640.
[138] *Ibid.*, I, pp. 657–658, 674–678; Price, *op. cit.*, p. 28ff.

Eastern trade.[139] The canal has been compared with the Trans-Siberian Railway since both functioned more to provide the means of reaching an objective than to serve the country through which they ran. This applies particularly to the canal, which was expected to give the United States a well-calculated advantage over her European rivals in Far Eastern trade. The trade and investment possibilities of Manchuria and Siberia were not forgotten in these plans. James J. Hill, in 1902, made plans for the construction of four large ships which were to connect the Pacific terminals of the Trans-Siberian and Great Northern railways.[140] E. H. Harriman made even larger plans. He hoped to purchase the Chinese Eastern Railway, acquire some interest in the Trans-Siberian Railway up to its port on the Baltic, and lay the foundation for a transportation system to encircle the earth.[141] Steamship lines would complete the circuit.

The financial offensive assumed a somewhat more substantial aspect in 1909 when the United States forced its way into the Hukuang financial group. This was accomplished against the strong opposition of Germany, France, and Britain and under the auspices of President Taft himself through a personal letter to the Chinese regent, Prince Chun. In the same year came the Knox proposals for the purchase by China, with the aid of the foreign financiers, of all Manchurian railways.

It has already been seen that the political situation in Manchuria was so tense that there was sentiment in both Russia and Japan in favor of getting rid of the railways. But there is no doubt that the building of competing railways or the purchase of existing railroads meant the ruin of the Russian and Japanese business and commercial future in Man-

---

[139] A. Viallate, *Economic Imperialism and International Relations During the Last Fifty Years,* New York, 1923, p. 84; B. Bakhmetev, "The Issue in Manchuria," *The Slavonic and East European Review* (London), VIII, No. 23, December 1929, p. 310.

[140] "The American Commercial Invasion of Russia," *Harper's Weekly* (New York), XLVI, No. 2361, March 22, 1902, p. 362.

[141] B. H. Williams, *Economic Foreign Policy of the United States,* New York, 1929, pp. 46–48.

churia.[142] All interested parties, therefore, were bound to oppose these schemes. In both countries there arose the strong opposition which presently resulted in further mutual understandings. One authority has characterized the situation aptly by saying that the chief value of the Knox proposals was to serve as a test case.[143] It tested "the value of the adherences of Russia and Japan to the policy of permitting unimpaired freedom of commercial and capital competition for the good of China in Manchuria." Both had given their sanction to this principle. But now both, supported by Britain and perhaps by the mutual determination to defy the implications of the world cruise of the United States fleet, drew together in a second set of mutual guarantees of their respective positions in Manchuria and Mongolia. On July 4, 1910, they signed what amounted to a defensive alliance.[144] Benedictory words about equal commercial opportunities and Chinese territorial integrity were conspicuously absent. The treaty frankly contemplated the protection of their spheres of interest against all intruders. The world saw the first tangible results of these treaties when, on August 22, 1910, Japan proceeded to annex Korea.

In 1911 the Chinese Revolution offered new opportunities for imperialistic adventures. In December of that year, Japan announced that the continuation of hostilities in China might make it necessary for her to intervene.[145] Finding the powers unreceptive to a sole intervention, however, she next proposed a joint intervention, first with Great Britain, and then jointly with both Great Britain and the United States. The intervention as proposed did not, of course, take place. But it is interesting to notice that within a mere six years these almost identical conditions would occur again and would be followed by the same proposals from Japan. On this occasion, however, the revolution occurred in Russia and the fact that the world was at war made it possible for Japan to obtain consent to the intervention she desired.

[142] Khodorov, *op. cit.*, p. 563; Grimm, *op. cit.*, p. 60.
[143] C. W. Young, *op. cit.*, p. 159.
[144] Price, *op. cit.*, pp. 43–46; MacMurray, *op. cit.*, I, pp. 803–804.
[145] Shuhsi Hsü, *op. cit.*, p. 348, Price, *op. cit.*, p. 71.

67

The Chinese Revolution presented Russia with a unique opportunity for expansion into Mongolia. In the first place Russian transactions with Mongolia enjoyed a measure of protection from interference by a third power—which, for example, was not true of her relations with Manchuria. Not only could Russia transact her affairs with Mongolia across a frontier that was remote and inaccessible to the rest of the world, but Mongolia was herself located beyond the immediate reach of Japan. Russia was also protected to some extent by the growing tensions in Europe which not only served to detract attention from her activities but gave her some promise that the European powers might be too occupied in the West to cooperate àctively with Japan against her. In Europe the years immediately preceeding the First World War were characterized by a series of international crises. In 1908 there was the annexation of Bosnia and Herzegovina by Austria-Hungary. In 1911 there was both a Moroccan crisis and an Italo-Turkish war. Then in 1912–1913 came the Balkan wars. Insofar as these events distracted Europe from active interference in Asia they acted as a shield for Russia. But, insofar as they might involve Russia herself, they acted as a restraint upon her.

The relations which arose in 1911 between Russia and Mongolia were the outgrowth both of the fear of Japanese power after 1905 and of the impotent efforts of China to recover her hold on Mongolia. The defeat in the Russo-Japanese War in 1905 settled the question of Russian pretensions to a monopoly in Korea and Manchuria. Her new policy was directed toward enchancing her position in Mongolia. In 1905 a new Russian consulate was opened at Uliasutai in western Mongolia.[146] In 1910 a Moscow trade expedition visited Mongolia to make a survey of commercial possibilities there. In 1911 another consulate was opened at Kobdo. Russian settlers in Mongolia, mostly merchants, increased during and after these years. The fifteen hundred Russians in Mongolia in 1912 had increased to about five

---

[146] I. Maisky, *Sovremennaia Mongoliia,* Irkutsk, 1921, p. 253.

thousand by 1919.[147] It was during these years, moreover, that China, engaged in a series of general reforms throughout her territories, began to take steps to tighten her grip on Mongolia. This included the encouragement of Chinese colonization along the Kalgan-Urga road, the strengthening of Chinese garrisons in various parts of Mongolia, and the construction of barracks at Urga for the permanent accommodation of additional garrison forces. Under the circumstances Russia feared the possibility of a complete absorption of Mongolia into China just at a time when she had become convinced that a forward policy there was her only salvation in the face of the increase of Japanese power. On the one hand, the new Chinese policy would strengthen Chinese power along a frontier that was always vulnerable and therefore raise the problem for Russia of additional defenses there.[148] On the other hand, it would deprive her of the freedom to shift her own power closer to the main centers of China where she could be prepared to counter any move Japan might make.

It was the good fortune of Russia that when the Sino-Mongol affairs reached a crisis in 1911 the Mongols turned to her for support against China. This was partly the result of the policy pursued under the Manchu rulers of China, of monopolizing to an extraordinary degree the economic life of Mongolia, and partly the result of Russian encouragement to look to her to counterbalance Chinese influence. Thus, a council of Mongol princes and lamas which met in Urga in July 1911 to consider the future of the country decided to send a delegation to St. Petersburg to ask for support for an independent Mongolia.[149] The delegation was received in St. Petersburg and the letter from the ecclesiastical head of Mongolia and the Khalkha princes, dated July 17, 1911, was carefully considered. On August 4 the Russian Council

[147] G. Cleinow, *Neu-Siberien (Sib-Krai); Eine Studie zum Aufmarsch der Sowjetmacht in Asien,* Berlin, 1928, pp. 112–113.
[148] W. W. Rockhill, "The Question of Outer Mongolia," *The Far Eastern Review* (Shanghai), XII, No. 1, June 1915, p. 1.
[149] S. Shoizhelov, "Avtonomistskoe Dvizhenie Mongolii i Tsarskaia Rossiia," *Novyi Vostok* (Moscow), No. 13–14, 1926, p. 352ff.

of Ministers decided upon general support for the Mongol cause. But the Russian policy also called for great caution. Then came the Chinese Revolution of October 1911 and, finally, the Mongol declaration of independence in December of the same year. In the end, not only Khalkha Mongolia, but all of Mongolia from the Khingan to the Altai Mountains joined in the new state which received the open support of Russia. The latter, at the time of the outbreak of the World War, was exerting every effort to monopolize Mongolia both politically and economically. By treaties of 1912 and 1913 respectively, Russia came to terms with Japan and China about the spheres of influence of these nations in the Mongol territories. The result, however, was to leave Russia in effective control of Outer or Northern Mongolia. It should be added that the year 1913 also found Japan actively trying to draw Outer Mongolia away from Russia by proposing a united Mongolia under Japanese protection.[150] During the intervention Japan returned to this proposal but without receiving any cooperation from Outer Mongolia.

The year 1914 found Japan still denied free access to the railway and loan opportunities in China proper. The Western powers still held the upper hand there in these lucrative fields. In March and July of 1914 Britain, for example, signed new agreements with China to finance the building of more railways.[151] Japan, because of her financial weakness as compared with the Western powers, had been a bystander in this rich field of investment and markets since 1895. But the outbreak of war promised to change this. The preoccupation of Britain, the financial and commercial leader in China, with the European war rendered her incapable of preventing Japan from making the obvious first move, the occupation of the German possessions in the Far East. This was

[150] Istoricheskie Uroki 15 Let Revoliutsii Doklad Predsedatelia Malogo Khurala Doksoma na Iubileinoi 21–i Sessii Malogo Khurala i Kratkoe Soderzhanie Doklada Amora," *Tikhii Okedn* (Moscow), No. 3(9), July-September 1936, p. 69.

[151] MacMurray, *op. cit.*, ii, pp. 1113–1121, pp. 1130–1148.

the beginning of a new relationship of the highest significance for the future of Japan on the Asiatic mainland. Britain was in effect in the act of retreating before Japan. The World War had indeed brought a new situation in the Far East. "Such an opportunity," said a memorandum of the Black Dragon Society of Japan, "will not occur for hundreds of years."[152]

[152] Williams, *op. cit.*, p. 316.

CHAPTER 3

Governments of Revolutionary Siberia

THE overthrow in 1917 of the established order in Russia provided the opportunity for an imperialistic venture for which Japan had been hoping for some years. For this reason efforts to establish an orderly government in Siberia were objectionable to Japan. This fact is reflected in the rise and fall of governments which characterized the political life of Siberia after the revolution of November 1917. Japan demanded an intervention. But before Allied consent could be obtained, the Bolsheviks were able to establish a Soviet government in Siberia. Prospective anti-Bolshevik governments arose in response to the desire of some of the Allied governments for an eastern front, for territorial or other concessions, or simply for internal opposition to the Bolsheviks.

In some cases these governments were organized to carry out a liberal program while others stood more or less openly for a return to many of the features of the old regime. All the proposed anti-Bolshevik governments had in common a dependence upon external support. The fact that a large number of governments were thus bidding for foreign support made them in time so completely the creatures of foreign or reactionary interests that they lost even the semblance of the popular appeal which some of them had had originally. The downfall of the Kolchak Government marked the end of the Allied effort to sponsor anti-Boshevik governments in Siberia. Events in Siberia which followed this overthrow reflected the continuing effort of Japan to establish herself permanently in Eastern Siberia.

The declining fortunes of the political and economic life of Russia between the years 1914 and 1917 were in part a result of the desperate struggle being waged against the Central Powers. But perhaps to an even greater degree it was also a result of the economic and political maladjustments already

72

pertaining within the Russian state itself. All the ills of the Russian monarchy were brought more and more clearly into focus as its meager strength became increasingly overtaxed by the war effort. The internal social discontent, the long-standing demands of the subject nationalities, the inefficient management of the government, the breakdown of the already inadequate industrial plants and of the transport system as well as the growing casualties, eventually brought on a complete collapse. A growing estrangement between the government and the people resulted in the isolation of the former to such a degree that its efforts at improvement had little relation to the ills they sought to remedy. Eventually things reached the point where patriotic and well-intentioned people felt that the interests of their country could best be served by opposition to the government, even while it struggled for its very existence.] In March 1917, the insufficiency of food and the high cost of living brought the riots in Petrograd which developed into the revolution.[1] On March 15, the day after the Provisional Government had already been established, the Tsar abdicated.

Advised by Ambassador Francis and other representatives in Russia, the American Government welcomed the revolutionary events there.[2] Seeing in this development only the removal from the Allied ranks of "an undisguisable autocrat whose presence had impaired the efficacy of the slogans of democracy . . . ," the United States gave official recognition to the new government on March 22.[3] Mr. Francis and others failed to realize that the attitude of the Soviet of Workers' and Soldiers' Deputies, which demanded "peace, bread and land," was a surer measure of the war weariness and desire for peace and economic rehabilitation than the determination of the Provisional Government to continue the war at all costs.

[1] Bunyan and Fisher, *op. cit.*, p. 2.
[2] P. C. Jessup, *Elihu Root,* New York, 1938, II, pp. 354–355; D. R. Francis, *Russia from the American Embassy, April 1916 to November 1918, New York,* 1921, pp. 90–91.
[3] Jessup, *op. cit.*, II, p. 354; Cumming and Pettit, *Russian-American Relations March 1917 to March 1920, Documents and Papers,* New York, 1920, p. 6 (hereafter cited as *R.A.R*).

On April 9, 1917 the Provisional Government issued a statement declaring bravely for a continuation of the war.[4] But the evidence could not be disguised by words. General Knox, the British military representative with the Russian general staff, saw the unmistakable signs of the disintegration of the Russian army, the decline in productive output and the lines of deserters moving eastward.[5] The members of the American Mission to Russia, headed by Elihu Root, also saw the evidence of what had happened in Russia. Passing along the Trans-Siberian Railway through Siberia in the summer of 1917 they saw law and order still preserved and property respected.[6] But they saw also the "tens of thousands of separate committees, having no established relations with each other and practically acknowledging little or no right of control on the part of the Petrograd government." Beneath this relatively quiet exterior, a revolution was slowly taking place. From March 14 on, the arrest of imperial officials had been going on throughout the towns of Siberia.[7] Clashes had already occurred between the local Soviets and the Committees of Public Safety. Illusive as it may have been to the traveler, the revolution which produced the abdication of the Tsar moved on relentlessly.

The official central organ of power in the Russian state after March 14, 1917 was the group of ten men known as the Provisional Government.[8] With Prince G. E. Lvov as Prime Minister this government succeeded nominally to the power of the Emperor, the Council of Ministers, the State Council, and the State Duma. Its subordinate administrative officers in the central government departments and in the localities were the commissars. They were, like the government itself, a transitional stage in the new revolutionary Russia.[9] N. A. Rusanov,

[4] *R.A.R.,* p. 10.
[5] A. Knox, *With the Russian Army, 1914–1917,* London, 1921, ii, pp. 625ff.
[6] "Report of the Special Diplomatic Mission to Russia to the Secretary of State," *Foreign Relations, 1918, Russia,* ii., p. 131.
[7] Maksakov and Turunov, *op. cit.,* p. 31.
[8] Bunyan and Fisher, *op. cit.,* pp. 3–4.
[9] F. A. Golder, *Documents of Russian History, 1914–1917,* New York, 1927, p. 504.

a former teacher in a trade school in Khabarovsk and a Socialist Revolutionary member of the Duma, was the Commissar for the Provisional Government in the Far East.[10] He arrived at Vladivostok toward the end of March and was able to give the Far East the first real information about the revolutionary events in the capital. Locally, Committees of Public Safety were elected in all the cities of Siberia.[11] These took over all local power and set up new militia forces to replace the old police which, in some cases, were actually a menace to public order.

In June 1917 the zemstvo institutions were introduced wherever they had not formerly existed, and thus for the first time in the Far East.[12] They were actually established there during the summer and fall of 1917. A zemstvo for the Maritime Province with headquarters at Vladivostok, headed by President A. S. Medvedev, assumed full power and, shortly after the November Revolution, Rusanov, the Commissar of the Provisional Government, left the Far East. Similar institutions were established in the other Far Eastern provinces.

The new institutions had greater powers than the old prerevolutionary zemstvos, having jurisdiction over the police and all questions of elementary education as well as medical and veterinary services. In addition to the provincial and district (uezd) zemstvo, there was now added one for the canton (volost), heretofore a purely peasant administrative division. Simultaneously with the establishment of the new local institutions, general suffrage was introduced for all persons over the age of twenty.[13] Since there were no residential qualifications, one could vote anywhere. By this means, areas where soldiers

[10] D. L. Horvath, "Memoirs," Ch. IX; E. K. Nilus, *Istoricheskii Obzor Kitaiskoi Vostochnoi Zheleznoi Dorogi*, 1896–1923 (Volume II ms. in Hoover Library), II, Ch. XX.

[11] Maksakov and Turunov, *op. cit.*, p. 31; F. Coleman, *Japan Moves North; The Inside Story of the Struggle for Siberia*, London, 1918, p. 73.

[12] E. Varneck and H. H. Fisher, *The Testimony of Kolchak and Other Materials*, Stanford, 1935, p. 235 n.151; T. J. Polner, *Russian Local Government During the War and the Union of Zemstvos*, New Haven, 1930, pp. 289–290; "Zemstvo," *Sibirskaia Sovetskaia Entsiklopediia*, Moscow, 1931, II, p. 151.

[13] Polner, *op. cit.*, p. 290.

were stationed became largely controlled by them. The new institutions were of particular interest to the Cossacks, who sought to use them to solidify their privileged position.

In January 1918 an effort was made to establish a general zemstvo government for the provinces of the Far East.[14] An administrative committee of six was selected and Blagovesh-chensk was chosen as a temporary capital. There was one member of the committee for each of the three continental provinces and one for each Cossack district. This will indicate the relatively greater strength of the Cossacks in this Zemstvo Assembly. Chosen to administer the area pending the establishment of new organs by the Constituent Assembly, they tried to obtain the cooperation of all political parties. In the long run, this of course proved impossible.

The original responsibility of the Provisional Government was to prepare for the Constituent Assembly and to govern until it met.[15] The convocation of the Assembly on January 18, 1918 must have brought an unpleasant surprise to those who expected support from this quarter for a renewal of the war effort. The German invasion had not yet begun and was therefore not registered in the sentiments of these representatives. For, like the Soviets, they expressed themselves in favor of a termination of the war and of a general peace.[16] The Assembly was disbanded by the Soviet Government, some of its members eventually going to Samara, where they established a government, held by them to be the only legal successor to the only legally elected government in Russia, the Constituent Assembly.

One of the characteristics of the new order in Siberia was the tendency of the inhabitants to dissolve into small regional and national groupings. General Siberian regionalism, the effort to establish an autonomous Siberia, will be more closely examined below. But there was also regionalism within regionalism such as that just noted of the zemstvo administrative

[14] *Foreign Relations, 1918, Russia,* I, pp. 25, 27.
[15] Golder, *op. cit.,* p. 315.
[16] *R. A. R.,* p. 76.

76

committee established at Blagoveshchensk. There were also Cossack congresses convoked for the purpose of maintaining unity and thus preserving their privileged status. Two such were held in August 1917, one at Chita for the Transbaikal Cossacks and one at Blagoveshchensk for the Amur Cossacks.[17] The Ussuri Cossacks held a similar one in October at Nikolsk-Ussuriisk. Another form of separatism is reflected in the various national congresses held to establish some type of autonomy. It has been seen that three Buriat congresses were held in 1917 which asked autonomy and, at the same time, favored zemstvo institutions, hoping to gain autonomy through them. In October 1917 a Moslem congress assembled in Tomsk, hoping to gain the same objective by supporting the Siberian Regionalist Government centered there.[18] Present administrative divisions of the Russian Soviet Federated Socialist Republic indicate the strength of some of these regionalist tendencies.

Meanwhile, preparation for the anticipated assumption of power by the Bolsheviks was begun at the same time as the establishment of the Provisional Government. The Petrograd Soviet of Workers' and Soldiers' Deputies was established on March 12, 1917.[19] In the same month the work was also begun in Siberia. Here the early Soviets were largely Socialist Revolutionary. Therefore, at the first congress of Soviets held in the Far Eastern Region, in April 1917, the Bolsheviks decided that, while forming their own party organizations, they would work in close harmony with the institutions of the Provisional Government which was predominantly Solialist Revolutionary.[20] The Soviets of Workers' and Peasants' Deputies were formed in towns and villages everywhere. With Vladivostok, the area containing the largest concentration of workers and the largest number of returning emigres,

[17] Maksakov and Turunov, *op. cit.*, p. 42.
[18] *Ibid.*, p. 45.
[19] Bunyan and Fisher, *op. cit.*, p. 4.
[20] A. Shurygin and Z. Karpenko, "Borba za Velikuiu Sotsialisticheskuiu Revoliutsiiu na Dalnem Vostoke," *Istoricheskii Zhurnal,* (Moscow), October 1937, p. 109.

as a center, a program of education was begun to change the political complexion of the Region.[21] The organ of the Vladivostok Committee, the *Red Banner*, was distributed to all parts of the Far Eastern provinces. In June a school was established there to prepare agitators and propagandists. Every opportunity—such as the mistreatment of workers or the counterrevolutionary activities of Kornilov—was used to bring home to both workers and peasants the identity of their interests with the Bolshevik program.

By the end of 1917 significant gains had been made among the population in preparation for the assumption of power by the Soviets. Meanwhile, some gains had also been made in organizing the higher Soviet bodies. Thus, in a Congress of Soviets of Workers', Soldiers' and Peasants' Deputies for Eastern Siberia at Irkutsk from April 20–26, 1917, the Bolsheviks were able to maneuver into the Presidium, chosen by this Congress, more Bolshevik members than those of any other party.[22] The Menshevik, and particularly the Socialist Revolutionary groups, however, remained strong throughout 1917. But by September, at the first Bolshevik Party Congress of the Far Eastern Region, the decision was made to break all connections with the other parties.[23] A Central Committee for the Region was established which included Nikiforov, Antonov, Sukhanov, Gubelman, Liubarsky, and Grossman, names which became prominent in the revolutionary history of Eastern Siberia.

On November 8, 1917 the All-Russian Congress of Soviets at Petrograd announced the assumption of power.[24] The Provisional Government had been declared deposed the day before. Also on the eighth a Soviet decree was issued calling for "an immediate peace without annexations and without indemnities."[25] It called for the self-determination of nations and the abolition of secret treaties. The earliest action in the

[21] Z. Karpenko, *Grazhdanskaia Voina v Dalnevostochnom Krae, 1918–1922,* Khabarovsk, 1934, pp. 23–25.
[22] Maksakov and Turnov, *op. cit.,* p. 34.
[23] Karpenko, *op. cit.,* p. 27.
[24] Bunyan and Fisher, *op. cit.,* p. 121.
[25] *R.A.R.,* pp. 41–44.

Far East came when, on November 21, 1917, an order was received from Lenin by the Harbin Soviet to assume power and to appoint commissars to the customs stations at Pogranichnaia, Khabarovsk, and Manchuli.[26] On the very next day the consular body acted to support General Horvath, the manager of the Chinese Eastern Railway and administrative head of the railway zone, against any such eventuality.[27] But, finding themselves with a Bolshevik majority, the Harbin Soviet, on December 12, 1917, declared itself the only organ of power in the railway zone. Horvath immediately appealed for help and by the end of the month Chinese troops had entered, disarmed, and deported the small Russian force and had itself taken over the duty of guarding Harbin.

From the first there was in the decrees and acts of the Soviet Government a sense of the inevitability of civil war and intervention. A strong hint of this was contained in a decree of the Petrograd Soviet on March 27, 1917, which explained that, "conscious of its revolutionary power the Russian democracy announces that it will, by every means, resist the policy of conquest by its ruling classes, and it calls upon the peoples of Europe for concerted decisive action in favor of peace."[28] In the Russian Far East there was a sense of impending danger both from within and without, and a corresponding willingness on the part of the Bolsheviks to compromise with other political parties.[29] But the beginnings of Bolshevik leadership were made in December 1917.[30] At the Third Congress of Soviets held at Khabarovsk during December, a proposal by the Bolsheviks that the Soviets assume power was adopted by the Congress. The Bolsheviks had carefully prepared for this by obtaining wide local support for the events in Petrograd, by propaganda to influence

[26] Horvath, *op. cit.*, Ch. IX.
[27] R. T. Pollard, *China's Foreign Relations, 1917–1931*, pp. 115–116.
[28] *R.A.R.*, pp. 7–8.
[29] P. Pozdeev, "Sovetizatsiia Zabaikalia v Usloviiakh Interventsii (1918)," *Proletarskaia Revoliutsiia* (Moscow), No. 34, 1924, p. 186.
[30] Iliukhov, *op. cit.*, p. 283; A. Shurygin and Z. Karpenko, *op. cit.*, p. 110.

the election of delegates, and by taking the first steps in the organization of a Red Guard to support the overturn when it came. In addition, armed demonstrations had been staged in Harbin, Khabarovsk, and Vladivostok.

At the Congress itself the Bolsheviks had forty-five of the eighty-two delegates. They were thus in a position to push through their program. Therefore, in addition to making a decision to proceed with the assumption of power, the Congress, under their influence, also decided to establish control over mines, factories, and, in general, all productive facilities. In line with the policy pursued throughout the Region, Krasnoshchekov, a leading figure in the Bolshevik movement in the Russian Far East and later head of the Far Eastern Republic, announced at this Congress that the Soviets would cooperate with the zemstvo and municipal institutions.[31] The latter were, accordingly, not all abolished. In January 1918 at Khabarovsk, in February at Blagoveshchensk, and in May at Vladivostok the Soviets assumed control of the administration. Then in April the liquidation of the zemstvos as organs of power began, and by June the entire Russian Far East was Sovietized. A regional executive committee in which the Bolsheviks had a majority had been chosen in January to guide these activities.

The only actually heavy fighting during this overturn in the Region took place at Blagoveshchensk in early March 1918.[32] Besides anti-Bolshevik Russian troops who constituted the so-called White Guardists, Japanese and Chinese militia troops also took part in this attack which was launched from Aigun, the Chinese town on the opposite side of the Amur River. Hence if the Chinese movement of troops into the Chinese Eastern Railway zone is considered the first armed interventionist clash in the Russian Far East and the invasion led by Semenov, to be explained presently, the second, then the attack on Blagoveshchensk was the third of a series of anti-Bolshevik attacks on the Region. The battle

[31] Karpenko, op. cit., p. 29.
[32] Norton, op. cit., p. 60; A. Bullard, The Russian Pendulum, Autocracy-Democracy-Bolshevism, New York, 1919, p. 174.

was furious while it lasted, but within a few days it was over, and the Soviets had won the day. At Irkutsk, outside the Region, during December 1917, a nine-day battle had attended the assumption of power by the Soviets.[33] But in the remainder of Eastern Siberia the overturn was relatively peaceful.

The Soviets proceeded to establish a complete provisional government for Siberia headed by Tsentro-Sibir, the central executive committee of the Soviets of all Siberia, and including the regional organization for the Far Eastern Region as well as the provincial, district (uezd), cantonal (volost), and village organizations. The first issue of the government organ, the Izvestiia of Tsentro-Sibir, was published on December 4, 1917.[34] On their visit to the Far East in April 1918 Captain Webster and Captain Hicks, two Allied officers sent to investigate the war-prisoner situation, found the whole area well controlled by the Soviets.[35]. The latter had beaten the attack at Blagoveshchensk as well as the Semenov attack launched from Manchuli. They were in fact urging recognition from the Allies as a means of protecting themselves against further attack from Manchurian territory. The Chinese, however, due to Allied or Japanese pressure, feared to negotiate with them regarding the nonviolation of Russian territory from Manchuria.

There were, however, serious charges against the Soviets which tended to make them unacceptable to the Allies. On March 6, 1918 Consul Caldwell at Vladivostok wrote to Secretary Lansing that the Soviets had arrested members of the Chamber of Commerce and had made demands on American business agents for financial contributions.[36] Businessmen of the city had resisted the Soviet program and were asking the aid of the consular corps. Soviet newspapers were, in turn, denouncing the Allies and their consular corps as

[33] Maksakov and Turunov, *op. cit.*, p. 53; V. Maksakov, "K Istorii Interventisii v Sibiri," *Krasnyi Arkhiv* (Moscow) No. 34, 1924, p. 131.
[34] Maksakov and Turunov, *op. cit.*, p. 51.
[35] *R.A.R.*, p. 123.
[36] *Foreign Relations, 1918, Russia*, II, p. 70.

the enemies of the Revolution. Thus, the implications of the Soviet regime for the business world were being reduced to simple and understandable terms. In a decree of October 30, 1918 the Council of People's Commissars at Moscow explained that during the recent war the bourgeoisie and Kulaks had grown rich by speculation on the necessities of life and would therefore be called upon now to disgorge their gains for the benefit of the revolutionary struggle.[37] They thereupon announced a levy of ten billion rubles on all propertied classes.

The forces protecting the Soviet regime were inconsiderable at the very time when the first Allied attacks against them began. Consisting for the most part; in the early months of 1918, of hastily assembled forces, they drew their principal strength from the weakness of their opponents. In some cases workers of the immediate vicinity were hastily organized when an uprising was imminent.[38] It was reported in June 1918, when troops were desperately needed to withstand the Czech attacks, that the Bolsheviks were stopping the westbound trains of the Chinese Eastern Railway at Grodekovo and removing all men between the ages of 18 and 35 who did not have foreign passports.[39] However, the prisoners of war of the Central Powers and the soldiers returning from the front, many of whom had brought home with them their guns and ammunition, were more dependable sources of recruitment.[40] Many of the prisoners and returning Russian soldiers had been propagandized by the Bolsheviks before coming into Siberia or were assisted in changing their minds by locally sponsored propaganda campaigns. But the ranks of the forces defending the new regime were unimposing until the late summer of 1918.[41] Decrees of late January

[37] J. Bunyan, *Intervention, Civil War and Communism in Russia, April–December 1918,* Baltimore, 1936, pp. 152–153.

[38] V. Vegman, "Kak i Pochemu Pala v 1918g. Sovetskaia Vlast v Tomske," *Sibirskie Ogni* (Novonikolaevsk), Nos. 1–2, Jan.–April 1923, pp. 136–137.

[39] *Foreign Relations, 1918, Russia,* II, p. 190.

[40] Pozdeev, *op. cit.,* p. 185.

[41] *Foreign Relations, 1918, Russia,* II, p. 236; W. H. Chamberlin, *The Russian Revolution, 1917–1921,* New York, 1935, II, pp. 25ff.

were ineffective in raising an army. But, under the threat both of the German invasion and of the Czech anti-Soviet rising as well as the propaganda value that these two sources of danger contained, a real force began to take shape sometime after the decrees of April 8, 20, and 22. By August 1, 1918 the Red army amounted to 331,000 and by December 1918 to 800,000.

Although both the Allied and the Soviet leaders were perfectly clear as to their respective objectives, each party was in many respects confused as to the way it could best achieve these objectives with reference to the other party. In the case of the Allies, not only was there a lack of understanding in political circles about the nature of the new Russian Government, but there was also a lack of reliable information about contemporary events in Russia. This was true even in the highest official circles. Arthur Balfour, the British Foreign Secretary, was uncertain of such important matters as the events then transpiring in various parts of Russia including Siberia, the real objectives of the Japanese, and the issues which divided the various contending parties in Russia.[42] What little information did come out of Russia originated for the most part from highly partial observers, for most of the Allied nationals living in Russia were likely to be associated with persons whose business or professional success was closely tied in with the old regime. This situation was equally true of diplomatic, commercial, or other business representatives in Russia. Hence, the possibilities of finding a basis for cooperation with a regime which would issue a decree such as that of February 8, 1918 repudiating Russian debts would hardly have been favorably reported in London. When, in addition, the regime completely repudiated all of its military obligations to the Allies, it was reasonable to expect that every potential friend of Russia would be alienated.

The division among the members of the British government and the British representatives in Russia is fairly typical of

[42] B. E. C. Dugdale, *Arthur James Balfour; First Earl of Balfour*, New York, 1937, ii, pp. 186–187.

this unfortunate situation. Thus, Bruce Lockhart, the unofficial British agent in Russia, worked for months trying to persuade his government that cooperation was the best policy. In London, however, Balfour saw the whole relationship hanging on the question of the Bolshevik action regarding peace with Germany.[43] The Soviet Government itself had, he felt, no claim to favorable treatment since its dispersal of the Constituent Assembly. Active support could hardly be expected from the Bolsheviks. David Lloyd George was in some respects quite favorable to cooperation with the Soviet regime since he saw in Bolshevism a menace to the fighting morale of the enemy nations.[44] General Knox, later so determinedly anti-Soviet, at first thought it might be better to write off the Russian army as an Allied force rather than endanger postwar relations with them.[45] British indecision reached a climax in July 1918, when, as the Czechs were besieging Kazan, and Boris Savinkov, financed by the French, was attacking Yaroslavl with his force, and the Allies were expected momentarily to land at Archangel, an official British Economic Mission arrived at Moscow.[46] The decision between opposition and cooperation had obviously not yet been made by all organs of the British Government.

Bruce Lockhart, it should be emphasized, was by no means the only one who endeavored to obtain the cooperation of the Bolshevik leaders in the Allied war effort. One of the most consistent advocates of this policy was Colonel Robins, the American Red Cross representative in Russia. It was his impression that the dissolution of the Constituent Assembly had raised no general protest in Russia, had, in fact, left the Soviet regime stronger.[47] It could be further strengthened either by drawing closer to Germany or to the Allies. Germany, he felt, (apparently unaware of the violent opposition

[43] C. Seymour, *The Intimate Papers of Colonel House,* Boston, 1928, III, p. 390.
[44] David Lloyd George, *War Memoirs of David Lloyd George,* Boston, 1936, v, pp. 124–125.
[45] Knox, *op. cit.,* II, p. 727.
[46] R. H. B. Lockhart, *British Agent,* New York, 1933, p. 303.
[47] *R.A.R.,* pp. 76, 69.

to the German occupation that had even then been aroused),
was sure to try increasing its strength in Russia by commercial relations as far more effective than military conquest.
He therefore advocated recognition and support of the Soviet
regime as the most effective means of restoring it to such
authority in Russia that it could once more place Russian
soldiers in the field against Germany. But the State Department did not agree. Indeed, Secretary Lansing expressed the
view in October 1918 that the "Bolshevik regime has been
preserved beyond its normal term by German support."[48]

The basis for cooperation with the Soviet Government
which Robins hoped the Allies, and particularly the United
States, would try, was economic reconstruction. In making
this proposal he was strongly influence by the encouragement
given him by Trotsky. On March 1, 1918, Trotsky explained
to Lockhart why he wished to cooperate with the Allies.[49]
While Anglo-American capitalism and German militarism,
he explained, were equally hateful to him, the latter was at
present the greater menace. Also, if the two were to unite,
Russia would be crushed. "So long, therefore, as the German
danger exists, I am prepared to risk cooperation with the
Allies, which should be temporarily advantageous to both
of us. In the event of German aggression, I am even willing
to accept military support." Trotsky probably also had in
mind recognition in exchange for the support he gave to the
Allied landings at Murmansk.[50]

Whatever his purpose, Trotsky asked openly for active
aid.[51] He requested an American Military Mission of ten
officers to organize and train a Russian force. He also asked
for American railway engineers and transportation experts
to reorganize the railroads. He offered to give the railway
mission complete authority in a specified area, making its
chief the Assistant Superintendent of Ways of Communica-

[48] *Foreign Relations, 1918, Russia,* iii, p. 158.
[49] *Ibid.,* p. 237.
[50] Bunyan, *op. cit.,* p. 132.
[51]*The New York Times,* March 21, 1918; W. Hard, *Raymond Robins'
Own Story,* New York, 1920, p. 98.

tion. The special objective of the mission would be the transportation of all available munitions to any place they wished, but in return the mission must assist the Russians to transport food to needed areas. While asking the United States to assume the responsibility for the training of the army, Great Britain was offered the opportunity of rehabilitating the Black Sea Fleet.[52] The French were also asked to assist in the rebuilding of the army. But none of these projected activities was ever realized, among other reasons because there was little confidence in the durability of the Soviet regime. But a more important reason was that the German and Austrian, as well as the Allied, interventions were already in progress and thus made the proposals coming from Moscow seem valueless.

This indecision and confusion in Allied thinking was one of the major drawbacks in their relations with Russia during the early Soviet period. There were among the Allies many who offered constructive and feasible suggestions as to the best attitude to assume toward the Soviets. But their plans were either based on insufficient information or were given overly prolonged consideration and, in the end, completely disregarded in favor of no course of action at all. Thus the Allies faced the crucial events in Russia without any real plan of action. The field was thereby left open to those whose views were more definite and, as it turned out, more harmful to the cause both of the Russian democratic elements and to that of the Allies. It will be seen presently, for example, that the Japanese ambitions in Siberia completely eliminated any possibility of success that the liberal parties in Siberia or their Allied supporters might have had.

The problem that confronted the Soviet leaders in March 1918 was, in a sense, almost insoluble. Their predicament, it must be said, was to some extent their own creation. By 1917 the Russian people had, it is true, suffered tremendously from the effects of the war. Both at the war fronts and in the fields there was one great desire–to end the war

[52] *R.A.R.,* p. 108.

86

as soon as possible. The Provisional Government, during its brief tenure of office, offered neither any outstanding leadership nor any startlingly new solution to the problems of political and military disintegration. The Bolsheviks, on the other hand, not only encouraged the collapse of the foundations of the old order, but actively encouraged it. Thus, the destruction of the army was an essential device as well as a natural by-product of the Bolshevik program of undermining the Provisional Government and winning the masses away from them. They identified themselves with the slogan "Peace, Bread, and Land" and with the policy implied in "Order Number One" which, as already described, was an efficient instrument for undermining the military authority both of the Provisional Government and of the whole officer class. Thus, the final extinction of the Provisional Government in November 1917 left to the Bolsheviks the most pressing problem of all—the collapse of Russian resistance in the face of unopposed German military might.

Under these circumstances, there were two general policies the Soviet leaders could adopt. One was the organization of resistance by every possible means; the other was the complete surrender to Germany. The Soviets adopted both these means of dealing with the situation. The rise of the Red Army, initiated well before the signing of the Treaty of Brest-Litovsk, has already been noted. On March 1, 1918 a statement by Lenin appeared in *Pravda* which explained the official Soviet attitude with respect to resistance. The general message of the article was that the immediate task of the Soviet regime was to repel the enemy with all the military force that could be mustered by the Russian people. But the problem was larger than the mere assembling of men bearing arms. In a statement issued some time later, Lenin recognized as in his previous statement that the basic duty was strenuous military preparation. But he also recognized that, "There can be no question of any serious military preparation before food difficulties are overcome, before the population is assured of the regular delivery of bread, before strict order in railway transportation is introduced, and before a true iron discipline is established among the entire population . . . ."[53] It was with respect to this problem that Allied help was sought by the Soviets.

The good faith of the Soviet leaders in asking for Allied assistance must be weighed against their own objective. This objective was quite simply the survival of the Soviet regime. In attaining it, they looked first of all to an expected German revolution which would result in the collapse of the German Imperial Government and the rise of a friendly workers' government which would annul all the benefits of the German victory. With the passage of time, however, this solution began to appear less likely. But there were other forces at work in the world which, though he was fully aware of the precarious position of Russia after the Treaty of Brest-Litovsk, nevertheless kept Lenin from viewing the situation as hopeless. One of these was the life-and-death struggle then taking place on the Western Front. Lenin saw in this the division of the imperialistic enemy into two contending factions, a situation which was duplicated in the Far East, also according to Lenin's analysis, in the American-Japanese rivalry.[54] The signing of the Treaty of Brest-Litovsk was expected to release Germany for the war on the Western Front and thus not only intensify the struggle but prolong it.[55] The continuation of the war would lead to the world revolution and the rescue of the Soviet regime in Russia.

The optimistic views of Lenin with respect to the long-range results of the Treaty of Brest-Litovsk were not shared by some of the other leaders of the Soviet Regime. In fact, as Krupskaia has characterized the situation, when the question of accepting the harsh German terms arose, "around Ilich there suddenly appeared a void."[56] In the final vote on this question in the Central Committee, Lenin received

[53] "Lenin's Theses on the Existing Political Situation, May 13, 1918, Presented to the Inner Circle of the Party," *Leninskii Sbornik*, XI, Moscow, 1931; as quoted in Xenia Joukoff Eudin, "Documents and Materials on Intervention," a manuscript collection in the Hoover Library.

[54] V. I. Lenin, *Sochineniia*, Moscow, 1929, XXII, pp. 478–479.

[55] D. Shub, *Lenin. A Biography*, New York, 1948, p. 415.

[56] *Ibid.*, p. 298.

a majority vote, but he was opposed by Bubnov, Uritsky, Bukharin, and Lomov while Trotsky, Krestinsky, Dzerzhinsky, and Ioffe refrained from voting. Furthermore, Karl Radek held views directly opposed to those of Lenin. To him the situation was full of danger for the Soviet regime. Faced by the French and British forces as well as the new American troops, Germany might well be expected to stamp out Russian resistance completely in order both to eliminate all danger to herself from the East and to give her complete access to the necessary raw materials of Russia.[57] As for the Far East, Radek continued, the development in the West could easily have the effect of freeing Japan from the restraints that fear of the Allies would otherwise impose and thus open the way for unrestrained aggression against the Russian Far East.

The Treaty of Brest-Litovsk was condemned by members of the Soviet regime for reasons other than those of mere expediency. There were those who shared with the White Russian elements a sense of guilt with respect to the treaty. In May 1918 at a meeting of the All-Russian Central Executive Committee of Soviets the Menshevik opposition made an open statement of their views.[58] It was their contention that, "Authority which has lost all moral influence upon the people cannot in the critical moment rally to itself the popular masses. Being guilty in the eyes of the people of the humiliation and destruction which Russia suffered from Germany at Brest and of the isolation from other capitalist countries in which Russia has found herself . . . the present government cannot arouse in the popular masses the desire to struggle for their freedom and independence." The statement continued by advocating nothing less than the convocation of another Constitutent Assembly, the restoration of the old institutions of local self-government, and the arming of Russia for the struggle against German enslave-

[57] "Vneshnaia Politika Sovetskoi Rossi," *Kommunist,* Moscow, No. 2, 1918, Eudin, *op. cit.*
[58] *Protokoly Zasedanii Vserossiiskogo Tsentralnago Ispolnitelnago Komiteta [Soveto] 4–go Sozyva,* p. 291.

ment. Circumstances made this prediction regarding the power of the Bolsheviks wrong in the end. But the contemporary view of a decision which time seems to have proved valid is important in considering the possible effects of Allied support of the Soviet regime.

It is also important when considering the third possible source of assistance to the Soviet Government against the menace of the Central Powers—direct cooperation with the Allies. Trotsky, it will be recalled, was willing to risk the effects this might have on the Soviet regime. Lenin, however, was more reserved in this matter. In March 1918, when both his leadership in the Soviet Government and even the survival of the regime itself was at stake, he had discussed the possibilities of aid with Colonel Robins. By May, when the Allies and the Soviets had grown further apart, he saw the problem differently. He was not opposed in principle to an agreement with one imperialist coalition against the other. But the implications of an agreement to cooperate with the Allies were such as to raise considerable doubt as to its real value in aiding the Soviet cause. In the first place, the reason the Allies wanted this cooperation was their hope of diverting German troops from the Western Front. Also, Lenin said, cooperation with the Allies would undoubtedly mean the advance of Japanese troops into Siberia.

It can be seen from these demonstrations of wavering, uncertainty, and division of opinion that the contemporary view of the Allied representatives who saw great opportunities in the harsh terms of the Treaty of Brest-Litovsk was not unjustified. The existing German occupation and the fear of an intervention by the Japanese Government was a constant and growing fear on the part of many of the Bolshevik leaders. It was at that time that they were actively interested in aligning themselves with the Allies if this could strengthen them economically or prevent further aggressions against them. On March 5, 1918 a note sanctioned by both Lenin and Trotsky was sent to the American Government by Colonel Robins asking what the United States would do if Russia should refuse to ratify the treaty.[59] The same note asked the other burning question: What would the Allies, particularly the United States, do if the Japanese should land at Vladivostok and seize the Chinese Eastern Railway? Lockhart and Harold Williams, both men of long experience among the Russian people, were of the opinion that the Bolsheviks would meet any obligations implied in this request. The note, however, remained unanswered. The treaty was duly ratified. Hearing that the Soviet delegates were instructed to ratify the treaty, Ambassador Francis telegraphed the State Department, "I fear that such action is the result of a threatened Japanese invasion of Siberia."[60]

Thus, the Soviet leaders weighed the two interventions, the German and the Allied, and found that the former could not be combatted unless by the aid of those who contemplated the latter. The Allies, lacking faith in the desire or ability (it is uncertain which) of the Bolsheviks to redeem their obligations, allowed matters to take their course and, as a result, the Soviet Government found itself confronted with both interventions. This development, in turn, helped to solidify the power of the extremist elements and make it impossible for more moderate groups to assert their views. In the opinion of Lockhart, the most intense and cruel events of the Russian Revolution and civil war resulted from this single fact.[61] Under date of March 2, 1918 he wrote, "I mention this comparative tolerance of the Bolsheviks, because the cruelties which followed later were the result of the intensification of the civil war. For the intensification of that bloody struggle, Allied intervention, with the false hopes it raised, was largely responsible."

But events, already in progress before these thoughts were expressed, moved on toward full-scale hostilities between the Allies and the Bolshevik-controlled Soviet Government. The removal of the diplomatic corps from Vologda to Archangel,

[59] Hard, op. cit., pp. 138ff.
[60] R.A.R., pp. 85–86.
[61] Lockhart, op. cit., p. 240.

July 25, 1918, was in fact interpreted by the Soviet Government as a prelude to a more active intervention.[62] On July 29, Lenin declared that Soviet Russia was in a state of war with Anglo-French capitalism. By this time the whole of Siberia was in Allied hands, an anti-Soviet military front was forming in the Volga region, and in a few days additional Allied forces would land at Archangel and Vladivostok. The ostensible reason for all this, the thing that had presumably made up the collective Allied mind, was the signing of the Brest-Litovsk Peace on March 3, 1918. But, in fact, it served as a reason rather than a cause. Efforts to bring the Russian armies back into the war continued right up until the end of June when the effort seemed wholly useless.[63] On March 12, nine days after the signing of the treaty, President Wilson sent a message of sympathy to the Russian people on the occasion of the opening of the Congress of Soviets at Moscow.[64] Lloyd George, perhaps expressing a stronger sense of realities than when he pretended to feel neutral toward the Soviets, explained Wilson's fine sentiments by the fact that "the American public had not the same cause for resentment against Russia as the European Allies, who had made great investments in Russia, and who had been deserted in the midst of the struggle." It is difficult to tell whether he was thinking primarily of the decree repudiating debts or the Treaty of Brest-Litovsk.

In mid-May 1918 General Stepanov sent a report to General Alekseev of the Imperial Army and then anti-Bolshevik forces, concerning conditions in Eastern Siberia.[65] All of the cities along the railway from Irkutsk to Vladivostok, he noted, were dominated by the Bolsheviks. About 15,000 Czechoslovak troops had reached Vladivostok. In the zone of the Chinese Eastern Railway he found that the Russian guards had been replaced by Chinese troops and that, in his opinion, general chaos prevailed there. It will be

[62] Bunyan, *op. cit.*, pp. 137ff.
[63] Lockhart, *op. cit.*, p. 268.
[64] D. Lloyd George, *op. cit.*, v, p. 128.
[65] Bunyan, *op. cit.*, pp. 314–315.

seen presently how the quiet conditions along the Trans-Siberian Railway were disturbed by the Czech forces which, after securing the towns of western and central Siberia, moved eastward where they formed a junction at Oloviannaia, in Transbaikal, with Semenov and then with the Allied forces which had recently landed at Vladivostok. The fall of Omsk on June 7, 1918 was the key factor in this eastward progress.[66] As elsewhere, the Soviet Government was replaced by the former local institutions. Toward the end of June the same overturn was brought about at Vladivostok by the Czechs who had already arrivèd there. On July 11 Irkutsk fell, and by August 16 the Soviet Government for Siberia, Tsentro-Sibir, had retreated to Chita. Finally, on September 18, a combined Czech-Japanese-White Guard force took Blagoveshchensk and the Soviet power in Eastern Siberia was totally extinguished.[67] The forces which had defended the Soviet regime disappeared into the forests and there formed partisan bands. The civil war had begun.

The confusion which presently resulted in Siberia after an interlude of relative stability under the Soviets was a result of forces that had been developing throughout the land for many months. One of these was the tremendous growth of population in Siberia. Refugees came from the disturbed areas of European Russia. Prisoners from several nations helped to swell the population. On the first news of the March revolution, emigres (refugees from the Tsarist police) returned in large numbers, especially from America.[68] They called street meetings and spoke to large crowds in Vladivostok, Harbin, and other centers, attacking public and political organizations at random. In their slogans they presumed to have condensed both cause and cure for the political ills of two continents. At every railway station there was sure to be at least one of these who could speak some

[66] L. Germanov, "K Istorii Chekho-Slovatskogo Nastupleniia i Sverzheniia Sovetskoi Vlast v Sibiri," *Proletarskaia Revoliutsiia* (Moscow), No. 4, 1922, p. 22; *Foreign Relations, 1918, Russia*, II, pp. 251, 252, 254.
[67] Maksakov and Turunov, *op. cit.*, p. 89.
[68] Nilus, *op. cit.*, II, Ch. xx; Ackerman, *op. cit.*, p. 64.

English. All in all, it is believed that the population of Siberia may have doubled as a result of these influxes.

In many parts of Siberia and Europe Russia there were foreign agents at work. The German espionage system was of long standing and centered around large business establishments, both German and others.[69] Its chief agent at Vladivostok was reported to be a Dane, at Khabarovsk a Swede, and at Omsk a Swiss. After the Armistice this system fell. French and British agents, however, were still at work all through Siberia as well as European Russia. It will presently be seen also how Japanese residents formed an infiltration force and how their agents sought out every pretender to power in Siberia who had any chance of success. A conspiracy between the Siberian Provisional Government and the major Allied nations to overthrow the Soviet Government was discovered in April 1918.[70] The Soviets considered the evidence strong enough to demand the recall of John Caldwell, the American consul at Vladivostock. Secretary Lansing, however, officially denied the charge and Caldwell remained at this post.

The military weakness of the Bolsheviks, particularly during the crucial first half of 1918, gave special importance to the secret officers' organizations which existed in the major centers throughout Siberia.[71] These organizations were a part of the Officers' Union which was formed at Moghilev in May 1917 with a Standing Committee under the presidency of Colonel Novosiltsev. According to General Denikin, the Union represented, initially at least, an effort to achieve some type of unity among officers who as a group were fast being isolated from the rest of the army by the military policies of the Bolsheviks. Their chief was, at least nominally, General Alekseev in South Russia and the activities planned for these groups were directed by a body known as the "National Center" having headquarters at Moscow, Samara, and

[69] Ackerman, *op. cit.*, p. 220.
[70] *R.A.R.*, p. 179.
[71] Chamberlin, *op. cit.*, II, p. 8; M. P. Price, *My Reminiscences of the Russian Revolution*, London, 1921, p. 327; A. I. Denikin, *Ocherki Russkoi Smuty*, Paris, 1921, I, Pt. 2, p. 106.

other places. These organizations were in touch with the Allies.[72]

In Siberia, the officers' organizations secured their arms by raiding depots of military stores and generally grew stronger as the weakness and lax discipline of the Red Army increased.[73] In the spring of 1918 Horvath was visited at Harbin by two of the traveling representatives of the officers' group, General Flug and Lieutenant Glakarev, who came disguised as merchants on a visit to the local organizations. Horvath made a contribution to their organization of 50,000 rubles. The French commercial agent at Irkutsk found that, while many of these officers claimed to be anxious to take part in any military action, the events of December 1917, when their whole regime fell, found most of them militarily noncommittal. Later, as members of the Kolchak forces, they showed an equally strong preference for the safety of the rear areas.

Politically the atmosphere in Siberia and the Volga region was as clouded as can be imagined. In the first place there was the rivalry between the governments pretending to power.[74] Between the Volga and the Pacific there were no less than nineteen governments hoping to succeed the defeated Bolsheviks as the recognized government in Siberia. There were, among others, the Amur Government of Blagoveshchenck, the Ural Government at Ekaterinburg, and the Horvath Government at Harbin. But the chief contenders for power were the governments established at Samara by the Committee of Members of the Constituent Assembly and that established at Omsk by the Siberian Provisional Government. The greatest rivalry was between these two. Each was reluctant to have its forces fight under the other. In fact,

<hr />

[72] V. I. Lebedev, *The Russian Democracy in Its Struggle Against the Bolshevist Tyranny*, New York, 1919, pp. 7–11; V. Maksakov, "K Istorii Interventsii v Sibiri," *Krasnyi Arkhiv* (Moscow), No. 34, 1929, p. 137.
[73] Horvath, *op. cit.*, Ch. xi.
[74] General Filatieff, "L'Admiral Koltchak et les Evenements Militaires des Siberie (1918–1919)," *Revue d'Histoire de la Guerre Mondiale*, x, April and July 1932, p. 170; V. G. Boldyrev, *Direktoriia, Kolchak, Interventy*, Novonikolaevsk, 1925, p. 30.

rivalry went so far that there was even talk of a proposed customs war between them which threatened to introduce economic contention between the regions they claimed to control. This situation, in effect, left the Czechs to do most of the fighting on the Volga front and made them deeply anxious to achieve unity between the two governments.

In addition to the rivalry of governments, there was the party strife within the governments.[75] It has been seen how the Bolsheviks spent the months preceding the overturn by December 1917 preparing the political ground upon which to establish a wholly Bolshevik regime. Their opponents, the Mensheviks, the Right Socialist Revolutionists, the Left Socialist Revolutionists, the Constitutional Democrats, and others contended against the Bolsheviks and against each other. In general the Socialist Revolutionaries stood for some type of a liberal regime, while there were Constitutional Democrats who wanted a monarchical restoration.[76] It was rumored at various times that Grand Duke Michael Alexandrovich, the brother of the ex-Tsar, was on his way to Samara or to Vladivostok to head movements backed by the Czechs or by the Japanese. All of this left a choice selection for a foreign nation with purely interventionist ambitions. But it made it extremely difficult for those who wanted a firm foundation to rebuild a Russian army for a new Eastern Front. In the opinion of Mr. Balfour, the most dangerous tendency exhibited by the anti-Bolshevik groups was the re-establishment of monarchy since this would make Russia a pawn of its neighbor, Germany, or, he might have added, Japan.

Harbin and the Chinese Eastern Railway zone was one of the most persistent centers of interventionist intrigue. It was a Russian area which, for interventionist purposes, was fortunately situated on Chinese territory—an anomaly which resulted from interventionist activities of the past, then carried on by Russia against China. In November 1917, it will be recalled, Lenin ordered the Harbin Soviet to assume

[75] Karpenko, *op. cit.,* p. 38.
[76] *Foreign Relations, 1918, Russia,* ii, pp. 235, 247, 279.

power. General Horvath was at that time strongly backed by business groups as well as by the Allied Consular Corps in his effort to retain his position as manager of the Chinese Eastern and Ussuri Railways and governor of the railway zone in Manchuria.[77] On December 25 the consular corps in Harbin, unable to cope with the growing strength of the Bolshevik movement, sent a request to the Chinese civil governor of Kirin Province for aid. On the 26th the Chinese troops entered, disarmed all the Russian troops, and dispatched them over the railway toward Manchuli. This is technically, therefore, the date of the first overt interventionist act against Eastern Siberia. As the intervention unfolded, China made further efforts to enhance her position in the railway zone and in Manchuria generally. On January 2, 1918, Kuo Hsiang-hsi, Civil Governor of Kirin Province, was appointed president of the Chinese Eastern Railway. In the fall of 1918 the reunification of Manchuria, divided since the Chinese revolution, was started by the appointment of Chang Tso-lin as Chief Military Inspector of the Three Eastern Provinces.[78] But the increase of Chinese authority was not viewed favorably by the powers. This was partly because they wanted to preserve the theory of the territorial integrity of Russia and partly because the collaboration of China and Japan was so close at this time that a gain for China was almost automatically a step forward for Japan.

At the outbreak of the revolution in March 1917 General Horvath was manager of the Chinese Eastern and Ussuri Railways and supreme administrator of the railway zone through Manchuria. Upon the advent of the Provisional Government he was confirmed in these positions and appointed Commissar of the Provisional Government in the railway zone.[79] During 1917 the revolutionary organs in Harbin, at first scattered and disunited, assumed not only unity but strength enough seriously to threaten Horvath's position. But, backed not only by the business and property

[77] Horvath, *op. cit.*, Ch. ix; Pollard, *op. cit.*, p. 117.
[78] Nilus, *op. cit.*, ii, Ch. xx.
[79] *Ibid.*

owning groups of Harbin but by the consular corps and the Chinese army, he survived and aspired to a wider expansion of his powers.

Harbin, situated on foreign soil and filled increasingly with large numbers of refugee conservatives from Siberia as the Bolsheviks assumed power there during the early months of 1918, was an ideal place to start an anti-Bolshevik government.[80] With this purpose in view, Horvath attended a conference in Peking, called by Prince Kudashev, the Russian Ambassador to China, on April 27. This conference was also attended by Admiral Kolchak and some Allied representatives. At the meeting a new railway managing board was formed with Kolchak as a member. The failure of the Semenov detachments in their efforts to push from Manchuria into Transbaikal against the meager forces of the Bolsheviks had led Horvath to the conclusion that Semenov was incapable and that it was necessary to have a military leader who would inspire greater confidence. This was the role intended for Kolchak.[81] He thus became a member of this board and was assigned the duty of forming a military force. As in the case of his later service at Omsk, Kolchak's position in the railway zone was part of the larger plan which has already been outlined.[82] General Alekseev was then engaged in an anti-Bolshevik movement in South Russia and a similar one in Manchuria was expected to form a part of a large anti-Bolshevik movement, coordinated in the East under the ambassador, Prince Kudashev, himself.

The whole movement foundered, partly because of the poor leadership contributed by Horvath (who by this time was associated in the popular mind with reactionary tendencies) and partly because it lacked the Allied support necessary to make it a success. Horvath asked frankly for Allied support but received little response except from the Japanese.[83] He received some support from France and Britain

[80] Varneck and Fisher, *op. cit.*, p. 234; Horvath, *op. cit.*, p. 117.
[81] *Ibid.*, pp. 110ff.
[82] M. I. Smirnov, "Admiral Kolchak," *The Slavonic and East European Review* (London), xi, No. 32, January 1933, p. 385.
[83] *Foreign Relations, 1918, Russia,* ii, pp. 141, 147.

and at least a million yen from Japan. But Japanese support was soon stopped when it was discovered he was unwilling to give them the compensation they wanted: free and exclusive mining rights in Eastern Siberia, free navigation of the Amur River, and other items which will be considered more fully later. Eventually all foreign aid was turned into what was to prove to be more promising channels, such as the attention concentrated on Semenov, Kalmykov, and others, and Horvath remained a local figure until he finally gave up his position and left for Peking on April 6, 1920.[84]

After the Vladivostok overturn of June 29, 1918 the Far Eastern Committee for the Defense of the Country and the Constitutent Assembly, a conservative group formed at Harbin in April 1918, urged Horvath to take steps to counteract the effect of the Socialist Derber Government which had risen to power at Vladivostok in the wake of the deposition of the Soviet Government there under Czech and general Allied auspices.[85] He therefore went to Grodekovo in the Maritime Province and on July 9, 1918 declared himself provisional ruler. His program called for the reestablishment of the pre-Bolshevik order, but said nothing about renewing the war against Germany although he advocated an army with strict discipline. As a ruler he had only a nuisance value, however, and when in September he was made the Far Eastern Commissioner of the All-Russian Directory at Omsk in the interest of unification, he had probably used his prestige somewhat beyond its real market value.[86] He seems to have been generally disregarded from this point on. The real power in the Far East was represented by Semenov, Kalmykov, Ivanov-Rinov, Rozanov, and others who were more willing to see the Japanese point of view.

One of the two major contenders for power in Siberia was the government established at Samara on May 9, 1918

[84] *Outline of the Activities of the Inter-Allied Railway Committee for the Supervision of the Siberian and Chinese Eastern Railways, 1919–1922*, p. 24. (Hereafter cited as *Outline*.)

[85] *Foreign Relations, 1918, Russia*, II, p. 277; Bunyan, *op. cit.*, pp. 320–321.

[86] *Foreign Relations, 1918, Russia*, II, 391; Horvath, *op. cit.*, Ch. xiv.

by the Committee of Members of the Constituent Assembly, referred to in Russian by the abbreviated title "Komuch."[87] This government was promoted by the French and supported by the Czech army. For a number of reasons it ought to have had a promising future. Its members were all ex-representatives in the Constituent Assembly, dispersed by the Bolshevik in the previous January. It was situated in a rich grain-growing area of relatively prosperous farmers who might have been expected to support it after experiencing the food and horse requisitioning of the Bolsheviks.[88] Insurrections had already occurred there during the Bolshevik tenure of office among both urban and rural classes. In the area, also, there was a great deal of army equipment brought from the German front. Furthermore, the Ural Cossacks were already engaged in an anti-Bolshevik war along the Volga River.

But the "Komuch" was actually a weak and vacillating government, destined almost from its inception either to fail or fall prey to the military elements supporting it. Since it regarded itself as only temporary until the reconvening of the Constituent Assembly, it avoided any definite measures and, therefore, lacked an adequate plan and showed no initiative. While it carried on propaganda, it failed to arouse any popular interest whatsoever. Above all, it lacked any definite land policy, since this was to be the subject of legislation by the Constituent Assembly when it convened. Under these circumstances, the way was open for the military element to have its way if it could find support. These military groups tried to get Czech assistance but were turned down at first by General Cecek. They tried to persuade General Alekseev to assume leadership should they succeed in overthrowing the "Komuch," but with no better result. They finally obtained a group of Annenkov's Cossacks to

[87] Maksakov and Turunov, *op.cit.*, p. 65; S. A. Pointkovsky, *Grazhdanskaia Voina v Rossii (1918–1921), Khrestomatiia*, Moscow, 1925, pp. 213–215.

[88] Price, *op. cit.*, p. 293; E. Varneck, "Siberian Materials and Documents" (a manuscript collection in Hoover Library).

help them in turning out the government. Some of these were seen arriving at Samara Station. Asked why they had come, the leader answered: "To scatter that Constituent business." The main success of the military group seems to have been the raising of an army, called the "People's Army," and even here progress was modest. After three months of existence they had only between 30,000 and 40,000 troops.[89] Most of these were conscripted though there were about 8,000 volunteers. The new army was formed by General Galkin and the officers of the old regime who had gathered in the area. It fought beside the Czech army and aided in the capture on August 7 of Kazan and the Russian gold horde worth 657,000,000 rubles.

During its existence the government restored the zemstvo and municipal institutions, established free commerce, denationalized the banks, and regulated the trade unions. Although it survived the various military efforts to overthrow it, it lost its separate existence in September 1918, when the conference held at Ufa made a strong and, outwardly, a relatively successful effort to unify the government of Siberia. Outward unity was achieved to some extent, but the inner conflict of indecisive politicians and determined military officers, inherent in the Samara Government, made the Kolchak overturn of less than two months hence almost a foregone conclusion. The "People's Army" became an integral part of Kolchak's army after November 18, 1918.

While the Samara Government came into being by virtue of the Czecholovak army, the Siberian Autonomist movement existed long before the Revolution, though it flourished on the support given it by the Czechs. The movement reflected the discontent of the Siberian intellectuals with the colonial status assigned to Siberia by the Imperial Regime.[90] It formed its first secret association in 1864. Its program was

[89] Filatieff, loc. cit., pp. 168–169; G. Stewart, The White Armies of Russia; A Chronicle of Counter-Revolution and Allied Intervention, New York, 1933, pp. 144–145.

[90] I. I. Serebrennikov, "The Siberian Autonomous Movement and Its Future," The Pacific Historical Review, iii (Glendale), No. 4, December 1934, pp. 400ff.; Horvath, op.cit., Ch. x.

characterized by demands for the extension to Siberia of the zemstvo institutions just established in Russia, for popular education and a Siberian university, for improved conditions for the native tribes and against filling Siberia with criminals from European Russia. These ambitions achieved greater prominence in the 1880's under two able leaders, N. M. Yadrintsev and G. N. Potanin, with the focal point at Tomsk, the home of Potanin and the seat of the only Siberian university. Additional strength was gathered after the events of 1905 and particularly after March 1917. As the influence of the Kerensky Government declined, the Tomsk group asserted its demands as the regional government of an autonomous Siberia.[91] In August 1917 a conference was held at Tomsk, the principal purpose of which was to plan the election of a Siberian Regional Duma. On this occasion, an organizing committee was established to plan another conference and a preliminary date set for October 21. In addition to adopting as its banner a green and white flag, it sent delegates to Kiev where another regional government was developing.

A Regionalist Conference attended by two hundred delegates from all parts of Siberia began its sessions toward the end of October and considered the peasant question, the formation of a constitution, and the economic problems of war and revolution.[92] But the events at Petrograd overshadowed all that was done. At an extraordinary session in December a Provisional Regional Council was chosen and the convocation of a Duma decided upon. But before the Duma was actually scheduled to meet, on February 9, the Bolsheviks had already occupied Tomsk. On the night of February 8, before the Duma assembled, several of its members were arrested by the Bolsheviks.[93] In a declaration of February 9, issued by a group of those still at liberty, it was

[91] Filatieff, op. cit., pp. 167–168; I. I. Serebrennikov, Moi Vospominaniia, Vol. I, Revoliutsii (1917–1919), Tientsin, 1937, pp. 34–35; Maksakov and Turunov, op. cit., p. 41.

[92] Serebrennikov, Moi Vospominaniia, I, pp. 44–45.

[93] Maksakov, "K Istorii Interventsii v Sibiri," op. cit., p. 130; Maksakov and Turunov, op. cit., pp. 143–144.

announced that, despite the fact that the Bolsheviks had not permitted the Duma to sit, it was the legally elected public body and possessed all power in Siberia.

After their dispersal, thirty-eight of the remaining members assembled in a private home and elected what became known as the Provisional Government of Autonomous Siberia. Twenty ministers were elected, with Peter Derber as Minister President.[94] Derber and a few others escaped and took refuge in Harbin, where General Horvath gave them a railway car in which to live. Vologodsky, Krutovsky, Serebrennikov, and others, not a part of the Derber groups, remained in or near Tomsk. Other members of the Siberian groups were scattered throughout various cities of Siberia. After the Czech rising in May 1918 they assumed administrative leadership in most of the cities of Siberia. After the combined Czech-White Russian army took Omsk on June 7, Ivanov-Rinov was made the temporary governor until the arrival of a Siberian Regionalist group headed by Vologodsky. The latter made Omsk the headquarters of the Siberian Provisional Government.[95] At the end of June the Czech overturn in Vladivostok permitted Derber and his group to establish themselves as a government in Vladivostok. On the 4th of July the Provisional Siberian Government declared its independence. Then, on September 22, an agreement was signed by Vologodsky and Derber by which the whole Siberian Government was unified under the All-Russian Directorate headed by Vologodsky.[96] Derber resigned, thus permitting the achievement, within the next few weeks, of what might be called, at least theoretically, unity in Siberia. The Provisional Siberian Government at Omsk ended its existence on November 3, 1918, after giving Russia four months of what Serebrennikov calls an independent Siberian Republic.[97] It was replaced by the All-Russian Provi-

[94] Horvath, *op. cit.*, Ch. x; Maksakov, "Vremennoe Pravitelstvo Avtonomnoi Sibiri," *Krasnyi Arkhiv* (Moscow), No. 29, 1927–1928, p. 86.
[95] Bunyan, *op. cit.*, p. 324.
[96] Karpenko, *op. cit.*, p. 56.
[97] I. Serebrennikov, "K Istorii Sibirskogo Pravitelstva," *Sibirskii Arkhiv* (Prague), No. 1, 1929, p. 21.

sional Government or All-Russian Directorate headed by Vologodsky, thus completing the unification of Siberia.

There are two features of this Siberian Government which are of considerable significance in the history of this period. The first is its international significance. The fact that it had or sought foreign support does not distinguish it from other non-Bolshevik Governments of Siberia. None of these governments, it must be added, had the slightest chance of survival without the acceptance of foreign support. The special feature of this government is that it compromised itself to such a degree that, at the price of accepting the dictatorship of Kolchak, it actually obtained foreign aid. The discovery of documents disclosing the efforts of the Siberian Government to obtain foreign support to overthrow the Soviet regime has been mentioned in another place. This discovery occurred in Vladivostok on April 25, 1918, and the one arrested was Kolobov, a member of the Siberian Government.[98] Kolobov was a member of the Derber group which had taken refuge in Harbin. It was from here that he was sent to Vladivostok, probably to sound out the Allied representatives in preparation for the overturn there two months later. When he was arrested he had on him documents showing that his mission was to request the United States to recognize the Russian Far East as a temporary administrative unit, to assume temporarily the administration of the Trans-Siberian and Chinese Eastern Railways, and, in cooperation with the other Allies, to send troops to guard these railways. This was neither the first nor the last time the United States was approached on this subject. At least as early as February 8, 1918 Ambassador Francis was approached by representatives of the same government with requests for commercial relations and loans.[99] A letter written by Ustrugov to Moravsky on April 10, 1918 indicates that their efforts in this direction were not discontinued.[100]

[98] Karpenko, *op. cit.,* p. 44; Maksakov and Turunov, *op. cit.,* p. 65.
[99] *Foreign Relations, 1918, Russia,* II, pp. 43–44.
[100] I. Mints, *Iaponskaia Interventisiia, 1918–1922, v Dokumentakh,* Moscow, 1934, p. 17.

Relations with the French Government agents were of a somewhat more active nature. Major Pichon, member of the French Military Mission, traveled through Siberia looking for a promising aspirant to power. His correspondence and that of Henri Bourgeois, French commercial agent at Irkutsk, reveals clearly the compromises required of a government seeking foreign aid. Thus, before their arrest on February 8, 1918, the Siberian Government had feared trouble with the Bolsheviks if they should try to convene the Duma.[101] They were therefore looking desperately for assistance. One of their hopes hung on the success of Semenov, who was then expected to take Chita in the near future. They not only maintained close liaison with him but proposed establishing duplicate governmental organs under his protection at Chita in order that, should their government at Tomsk be arrested, the government at Chita could carry on. In a letter to the French Foreign Minister on February 16, 1918, Bourgeois, having still to hear the news of the arrest at Omsk, advised his government that he personally considered the Siberian Government a bad risk.[102] It had, he continued, neither consultative organs nor a fixed place to conduct its business but was forced to wander from place to place. Should it actually go to Chita it would be near the Manchurian border and there would undoubtedly fall into the hands of military chiefs who would use it for their own purposes. This advice was given because Derber had approached Bourgeois for a French loan. Derber, it will be recalled, did not actually go to Chita but to Harbin. Here he continued his efforts to obtain support. By April 3 he had not succeeded in persuading the Allies to support him but he had a promise from Gamov, one of the Cossack leaders of bad repute, to help him in raising an army.[103] He was able, however, to take advantage of the Czech rising on June 29 to establish himself at the head of

[101] V. Maksakov, "K Istorii Interventsii v Sibiri," *op. cit.*, p. 158.
[102] *Ibid.*, p. 148.
[103] V. Maksakov, "Vremennoe Pravitelstvo Avtonomnoi Sibiri," *Krasnyi Arkhiv* (Moscow), No. 29, 1927–1928, p. 107.

a government at Vladivostok. But the need for support continued. In August a special mission was sent to Japan for this purpose but the results were the same.[104] Only when the government achieved complete unity under Kolchak was Allied assistance forthcoming and even then it came almost entirely from Britain.

The second fact to be particularly noted regarding the Siberian Government is that the hopes for a democratic government in Siberia depended entirely upon its success. Its compromises were, therefore, the compromises of democracy in Siberia. The political complexion of the men who organized and carried on the whole movement was overwhelmingly Socialist Revolutionary.[105] The first and only Siberian Regional Duma ever actually held was convened on August 15, 1918. Out of its ninety-two delegates, forty-six were Socialist Revolutionaries. No other bloc had more than seven members. When we are considering the Siberian Government, therefore, it is important to bear in mind that its members constituted the elements in Russia which had the most democratic leanings. Moreover, the program which the Government announced on July 8, 1918 shows that their intentions were in the tradition of Russian democratic developments of the past.[106] They wanted, according to this declaration, to establish a democratic federal republic which would later become part of a Russian republic. They wanted the restoration of the zemstvos and municipal dumas, of private property, personal liberty, and freedom of commerce. They wanted to base their authority on a freely elected Duma. They wanted to recognize all Russian treaties before Brest-Litovsk and, therefore, to resume the war against the Central Powers.

Why did they fail? The reasons are not difficult to determine. In the first place, the very thing without which a government of any type, liberal or otherwise, cannot exist

[104] *Ibid.*, No. 35, 1929, p. 53.
[105] Maksakov and Turunov, *op. cit.*, p. 203; "Materialy i Dokumenty," *Sibirskii Arkhiv* (Prague), No. 1, 1929, pp. 43–44.
[106] *Foreign Relations, 1918, Russia,* ii, pp. 293, 295; Maksakov and Turunov, *op. cit.*, pp. 181–185.

is a regular source of revenue, and this they did not have. By mid-September 1918, they were able to begin to collect taxes.[107] But the receipts remained small and the need for funds continued as before. Meanwhile, Semenov robbed and looted and showed the only way to success in a society whose political and economic framework had been wrecked. In the midst of this ruthless warfare, democracy could hardly hope to flourish unless supported by those who recognized its existence and wished it well. The peasantry were too backward to give it support and its leaders were emotionally and mentally too far from them to explain the significance of the government they stood for. The struggle was harsh and, under the circumstances, it could be carried on better by such men as Denikin and Kolchak than by such as Avksentev and Zenzinov. Furthermore, the price of British or French aid was complete unity and of Japanese aid complete disunity. Kolchak was the answer to the former demand, Semenov and Kalmykov to the latter. This is why Russian democracy, "the only movement of that kind that developed from within Russia," in the words of Paul Miliukov, failed.[108]

One of the major efforts of the Siberian Government, as it sought to enhance its position domestically and internationally, was to unify itself more and more, until the ultimate was reached on November 18, 1918, with the advent of Admiral Kolchak to supreme power. This act represented politically the victory of the conservative "National Center" group whose representative, Victor Pepeliaev, was shot on February 7, 1920, with Kolchak, his associate in the government of Siberia. But much of the impelling force toward unification undoubtedly came from the Allies, particularly the Czechs without whom the Siberian Government could not have hoped to exist, much less carry on a struggle against the Bolsheviks.[109] The organization of a

[107] Bullard, *op. cit.*, pp. 157–159.
[108] P. N. Miliukov, *Russia Today and Tomorrow*, New York, 1922, p. 136.
[109] R. Medek, *The Czechoslovak Anabasis Across Russia and Siberia*, London, 1929, pp. 2–3.

strong national army to replace the all-important Czech Legion became the objective. For this a government was necessary that could command universal respect among the people and at the same time convince the Allies of its stability, in order to receive their aid. A government which would fill these requirements was assumed, even by the representatives of democratic nations, to be a strongly centralized or dictatorial government. In any event, this was the direction taken by the Siberian Government.

A series of conferences among the various governments in Siberia and a series of efforts to effect a change in the Siberian Government itself took place which ended in the Kolchak triumph of November 18, 1918. The first of the conferences was held at Cheliabinsk on July 15 and 16 with the deliberations conducted under the sponsorship of the French and Czechoslovak representatives.[110] A united military command, under the Czech Lieutenant Syrovy, now raised to a general, was agreed upon by General Galkin of the Samara Government and General Grishin-Almazov of the Siberian Government at Omsk. To carry the unification into the administrative field, another conference was planned for August. It met in Cheliabinsk between August 23 and 25. One hundred and fifty delegates attended, representing the various governments and, as before, the chief sponsors of the Assembly were the French and Czech representatives. Only preliminary work for the coming conference to be held in September was carried on at this time.

But the military officers, whose program called for the type of government desired by the Allies and, they hoped, by the Czechs, were becoming impatient. The very foundations of the Samara Government were, from its inception, weakened by the desire of the military element to establish a government more decisive in its aims and purposes and, in general, more congenial to their own ambitions. The same was true of the Siberian Government at Omsk.[111] Here the

---

[110] V. B. Boldyrev, *Direktoriia, Kolchak, Interventy,* Novonikolaevsk, 1925, p. 33; Maksakov and Turunov, *op. cit.,* p. 76.
[111] Miliukov, *op. cit.,* pp. 150–151.

military groups had given their support to the less radical politicians in establishing the government that grew up in June following the overthrow of the Soviets by the Czechs and White Guard detachments. Their efforts at unification made the government constantly unstable and forced it to send delegates to the conferences called to unify all government in Siberia. The first large-scale attempt of the officer group to effect an overturn was on the night of September 20–21 while the conference was in session at Ufa.[112] The reactionary officer group actually arrested several of the more extreme Socialists. But the Czechs intervened and they were released and given twenty-four hours to leave Omsk. The Czechs forced the government to compromise until the Directorate, the government agreed upon by the conference at Ufa, arrived in Omsk on October 9 to assume charge.

The conference at Ufa, meanwhile, had been in session from September 8 to 23, 1918. It met under circumstances that demanded action. The anti-Bolshevik front in the Volga region was in danger of collapsing because the Czechs, receiving none of the promised help either from the Allies or the Russians, were threatening to abandon it altogether. The military element was pointing to the disunity as the reason for the lack of Russian fighting strength. Vologodsky had left for the Far East on September 10 in a frantic effort to achieve unity in that area.[113] On September 22 Derber resigned at Vladivostok and on the following day Horvath agreed to give up his pretensions to a separate government and act as the Far Eastern Commissioner for the Omsk Government. Victor Pepeliaev, the representative of "National Center," played some part in this agreement, and on October 11 left for Omsk with two members of Horvath's former government.

The one hundred and seventy representatives who gathered at Ufa on September 8 were thus almost bound to come to some settlement. In deference to the Samara Government, the Constitutent Assembly of January 1918 was recognized

[112] *Foreign Relations, 1918, Russia*, II, p. 392.
[113] Maksakov and Turunov, *op. cit.*, pp. 88ff.

as the source of authority.[114] In exchange for this, the Samara Government transferred to the Directorate the Russian gold hoard captured at Kazan. The new government was to be the sole trustee of sovereign authority in the Russian state until the convocation of the new All-Russian Constituent Assembly. An army was to be organized with strict discipline for the purpose of carrying on a war against the Central Powers and the Bolsheviks. Democratic city and zemstvo institutions were to be organized in all regions liberated from the Bolsheviks. Civil liberties, private enterprise, and recognition of unions were also included in the agreement. To carry on the administration, an All-Russian Provisional Government or Directorate of five members was chosen, each with an alternative member to function in his absence. The principal members of the Directorate were Avksentev, Astrov, General Boldyrev, Vologodsky, and Chaikovsky. On October 9 it moved to Omsk to carry on the government of all Siberia, and on November 3 it formally assumed direction of a theoretically united Siberia.

As might be expected in the case of a government which was overthrown, a controversy has raged as to the cause of its fall.[115] Its opponents urged that it was incapable of raising an army and of coping with the many complex problems then demanding a solution. It has also been charged that the reason for its inherent weakness was the obstinate refusal of the Socialist members of the new government to agree to any compromise with their more conservative colleagues. It has been asserted with respect to an alleged socialist plot to obstruct the work of the Directory, however, that this was a pure fiction, an invention of the conservative and the military element who were themselves systematically engaged in undermining the Directorate and preparing for the overturn which they finally accomplished on Novem-

[114] Bunyan, *op. cit.*, pp. 352ff.; *Foreign Relations, 1918, Russia*, II, pp. 406–409.
[115] C. Nabokov, *The Ordeal of a Diplomat*, London, 1921, p. 272; Bullard, *op. cit.*, p. 169; Chamberlin, *op. cit.*, II, p. 204; V. Gurevich, "Realnaia Politika v Revoliutsii," *Volia Rossii* (Prague), No. 14, 1923, pp. 20–21.

ber 18 by the installation of Kolchak as dictator. On the other side, it has been urged that the conservatives in the government openly violated some parts of the Ufa agreement, in particular those concerning personal liberties and freedom of speech and press, and that the growth of the new army brought about the reestablishment of epaulettes as well as the hated army discipline of the old type. While remembering that many of the Russian Socialists were highly doctrinaire and unaccustomed to the day-by-day processes of public administration, it must also be remembered that the conservatives not only tried but succeeded in seizing the government. Also, it should not be forgotten that General Alekseev and General Denikin, the acknowledged leaders of the military party in Russia, withheld recognition from the Directorate.[116] Finally, the defeat of the democratic groups represented not only the defeat of what might have become a liberal government, but the triumph of reaction. It was, therefore, the central tragedy of the intervention in Siberia.

It has been mentioned that Viktor Pepeliaev was the representative of the "National Center" and that he was instrumental in obtaining an agreement between Volgodsky and Horvath which brought unity into their effort to govern Siberia. While still in the Far East, Pepeliaev had met Horvath and Gaida at Borzia station in Transbaikal.[117] This group agreed that a dictatorship was the best solution to their political problem of achieving unity. But, since a dictatorship seemed out of reach at the moment, they agreed to support the Siberian Government. According to Horvath, Vologodsky shared this view. Later, when a dictatorship appeared more possible, it was this same Pepeliaev who carried out the will of the National Center and of the Allied supporters and announced the choice of Kolchak.[118] The first choice had been General Alekseev, but he was not only unavailable in Siberia but his death on September 25 eliminated him as a candidate. The choice thus fell on Kolchak.

[116] Filatieff, *op. cit.*, pp. 171–172.
[117] Horvath, *op. cit.*, Ch. xiv.
[118] Maksakov and Turunov, *op. cit.*, p. 92.

At the time of his choice for the role of dictator, Aleksander Kolchak was forty-five years old and a vice-admiral in the Russian Navy.[119] He had served with distinction both as an active commander with the fleet in the Russo-Japanese and World Wars and as a staff officer and arctic explorer before and after the war of 1904–1905. During the British cooperation in the reconstruction of the Russian fleet after its devastating defeat in the Russo-Japanese War, he was closely associated with the British naval advisory staff and was, in fact, something of a Anglophile himself.

During Kolchak's regime in Siberia, one of his closest advisors was a Mr. Fedosev, managing director of the Irtysh and Tanalyk Corporations, British mining firms, the chairman of which was Mr. Leslie Urquhart, also a close friend of Kolchak.[120] The varying fortunes of these mining activities through the succeeding periods of war, revolution, and intervention form an interesting commentary on the British interests in the West Siberian-Ural region and throw light on their reasons for supporting Kolchak. These corporations, the Irtysh and Tanalyk, had early in the war acquired properties formerly belonging to Russian corporations.[121] The mining properties included deposits of coal, copper, iron, and other valuable resources. By gaining the support of the local population, many of whom were Moslem in the areas where these mines were located, the British managed to survive the efforts of the Bolsheviks to nationalize their mines. The rise of the Czechs provided a respite from Bolshevik attack and from the disturbances of civil war. Recovery in production was becoming a reality by August 1918. By November, the month which saw the rise of Kolchak to supreme power, coal production in the Irtysh Corporation

---

[119] Varneck and Fisher, *op. cit.*, pp. 9ff.

[120] F. S. Cocks, *Russia and the Allies,* London, 1919, pp. 4, 10 (information taken from *The Daily Mail*, London, *Sept.* 12, 1917).

[121] "Mining Enterprises in Siberia," *The Far Eastern Review* (Shanghai), xv, No. 4, April 1919, pp. 334–338; P. Polevoi, "Mines and Mining in Siberia," *The Far Eastern Review* (Shanghai), xvi, No. 6, June 1920, pp. 277–286.

112

mines of Western Siberia had made rapid strides and coke was again being produced.

In addition to the mines of the Irtysh and Tanalyk Corporations, located in the general region of Ust-Kamennogorsk as well as in the south Ural region, there was also the British Kyshtim Corporation with important interests centered in the Urals. The chairman was C. J. Carter-Scott; the corporation showed gross profits for the year 1916 amounting to six million rubles.[122] During the chaos that followed the events of March 1917, however, the output declined sharply. The corporation had a copper business including mines, smelters, and refineries, as well as a sulphuric acid plant with an annual capacity of eight thousand tons; it also owned iron mines. These mines and production plants had reflected the rise and fall of events in Siberia and had felt the beneficent effects of the anti-Bolshevik uprising of the Czech Legion and the resulting Allied control in the Ural region.

Since all of these interests lay within the territory where the armies commanded by Kolchak took their stand against the Bolsheviks, it is not surprising that he should have been so strongly supported as head of the Russian Government in Siberia by the British and their representatives. In October 1918 General Boldyrev told Colonel Ward, the commander of the British forces, quite plainly how he felt about Kolchak's relations with Britain. He said, "that the Social Revolutionary group had been forced by one of the Allies to accept the Admiral as a member of the Government; that they had done so merely to secure Allied support!"[123] That he meant Britain, all available evidence leaves unquestioned. Boldyrev and Kolchak discussed this very question, and Kolchak explained frankly how he saw the problem.[124] There were, he thought, two coalitions among the Allies: the Anglo-French and the Japanese-American. The former were friendly to Russia while the latter two were proceeding rapidly

---

[122] "Mining Enterprises in Siberia," op. cit., p. 336.
[123] J. Ward, With the "Die-Hards" in Siberia, London, 1920, p. 114.
[124] Boldyrev, op. cit., p. 125.

with the economic conquest of the Far East. There is reason to believe, therefore, that entirely apart from his other predilections, his strong sense of patriotism somehow influenced him to see in Britain the nation from which the most impartial assistance could be expected. The alternative, as Kolchak saw it, was a Japanese victory.

Admiral Kolchak was a man of the finest character and, by most accounts, a naval officer of high attainments, greatly respected in naval circles in Great Britain and the United States. At the invitation of Admiral Glennon, a member of the Elihu Root mission to Russia in 1917, he went to the United States.[125] The United States was then considering plans for an attack on the Dardanelles and, knowing that Kolchak had already elaborated such a plan, desired his advice. He was well received and entertained during his trip to America and was received by President Wilson on October 16, 1917.[126]

Politically, however, the admiral's views were less firmly grounded. In answer to a question of one of his prosecutors during his rather summary trial, he spoke of his brief experience with labor and social questions.[127] His active experience, he indicated, had been concerned largely with technical pursuits and hardly at all with social or political questions. "So far as I can tell," he added, "I remember nothing at all [during duties in the Obukhov plant] concerning questions of a political or social nature." His later experience as Supreme Ruler indicate that in the administrative and political field he was entirely inept. The American ambassador to Japan, Roland Morris, a careful observer of all that concerned him during his tour of duty in the Far East, bears out this conclusion. "Admiral Kolchak," he wrote to Lansing, "is, in my judgment, an honest and courageous man of very limited experience in public affairs, of narrow views and small administrative ability."[128]

---

[125] Varneck and Fisher, op. cit., pp. 85ff.
[126] R. S. Baker, *Woodrow Wilson, Life and Letters*, New York, 1927–1939, VIII, p. 309.
[127] Varneck and Fisher, op. cit., p. 39.
[128] *Foreign Relations, 1919, Russia*, p. 403.

Bernard Pares saw Kolchak's position in a highly dramatic light, as the fledgling politician surrounded by hardened men of affairs who used him for foul purposes.[129] "Everywhere," continues Pares, "he found around him a fluid world in which personal character and initiative had almost disappeared." This, it must be said, is the standard apology for the Kolchak regime. But it leaves unexplained why men presumably desiring the well-being of their country should choose an incapable administrator or why an otherwise honest man would presume to accept or retain a position of such supreme importance for his country to which he felt so patriotically attached. The answer will become evident in succeeding pages. The tragedy of Kolchak was not the unequal political position in which the admiral found himself during his experience at Omsk, but the fact that the Russian people were reduced to such a low political state that men so devoid of vision and a sense of good will toward their country as those who surrounded Kolchak were able to seize power and entrust it to him.

The overturn which placed Kolchak in power began on the night of November 17, with the arrest by a detachment of Cossacks belonging to the command of Colonel Krasilnikov, of four socialist members of the government—Avksentev, Zenzinov, Argunov, and Rogovsky.[130] These were later conveyed to Chang Chun in Manchuria under joint Russian and British guards. Ward explains that it was intended they should be shot but, if this were done, it would have made Kolchak appear as a dictator to the British people, which would have compromised seriously his chances of receiving aid and of being recognized by Britain.

With the most vocal opposition thus cleared away, the Council of Ministers, a body heretofore subordinate to the Directorate, assembled on November 18 and announced, over the signature of Peter Vologodsky, that they had as-

[129] B. Pares, "Dopros Kolchaka, *The Slavonic and East European Review* (London), xiii, No. 39, April 1925, p. 229.
[130] Ward, *op. cit.*, pp. 136–138; *Foreign Relations, 1918, Russia*, ii, p. 439.

sumed all governmental power.[131] The next step was to promote Kolchak to full admiral. Then, by decree, they transferred "for the time being" all their governmental authority
to Kolchak with the title of "Supreme Ruler." This entitled him to all civilian governmental power and supreme
command of all the armed forces of Russia. However, any
exercise of authority by Kolchak was subject to examina-
tion by the Council of Ministers and had to be countersigned
by the appropriate member of the Council.[132] On the same
day Kolchak announced the acceptance of the power thus
conveyed, which was obviously little more than a title. In
the same announcement he stated the purpose of the overturn—the formation of an army and the overthrow of Bolshevism. When this objective had been achieved, he indicated, the people would be allowed to choose freely the
type of government they desired. Ernest L. Harris, the
United States Consul General at Irkutsk, interpretated the
events of November 18 to mean that Kolchak was the legal
successor "to all lawful Russian governments which existed
up to the end of October, 1917."[133] This is an unusual interpretation to give to an assumption of power possible only
after the arrest and overthrow of the government which had
the only existing legal claim to such a precedent.

Once in power, Kolchak organized a special Council of
the Supreme Ruler consisting of Vologodsky and four others.
On November 29, 1918 he announced his recognition of all
the liabilities of the Russian State Treasury and declared
illegal all financial obligations of the Soviet Government.[134]
He had thus established a government which had all the
appearances of unity and of being pleasing to the Allies. In
effect, however, his advent to power was the signal, or the
excuse, for the opening of a new and more violent phase
of the civil war. Many socialist groups opposed him. The

[131] United States Department of State, *Russian Series*, No. 3, p. 1
(hereafter cited as *Russian Series*); Maksakov and Turunov, *op. cit.*,
pp. 264–265.
[132] *Russian Series*, No. 3, p. 1.
[133] *Foreign Relations, 1918, Russia*, II, p. 447.
[134] *Russian Series*, No. 3, p. 2.

Japanese as well as their hirelings, Semenov and Kalmykov, opposed him under various pretexts. Representatives of the United States began to see in his regime the beginnings of a reestablishment of a monarchy. Above all, Bolshevism found increasing popular support as Kolchak's regime disclosed to the people its real nature and purpose. Moreover, his regime lacked any real basis of authority. As Winston Churchill has expressed it so aptly, "He possessed neither the authority of the Imperial autocracy nor of the Revolution."[135] He dared not antagonize his military supporters by punishing their excesses. For this reason, all of the declarations calculated to enlist general support were useless since those who would normally have effectuated these pronouncements openly made a mockery of them.[136] Writing in August 1919, Baron Budberg expressed succinctly his opinion of all that he saw around him. "In the army," he wrote, "decay; in the Staff, ignorance and incompetence; in the Government, moral rot, disagreement and intrigues of ambitious egoists; in the country, uprising and anarchy; in public life, panic, selfishness, bribes and all sorts of scoundrelism."[137]

According to General Knox, the original Allied plan was to make the French General Janin the commander of all forces in Siberia, both Russian and Allied.[138] But Knox himself did not think there was the slightest chance that the Russians would have fought a war of liberation on their own soil under a foreign commander. This was precisely Kolchak's reaction.[139] He emphasized that confidence in himself was itself an important factor in fighting a civil war and objected strenuously to any division of authority. In the end, Kolchak remained commander of all Russian forces and Janin of all Allied, including Czech forces west of Lake Baikal. By all reports, Kolchak was unable to make much of his command.

[135] W. S. Churchill, *The Aftermath,* New York, 1929, p. 181.
[136] *Foreign Relations, 1919, Russia,* pp. 403–404.
[137] Chamberlin, *op. cit.,* II, 195.
[138] A. W. Knox, "General Janin's Siberian Dairy," *The Slavonic and East European Review* (London), III, No. 9, March 1925, p. 724.
[139] M. Janin, "Fragments de non Journal Siberian," *Le Monde Slave* (Paris), No. 2, 1924, pp. 227–228.

The army staff and supply departments were badly disorganized and inefficient and, worst of all, nothing was ever done about these fatal defects.[140] Just as they had been reluctant to fight for what was presumably their cause at Irkutsk in December 1917, so now the officers held back and swelled the ranks of the staff of Osmk to fantastic proportions while the front lines suffered from want of officer personnel.

In Eastern Siberia the Kolchak regime was at its weakest and worst. Here his authority was rendered entirely ineffective by the Japanese and their agents Semenov and Kalmykov, who not only refused to cooperate with Kolchak but took active measures to obstruct every effort of the Kolchak Government to enforce his authority east of Lake Baikal. This was relatively simple since Semenov established himself at the junction of the Chinese Eastern and Amur Railways, where he could entirely control the passage of supplies moving westward. Furthermore, the Kolchak representatives in the Far East soon found it both wise and profitable to come to an understanding with the Japanese. They, therefore, became of no more value to Kolchak then Semenov or Kalmykov while, as his official representative, they helped to make the name of Kolchak synonymous among the people with the blackest reaction. General Ivanov-Rinov came to the Far East on October 24, 1918 under the Directorate to take command of all Russian forces there.[141] While Horvath remained nominally the regional authority, in practice Ivanov-Rinov carried on as he saw fit. His searches for recruits and weapons among the villages became terror campaigns which in time swelled the ranks of the partisan forces. Possession of weapons—even if the people were on the way to turn them in—called for torture and killing of those caught. Ivanov-Rinov was recalled in May 1919, and Horvath left in nominal control until the arrival of General Rozanov in September 1919.[142] In sheer ability to

[140] *Foreign Relations, 1919, Russia,* p. 401.
[141] Graves, *op. cit.,* p. 143.
[142] *Foreign Relations, 1919, Russia,* pp. 497, 501, 521; Stewart, *op. cit.,* p. 293.

inflict cruel treatment, General Graves rated Rozanov second only to Semenov and Kalmykov. But by this time Kolchak was no longer able to recall anyone. Rozanov was removed by the partisan forces themselves on January 31, 1920.[143]

Kolchak's relations with the people were his great and fatal weakness. So harsh were the measures by which he tried to control them that the Bolshevik appeal to join the partisan forces received increasing support. It can therefore be said without exaggeration that the Kolchak regime signified not only the separation of the Far East from the rest of Siberia but of the people from the government and all it stood for. Unable to govern actively, the Kolchak representatives antagonized the people by appearing with knout and gun only when they wanted recruits or money.[144] In particular, they completely alienated the zemstvo and municipal institutions which should have been the cornerstone of his regime. Nothing interposed between the people and the Cossack whips. In his discerning report to the State Department, Ambassador Morris reported from Omsk that the utter insecurity of person and property was the cause of the political instability and revolt in Siberia.[145] "All over Siberia," he continued, "there is an orgy of arrest without charges; of execution without even the pretense of trial; and of confiscation without color of authority. . . . Fear-panic fear has seized everyone. Men suspect each other and live in constant terror that some spy or enemy will cry 'Bolshevik' and condemn them to instant death."

Only against this background can the irony of Kolchak's appeal for popular support be appreciated.[146] "The time has passed, never to return," said he to an assembly of representatives of local governmental institutions held in March 1919, "when state authority places itself in opposition to public opinion as a force to which it is distant and even hostile."

[143] G. Reikhberg, "Partizany Dalnego Vostoka v Borbe s Iaponskoi Interventsiei (1918–1920)," *Istoricheskii Zhurnal* (Moscow), IX, 1938, p. 70.
[144] Nabokov, *op. cit.*, p. 243; Graves, *op. cit.*, p. 227.
[145] *Foreign Relations, 1919, Russia*, p. 400.
[146] *Ibid.*, p. 347.

He went on to describe the democratic government he proposed to foster once the Bolsheviks were beaten. Later as the situation grew desperate, as his armies melted away and the British uniforms of his troops began to appear in greater numbers among the Bolshevik forces, his appeals grew more desperate. By July he wanted a definite propaganda program to raise the morale of his own troops and convince the Bolshevik troops of his good intention.[147] By fall the sight of his retreating army had brought him to make a conciliatory gesture toward the local institutions which he had disregarded. But it was much too late. Even the speaking tours of Sir Bernard Pares and Colonel John Ward, earlier in the year, were forgotten in the events that had passed since then. Colonel Frank, the Russian officer who had accompanied Colonel Ward on his tour (which of all things aimed at enlisting for Kolchak the support of labor), had more recently been known as the aide of Rozanov, who had devastated entire villages in his attempt to recruit soldiers.[148] A Jewish pogrom carried out in Ekaterinburg in mid-July 1919, with 2,000 persons killed, must have been strangely reminiscent of the Tsarist regime. No mere hasty appeal could either blot these things out of the minds of the people or draw away from the Red Army the Kolchak deserters who were filling its ranks. It is thus not difficult to see that there is considerable truth in the conclusion which Sidney Graves, who served with his father in Siberia, draws from the Kolchak episode. Kolchak's failure was not, Graves concludes, the result of Allied failure to support him, but the failure of the government itself.

The most important military aspect of the Kolchak regime is of course the fact that he lost the war. In a fluid situation where each side could either make or break itself and nothing was predetermined, this fact alone is significant. According to

[147] P. Miroshnichenko, "Iz Istorii Kolshakovschchiny," *Krasnyi Arkhiv* (Moscow), No. 28, 1928, pp. 225–226.

[148] Ward, *op. cit.*, Ch. xviii; S. C. Graves, "The Truth About Kolchak," *The New York Times Current History* (New York), xiv, No. 4, July 1921, p. 671.

the estimate of Winston Churchill, Kolchak had available in November 1918 about 243,000 troops of all nationalities.[149] By June 1919, in spite of the loss of the Czechoslovak army as well as a huge number of deserters, General Filatieff estimated that the Kolchak forces still numbered about 800,000 men.[150] The main offensive occurred in March and early April 1919; by the end of April it was over. The strategy had called for a junction with the Allied armies moving south from Archangel and those of Denikin moving north from South Russia. But, because of the presence of Semenov astride the tracks in Transbaikal and other factors, the supply was bad. In the retirement that grew into a retreat during the summer, desertion became a growing problem. A new recruit waited only long enough to receive his new British uniform before deserting to the Red Army.[151] During September there was a lull in the retreat, the Kolchak reformed and advanced against the Red Army for a few weeks. But in October the retreat, now a rout, resumed. On November 11, Omsk was abandoned after the loss of 40,000 men and entire trainloads of supplies in the effort to defend it.[152] On January 15, 1920 Admiral Kolchak surrendered and on the morning of February 7 he and Viktor Pepeliaev were shot.[153] Kolchak had already resigned his power in favor of General Denikin in European Russia and Semenov in Eastern Siberia. In Western Siberia there was no need to make a transfer since the Red army had moved eastward behind Kolchak and occupied Siberia up to Lake Baikal.

In the Far East four governments sprang up on the ruins of the Kolchak claims. By an order of January 5, 1920 Kolchak transferred all power in the Far East to General Semenov until General Denikin should order otherwise.[154] Semenov established a government at Chita and maintained

[149] W. S. Churchill, *op. cit.*, p. 46.
[150] Filatieff, *op. cit.*, p. 185.
[151] W. S. Graves, *op. cit.*, pp. 201–202.
[152] S. C. Graves, *op. cit.*, p. 669.
[153] Varneck and Fisher, *op. cit.*, p. 217, n. 3; p. 222, n. 46.
[154] P. S. Parfenov, *Borba za Dalnii Vostok, 1920–1922*, Leningrad, 1928, pp. 41–42; *Foreign Relations, 1920*, III, pp. 555–556.

himself there as long as he had Japanese support. But after they left, the government at Verkhne-Udinsk made a vigorous drive against him and by October he had been driven into Manchuria, leaving the Verkhne-Udinsk Government supreme in Transbaikal. The government at Verkhne-Udinsk was established by agreement with the government at Moscow to serve as a buffer state between the Soviets and Japan. It eventually grew to include all of the Far Eastern Region except the part of the Maritime Province which was under Japanese occupation, and which was known as the Far Eastern Republic. At Vladivostok the career of Rozanov was brought to an end on January 31, 1920 when a partisan force entered the city under Shevchenko and, by a bloodless overturn, reestablished A. Medvedev and the zemstvo institutions in power.[155] Graves observed the new institutions at Vladivostok during the following two months and found that they made genuine efforts at good government. The type of government established at Blagoveshchensk resulted from the circumstance that partisan activities had been particularly strong in the Amur Region and soon after the fall of Kolchak forced the retirement of Japanese troops toward Khabarovsk.[156] Thus, while the Maritime Province remained under threat of Japanese and other forces and Transbaikal remained under the shadow of the pretensions of Semenov, the Amur Province was free to act as the partisan and Soviet leaders desired. It therefore established on February 6, 1920 the most openly Bolshevik of the four governments of the Region.

The Verkhne-Udinsk Government eventually became the Far Eastern Republic and came to include all of the Far Eastern Region not held by Japan. It was originally conceived as a buffer against Japan to operate with head-

[155] A Iaremenko, "Partizanskoe Dvizhenie v Primorskoi Oblasti, (1918–1920), *Proletarskaia Revoliutsiia* (Moscow), No. 7, 1922, pp. 82–83; W. S. Graves, *op. cit.*, pp. 317, 324–325.
[156] G. Reikhberg, "Dalnevostochnyi Proletariat v Borbe s Iaponskoi Interventsiei," *Istoriia Proletariata, S.S.S.R.* (Moscow), No. 2, 1934, p. 164; *Foreign Relations, 1920*, III, pp. 557–558.

quarters at Irkutsk.[157] But the Red armies moved on to Lake Baikal in order to hold the strategic tunnels south of the lake, thus forcing the "Political Center," the coalition group which had arrested Kolchak, to move to Verkhne-Udinsk, east of the lake. It was finally abolished in November 1922 when the last Japanese forces had left. At the same time all zemstvo institutions were abolished, and once more the Soviet power extended to the Pacific Ocean.

[157] F. B. Kirby, "Siberia's New Republic: Its Standing," *The New York Times Current History* (New York), xiv, No. 3, June 1921, p. 476; Polner, *op. cit.*, p. 291.

CHAPTER 4

The Siberian Railways

AFTER the collapse of the Imperial Russian Government, the United States planned to undertake a program of railway control and management which had as its objective the preservation of both the important railway communications and the territorial integrity of the Russian State. In the past, the struggle for the territorial integrity of China had resolved itself into a contest for control of railway lines and the making of loans to the government. In the early part of the First World War the effort to place these two forms of economic control upon a consortium or cooperative basis had lapsed and Japan had enhanced at will her position in China while her allies were occupied in the war. But when the Russian Revolution evoked the threat, not only of a breakdown of the Eastern Front against Germany, but of the opening of a new theater of action for Japanese imperialistic adventures, the United States took steps to prevent both these eventualities.

The American attack upon this problem took the form of a number of missions which were sent to Russia to revive the active interest of the Russian people in the Allied war effort and to aid the Russian Provisional Government in retaining its hold upon the whole country by granting it loans and by improving the railway facilities in order that economic and political stability might be possible. These measures constituted the first step in a program which was designed not only to eliminate the Japanese threat to Russian territory but, in its wider implications, to reduce the Japanese gains in China. The effort to control the railways was therefore followed by the development of a new consortium to make loans to China, the stipulation that a Siberian intervention, if it had to come, must be an Allied intervention and the insistence upon the return of Shantung to China by Japan. These projects were evidences of the determination of the United States to prevent Japan from undermining the balance of power in the Far East by encroaching any further upon her continental neighbors—China and Russia.

One of the significant results of the First World War was the transformation of both Japan and the United States from the category of debtor to that of creditor nations. The United States, for example, overcame—in the course of the war and the period immediately following—a foreign debt of more than $2,000,000,000 and by 1928 had accumulated a foreign credit of more than $8,000,000,000.[1] Both had formerly been competing unequally in China with the great European capitalist nations, especially France and England. The war left Japan free to seize territories and acquire rights by the crude methods she had seen practiced in China for so long; it also left her in a position to invest her great war earnings with diminishing competition from France and England, whose wealth was then being absorbed by the war in Europe.

The rapid acceleration of the economic development of Japan during the war was accompanied by equally strenuous efforts to acquire control of economic resources and outlets in China before the prewar competitors had a chance to return to their former field of activity. In general, the trend within Japan was to greater production and larger raw material requirements. Greater production demanded additional markets to replace those to which Europe and America would return after the war. The larger requirements in raw materials made increasingly evident the Japanese poverty of raw materials and the necessity of finding new sources of supply. The industrial and commercial growth which produced investment capital produced also a growing working class whose demands grew louder and more insistent. If there was a basis for Japanese continental expansion before 1914, it increased many times after that date. The great

[1] B. H. Williams, *op. cit.*, p. 19.

opponent of a Japanese expansion policy in the Far East continued, as before the war, to be the United States. Therefore, while the United States was absorbed in the war, Japan contracted a series of loans intended to draw China into closer dependence upon her and obviate not only the reentry of the United States into the China loan market, but the revival of anything like a consortium. Nishihara Kamezo, acting for the Premier, Count Terauchi, and the Bank of Chosen, proceeded to negotiate during 1917 and 1918 a series of loans to the Central Government, as well as some provincial governments, of China.[2] But, instead of providing against the rise of a new consortium or the return of the United States to the Chinese investment market, the loans gave rise to a new consortium headed by the United States.

Meanwhile, the United States had emerged as the persistent rival of Japan in precisely those lines of advance which Japan considered most feasible for herself after the European withdrawal. A new trend in financing was introduced when, during 1916, the American firms of Lee, Higginson and Company and the Continental and Commercial Trust and Savings Bank of Chicago had made nonconsortium loans to China.[3] In the spring of 1917, however, the United States entered the war. Absorption of American efforts in the war and the temporary inability to make private loans or compete with the Japanese in China was reflected in the withdrawal of America from the China loan market and in the Lansing-Ishii Agreements recognizing the Japanese "special position." Japan, left in a better position than ever, pursued the loan policy already noted. But by 1918 the United States had returned to the offensive and in the course of the succeeding four years threatened seriously the Japanese program of expansion in the Far East.[4] She took the lead in the new consortium which aimed at forcing Japanese loan policies to function within a cooperative framework. She also participated in the Allied intervention in Siberia, as she had in the

[2] C. W. Young, op. cit., pp. 244, 340.
[3] T. E. LaFargue, China and the World War, Stanford, 1937, p. 124.
[4] Griswold, op. cit., p. 223.

Portsmouth Conference of 1905, to prevent Japan from taking over the Chinese Eastern Railway or detaching the Russian Far Eastern areas from Russian administration. She insisted, furthermore, upon the restoration of Shantung to China and upon placing in treaty form the principles of collective security in the Pacific Ocean. The United States was in this way moving toward the attainment of equal commercial and financial opportunity which she had seen as both wise and profitable during more than a century. Past experience had demonstrated beyond question that "the ownership by a foreign government of a railway in any country in practice destroys equality of commercial and industrial rights."[5] This was as true of the Trans-Siberian and Chinese Eastern Railways as of the railways of Southern Manchuria or China where the principle had been tested. It is not surprising, therefore, that the United States should see her own advantage in the security of the Trans-Siberian Railway and the territorial integrity of Russia when confronted by the Russian Revolution of 1917.

It has been said that the policy which the various Allied nations pursued during the intervention reflected their several economic interests.[6] Thus French capital investments in the railways of Russia gave her an intense interest in promoting intervention and in ousting the Soviet Government, which had repudiated all financial obligations. Britain, primarily interested in raw materials and markets, long pursued a wavering policy toward the Soviets since by establishing friendly relations her objectives, some believed, might even be achieved under a Soviet Government. The United States, according to this analysis, was interested in preserving a place for herself in the Far East or at least in reducing the danger of overwhelming competition there. This objective could be achieved most advantageously, not by military intervention,

<hr />

[5] P. S. Reinsch, "Japan's Lone Hand," *Asia* (New York), xx, No. 2, February–March 1920, p. 171.
[6] "K Istorii Interventsii—Pravitelstvo Kolchaka i Soedinenye Shtaty," *Vestnik Narodnogo Komissariata Inostrannykh Del* (Moscow), Nos. 9–10, December 15, 1920, p. 54.

but by the maintenance of stable political and economic conditions. It has been seen how the railways of Siberia and North Manchuria both created and maintained the economic life of those areas. Preserving the ordered life of Siberia thus depended to an unusual degree upon the normal operation of the railways. In her attempt to forestall the break-up of the economic and political life of Siberia by assisting Russia in operating these essential communication lines, the United States took what might be termed the first step toward preventing intervention.

American business had for years been active in the economic development of Siberia. The building of railways of continental dimensions had given American railroad men the experience and technical knowledge from which long-distance railway builders of Russia could benefit. Prince Khilkov, a Minister of Ways of Communication under the Tsar, had learned about railways in an American railway machine shop.[7] Both E. H. Harriman and J. J. Hill had aspired to make the Trans-Siberian a link in a round-the-world transportation system. Steel manufacturers had sold rails, cars, locomotives, and other equipment for the building of the Chinese Eastern Railway. The building of trolleys, ships, bridges, dry docks, and other essentials for the growing industrial order in Russia had been participated in by American manufacturers. The International Harvester Company, the builder of equipment geared to the plains of the American Middle West, had supplied agricultural equipment of all types to Siberia and had its own plants in Russia. The Westinghouse Company had a large factory in Petrograd and was making air brakes for the railway cars of Russia. In July 1918 the J. M. Coates Company was still producing sixty percent of all the cotton thread used in Russia.[8] In April 1918 Madden Summers, the American Consul General at Moscow, was reporting the arrests and the demands for special contributions made by the Bolsheviks against the

[7] "The American Commercial Invasion of Russia," *Harper's Weekly* (New York), XLVI, No. 2361, March 22, 1902, p. 362.
[8] *R.A.R.*, p. 215.

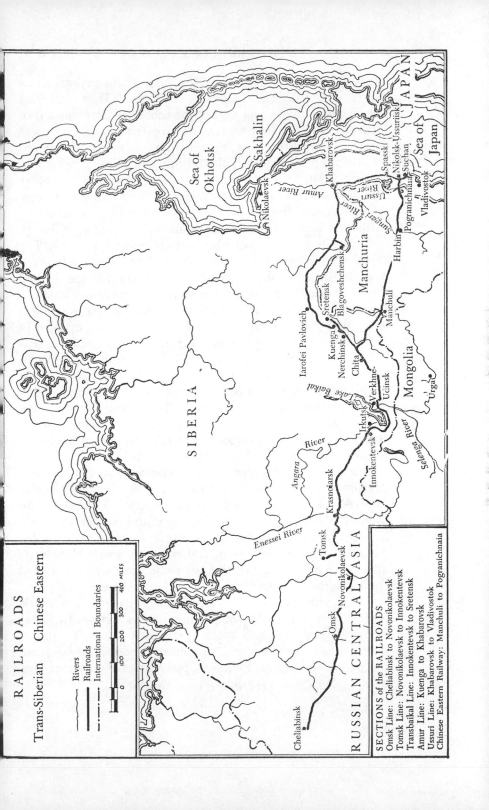

RAILROADS

Trans-Siberian   Chinese Eastern

— Rivers
━ Railroads
—··— International Boundaries

0   100   200   300   400 MILES

SIBERIA

Sea of
Okhotsk

Sakhalin

Nikolaevsk

Amur River

Khabarovsk

JAPAN

Spassk
Nikolsk-Ussuriisk
Suchan
Pogranichnaia
Vladivostok

Sea of
Japan

Ussuri River

Sungari River

Manchuria

Harbin

Manchuli

Blagoveshchensk

Sretensk

Iarofei Pavlovich

Kuenga
Nerchinsk

Chita

Verkhne-
Udinsk

Mongolia

Urga

Lake Baikal

Irkutsk

Angara River

Innokentevsk

Selenga River

Krasnoiarsk

Enessei River

Tomsk

Novonikolaevsk

Omsk

Cheliabinsk

RUSSIAN CENTRAL ASIA

SECTIONS of the RAILROADS
Omsk Line: Cheliabinsk to Novonikolaevsk
Tomsk Line: Novonikolaevsk to Innokentevsk
Transbaikal Line: Innokentevsk to Sretensk
Amur Line: Kuenga to Khabarovsk
Ussuri Line: Khabarovsk to Vladivostok
Chinese Eastern Railway: Manchuli to Pogranichnaia

agents of the Singer Sewing Machine Company at Krasnoiarsk and other railway towns of Siberia.[9] Thus American business was an integral part of the economic development of Siberia during the very years of her greatest expansion. It was therefore hoped that this valuable market could be preserved by the simple expedient of keeping the railway open and preventing its falling into the hands of Japan or any other nation desiring to enforce a monopoly by the use of troops.

Between the effectuation of the American Open Door policy in Siberia and in China there is an unmistakable similarity, not only in purpose, but also in time and in methods. The threat of Japanese armies extending their hold in Northern Manchuria and Siberia made it necessary for the United States to send forces to aid the railway commission in maintaining the railways in operation. Corresponding almost exactly with the period when these American forces were in Siberia were the negotiations for the formation of a new consortium for making loans to China. Both began to be the subject of discussion shortly after the conclusion of the Lansing-Ishii Agreements. Both had their actual beginnings in the summer of 1918. In 1920 the American troops were withdrawn early in the year after the main features of the consortium had been elaborated while the actual signing of the consortium agreement came somewhat later.

During the negotiations for the consortium, the Japanese developed a theory which forms a kind of ideological bridge between the consortium and the intervention. In a memorandum of March 2, 1920, the Japanese ambassador at Washington sought to explain to the State Department why the Japanese were entitled to special rights in South Manchuria and Inner Mongolia and to have these areas exempted from the consortium restrictions. "From the nature of the case," read the memorandum, "the regions of South Manchuria and Eastern Inner-Mongolia which are contiguous to Korea stand in very close and special relation to Japan's national defense and her economic existence. Enterprises launched forth in these regions, therefore, often involve questions vital

[9] *Foreign Relations, 1918, Russia,* i, pp. 501–502.

to the safety of the country. This is why Japan has special interest in these regions and has established there special rights of various types."[10] This argument was used, it should be noted, not only to prove the necessity for exclusive Japanese financial rights in South Manchuria and Inner Mongolia but also to explain why Japanese troops should remain in Siberia to protect these areas against the Soviet Government, then extending its influence eastward through Siberia. Also, by an interesting coincidence, on April 3 the United States accepted the Lamont compromise on the consortium agreement, a compromise favorable to Japanese continental pretentions, while on April 4 the Japanese renewed their aggressive operations in Siberia by the attack staged in Vladivostok. One victory perhaps encouraged the hope of another. All in all, it may be said that the vital interests of China and Siberia must have been closely associated in the minds of both Japanese and American leaders of the period of the intervention.

The consortium principle is the very core of American policy in the Far East.[11] In it is reflected the most-favored-nation treaties of the earlier relations with China, the fear of the rise of competing imperialisms and of the threat to partition China into exclusive preserves, as well as the concern which this threat raised regarding the right to conduct free and competitive business enterprises in China. It is, in fact, a financial version of the Open Door policy of John Hay and his predecessors. The first consortium agreement, signed June 8, 1912, grew most immediately out of the policy pursued by Japan and Russia in Manchuria and Mongolia after 1905.[12] Up to 1910 the Japanese policy was defensive and aimed at preventing other nations from encroaching on these areas. But by 1910, not only had other nations failed to break through the protective barrier, but the theory of special rights had become a more definitive and aggressive attitude toward the territories in which the passage of time

[10] *Foreign Relations, 1920,* I, p. 516.
[11] Viallate, *op. cit.,* p. 90.
[12] La Fargue, *op. cit.,* p. 123.

131

was rapidly giving Japan well-understood prescriptive rights. The consortium was formed in the course of 1911 and 1912 during the Chinese Revolution. In 1913 President Wilson was instrumental in withdrawing American support from the consortium because, as he told the press on March 18, 1913, "The conditions of the loan seem to us to touch very nearly the administrative independence of China itself . . . ."[13] After the withdrawal of the European members in 1914, Japan was left alone to provide loans for China. This fact in itself was a major upset to the balance of power in the Far East. The effects were soon evident in the Nishihara loans of 1917 and 1918, which helped to make China an appanage of Japan. The result was the growth of a new consortium group.

The new consortium, initiated in 1918 and signed in New York on October 15, 1920 by representatives of France, Britain, Japan, and the United States, is more important in showing intentions than in tracing gains. It was never used.[14] Its chief feature was the recognition of the cooperative principle in financing all loans to China.[15] A pool of seventeen Japanese, thirty-seven American, seven British, and nine French banks was established through which the necessary funds were to be raised. Money was to be raised wherever it was most easily accessible, but the actual loans would be made in the name of the four member nations. This was a concession to Japan, whose available investment capital was slight compared to that of the United States, a fact which threatened in time to diminish the Japanese political influence in China. Another concession to Japan was the Lamont agreement, which recognized the special position of Japan in Mongolia. In fact, of course, the failure to use the consortium in Manchuria was the greatest asset of all to Japan. With the exception of the British investment in the

[13] B. H. Williams, *op. cit.*, p. 85.
[14] C. W. Young, *op. cit.*, p. 297.
[15] Jumpei Shinobu, *Taisho Gaiko Jugonen Shi*, Tokyo, 1929, pp. 55–56; Carnegie Endowment for International Peace, *Treaties and Agreements with and Concerning China. 1919–1929*, Washington, 1929, pp. 32–36; F. V. Field, *American Participation in the China Consortiums*, Chicago, 1931, pp. 165–166.

Peking-Mukden Railway, no foreign money except Japanese was ever again directly invested in the railroads of Manchuria. At close range it seemed to have halted the scramble for concessions and the danger of a partition of China. But the events of the fall of 1931 are a better commentary on the effectiveness of agreements which try to stop aggression with words. These events also demonstrate the wisdom of sending troops to Siberia in 1918 to preserve the railways for Russia.

Whether in its consideration of foreign railways, or in the making of international loans, the policy of the United States in the Far East has stressed the preservation of an open market for commercial activity, and the avoidance of monopoly. The building of the Panama Canal, it has been noted, was a reflection of the American interest in bringing the commercial ports of her Atlantic seaboard closer to the markets of the Far East. Some students of this phase of the foreign relations of the United States have found in the opening of the Panama Canal in 1914 a symbol of a consistent American plan to carry forward aggressive action in the whole Pacific basin.[16] But this is a misconception which fails to take into account the inconveniences faced by a federal, democratic government in its relation with more centralized regimes. The latter have greater freedom of action in international affairs than the democratic state. This is why the United States Government, knowing that the American people would be very unlikely to support an aggressive policy, has been forced to find peaceful means of maintaining her commercial position in the Far East.[17] Therefore, such concepts as the preservation of the territorial integrity of a nation or the maintenance of the "open door" in trade relationships have been found useful because they are intended to enlist the general support of all interested nations in protecting their own positions.

It is not surprising, therefore, that the United States,

---

[16] M. Pavlovich, "Tikho-Okeanskaia Problema," *Novyi Vostok* (Moscow), No. 1, 1922, p. 21; A. E. Khodorov, "Manchzhurskaia Problema," *Novyi Vostok,* (Moscow), No. 2, 1922, p. 563.

[17] Viallate, *op. cit.,* p. 78.

faced by the possibility of a decline in Russian power in the Far East and a consequent encroachment of Japan upon her territory, should have turned again to these traditional policies. The preservation of the territorial integrity of Russia and of the open door there were, in fact, the objectives to which the United States turned first when the March Revolution gave warning that the condition from which China had so long suffered might shortly be the fate of Russia. This remained the basic American policy with respect to the Siberian intervention. In his instructions for Ambassador Morris regarding the visit of the latter to Omsk in July 1919, President Wilson wrote, "I am also desirous that Ambassador Morris should so utilize his visit to Omsk as to impress upon the Japanese Government our great interest in the Siberian situation and our intention to adopt a definite policy which will include the 'open door' to Russia free from Japanese domination."[18]

It was thus no new departure in American policy that John Stevens and a number of other railway experts were sent to Russia in the summer of 1917 to remain there for over five years. If his instructions had not done so, Stevens' experience would have made him abundantly aware of the role he must play in Siberia and Manchuria if he were to do anything at all. In a memorandum written after his return he tells that after long experience, "I may be supposed to know what I was there for. And I am very free to say however egotistical it may sound, that after matching wits for four long years—secretly of course—I prevented the Japanese from taking the Chinese Eastern Railway."[19] It is also not surprising to learn that it was Stevens, who on the basis of this long and intimate association with the Far Eastern railway problem, proposed that, as a means of preventing its seizure by some other country, the Chinese Eastern Railway should be internationalized.[20] Similar conditions had merely

[18] *Foreign Relations, 1919, Russia,* p. 388.
[19] John F. Stevens, "Memorandum."
[20] S. V. Vostrotin, "A Russian View of Manchuria," *The Slavonic and East European Review* (London), No. 31, July 1932, p. 25.

made clear the soundness of the cure proposed more than a decade before by Willard Straight, Secretary Knox, and others. This is why Japan came to consider the work of Stevens and the Inter-Allied Railway Commission, insofar as it was able to fulfill its intended function, as a great bloodless victory for the United States.[21]

It is undoubtedly true that, in the American view, the intervention which developed during the course of 1918 was essentially an economic problem. In preparing to take the whole intervention question before Congress in early 1919, Secretary Lansing instructed Frank Polk, the Acting Secretary of State, to stress precisely those points already mentioned: the importance of the railways in the future development of American commerce and the related necessity of keeping them from the exclusive domination of any single power.[22]

Yet it should not be assumed that this was the exclusive reason for American interest in Siberia. Cut off from the West by Turkey and the Central Powers, the Trans-Siberian Railway, insufficient as its contribution might have been, became for Russia one of the chief means of communication with the outside world. The outbreak of the March Revolution meant to all the Allied nations the possible loss of the Russian Army in the struggle with Germany. One thing at least was certain—if the Trans-Siberian Railway should for any reason become unavailable for the use of Russia and her Allies, fighting on the Russian front would be materially weakened. The maintenance of railway service was a major contribution which American experience and past interests could make to the Allied cause. How determinedly the American leaders intended to perform this service can be judged from a letter written by Secretary Lansing to Secretary of War Baker on March 31, 1917.[23] He wrote: "I hope you will agree that no contract for delivery of railroad

[21] "K Istorii Interventsii—Pravitelstvo Kolchaka i Soedinennye Shtaty," *op. cit.*, p. 64.
[22] *Foreign Relations, 1919, Russia,* p. 246.
[23] *Foreign Relations, 1918, Russia,* III, p. 183.

material, whether locomotives or cars, should be made with Russia, which does not stipulate that the duration of the agreement is contingent upon Russia's continuing active in support of the war against Germany."

The wartime economic problems of Russia arose to a considerable extent from the failure of transportation. In a letter of September 13, 1918, Secretary Lansing summarized the situation which had resulted in sending the railway experts to Russia in the summer of 1917.[24] The revolution, he wrote, was precipitated by the demand of the people of Petrograd for food. The available food throughout the country was apparently adequate, but the machinery of distribution had broken down. Therefore, the Provisional Government recognized this state of affairs as one of its first problems and invited the United States to send experts to propose a solution. This analysis is as accurate for Siberia as for the rest of Russia. Western Siberia had abundant wheat crops, at least before the civil war began in earnest. Travelers passing through the Ussuri Valley in 1918 found untouched crops of wheat standing in the fields.[25] The problem was so urgent that it was among those which the Soviet Government was willing to entrust to the Allies. "It is urgently necessary," Lenin told Robins in May 1918, "to put transportation in order for the reestablishment of proper exchange of commodities . . . ."[26] Transporting this food to areas where it was needed was therefore the most immediate Russian problem with reference to the railroad. The failure to restore railway traffic to a normal condition was largely responsible for the starvation which eventually overtook this land of grain, dairy products, fish, and livestock.

In addition to the American interests in the railways, there were other important foreign interests to be considered. The most important, that of Japan, has already been discussed. It remains, however, to mention that the Trans-

[24] *Ibid.,* III, p. 250.
[25] Maksakov and Turunov, *op. cit.,* p. 47; F. F. Moore, *Siberia Today,* New York, 1919, p. 41.
[26] *R.A.R.,* p. 205.

Siberian Railway tapped the trade of all Siberia and brought it not only to Vladivostok but also to Harbin as well as to Dairen by way of Kuan Cheng-tze, the point south of which the railway became the Japanese South Manchuria Railway. Japanese Dairen was thus a business competitor of Vladivostok and Japan was an interested party on this score alone.[27] China, moreover, was vitally interested because the Chinese Eastern Railway ran across her soil. France had a double interest. She was concerned about the railway as one of her important foreign investments, the security of which was shaken by the revolution. This in turn raised her determination to intervene in order to overthrow the Soviet Government which cancelled its debts and left the German armies free to move in increasing numbers toward France. Therefore, the intervention plan drawn up by Major Pichon, a French agent in Russia, called for the seizure of the entire railway.[28] Finally, a German effort to seize the railroad was considered a distinct possibility as the Russians negotiated peace at Brest-Litovsk.[29]

Besides these more basic Allied interests, one of the official reasons given by the Allied Governments for sending military forces to Siberia was to guard the stockpile of materials accumulated at Vladivostok. Estimates place this accumulation at 700,000 to 750,000 tons of goods.[30] The stocks had originally been placed in warehouses. But, as the flow of war shipments to Vladivostok increased, the railway became more and more overburdened and less able to handle the materials flowing westward. They were then left piled on the docks and eventually newly received stocks had to be taken back toward the hills near the city and left in the open, frequently without any covering. At the time of the arrival of the American forces, in the fall of 1918, observers

[27] "American Engineers in Siberia," *The Far Eastern Review* (Shanghai), XVII, No. 4, April 1921, p. 246.
[28] V. Vilensky-Sibiriakov, *Soiuznicheskaia Interventsiia na Dalnem Vostoke i v Sibiri,* Moscow, 1925, p. 50.
[29] *Foreign Relations, 1918, Russia,* III, p. 224.
[30] J. E. Greiner, "The American Railway Commission in Russia," *Railway Review* (Chicago), LXIII, No. 5, August 3, 1918, p. 171.

137

estimated the value of this vast accumulation at between 750,000,000 and 1,000,000,000 dollars.[31] There was a hill of cotton, 37,000 railway truck wheels, a submarine, millions of rounds of ammunition, automobiles, shoes, tremendous quantities of barbed wire, agricultural implements, field guns, and other materials. The sight of this tremendous stock of necessary goods accumulated here because of the inadequacy of railway service must have made many Allied observers realize the impossibility of supplying a new Eastern Front by means of this railroad alone. Perhaps some even remembered the advice Robins had once given that a real revival of the Eastern Front depended upon internal economic and political revival. Instead, guards were posted over the stock to keep it from being used. This did not, however, prevent its use, by the very ones best able to use it most effectively, the Japanese.

The causes of this unfortunate situation were partly historical. The Siberian railways had always run at a loss. After the revolution the decline in tax receipts rendered the government incapable of making up these deficits.[32] The result was a steady deterioration of rolling stock and equipment, as well as the accumulation of more and more back pay owed to the employees. Thus there grew up side by side a technical and a social problem. Lack of spare parts, shortages, and the absence of lubricating oils and cotton waste took an increasing number of cars out of service.[33] Growing unrest among the workmen lengthened the period required for the repair of a car or locomotive. By early 1918 the needed replacement of rolling stock alone was so great that it was estimated that the services of three hundred ships would be required for six months in order to bring it in sufficient quantities to Vladivostok. In addition, there were matters of engineering which rendered the railway less efficient. Joseph Greiner, one of the American experts, felt that

[31] Ackerman, *op. cit.*, p. 42.
[32] Bullard, *op. cit.*, p. 187.
[33] O. Gilbreath, "The Sick Man of Siberia: The Story of the Trans-Siberian Railroad," *Asia* (New York), XIX, No. 6, June 1919, p. 548.

the way the coal supply was handled on the Tomsk line was alone responsible for much of the accumulation at Vladivostok.[34]

Only against this background is it possible to understand in proper perspective the significant events of early 1917, the Russian Revolution, the entry of the United States into the World War, and the sending of special missions to the new Provisional Government of Russia. Basically, this series of events represented the recognition of the incipient depreciation of Allied fighting power due to the growing decline of Russian military strength and the realization that, because of the revolution, a possible defection of Russia from the Allied ranks must be anticipated. But the events indicated also the American and Allied concern with the question of the threat of encroachment upon a weakened Russia by two of her greedy neighbors, Germany and Japan. In addition, to President Wilson they meant the elimination from among the Allies of a hated autocracy and the addition of a new revolutionary democracy. With reference to this last point, however, it should be emphasized that the occurrence of the Russian Revolution was only one of a number of causes for the entry of the United States into the war. The preceding causes for war, it must be remembered, were of such importance that, even before the Russian Revolution, an American declaration of war was momentarily expected. Therefore, suggestive pronouncements to the effect that the entrance of the United States into the war was actuated solely by the fear of a Russian departure from the eastern battlefields must be accepted with reserve.[35]

The Revolution was, however, an extremely important element in the rapid maturation of American plans. By this time overt acts on the part of the German submarine fleet were no longer novelties either to the United States or the Allies. The severance of diplomatic relations with Germany,

[34] J. E. Greiner, "The American Railway Commission in Russia," *op. cit.,* p. 171.
[35] S. Katayama, "Fevralaskaia Revoliutsiia i ee Vlianie v Iaponii na Dalnem Vostoke," *Proletarskaia Revoliutsiia* (Moscow) Nos. 2–3 (61–62), February–March 1927, p. 212.

moreover, had already occurred on February 3, though it was not followed by the anticipated declaration of war. President Wilson had, as a matter of fact, been trying to avoid war in spite of the accumulation of events pointing to such an outcome and of the growing conviction in many quarters that war was, in the long run, unavoidable. But the occurrence of the Russian Revolution was the real turning point in the development of American determination to participate in the war and in the mind of President Wilson, whose leadership would be necessary to carry out a declaration or a prosecution of war. While the President could not have overlooked the implications of the Revolution to the Allied cause, the Russian developments provided him that other thing he needed so much—a real ideological basis for a declaration of war. With reference to this point, Ray Stannard Baker wrote: "Nothing, perhaps, better fitted in with Wilson's conviction that war, if it were accepted, must be based upon constructive ideals, than the amazing news that came out of Russia on March 15th—while he was seeking a decision as to his own course. The Russian autocracy fallen! A new democratic regime in control!"[36]

The next two weeks witnessed the development of the crucial steps which led the United States toward full participation in the Allied war effort. On March 21 Congress was convened for April 2 to hear a Presidential message. On the following day, March 22, the President approved the granting of immediate recognition to the new Provisional Government of Russia, thus making the United States the first nation to take this step. Then, on the evening of April 2, in the tense atmosphere which pervaded the nation, the capitol, and the House of Representatives, the President ascended the rostrum of the House to deliver his momentous message. After recounting the provocations of the past months and years, he came to the startling though fully anticipated proposal that "the Congress declare the recent course of the Imperial German Government to be in fact

[36] Baker, op.cit., vi, p. 501.

140

nothing less than war against the government and people of the United States."[37] He passed on to outline his plan, coming in due course to the role of the new Russian democracy in the struggle against German autocracy. Now all the Allies, he said significantly, were fighting for freedom. "Here," he concluded, "is a fit partner for a League of Honor."[38] These two events—the revolutionary developments in Russia and the American entry into the war—both so closely associated in time and in the mind of the President, provided for him a single significant and just cause to which he could now, by leave of his highly critical conscience, devote himself wholeheartedly.

Within a few days the President turned to another aspect of this same problem, the sending of two different types of missions to Russia. Both of these missions, in a sense, grew out of the idea proposed to President Wilson by Secretary Lansing in a letter of April 11 that the United States "do something to prevent the socialistic element in Russia from carrying out any plan which would destroy the efficiency of the Allied Powers."[39] Yet the two commissions were separate and distinct. The first was headed by Elihu Root, a former Secretary of War and Secretary of State, who for the purpose was given the rank of ambassador. The special purpose of this mission was to give moral support to the new Russian regime and to discover, through a general survey, what material support Russia needed to carry on as an ally in the struggle against Germany. For this reason men representing various special fields of interest were included in the mission. There was, for example, Admiral Glennon. One of his duties was to consult with Admiral Kolchak and, invite him to come to Washington for conferences with the Navy Department.[40] The United States Government was then considering a naval operation against the Dardenelles and,

[37] *Ibid.,* vi, p. 511.
[38] *Ibid.,* vi, p. 513.
[39] United States Department of State, *Papers Relating to the Foreign Relations of the United States. The Lansing Papers,* 1914–1920, ii, p. 325 (hereafter cited as *The Lansing Papers*).
[40] Smirnov, *op. cit.,* pp. 383–384; Varneck and Fisher, *op. cit.,* p. 85.

141

knowing that Kolchak had functioned effectively as the commander of the Russian Black Sea Fleet and had himself elaborated a plan for an operation against the Straits, wished to consult with him in this matter. Besides Glennon there was included on the Commission such persons as Cyrus H. McCormick, a businessman with important Russian economic interests and an understanding of Russian requirements, S. R. Bertron, a financier, as well as others representing the army, labor, and other important aspects of the wartime Russian scene.

The role of the Root Mission as a stimulant to Russian morale and to Russian determination to continue the war against Germany, if this latter could still be considered possible, was well served by the presence on it of well-known and important persons and particularly by the fact that the chairmanship of the Commission was entrusted to one of America's most distinguished elder statesmen. It was obviously intended that these men should serve as proof to the Russian people that, whatever message the members of the mission brought or whatever proposals they made, these transactions were intended to represent the most serious intentions of the government of the United States. Upon the arrival of the mission at Vladivostok on June 3, Root expressed his first message to Russia.[41] "It is our aim," he said, "to convey to the Russian democracy the good will of America, her sister democracy; to seek to establish closer cooperation and friendship between the two nations, and to learn what the needs of Russia are and to assist her in every way possible." Going on across Siberia, he arrived at Petrograd, where on June 15 he addressed an even more pointed message to the Russian Government.[42] "As we look across the sea," he said, "we distinguish no party, no class. We see great Russia as a whole as one mighty, aspiring democracy . . . . One fearful danger," he continued, "threatens the liberty of both nations. The armed forces of a military autocracy are at the gates of Russia and of her Allies. . . .

[41] Jessup, *op. cit.*, II, p. 353.
[42] *R.A.R.*, p. 29.

142

So America sends another message to Russia—that we are going to fight for your freedom equally with our own, and we ask you to fight for our freedom equally with yours." Here, in the well-phrased language of an official message was the American proposal for continued Russian cooperation in the Allied war effort. America was asking Russia to perform her rightful obligations toward herself and her allies and thus not only continue to provide her share in the war against the Central Powers but, at the same time, avoid becoming a prey to the territorial ambitions of her neighbors whether near or distant.

In his reports on the mission, Root suggested the expenditure of 5,000,000 dollars in propaganda, the object of which would be to bolster the morale of the Russians by showing them that America was fighting beside them and that they were not alone, as they had been told.[43] Through fraternization at the front, Root reported, the Russians had been subjected to considerable adverse German propaganda. He suggested newspapers, pamphlets, posters, Y.M.C.A. stations, moving pictures, and other means of bringing the Russian people closer to the United States. In all this, it has been suggested, he reckoned without the most important factor of all—the determination of the Russian people to end the fight regardless of who stood beside them.[44] Those he met were sympathetic toward him and his purposes. The radicals who opposed all he stood for not only attacked him in the press, but—what was far more fatal to his cause— perhaps represented the will of the people more accurately than those who befriended him. In any case, Edgar Sisson, the General Director of the Foreign Section of the Committee on Public Information, and others were later sent to Russia by the American Government with the object of effectuating the various types of good-will publicity recommended by Root, but without any ultimate success.

In addition to the Root Mission, there were, both from

[43] Jessup, op. cit., II, p. 364.
[44] F. L. Schuman, *American Policy Towards Russia Since 1917*, New York, 1928, p. 43.

the standpoint of objectives and of administrative organization, two separate railway missions sent to Russia in the spring of 1917. In the words of President Wilson himself, the two railway missions were clearly distinguished from the Root Mission by the fact that the former were concerned exclusively with assisting Russia in working out her difficult transportation problems.[45] It is interesting to note that both Root and Stevens, the latter being the chairman of the first of the railway missions, were somewhat confused on this point. Root at first feared that the whole purpose of his mission would be undermined if the discussion of the railway situation were entrusted to a separate delegation under Stevens.[46] Stevens, on his part, began to assume such large powers and make such unwarranted promises that the President himself found it necessary to remind him of the technical and specific nature of his duties.[47] Meanwhile, recognizing that eventually the improvement of Russian railway service would necessitate not only expert advice, but replacement and repair of equipment, large stocks of railway materials and rolling stock were made available by the American Government for shipment to Russia when needed.[48] In addition, on May 16, an initial credit of 100,000,000 dollars for the purchase of supplies was extended to the Provisional Government.[49]

The members of the railway missions, it should be noted, were to achieve an unusual record in maintaining neutrality even in the complex and all-pervading political conflicts within revolutionary Russia. So supercharged with far-reaching implications was every act and so nearly impossible was the idea of remaining unentangled in the factional strife that, after November 18, 1918, the very act of maintaining efficient railway service was itself not only a contribution to the Kolchak cause but—what was perhaps even more

[45] *The Lansing Papers,* II, p. 331.
[46] *Ibid.,* II, p. 329.
[47] *Ibid.,* II, p. 339.
[48] *The New York Times,* May 10, 1917.
[49] Committee on Russian-American Relations; the American Foundation, *The United States and the Soviet Union,* New York, 1933, p. 24.

disturbing—it also constituted a definite alignment against the deadly and determined enemies of Kolchak, the Japanese and the Cossack leaders of the Far Eastern Region as well as the Bolshevik-led partisan forces. Moreover, the members of the railway missions were subject to constant political pressure from their own colleagues, from the other Allied nations and Russia, as well as from the American State Department itself. In the case of the State Department, this pressure was particularly brought to bear in the course of summer of 1919 during the Kolchak retreat. The State Department urged, undoubtedly moved to do so by tardy or false information, that Kolchak should be openly supported since he would shortly be victorious anyway.[50] It must therefore be considered a compliment of the highest value that General Horvath, himself a partisan contender for power, should see fit to accuse the railway experts of remaining completely neutral and refusing to take sides in the vicious partisan strife which characterized Siberia during the civil war and intervention.[51]

The first of the two railway missions was called "The United States Railway Advisory Commission to Russia." Its chairman was John F. Stevens, who was at the same time in general charge of all American railway activities in Russia. Stevens had in the past been prominently connected with the building both of the Panama Canal and of the Great Northern Railway.[52] During his five years in Russia he was answerable only to the Secretary of State or to the President himself.[53] Under the Russian Provisional Government his official position was that of director general of all railways, though his salary and the salaries of the members of his staff were paid by the United States Government. Under his supervision were such capable men as Henry Miller of St. Louis, an expert in railway operations; George Gibbs of

[50] C. H. Smith to H. H. Fisher, February 14, 1931; J. F. Stevens, "Memorandum."
[51] Horvath, op. cit., Ch. x.
[52] Foreign Relations, 1918, Russia, III, pp. 189–192.
[53] Stevens, "Memorandum."

145

New York, expert in mechanical equipment; W. L. Darling of St. Paul, a specialist in railway maintenance; Joseph E. Greiner of Baltimore, an expert in railway structures.[54] In Russia the delegation was joined by Charles H. Smith, who had gone to Russia in 1916 in a professional capacity.[55] Urged by David R. Francis, the American Ambassador in Russia, to remain after the United States entered the war in 1917, Smith became an aide to L. A. Ustrugov, the Assistant Minister of Communications under the Provisional Government. He was later to become the American member of the Inter-Allied Railway Committee, formed in January 1919. It should be added that Mr. Smith has left some of the most enlightening and penetrating observations on the experiences and activities of himself and others in Siberia.

The specific assignment of the United States Railway Advisory Commission to Russia was to make a complete survey of all Russian railways in order to make recommendations regarding improvements in management and technical changes, as well as to ascertain the existing requirements as to supplies and equipment.

The members of the Railway Commission under the direction of Stevens conducted an inspection of Russian railways lasting some fifty days.[56] Landing at Vladivostok on May 31, 1917, they conducted a thirteen-day inspection of the railway to Petrograd, traveling only by day. After this they inspected the railways of European Russia. Mr. Darling undertook the inspection of progress made on the Petrograd-Murmansk line, construction on which was interrupted by the Revolution. He decided that, due to the work remaining to be done on it and the fabulous sum required to complete it, the use of this line would have to be considered questionable. The Commission announced its conclusion that the only usable railroad into Russia from the outside world was the Trans-Siberian.

[54] J. E. Greiner, *The Russian Railway Situation and Some Personal Observations*, p. 7.

[55] Smith to Fisher, *op. cit.; C. H. Smith*, "What Happened in Siberia," *Asia* (New York), XXII, No. 5, May 1922, p. 373.

[56] J. E. Greiner, *The Russian Railway Situation, op. cit.*, p. 8; Stevens, "Memorandum"; *The Lansing Papers*, II, pp. 340–341.

The inspection disclosed that, while the Russian railways were basically in good physical condition, their management was poor and the equipment was not only antiquated but much of it was in desperate need of repair or replacement. Generally speaking, the workmanship in the building of the railway was excellent even by American standards, while the engineering was often very poor.[57] Thus, the forty-one tunnels south of Lake Baikal, the Commission found, could have been avoided by the simple expedient of laying the tracks farther to the South. Another engineering problem which had been poorly solved by the Russian builders was the efficient use of mines. Thus, there were two coal mines on the Tomsk line, one at Taiga and one at Cheremkhovo.[58] The use of the latter reduced traffic to a mere five or six trains a day. If the Taiga mine 950 miles to the west were used, it could have increased the train capacity of the line to about fifteen each day. But the miners at Taiga had gone on strike and the officials were hesitant and uncertain about trying to force them back to work. Another difficulty was the use of locomotives and cars which were antiquated and extremely small and inefficient. The car shortage, for example, was estimated at about 88,000. Further difficulties were found in the inefficient divisional organization, the failure to make full use of available cars and locomotives, and, finally, the inefficient location of railway repair facilities.

The second group of railway experts was called the Russian Railway Service Corps and was under the direction of Colonel George Emerson, the general manager of the Great Northern Railway.[59] The Corps consisted of about three hundred officers and skilled mechanics, all of whom held United States Army commissions or warrants. They were not, however, ordinary members of the army, but were a group organized under a special act to permit them to receive salaries higher than those of regular members of the armed

[57] B. O. Johnson, "Sidelights on the Railway Situation," *The Railway Age* (Philadelphia), LXVI, April 25, 1919, pp. 1063–1064.
[58] Greiner, *op. cit.*, p. 13.
[59] *Foreign Relations, 1918, Russia,* III, pp. 222–223.

forces. On November 18, 1917 Colonel Emerson and the first contingent of his Corps left San Francisco.[60] In pursuance of recommendations made by the Railway Commission, it was contemplated that upon arrival in Siberia the Corps would be organized into units of about fourteen men each. According to this plan, a unit would consist of a superintendent, a dispatcher, a yardmaster, a trainmaster, and all the other key positions in railway operation. The function of the members of these units was to instruct and supervise the Russian railway men in the revised and more efficient methods. The November Revolution in Russia prevented the immediate assignment of these units to the railways of Siberia and North Manchuria. Meanwhile they waited in Japan. Then, in March 1918, the first one hundred and ten engineers went to Harbin for assignment to duty on the Chinese Eastern Railway.[61]

After the arrival of the Allied (particularly the Japanese) forces in the summer of 1918, the condition of the Russian railways became increasingly chaotic. The open revolt in the Far Eastern Region following the rise of Kolchak and the serious beginnings of partisan activities there made conditions increasingly worse. It was not until January 9, 1919 that the United States was able to force acceptance by the Allies of a plan which Stevens felt was at all workable.[62] The plan called for general supervision of the railways by an Inter-Allied Railway Committee whose chairman would be a Russian. Each Allied nation concerned would have a representative on the Committee. The chairmanship was first assumed by Ustrugov after which Horvath, Klemm, and other prominent Russians held it.[63] The original Allied members of the Committee were Matsudaira for Japan, C. H. Smith for the United States, Girsa for the Czechoslovaks, Liu Tsin Yen for China, Sir Charles Eliot for Great Britain, Count de Matelle for France, and Gasco for Italy.

[60] Ibid., II, p. 208.
[61] Ibid., III, p. 251.
[62] Ibid., III, p. 301.
[63] Outline, p. 7.

All agreements of the Committee were arrived at by a majority vote, and no discriminations were to be made in favor of any nation. The Committee assumed charge of all railway materials and rolling stock. It held its first meeting on March 5, 1919, and until its dissolution in 1922 held a total of two hundred and thirty-four meetings. Its jurisdiction theoretically ran to the Ural Mountains and was intended to run farther west as Kolchak moved into Europe. But since he moved the other way, its jurisdiction was limited by Lake Baikal after January 1920. As to the type of questions it was called upon to decide, those of a technical nature were of most frequent occurrence, those concerning internal organization next, while problems having to do with the military guard were third in number of cases.[64]

Since the Inter-Allied Railway Committee was theoretically a policy-making body, though actually a mere front for the management of the whole railway enterprise by John Stevens, the actual administration was carried out by a number of specialized agencies. The most important of these was the Technical Board. Although theoretically subordinate to the Committee, this Board was really the heart of the entire plan. In fact, it could be said that the railway plan was found acceptable to the United States only because it was understood that John Stevens would be named as president of this Board.[65]

Each of the Allied nations named a technical representative to the Board. Its duties comprised all technical and economic questions, and its decision was usually final, even though the question might still be heard before the Committee. A Military Transportation Board also functioned under the Committee. Its duties were to coordinate military transportation though its arrangements were not final until passed upon by the president of the Technical Board. Each of the Allies had a military representative on the Military Transportation Board and its chairman was always a Japanese, of whom General Takeuchi was the first. The fact that

[64] *Ibid.*, p. 5.
[65] *Russian Series,* No. 4.

the Japanese held the permanent chairmanship of this board, it must be emphasized, was of great importance to them, since, not hesitating to exceed the contemplated quota of seven thousand troops, they had over seventy thousand men in Siberia within three months after the Allied landing at Vladivostok. As against this, the Americans at the time of the railway agreement numbered approximately eight thousand. Under the Technical Board was an Inter-Allied Purchasing Board which had exclusive charge of all financial obligations contracted by the Committee.

An indispensable element in the administration of this plan was the guarding of the railway so that the orders of the various boards could be made effective. This guarding was put into practice by assigning a specific section of the railway to the military forces of each nation represented in Siberia.[66] Thus, the guarding of the Chinese Eastern Railway from Nikolsk-Ussuriisk (inclusive) to Manchuli (exclusive) was assigned to the Chinese in order to keep the Japanese troops away from it since their conduct there was assuming all the disturbing features of permanency. The Chinese troops also guarded the branch line between Harbin and Kuan Cheng-tze as well as the section of the Ussuri line between Ussuri and Guberovo. The Japanese were persuaded to take over the sections of railway lying between Nikolsk-Ussuriisk and Spassk and between Guberovo and Khabarovsk on the Ussuri line, between Khabarovsk and Karymskaia on the Amur line, and the strips running from Manchuli (inclusive) to Verkhne-Udinsk (exclusive) on the Transbaikal line. Interspersed between these sections were those assigned to the American forces. They guarded, for example, the Ussuri line from Vladivostok (inclusive) to Nikolsk-Ussuriisk (exclusive) along with the branch line to Suchan and the section running from Spassk to Ussuri. On the Transbaikal line they guarded the section between Verkhne-Udinsk (inclusive) and Baikal City (inclusive). In addition, the American forces maintained a garrison of one thousand men at

[66] *Outline,* p. 20; *Foreign Relations, 1919, Russia,* pp. 555–556; Mac-Murray, *op. cit.,* I, pp. 83–84.

Harbin. To the west there was a Russian force between Myssovaia and Irkutsk, a Czechoslovak force between Irkutsk and Novonikolaievsk, and a Polish force west of Novoniko-laievsk.

All guards posted west of Lake Baikal were under the command of General Janin; those east of the lake were nominally under the Japanese commander, initially General Otani. Actually, General Graves refused to recognize the right of General Otani to assume command of the American forces in spite of his seniority in rank. The American force therefore retained its independence and remained clear of the many troubles that would undoubtedly have arisen had the Americans been subject to Japanese command.

One of the many difficulties encountered in trying to run the Russian railways was that of obtaining financial support. By February 1920 China had contributed 500,000 gold dollars; Japan, 8,000,000 gold yen; and the United States 5,000,000 gold dollars.[67] Britain had hedged on the question of support, while France and Italy refused altogether to pay the requested amounts By March 1 all Russian funds set aside for railway purposes by the Provisional Government had been exhausted. One source of new funds available to the Russian Embassy at Washington was the sale of railway stock. On July 14, 1917 the Provisional Government had placed orders in the United States for 500 locomotives and 10,000 cars and had under consideration additional orders for 1,500 locomotives and 30,000 cars.[68] On April 1 and 2, 1919 *The New York Times* announced that the Russian Railway Mission at Washington was disposing of some of these unused purchases to China. The stocks of cars, loco-motives, and rails thus available at Vancouver and Seattle for immediate shipment were valued in excess of 6,000,000 dollars. Yet it is not evident that any part of these funds was ever contributed by the Russian embassy to the expense of preserving their own rights in these railways. In fact Stevens' financial statement indicates definitely that no funds

[67] *Outline*, p. 20; *Foreign Relations, 1919, Russia*, pp. 262, 265, 266.
[68] *Foreign Relations, 1918, Russia*, III, p. 194.

were ever paid over to him by the Russian Embassy at Washington.[69] Instead, with much larger sums estimated as necessary for efficient railway operation, Mr. Stevens carried on his work with the funds contributed by the United States, Japan, and China. Meanwhile, the defeat of Kolchak reduced the area of jurisdiction of the Committee so that Stevens was able to return 917,000 dollars to Secretary Hughes after his five-year tour of duty.

Technical as well as other difficulties prevented the railway from running smoothly, even with some of the best American engineering talent supervising the operations. Dispatching was introduced, repair-shop practices revised, train sheets made up for operating officers, and other improvements carried out under the direct supervision of Colonel Emerson, later replaced by B. O. Johnson. One of the first obstacles the engineers met with was the attitude of their Russian colleagues. The Russian Railway Technical Board with which Stevens had to deal at first consisted of fifteen or twenty very learned professors with little practical railway experience. One of these remarked to Stevens: "Yes, Mr. Stevens, these things which you propose [to] put into effect, would better the service, move our trains, and result in economy, but what object is that to us. We have life positions, and if there is a deficit, the National Treasury makes it up."[70] It was in this spirit that the Russians felt doubtful about the benefits of American efficiency. Ustrugov and his clique were all graduates of the same technical college in Russia and feared the undermining of their positions should novel techniques be introduced on the railways.[71] Blocked by this often unspoken opposition, the engineers came at times to feel their work useless and the desire to leave was frequently expressed. They had also to put up with the results of sheer lack of funds.[72] Engineers, trainmen, and mechanics would sometimes work without pay for several months and

[69] Stevens, "Memorandum."
[70] Ibid.
[71] Foreign Relations, 1919, Russia, p. 534.
[72] Foreign Relations, 1918, Russia, III, p. 283.

would frequently leave the service in disgust. A large percentage of locomotives remained out of repair. Thus it was not unusual to find a complete stoppage of all but purely military traffic. The feud between Kolchak and Semenov had the same effect expect that all traffic would be affected during its worst periods.

The management and guarding of the railroads cannot be considered apart from the various aspects of the civil war, which formed a backdrop for events during most of the intervention, though its real beginnings came in the fall of 1918 and it rose to a climax at the close of 1919. The feud between Kolchak and Semenov had particular importance because the Japanese were the backers of all the foul activities carried on by Semenov during and after the intervention. The partisan activities which so disturbed railway traffic during the period were themselves an outgrowth of this and other military excesses perpetrated under the sponsorship of foreign governments. In a very real sense, therefore, it was basically the intervention which defeated the efforts of the railway experts. When, in late 1919 and early 1920, the Red Army pushed the Kolchak forces and other forces eastward, then the worst of all railway problems resulted. The panic was increased by the Czech seizures at that time of a large number of trains for their own exclusive use.[73] Hated by the Kolchak forces because of their withdrawal from the front line and opposed by the Japanese who sought to hold them back lest their going remove the Japanese excuse for remaining in Siberia, the Czechs decided to move through against all opposition. This Czech move, it should be added, was one of the only points on which Kolchak, Semenov, and the Japanese saw eye to eye.

Severe dislocations of railway traffic resulted from this confusion. The Allies lost one hundred and twenty trains to the advancing Red Army as a result of the Czech activities alone.[74] Another result was that the Japanese were able to control 8,000 cars which had accumulated on the Ussuri

---

[73] *Outline*, p. 11.
[74] *Foreign Relations, 1919, Russia*, p. 232.

line in the course of the evacuation.[75] Thereupon, the Japanese established the convenient rule that no cars would be allowed to leave the coast unless an equal number were brought out in exchange. The result of this rule was effectively to shut off Siberia from the outside world and to keep other countries from trading with the Soviet Union through this only remaining means of entry.

The Russian attitude toward this Japanese-American duel for the railway was by no means uniform. From the Soviet point of view, the hopeful aspect of the problem, as already noted in a previous chapter, was voiced by Lenin in a speech on May 14, 1918.[76] There were two fundamental contradictions, he said, which determined the present position of Russia. The first was the struggle between Germany and England, the fierceness of which prevented their union against Russia. This eventually proved more logical than true, as will be seen presently. The second factor, Lenin continued, was the rivalry between Japan and America. The economic development of these two, he believed, rendered inevitable a struggle for supremacy. This statement, though somewhat lacking in logic, was, in the long run, true. In the light of the Portsmouth Conference more than a decade before and the Second World War two decades in the future, the fundamental soundness of this analysis can be seen, though its inevitability is quite another matter. This rivalry was frequently mentioned by members of the new Soviet Government as the one thing that stood between them and the loss of their Far Eastern Region. Of the two rivals they placed their only real reliance on the United States. The rivalry, already seen to have been evident in the railway and military fields, was also keen in the field of commercial enterprise. One of the outward evidences of the rivalry, it may be added, was the increase at this time in consular representation by both the United States and Japan.[77]

[75] C. H. Smith, "What Happened in Siberia," *Asia* (New York), XXII, No. 5, May 1922, p. 483.

[76] Bunyan, *op. cit.*, p. 117.

[77] Kamido Masao, "Beidoku no Shibiria Hatten ni tai suru Waga Keizaiteki Hatten," *Chuo Koron* (Tokyo), No. 356, May 1918, p. 51; Yamasaki Kakujiro, Ogawa Gotaro, *The Effect of the World War Upon the Commerce in Industry of Japan*, New Haven, 1929, p. 31.

It would be too much to expect that Japan would stand idly by while the United States placed its experts in strategic locations along the railway. Japan had, as a matter of fact, been deeply stirred by the growth of American business in Siberia during the earlier years of the century.[78] In particular, the years 1908 to 1911 had seen an impressive growth of American imports into Siberia. The International Harvester Company had come to have over two hundred branches throughout Siberia. The agricultural experiment stations scattered through Siberia were so largely stocked by International Harvester that they must have seemed like branches of the company itself. The presence on the Root Mission of Cyrus H. McCormick brought back the memories of his business activities in Siberia and raised suspicions in the minds of the Japanese as to the whole purpose of the Mission.[79] The Root Mission, it was feared, was simply an excuse to bring businessmen into the country in order to foster the long-standing American plans to increase her investment in mines, railways, forest, and other available enterprises. Moreover, the very fact that the Root Mission went directly to Siberia without stopping in Japan seemed to Iichiro Tokutomi ample evidence of American bad faith and sinister intentions.[80]

In July 1917, according to a Soviet revelation nearly a year later, the Japanese had broached the question of financial competition to the Russian ambassador at Tokyo.[81] If, a Japanese statement to the Russian ambassador read, it were actually true, as rumor had it, that Russia was contemplating the granting of concessions to Americans in the Maritime Province or Sakhalin, then it must be stated that this would create a grave reaction in Japan. Japanese capitalists, the Russian Government was reminded, had long aspired to share in the exploitation of the mineral wealth of these

[78] Abe Hidesuke, "Shibiria ni tai suru Waga Keizaiteki Hatten," *Chuo Koron* (Tokyo) No. 356, May 1918, pp. 57–58.

[79] Hattori Bunshiro, "Wa Tai Shibirisaku no Kompon wo Keizaiteki ni Oke," *Chuo Koron* (Tokyo), No. 356, May 1918, p. 54.

[80] Iichiro Tokutomi, *Japanese-American Relations*, New York, 1922, p. 117.

[81] *Izvestiia*, April 7, 1918.

regions and were even now prepared to form Russo-Japanese companies for this purpose. Only recently, Motono, then the Japanese ambassador to Russia, was informed, the statement continued, that the law prohibited the participation of foreigners in the mining enterprises of these areas. If this law had been altered in the meantime, Japan desired to be apprised of this fact.

The arrival in Siberia of the Stevens and then the Emerson groups confirmed the suspicions roused in Japan by the Root Mission.[82] The large quantities of railway materials and rolling stock simultaneously placed on order in the United States immediately raised the question of how Russia would pay for these goods. Undoubtedly, wrote Oyama Ikuo, large advantages had been given for these things. Perhaps Americans had obtained railway construction contracts, rights to railway loans, shipping advantages, mining and timber rights, and probably the right to build municipal electricity and water systems as well. Then, continued Mr. Oyama, referring perhaps to an old Russian-American plan for joining the two countries together by telegraph and cable through Siberia and Alaska, the United States was probably even then establishing wireless stations in Alaska for communication between the United States and Russia.[83] It was hard to prove these things, continued Oyama, but he held that they were real possibilities. The State Department, it must be said, made no effort either to confirm or deny these various accusations in detail. In a communication to Ambassador Morris in December 1918, the Acting Secretary of State merely took general note of all the worst fears of the Japanese and denied them all flatly.[84] The members of the Russian Railway Corps were not, he wrote, agricultural experts, industrial promoters, or any other types of experts in disguise, using the railway work as a cloak for other activities.

[82] Oyama Ikuo, "Beikoku no Tai Ro Seisaku no Seiko," *Chuo Koron* (Tokyo), No. 356, Part 2, May 1918, p. 65.

[83] For a description of this interesting Russian-American project see, Richard L. Neuberger, "The Telegraph Trail," *Harper's Magazine* (New York), October 1946, pp. 363–370; Also S. R. Tompkins, *Alaska, Promyshlennik and Sourdough*, Norman, Oklahoma, 1945, pp. 180–182.

[84] *Foreign Relations, 1918, Russia*, III, p. 294.

One of the evidences of the intentions of America, according to Hattori Bunshiro, was her strong opposition to the sending of Japanese troops to Siberia.[85] This, it was seen by Hattori and others, suggested the difference between Japanese and American methods of penetration of Siberia. The difference was not in objectives but rather in methods. While the United States was able to make satisfactory progress by establishing and enlarging her commercial and investment interests, Japan tried to achieve the same objective by military means. Therefore, instead of creating good will and a sense of mutual advantage, Japan suceeded only in arousing popular opposition and suspicion. Unless Japan were able to find a less aggressive policy, wrote Kamido Masao, she could not in the long run compete with the United States or, for that matter, with Germany. The latter, he continued, would undoubtedly penetrate Russian life by the wiser and surer method of commercial and financial leadership in a war-ravaged country and would eventually extend her control eastward. It was evidently not known that, at the very moment of writing, the Germans in the West were pursuing a high-handed policy in Russia suitable only to a nation completely and finally subjugated.[86] However, the desperate determination with which the Russian people were shortly to fight and drive out all foreign invaders demonstrated how correctly these writers had seen the results of Japanese policy and the impossibility of establishing confidence by military methods.

That the Japanese hoped that by intervention they could not only counter American efforts to run the Russian railways for the benefits of Russia, but actually seize and control the railways themselves, is beyond question. Ambassador Morris reported to Lansing in November 1918 the elaborate preparations the Japanese had made with this expectation.[87] They had established a school at Mukden to teach the Russian language and Russian railway methods. In a single day five carloads of these prospective railway officials and opera-

[85] Hattori, *op. cit.*, p. 54.
[86] *Foreign Relations, 1918, Russia*, ii, p. 221.
[87] *Ibid.*, iii, p. 280.

tives passed through Harbin on the way to Chita. Not only did the Japanese bring in all the necessary materials for changing the railway gauge but, when they saw that they would be forced to relinquish the guarding of the Chinese Eastern Railway due to the Inter-Allied Railway Agreement of January 1919, they ran their own field telephone along the railway, thus requiring soldiers to guard it.[88] Without any previous consultation with Allied representatives they made a loan of 1,000,000 yen to the railway. They went even beyond these preparatory acts. A United States Army intelligence investigation in November 1918 disclosed that the Japanese had openly demanded from the Chinese Government the surrender to them of the Chinese Eastern Railway.[89] At this very time the early efforts to force a common Allied agreement for controlling and guarding the railway were being made. The earlier Japanese plan had been to let Horvath fail because of lack of support and military forces, thus opening the way for a Japanese occupation to restore order. But the current effort to make the restoration of order a common project threatened to frustrate this desire. They were, therefore, resorting to more direct measures. However, the Inter-Allied Agreement was forced through and for the time being the Japanese aims were thwarted.

The year 1919 was filled with outbreaks and imminent outbreaks between the United States and Japan over the railway. Either directly or through Semenov, the Japanese made it abundantly evident that the only change in their ambitions was an unavoidable postponement. In early 1920 as the Allies prepared to leave the fight for the railway was renewed, this time as a three-cornered struggle between Japan, China, and the Inter-Allied Railway Committee. How completely Japan had prepared for the anticipated acquisition of the railway can be seen from an incident related by Charles Smith.[90] Arriving at Pogranichnaia on April 14, 1920

[88] *Ibid.*, III, p. 239; M. Pavlovich, "Iaponskii Imperialism na Dalnem Vostoke," *op. cit.*, p. 55; Graves, *op. cit.*, p. 182.
[89] *Foreign Relations, 1918, Russia*, III, p. 287.
[90] C. H. Smith to H. H. Fisher, February 14, 1931.

on one of his official tours of inspection, he found that in the thirteen days since General Graves and the last of the American troops had left, the Japanese had taken over the line from Pogranichnaia to Vladivostok in a most complete manner. All the trains were being run by Japanese trainmen. Even the names of the stations were written in Japanese. Not until May 22, after many conferences, was the line restored to Russian hands. It was perhaps in anticipation of these aggressive moves that the Chinese began to assume new powers over the railway 'at the first word of the collapse of Kolchak.[91] During the course of 1920 the Chinese enhanced considerably their position in the management of the Chinese Eastern Railway.[92] By a supplement to the basic agreement of 1896 China obtained a larger representation on the Board of Directors, the Audit Commission, and among the officials of the railway generally. For the time being, however, the Inter-Allied Committee remained in charge.

The capture of the railways, the economic key to North Manchuria and Eastern Siberia, failed in spite of all Japanese efforts whether military or commercial. In Japan there was little quarrel among economists with the general objectives of the Siberian adventure. But, as already noted, the methods used were sharply criticized. The commercial relations Japan had carried on with Siberia during the intervention were to a large extent the result of the presence of a large army.[93] Goods of other merchants were shunted off onto a siding while Japanese goods were hurried through in sealed, uninspected cars, commandeered as though for military purposes. Customs duties and license fees were evaded. The people of Siberia, starved for necessary articles, bought without question. But the troops which alone made this possible were an expensive item. One of the arguments against sending Japanese troops to Siberia had been the expense it in-

[91] Vostrotin, *loc. cit.*, p. 23.
[92] "China's Effort to Recover Control Over the Chinese Eastern Railway," *The Far Eastern Review* (Shanghai), xvi, No. 11, September 1920, p. 606.
[93] D. P. Barrows, "Japan as Our Ally in Siberia," *Asia* (New York), xix, No. 9, September 1919, p. 930.

volved.[94] Japan, it was true, had become a creditor nation during the war. But thus far the total accumulations were modest compared with those of the major capitalist powers. Previous experience with the military solution to the problem of continental expansion had shown that, once introduced, troops must remain and that the expense of such a program was great. To attempt such an expensive exploit in Siberia would seriously deplete all the wartime profits. The establishment of good will would have been much less expensive and undoubtedly far more profitable. But this was an economist's point of view. The businessmen whose goods were favored by the interventionist policy took a more restricted and, for them, more profitable view of the matter.

The Japanese-American struggle for control of the railways constituted the basic economic aspect of the Allied intervention in Siberia. In the end it proved also to be the decisive phase of the Japanese efforts to control Eastern Siberia. The next phase—the attempt to strangle the economic life of Siberia by control of railway terminals and strategic harbors and rivers—came too late to achieve the conquest for which Japan hoped. By this time the Soviet Government had survived the main force of the civil war and intervention. There was revolt in China and criticism against the government in Japan itself. Finally, the United States was by that time strong enough to force her "open door" policy upon the other powers in the Far East. In the long run, therefore, the Japanese-American duel for the railway proved as decisive for the future of the Soviet Far East as the Allied victory on the Western Front had the success of the Bolshevik Revolution.

[94] Hattori, *op. cit.*, pp. 56–57.

CHAPTER 5

The New Inland Sea

THE period of Russian participation in the First World War marked the beginning of Japanese encroachment upon the Russian Far East. It was then that the Japanese expansionists formulated their plans for acquiring the natural wealth, the strategic base, and the gateway to markets farther west which would be theirs if they could find a way to drive Russia back from the shores of the Pacific. Before its demise, the Tsarist regime had already had occasion to resist Japanese demands for the surrender of territorial or other concessions. Upon the collapse of the Imperial and Provisional Governments, therefore, Japan endeavored to make the rise of any other government in Asiatic Russia contingent upon the satisfaction of her own territorial demands. In accordance with this policy, the Japanese Government sponsored a number of aspirants for governmental power with the hope that out of the confusion there might arise a desire to accept any government which could restore order, even one which willingly surrendered territory to Japan. The Siberian intervention was, in its political and military aspects, essentially the story of the Japanese effort to carry out this policy.

It has been emphasized that the expansion of Japan onto the Asiatic continent was not the result of an adventuresome urge on the part of the leaders of the army and the navy. The reasons were, indeed, far more fundamental and vital than this. Only by realizing the growing size and power of the urban and industrial classes can these reasons be made entirely comprehensible. While the industrial development that occurred during the First World War did not initiate this growth, it accelerated it tremendously. Between the years 1908 and 1912, while the rural population increased 7.8

161

percent, the urban population grew 8.4 percent.[1] Between 1912 and 1918 the corresponding figures were 0.8 percent and 17.3 percent. It can be seen from this how much more dependent on commercial and industrial sources of wealth the Japanese people had grown by 1918. Against this fact the business leaders had to weigh the effects of a termination of the war—the return of the old competitors to the world markets with a corresponding loss of Japanese business, the increase of colonial industries whose products supplied a market no external competitors would ever again fill, and, finally, the increased productivity of Japanese industry which had to find markets or face a depression. In this situation the industrial and commercial classes were by no means inclined to sit quietly while the gates of opportunity closed in their faces. They made use of the military forces to find new sources of wealth. Their view of this relationship with the army and navy is well stated in a book by a member of the industrial class, Fujihara Ginjiro.[2] "Diplomacy without force," writes Fujihara, "is of no value. Now the greatest of forces is military preparedness founded on the army and navy. . . . In this sense, an outlay for armament is a form of investment." While this reflection was written some years later, it expresses the demands which were answered in 1918 by the Siberian intervention.

One of the results of the industrial growth was to widen even more the existing chasm between the upper and lower classes in Japan. This chasm was reflected in the doctrine that each of these classes espoused during these years of war and intervention. It was at this time that Communism became popular among professors, intellectuals, and radical leaders.[3] The first May Day parade was held in 1920 and the first actual Communist Party formed in 1922. But "dangerous thoughts" began to give the government increasing trouble.

[1] U. Kobayashi, *The Basic Industries and Social History of Japan, 1914–1918*, New Haven, 1930, p. 108.

[2] Fujihara Ginjiro, *The Spirit of Japanese Industry*, p. 143 as quoted in T. A. Bisson, *Japan's War Economy*, New York, 1945, p. 134.

[3] H. Borton, *Japan Since 1931—Its Social and Political Development*, New York, 1940, p. 27.

An army officer was forced to divorce his wife because her sister was married to a well-known Socialist.[4] The translation into Japanese of some of the writings of Kuropatkin brought a prison sentence for a young professor at the Imperial University at Tokyo. Moreover, the same period which saw the rise of the radical protest against conditions which had become aggravated by war, saw also the rise of the ideology of suppression. The intensified nationalistic doctrines which were crystalized in a somewhat later period grew out of this era of change.[5] Societies arose which were closely connected either with the leaders of the older Black Dragon group or with the management of the South Manchuria Railway. The Dai Nippon Sekkaboshidan or Great Japan Brigade for Combatting Bolshevization was of the former class while the Odogikai or Society of the Royal Road belonged to the latter class and was closely connected with foreign aggression.

The growing intensity of the social struggle naturally roused a strong clash of opinion in Japan. The expansionists carried on their part of the struggle largely by initiating expansionist acts without any previous consultation. The opposition was strongest when appearing in print or making an interpollation in the Diet. One of the most persistent opponents of the official policy of the government was Yoshino Sakuzo. In an article in the May 1918 issue of the *Chuo Koron* he made three strong points tending to show that the government had displayed bad faith with respect to the people.[6] In the first place, he wrote, the government was fully aware that the question of a possible intervention was being widely discussed among the people. Ambassador Uchida had recently returned from Russia and so had a number of Japanese residents from abroad. Coming so closely after the signing of the peace of Brest-Litovsk, these arrivals had

[4] A. M. Young, *Japan Under Taisho Tenno, 1912–1926,* London, 1928, p. 194.
[5] O. Tanin and E. Yohan, *Militarism and Fascism in Japan,* New York, 1934, pp. 72ff.
[6] Yoshino Sakuzo, "Tai Ro Seisaku ni tai suru Kokumin to shite no Kibo," *Chuo Koron* (Tokyo), No. 356, May 1918, pp. 42ff.

made the public anxious about the events that they might presage. Yet on March 26, Yoshino continued, Motono in the Diet and Terauchi in the House of Peers had refused to commit themselves to any definite statements regarding the policy of the Government. The latter had made veiled hints as to the effect that the Treaty of Brest-Litovsk might have on future Japanese policy. Should German influence extend eastward and thus threaten Imperial or Allied interests, Japan would be forced to take suitable measures. This was all he admitted.

In the second place, wrote Yoshino, the dangers of the Russian situation were greatly exaggerated. Reports of April 14, both from Major General Ishisaka and from the special correspondent of the *Asahi*, showed that the danger from armed war prisoners was purely imaginary. A group of not more than two thousand prisoners had been reported near Krasnoiarsk. They were internationalists who had sworn to fight all enemies of the Bolsheviks. But this, continued Yoshino, was not a menace to Japan either in itself or as an extension of German power eastward. The prisoners would become a danger to Japan only if the Soviet regime were itself to be made an enemy by some aggressive move. The extension of German power eastward by means of the sworn enemies of Germany was an impossible contention. Finally, according to Yoshino, the absence of any threat from the Soviet Government was proved by the fact that, according to the latest reports, the Soviet was just then arming itself, not for aggression, but to protect itself against foreign aggression. In these respects, Yoshino, among others, found the official reasons for intervention unacceptable. It will be seen presently that the same thing puzzled General Graves, who found the official reasons for intervention totally invalid. But he was not as close to the source of Far Eastern aggression as Yoshino, and he was therefore unable to see as clearly the long and continuing struggle cloaked behind the formal words of the official pronouncements.

The pressure on the guardians of the Japanese state was increased by the condition of the rural population and the rising cost of living. The farmer, it will be recalled, was the foundation stone of the Restoration settlement. His labor furnished the capital for the new state and as the new capitalist class rose to greater strength his condition grew steadily worse. The lag in farm prices and the increasing cost of farm labor made the war years a period of particular hardship for the farmer. The result was the consolidation of farms and the growth of tenancy during the war.[7] The short-term leases and consequent power to evict made the position of the farmer difficult indeed. The sharply rising cost of living, moreover, gave the internal problem a range far beyond the countryside. Taking the year 1900 as 100, the index figure of the rise of prices was 120 in 1914 and 283 in 1918.[8] As soldiers returned from Siberia, the people learned the slogans and formula: of protest and revolt. The leader of an agrarian disturbance in Gifu Perfecture in 1921 was a noncommissioned officer returned from Siberian duty.[9] Strikers learned to ask for more than an increase in wages. They began to demand recognition of unions, annual contracts, and other things which labor in other countries had attempted to achieve long before.

Against this background, the rice riots of 1918 can be seen as a climax of the events of preceding decades intensified by the developments of the war period. With the growth of a labor force during the war, there was an increase in the consumption of rice and at the same time an insufficiency of foreign supply.[10] In addition, there was a lack of substitutes, considerable speculation, and a rising cost of the price of rice.

The riots began in July and lasted through August 1918.[11] The large cities of Tokyo, Osaka, Nagoya, Kobe, Kyoto,

[7] U. Kobayashi, *The Basic Industries and Social History of Japan,* 1914–1918, pp. 101–102.
[8] K. Yamasaki and G. Ogawa, *op.cit.,* p. 51.
[9] M. Pavlovich, "Iaponskii Imperialism na Dalnem Vostoke," *op.cit.,* p. 48.
[10] K. Yamasaki and G. Ogawa, *op.cit.,* p. 63.
[11] U. Kobayashi, *op.cit.,* pp. 272–273; B. Z. Shumiatsky, *Borba za Russkii Dalnii Vostok,* Irkutsk, 1922, p. 76; *The Japan Chronicle,* Weekly Edition, August 15, August 22, August 29, September 5, September 19, 1918.

and others were affected. In all, 162 cities were affected, in twenty-three of which the army was used to quell the disturbances. Stores and newspaper offices were burned and firemen were prevented by crowds from extinguishing fires. Arrests carried out during these disturbances were estimated at 7,000 and some of the trials lasted a year and a half. The climax of the whole disturbance was the resignation of the Terauchi Cabinet on September 21, 1918. This event, followed by the Armistice in the West less than two months later, forced the Japanese to relax their pressure in Siberia, thus opening the way for the signing of the Inter-Allied Railway Agreement of January 9, 1919. Because the masses felt for the first time their power to. influence events—and therefore the value of organization—it has also been held that this internal weakness of Japan eventually forced the expansionists to observe the popular will, particularly in the face of their own continuing failure, and thus became one of the factors which caused the Japanese withdrawal from Siberia in 1922 at the demand of the United States and Britain.[12]

Before the war the foreign trade of Japan had developed in the direction of increasingly close ties with the Asiatic market.[13] The European trade fell while the Asiatic trade rose. Simultaneously, the export of raw materials fell while the import of the same rose. Japan was becoming the manufacturing center of Eastern Asia. When the war came she was in many ways prepared to take over the markets of North and South America, Africa, the Malay States, India, and China which were left open by the European and American exporters whose productive strength became absorbed in the war. Besides the expanded market there were several notable features about the new wartime trade. In the first place, as against the usual prewar unfavorable balance of trade which necessitated the balancing of the budget by means of foreign loans, there appeared a constant favorable balance and the accumulation of a growing surplus.[14] Secondly, the

[12] O. Tanin and E. Yohan, *op. cit.*, p. 72.
[13] U. Kobayashi, *op. cit.*, pp. 3–4.
[14] K. Yamasaki and G. Ogawa, *op. cit.*, pp. 33–34.

166

large demands made upon the productive resources of the United States, Great Britain, and other nations necessitated their prohibition of the export of certain materials such as iron, iron manufactures, wool, raw cotton, chemicals, and others which had heretofore been required by Japan. This prohibition forced Japan to find them elsewhere, preferably as near home as possible. Finally, one of the outstanding features of the wartime trade was the rise of commercial relations with Asiatic Russia, particularly in exports to that area, and their sharp reduction upon the coming of the Revolution.

The end of the war was even more disastrous for Japanese foreign trade than had been anticipated. Besides the worldwide decline in purchasing power, the disappearance of the market for war materials, and the reappearance of the European and American manufactures in the markets, Japan found, in addition, that the Russian Revolution and the resulting political and financial chaos, the Chinese boycott, the decline in the value of silver affecting the trade with India and China, and, finally, the high prices prevailing in Japan, were deterents to recovery.[15] It was in anticipation of these developments that Japan looked to Asiatic Russia and saw the possibility of creating markets there, by force if necessary.[16] Japanese agents, investigators, merchants, not to mention soldiers, were seen in every town along the railways. Trade with Eastern Siberia was by no means the only possibility. Control of the railway would open up the road to Western Siberia and even European Russia. Japan could replace the United States, Germany, and European Russia as the manufacturer for Siberia and could even invade the markets further westward. This, writes Mr. Hodges, is why Japan entered Siberia and why she left. The businessmen of Japan saw what appeared to be an opportunity for expansion if it were grasped quickly and forcefully enough. They joined forces with the army in a desperate effort to

---

[15] *Ibid.,* p. 113.

[16] J. Spargo, *Russia as an American Problem,* New York, 1920, p. 217; C. Hodges, "Siberia—A First Lesson in International Politics," *The Outlook* (New York), cxxxiii, No. 2, January 10, 1923, p. 69; Ackerman, *op. cit.,* p. 44.

seize Siberia from what they chose to consider American enroachment. But the struggle was so long and so costly that the advantages of the war boom were rapidly being lost. For this reason, Japanese business interests, seeing the cost of forcing their goods upon Siberia exceeding their profits, decided to withdraw. Thus business added its voice to labor in dictating the eventual conclusion of the Siberian adventure.

In a book written after his experience in revolutionary Russia, Mr. Arthur Bullard made an interesting comment on the nature of intervention in general.[17] In one form or another, he thought, it is a part of modern international life. "Nations can hold it in check," he continues, "only when they are themselves strongly organized. . . . Weak nations cannot resist intervention." The opening of the World War and the subsequent weakening of Russian strength in the Far East saw this very tendency begin to materialize in Eastern Siberia.[18] Japanese surveyors and investigators went there to check up on the Russian reports regarding the mineral, forest, petroleum, and other wealth of the region, particularly along the coast and in Sakhalin. In 1916 the Terauchi Government came into power. This government, in the course of its tenure of office, was to represent a "positive financial and economic policy" toward China.[19] The policy was carried out in behalf of the Bank of Chosen, the Industrial Bank of Japan, and the Bank of Taiwan through the notorious representative, Nishihara. Japanese banking operations, it should be added, followed in the wake of the interventionary armies that entered Siberia in August 1918.[20] They engaged in the exchange of official military notes as well as other financial business and established branch offices not only in Tsitsihar and Manchuli in northern Manchuria but in Chita, Khabarovsk, Blagoveshchensk, and Spassk in the Russian Far East. Furthermore, it is perhaps not too

[17] Bullard, *op. cit.*, p. 206.
[18] Miliukov, *op. cit.*, p. 314.
[19] C. W. Young, *op. cit.*, p. 242.
[20] "Bank of Chosen Enjoys Prosperous Year," *The Far Eastern Review* (Shanghai), xv, No. 4, April 1919, p. 338.

widely appreciated to what extent the Japanese venture into the field of foreign investment affected Russia. Yet more than a third of the total foreign bonds sold in Tokyo were those of Russia.[21] They amounted to more than twice the amount of Chinese bonds purchased in Japan. Furthermore, a number of Japanese factories were geared to the manufacture of Russian armaments. Such was the Aichi Tokei Denki near Nagoya, a city which felt most severly the loss of Russian business.

The revolution in Russia could not possibly have been disregarded by Japan. The March Revolution provided a basis for the talk of sending armies to preserve order in Siberia. But the November Revolution provided the Japanese imperialists with a large, discontented Russian element willing to help in the promotion of interventionist schemes. It provided also the convenient charge that the Bolsheviks had repudiated their debts and that, in compensation, Japan should be allowed to annex Siberia as far as Irkutsk.[22] Other charges and accusations were invented or repeated from time to time. There was the rumor, for example, that a German submarine had been transported over the Trans-Siberian Railway and assembled at Vladivostok for action in the Pacific. It was also said that German planes could threaten Japan through Siberia and that the German armies might be expected to launch an attack from the same direction. One Japanese writer, seeing the humor of these assertions, mockingly compared the threat from the German Army, engaged in a life-and-death struggle in the West, to the threat from the Russian fleet during the Russo-Japanese War.[23] The charges and excuses changed from time to time, but the reason remained the same.

During the war Japan had occupied herself with a series of bargains in which she had been relatively successful, so that she approached the end of the war with something like

[21] K. Yamasaki and G. Ogawa, *op. cit.*, p. 38.
[22] A. M. Young, *op. cit.*, p. 124.
[23] Horie Kiichi, "Tai Shibiria Keisaisaku," *Chuo Koron* (Tokyo), No. 356, May 1918, p. 60.

169

hegemony in China. Her initial project had been the attack on Tsingtao, which was followed by the presentation of the Twenty-One Demands early in 1915. In neither of these had the British partner of the Anglo-Japanese Alliance given anything more than forced acquiescence.[24] In 1916 Japan looked to Russia for support and received it in the Russo-Japanese Treaty of that year. Then came the Russian Revolution and the renewal of the search for support. The United States gave the desired sanction to Japanese activities in the Lansing-Ishii Agreements. The desperate condition of British shipping, resulting from the submarine warfare, was another Japanese opportunity. In exchange for furnishing destroyer escort in the Mediterranean, Japan received both British and French support for the retention of German possessions in the Far East and the Pacific.[25] With these wartime successes, it is easy to see why Japan saw the Armistice as a hindrance to the fulfillment of her program of complete consolidation in the Far East and the prospect of a League of Nations as the negation of all Japanese aims. On November 27, 1918, shortly after the Armistice, Ambassador Morris reported to this effect from Tokyo.[26] Hayashi Kiroku, a member of the Diet, it was reported, feared that the establishment of a League of Nations would mean the establishment of the status quo and would thus be "a source of affliction to nations with limited areas that contemplate future development." This idea Morris found common among journalistic writings of the time.

Economic conditions, geography, international politics, and even race joined to give Japan a perfect and almost unimpeachable set of reasons for remaining at peace during the war and consolidating her position. One of these was the frequently reiterated contention that the military officers constituted an uncontrollable clique which started foreign

[24] J. Fleming, "A Counter-Thrust for Russia; World Democracy Must Strike Germany in Asia," *Asia* (New York), xviii, No. 7, July 1918, p. 539.

[25] T. A. Bailey, *Woodrow Wilson and the Lost Peace,* New York, 1944, p. 143.

[26] *Peace Conference Papers,* i, p. 491.

incidents which the civilian members of the government, in turn, found it embarrassing to explain abroad.[27] Mr. Smith of the Inter-Allied Railway Committee was approached by Japanese businessmen in Siberia with this complaint. The militarists, they said, were pro-German and were out for territorial aggression. These businessmen did not mention whether they themselves were among those who had failed to obtain a share in the Siberian business or had obtained a share and found it unprofitable. Another explanation of the fact that Japan concentrated her efforts in the East instead of sending troops to Europe as readily as she had to Kiaochow had to do with the poverty of Japan.[28] Adachi Kinnosuke, in an article written for *Asia* magazine, explained that Japan was not wealthy enough to dispatch and supply an army either in Western Europe or on the Eastern Front. Moreover, he continued, there would be racial objections to the presence of these troops on the Western Front. Besides, Adachi implied, perhaps thinking of the international guarantees already given for the Japanese wartime gains, what could Japan gain by such an expedition that she would not otherwise gain from the war? It was much better, he concluded, that Japan remain in the Far East, and, in the case of Siberia, protect the stores at Vladivostok, prevent the eastward extension of Germany, and guard the Trans-Siberian and Chinese Eastern Railways.[29]

Behind a smoke screen of official reasons, used also by France, Great Britain, and even the United States, the Japanese maintained that the intervention was necessary to preserve order in Siberia, but that it had been carried out in such a manner that this objective had not been achieved. Few disputed the fact that the intervention had been a failure. But anyone who had an opportunity to observe the

[27] Ishii, *op.cit.*, pp. 369–370; C. H. Smith to H. H. Fisher, February 14, 1931.

[28] Adachi Kinnosuke, "Why Japan's Army Will Not Fight in Europe," *Asia* (New York), xviii, No. 2, February 1918, pp. 118–120; "Concerning Japan and Siberia," *Asia* (New York), xviii, No. 8, August 1918, pp. 637–639.

[29] "Japan to Aid Her Allies Against Germany," *The Outlook* (New York), cxviii, No. 11, March 13, 1918, p. 401.

activities of the Japanese troops in the Far Eastern Region would hardly be inclined to agree with the reason assigned by Japanese apologists for its failure. The reason they gave was that it came too late.[30] Had it come in the spring of 1918, it was asserted, there would have been some reason to anticipate success. In this way the blame for the whole episode was cleverly placed upon the United States, which had tried to prevent the military intervention as long as possible. Defense against the charge was of course impossible because the real reason for the intervention—the Japanese-American rivalry—was not admitted in official communications between the two governments.

The American part in the intervention was also emphasized in another way. While reiterating the contention that Japan had entered Siberia for the purpose of aiding the Czechoslovaks to leave Russia and of restoring order in Siberia, the Japanese always emphasized the fact that they had entered upon these duties at the express proposal of the United States.[31] This was a statement which probably, in its ultimate significance, was intended to emphasize the Japanese share in the prewar and wartime system of treaties which bound her closely to Imperial Russia as well as to the other Allies. To permit the Bolshevik Government to survive and disregard these might prove dangerous to the Japanese position and perhaps to that of other Allied nations. This network of public and secret agreements had bound the Allies together before the intervention and must certainly have been one of the factors behind the Allied solidarity which forced the United States to invite Japan to send an army to Siberia. In this way, Japan, fortified by her fortunate remoteness from the centers of warfare and by a smoke screen of alibis and defenses, was in a perfect position to act in behalf of expansion into Siberia and yet throw off all responsibility for her acts.

The involvement of Japan in the intricate network of

[30] K. K. Kawakami, *Japan and World Peace,* New York, 1919, pp. 82–83.
[31] H. Kobayashi, *Shosetsu Nippon Rekishi,* ii, pp. 518–519; A. L. P. Dennis, *The Foreign Policies of Soviet Russia,* New York, 1924, p. 270.

international alliances made her position more secure than might be supposed. It should be noted, for example, that the weakening of Russia was the original objective of the Anglo-Japanese Alliance and that this objective was one common ground upon which there could be a meeting of Japanese and British minds. Keeping Russia back from the sea would, even after 1914, still be to the advantage of Britain as it was to Japan.[32] In this respect the Alliance was as valid as ever. The Soviets feared that the French were also ready to strike a bargain with Japan on the basis of their financial interests in the railways.[33] It may be added that the French and Japanese did strike such a bargain after the termination of the Allied intervention. In exchange for the security of their investments and their other objectives in Russia, both France and Great Britain proved willing to support a Japanese seizure of natural resources. This, it was feared, was the way in which Japan might be able to divide the Allies and paralyze the opposition of the United States—which was, of course, the way it turned out. It is significant in this regard that Colonel Ward, the British commander, assumed that the Allies were prepared to concede Eastern Siberia to the Japanese.[34] Moreover, there was even a body of American opinion which felt the same way. An editorial in the *Detroit Free Press* on January 27, 1921 concluded that a growing Japan must expand somewhere.[35] It continued: "If the Japanese go into eastern Siberia and devote their energies to development of that country they are likely to look less longingly at the Philippines, and at Hawaii, and at South America, and at Australia, and at New Zealand, yes, and at the west coast of the United States." Besides, adds the editorial, the Siberian question is none of our business. It should be noted that the *Review of Reviews* agreed substantially with this editorial.[36] Here was a type of isolationist

[32] L. Fischer, *The Soviets in World Affairs*, New York, 1930, I, p. 101.
[33] Dennis, *op. cit.*, p. 285.
[34] Ward, *op. cit.*, p. 90.
[35] "America and Japan; The Swing of the Pendulum," *The Far Eastern Review*, (Shanghai), XVII, No. 5, May 1921, p. 332.
[36] "An American Solution to Japan's Problem," *The Far Eastern Review* (Shanghai), XVII, No. 7, July 1921, p. 419.

sentiment that must have given comfort and reassurance to the Japanese expansionists of 1918.

As already indicated, there was some division of opinion among Japanese leaders as to whether military or economic penetration was the more effective method of satisfying the needs of Japan. But the lesson of the war years was clear to all. "The War and America's steel embargo," writes the economist Kobayashi, "indelibly impressed on the mind of the Japanese the unfortunate position of a nation insufficiently endowed with iron ore, and the immediate necessity of finding a way out."[37] It was pointed out by those who had opposed military intervention that the coal and oil of Sakhalin and the fish of Kamchatka were the natural sources of supply for Japan.[38] Moreover, with some expenditure of capital the riches of the Siberian hinterland could be tapped and would be found to contain ample resources for the needs of the country. Japanese capitalists must be willing to make the long-term investments and to go into undesirable climates to realize the rewards this policy would bring. But it had to be done, a writer in the *Kokumin* emphasized, in cooperation with the Russian people if it was to be effective.[39]

Furthermore, it was urged, the privilege of exploitation belonged to Japan by right of the proximity of Siberia to the home country.[40] American efforts at commercial penetration of Siberia, one writer warned, would have serious effects upon Japanese-American relations because, instead of confining herself to fields of development close at hand, the United States insisted upon entering a territory which had special interests for Japan. America should seek outlets in Alaska, Canada, or Central and South America, where opportunities were doubtless not inferior to those of Siberia. This sentiment found strange corroboration in the *Boston Transcript*, which said: "American economic flirtation with the resources of Siberia, while Alaska lies undeveloped at our

[37] U. Kobayashi, *op. cit.*, p. 157.
[38] Abe, *loc. cit.*, p. 58.
[39] Quoted in P. S. Reinsch, "Japan's Lone Hand," *Asia* (New York), xx, No. 2, February–March 1920, pp. 166–167.
[40] Horie, *op. cit.*, p. 61.

doors, seems to be decidedly a case of fields being green that are far away."[41]

In his *Diplomatic Notes,* Viscount Ishii mentioned a fact which was of considerable interest in connection with the intervention.[42] Traditionally, he explained, Japan had been faced with two defense problems which ingrained themselves deeply on the Japanese consciousness. One was the defense of the north, Sakhalin and the region of the Maritime Province, while the other was the defense from the direction of the Korean peninsula. In earlier centuries the external attacks came from these directions and, at the same time, the Japanese learned to fight off their enemies from these directions. The growth of a power there in modern times was only the latest development of this traditional fear of the menace that might rise on the adjacent continental areas. Part fact and part convenient fiction, this idea, understandable if the history of Russo-Japanese is recalled, might explain why the average soldier could be so effectively schooled in this ideological background of imperialistic adventure as to perform his task with such a will that the Russian fear and hatred for the Japanese soldier present in Siberia since 1905 was increased many times during the intervention.

It has been noted that Japan looked to Siberia and North Manchuria for the satisfaction of certain specific requirements of her national life. These could be fulfilled to some extent by the investment of capital and the development of natural resources for Japan. In addition, the seizure of the Chinese Eastern Railway would also give Japan control over valuable areas and resources, not only in North Manchuria but in Siberia as well. But those who thought in terms of the imperialistic struggle of the past in which Japan had won her continental position only against the greatest international opposition, saw the hazards of the long-term, purely economic approach to a stronger continental position. To these the presence on the shores of the Pacific of possessions

[41] "An American Solution to Japan's Problem," *The Far Eastern Review* (Shanghai), xvii, No. 7, July 1921, p. 419.
[42] K. Ishii, *Gaiko Yoroku,* pp. 2–4.

175

or interests of Russia and the United States was a constant threat, not merely to Japanese growth but even to what she looked upon as the status quo.[43] Protection against these nations or preparation to attack them could, therefore, be enormously enhanced by the expedient of either controlling or occupying Siberia east of Lake Baikal.

It was in accordance with these objectives that plans were formulated in Japan which became known as blueprints for the policy of the "New Inland Sea." The Inland Sea of Japan is the body of water which lies between the island of Shikoku and southeastern Honshu. Since all its shores are in Japanese hands, it provides a closed area of complete safety for those who live or travel within it. When, therefore, a writer of the intervention period spoke of the Japan Sea as the New Inland Sea he used a phrase which would make a significant appeal to all Japanese.[44] It meant the control by Japan of the areas surrounding the Japan Sea, i.e. Manchuria, the Maritime Province, Sakhalin, and as much territory further back as seemed to be necessary to make these areas safe as Japanese possessions. That this represented the program of the Japanese intervention is beyond question. During his tour of duty in Siberia, Charles Smith was approached by an English colonel who showed him a map of the "new Japan."[45] On it was a line running northward from the Yangtze River and passing through Kalgan and Urga, thence up to and along Lake Baikal, and from here northeastward to the Sea of Okhotsk. Within this line was the area intended to be included in the Japanese Empire, the area which would surround the New Inland Sea. A slightly more restricted area was marked out on a map appearing in the *Yomiuri* in April 1922,[46] The objectives exemplified in these documents were not only suspected but openly feared by other participants in the intervention. Many of those

[43] S. C. Graves, "Japanese Aggression in Siberia," *The New York Times Current History* (New York), xiv, No. 2, May 1921, p. 244.

[44] Y. S. Kuno, *What Japan Wants,* New York, 1921, p. 93.

[45] C. H. Smith to H. H. Fisher, February 14, 1931.

[46] M. Pavlovich, "Iaponskii Imperializm va Dalnem Vostoke," *op. cit.,* p. 57.

who represented their governments in Siberia were perfectly aware of the Japanese aims and acted or planned accordingly.[47]

The program just described represents the most extreme demands actually made by the Japanese at the time of the intervention. Had the intervention been successful for Japan it would have constituted a stroke of tremendous strategic significance in her future struggle with the United States. One Soviet historian believes it would under conditions prevailing at the time have paralyzed entirely any future military activities the United States might have launched even from Alaska.[48] At the very least it would have changed the balance of power between these two nations, particularly in regard to China. The territorial encirclement of Manchuria would have made its absorption possible ten years before this actually happened. But most of the struggle during the intervention was fought for far fewer gains than this. The immediate aims of the Japanese appeared to be to control the area through puppet rulers who would pledge resources and other rights to Japan in exchange for Japanese support. It was the reliable method of "divide and rule" tested by Japan in China and by other rulers since the beginning of time.

The practice of bargaining for advantages was not an innovation of the First World War. The prewar imperialism out of which widespread international hostilities grew was based upon it. The bargaining of the war period was itself but a continuation of this era of imperialism. In fact, as one writer has aptly summarized the situation, there is little reason to believe that such nations as Italy and Japan would have entered the war but for the promises extended to them and their hopes to gain from their association with the Allies. On the other hand the fact should not be ignored "that the Allies probably would have lost the war if they had not made these clandestine bargains."[49] Bargaining was, therefore, of

[47] V. Vilensky-Sibiriakov, *Soiuznicheskaia Interventisiia na Dalnem Vostoke i v Sibiri*, Moscow, 1925, p. 8; J. Stevens, "Memorandum."
[48] A. Kantorovich, *Amerika v Borbe za Kitai*, Moscow, 1935, p. 290.
[49] Bailey, *op. cit.*, p. 144.

the very essence of international relations during the war
and those subject to the most severe pressure were forced
to consent to the hardest bargains. All through the war
Japan was able to find formulas for avoiding the front
battle lines and for concentrating on the development of her
own advantages in the Far East. The first Japanese step in
the war—the attack on the German possessions in Shantung—was taken under cover of the Anglo-Japanese Alliance.[50] Yet not only did Britain not want Japan to enter
the war, but before entering it Japan offered terms to Germany which, if complied with, would have left Japan
neutral.[51]

It is not surprising, therefore, that Japan, after acting
with this degree of independence throughout the war, should
have looked upon prospective White Russian aspirants to
power in Siberia entirely in terms of the concessions they
would be willing to promise to Japan. Each was sounded
out to learn how far he would lean in the direction of complete Japanese hegemony in Siberia. Then, it was anticipated, just as was the case with the secret arrangements
made by Nishihara in China, when the outcome looked
certain for any one of the various candidates, it would be
possible for Japan to announce officially the concessions he
had made.[52] Unfortunately for Japan, none were as successful as the clients of Nishihara had been in China.

In addition to the military, diplomatic, and economic
bases for foreign aggression, the social and political development of modern Japan provided other incentives for imperialistic adventures. The nature and development of the
transitional Meiji Restoration period left both a model and
a social base for the growth of the secret societies which
assumed leadership in the expansionist plans and activities
of succeeding years.[53] The noted Restoration leader, Saigo

[50] H. Kobayashi, op. cit., III, p. 516.
[51] F. R. Dulles, Forty Years of American-Japanese Relations, New
York, 1937, p. 103; A. M. Young, op. cit., p. 218.
[52] P. S. Reinsch, "Japan's Lone Hand," Asia (New York), xx, No. 2,
February–March 1920, p. 166.
[53] E. H. Norman, "The Genyosha: A Study in the Origins of Japanese
Imperialism," Pacific Affairs (New York), xvii, No. 3, September 1944,
pp. 267ff.

Takamori, had been the organizer of a school for the training of the militant and rebellious samurai who were dissatisfied with the reluctance of the new Japanese government to embark upon a program of continental expansion.
His school, which appealed to the aristocratic samurai, became a model for the policy of various secret societies in that
their work was carried on by an elite group whose role was
"to command, guide, instruct, beguile or cajole the docile
masses." In passing, it is interesting to note that these societies carried on their work, among other places, in Siberia,
where in the course of time the opposition to them was led
by the Bolsheviks whose organization was also based upon
the leadership of the elite group.

The failure of the rebellion of 1877 inspired by Saigo and
his disciples served as a lesson to the dissident samurai which,
in its ultimate effect upon their future activities, Mr. Norman finds similar to the lesson of the Munich Putsch of 1923.
Expansionist groups in Japan henceforth sought to achieve
their objectives by working within the constitutional framework of the state even though the cooperation of individual
members of the government might at times have to be obtained by a liberal use of terror, blackmail, and various
kinds of intrigue. In time these secret societies became
closely associated with various organs of the government
and with business firms. The societies maintained language
schools, sent agents abroad to gather information, carried
on intrigue, and, as in the case of the Russian Far East,
established strategic settlements. They provided for their
clients not only intelligence information but also interpreters
and translators for all foreign relationships. Their field of
interest included Siberia, China, Southeastern Asia, and
reached as far as Afghanistan. The large circle of friends
whom they cultivated included Sun Yat-sen, Chiang Kai-
shek, Wang Ching-wei, Aguinaldo, and Kurban Galev, a
former Russian Moslem leader.

One of these societies, the Kukuryukai or Black Dragon
Society, was organized in 1901 by Uchida Ryohei, a leader
of the Genyosha or Black Ocean Society, organized some

twenty years before.[54] The society took its name from the Amur River, which in Japanese is called the Kokuryu. The society thus had from the first an anti-Russian orientation and began to prepare for a war with Russia by agitation at home and by espionage in Siberia. It maintained a Russian language school in Tokyo, made maps of Siberia, and, according to Tanin and Yohan, sent hundreds of residents into the Transbaikal, Amur, and Maritime provinces. The society organized the Hung Hu Tze, the Chinese roving bands already noted as active in the Russian Far East, into a guerrilla force which assisted the Japanese against the Russians in 1904–1905. The Japanese agents who, as previously noted, observed the progress of the building of the Amur Railway in the years preceding the First World War represented one aspect of the work of the Kokuryukai. Another reflection of its careful planning materialized in the large number of Japanese residents in the cities of the Russian Far East who joined the anti-Bolshevik militia organization at the time of the Revolution. Such a group, for example, took part in the attempt to prevent the Soviet Government from assuming power in Blagoveshchensk in February 1918.

Another means of achieving close relationships with the Russian scene both before and during the intervention was the Russian Orthodox Church.[55] The Orthodox Church was first established in Japan in 1858 when its work was begun in the city of Hakodate. By the end of the 1860's there were twelve Japanese converts. The real foundations of the church in Japan were laid by Ioann Kosatkin, known as Nikolai, who served in Japan from 1860 until his death on February 3, 1912. He was made a bishop in 1880 and an archbishop in 1906. In 1915 the mission in Japan numbered one hundred and seventy-eight including the Japanese priests. By this time there were 37,000 Japanese members of the church and there were three journals being published in the Japanese language. A considerable church literature in the

[54] O. Tanin and E. Yohan, *op. cit.*, p. 44.
[55] B. Kandidov, *op. cit.*, p. 50.

Japanese language had been developed during the intervening years. Support for the large mission establishment, it should be added, came almost entirely from the Russian Government.

The Orthodox Church in Japan performed many important services for the Japanese during the intervention.[56] The priests acted as intermediaries between the government and some of the anti-Bolshevik leaders who came to Japan seeking support for their movements. They were able to give valuable advice with respect to propaganda and general plans for the various Japanese interventionary activities in Siberia. Also, their relationships with the Russian clergy as well as other White leaders in the Russian Far East were very close. They are said, for example, to have performed valuable liaison services for Japanese business firms through these relationships. Finally, their services as interpreters for the Japanese civil and military representatives in Siberia were of great importance. Thus, Professor Higuchi, a former student at the Kiev Ecclesiastical Academy and then a teacher at the seminary at Tokyo, was one of those who served in this important capacity. His acquaintances among the conservative circles in Vladivostok were of great value to the interventionary forces. He also served on the Russo-Japanese commission which carried on the fatal negotiations on the night of April 4–5, 1920.

It can be seen from these developments that Japanese expansionist aims were formulated long before the intervention. A statement of Japanese policy with respect to Siberia as formulated during the Russo-Japanese War has appeared in a recent Russian periodical.[57] It was to the effect that, "In the first war it will be enough for us to reach Baikal. In the second war we shall plant our flag in the Urals and water our horses in the Volga." The events, however, developed somewhat less rapidly than this. But Japanese

[56] *Ibid.*, pp. 58–59.
[57] *Gaiko Jiho,* October 20, 1904 as quoted in, "Japanese Imperialism and the Peoples of Asia," *New Times* (Moscow) No. 10 (20), October 15, 1945, p. 17.

encroachment upon Russian rights in the Far East was, in any case, in full swing by 1916. In the secret Russo-Japanese Treaty of that year the habit of making demands from Russia was started—on this occasion in payment for extending to her Russian ally the privilege of buying the munitions of war which were making Japan prosperous.[58] In exchange for these munitions Russia agreed to make over to Japan a portion of the Chinese Eastern Railway north of Kuan Cheng-tzc and not to oppose the Japanese demands in China. In the summer of 1916 a strong press campaign was waged to urge Russia, "in compensation for the freedom of action accorded to Russia in the west," to cede to Japan North Sakhalin or even the whole Siberian territory east of Lake Baikal.[59] Judging from a statement made by Viscount Ishii in his *Diplomatic Notes,* it is evident that Russia was under considerable pressure from Japan which undoubtedly nothing less than fear of Allied or American retaliation could have counterbalanced.[60] He says that the only reason Russia did not sign a separate peace sooner was her fear of a Japanese invasion of Siberia if she did. This would be true only if the possibility had been made clear to the Russian Government beforehand. In other words, it would seem that Russia could feel free from this threat only if she remained in the Alliance. But, once having transgressed the most compelling of all war agreements between allies, she would place herself outside Allied or American protection and make herself liable to Japanese invasion.

This conjecture is largely borne out by the negotiations carried on in 1917 in an effort to obtain the active military cooperation of the Japanese army in the war against Germany. In January and February 1917 conversations were held in London with General Dessino and Constantin Nabokov, the Russian chargé d'affaires, representing Russia, General Inagaki representing Japan, and Colonel Repington

[58] P. Krainov, *op. cit.,* p. 75; Ishii, *op. cit.,* p. 129; Griswold, *op. cit.,* p. 229.
[59] Miliukov, *op cit.,* p. 316.
[60] Ishii, *op. cit.,* p. 129.

of the British Imperial Staff acting for Britain.[61] In exchange for 500,000 Japanese troops, General Dessino was willing to recommend the cession of North Sakhalin. But Japan was asking more. The control of the Chinese Eastern Railway as far as Harbin and the dismantlement of the fort and naval base at Vladivostok were conditions mentioned by General Inagaki. Balfour examined these terms and found them too harsh. It is notable that General Inagaki remarked at the time to Colonel Repington that before this occasion only France had mentioned the dispatch of Japanese soliders to the West and that was two years before. But it is known that the conversations with the Allies were resumed in the summer of 1917.[62] Negotiations were either continuous from this point or were resumed again soon after the November Revolution. In any case, the objectives of Japanese bargaining were the same up to and throughout the intervention.

The development of a Siberian intervention movement brought forth from the Soviet Government an appeal quite different from the one used in European Russia.[63] An appeal for Siberian support against a possible intervention appeared on March 9, 1918 in *Izvestiia*, which struck a patriotic note and asked for support of the "Soviet Fatherland," Dennis points out that this is in contrast to the appeal to the proletarian class feelings in other parts of Russia. The notable weakness of the proletariat in Siberia may be the explanation. But Dennis thinks it was particularly due to the approach of intervention there by Japan. Sole Japanese intervention was looked upon as a calamity by Russians of various classes and political parties. But to the Bolsheviks it had a particular horror. In a speech of June 16, 1918 Trotsky explained why, in case a choice were forced upon him, he preferred the Germans to the Japanese.[64] Among the Germans, he said, there were more class-conscious workmen than among the

---

[61] C. C. Repington, *The First World War, 1914–1918, Personal Experiences*, Boston, 1921, I, pp. 442–443, 469–471.
[62] C. Nabokov, *op. cit.*, p. 244.
[63] Dennis, *op. cit.*, p. 284.
[64] *Ibid.*, p. 286.

Japanese. Therefore, a revolutionary movement was possible among the former that would terminate their occupation. This was not true of the Japanese, whose coming was therefore far more to be feared.

Although there is reason to believe that negotiations in some form were carried on before, the earliest definitely known exchange of conditions between Japan and the Allies concerning intervention occurred in December 1917.[65] The Japanese proposed sending a force to Siberia or even to both Siberia and Europe provided that the forces in Siberia were exclusively Japanese, that the Japanese position in China was recognized, and that the Japanese receive exclusive concessions in Eastern Siberia for mining, lumbering, and fishing. France and Britain, desperate for aid against Germany, accepted the conditions. But the United States vetoed the whole suggestion. After this the international negotiations for an intervention continued.

The efforts to promote intervention through individual Russian leaders also continued, at first with more success than in the case of the efforts to achieve an Allied intervention. As Russian emigres moved eastward, Harbin and even Peking became centers of intrigue between them and the Allied representatives. By February 1918 the emigres at Peking had formed a committee whose purpose was to seek Allied aid.[66] Here also the French mission through its agent Major Pichon kept in close touch with the situation in Siberia. Above all, it was in the Far East that the Japanese agents, especially General Nakashima, watched closely for the opportunity to promote their interests. Candidates such as Kolchak who desired aid but refused the Japanese terms were remembered for their obstinacy.[67] It was even before this time, in early December 1917, that the Far Eastern

[65] Miliukov, *op. cit.*, p. 317; R. Wilton, "The Rush for Siberia: Causes of the Present Crisis in the Pacific,". *The Fortnightly Review* (London), cx, No. 659, November 1, 1921, pp. 782–783; V. P. Potemkin, *Istoriia Diplomatii*, Moscow, 1945, II, p. 318.

[66] Karpenko, *op. cit.*, p. 43; V. Avarin, *Imperializm v Manchzhurii*, Moscow, 1934, II, p. 185.

[67] Filatieff, *op. cit.*, p. 178.

Congress of Soviets discovered a plot among the Russian military commanders in the Maritime Province to come to an understanding with the Japanese.[68] At the time that he was a delegate to the Congress of Soviets in session at Khabarovsk, Alexander Krasnoshchekov discovered these negotiations and obtained the arrest of the guilty ones. But the Japanese, in reprisal for this act, dispatched a warship to Vladivostok without any previous consultation with the Russian authorities. Japan had given the first open manifestation of her intention.

But the first active use of troops against Communist Russia took place in the Chinese Eastern Railway zone of North Manchuria. It will be recalled that the first actual dispatch of troops onto Russian soil in the Far East was made by the Chinese when in December 1917 they sent a detachment into the zone of the Chinese Eastern Railway at the invitation of General Horvath and the Allied representatives. Most of the Chinese troops had withdrawn by the end of January 1918, and thereafter the Chinese played a relatively passive role in the intervention.[69] But General Horvath continued to be the center of intrigue for some time. This was natural since, as the only surviving Imperial official of such stature in all of the Far East, he was a man of considerable influence. The business groups at Harbin and the upper classes who fled from the Bolsheviks in Siberia gave him their support and encouragement in his efforts to build up an anti-Bolshevik force in the railway zone which, it was intended, would move into Siberia when all preparations were made. The Russian capitalists, including Putilov, who formed a part of the group supporting Horvath, gave him considerable aid from funds available to them in the Far East. But foreign support remained a necessity.

Among the Japanese, Horvath had acquired an unfortunate reputation during the war. He himself explains that he was a member of the party headed by Grand Duke Georgii Mikhailovich which went to Tokyo in the summer

[68] Norton, *op. cit.,* p. 54.
[69] La Fargue, *op. cit.,* p. 163.

185

of 1916 to ask for increased aid for Russia.[70] As already noted, the aid was given in exchange for the section of the railway north of Kuan Cheng-tze. But the Imperial Government fell before the agreement regarding the section of the railway was fully settled. Horvath, therefore, did not feel obliged to turn it over to the Japanese, and consequently he acquired the reputation of being reluctant to surrender Russian rights freely to the foreigners. About the end of March 1918 it became known that the Japanese, through General Nakashima, had approached Horvath some time before with a rather definite proposal.[71] They offered support in exchange for the demolition of the fortifications of Vladivostok and the creation there of an open port, the granting of full fishing rights to Japanese subjects in all Siberian coastal waters, the opening of the Amur to Japanese navigation, and the exclusive concession for the Japanese exploitation of Siberian mines and forests. But the suggestion received no response either from Horvath or the Far Eastern Committee. Japanese support was, therefore, thrown increasingly to the Cossack atamans who were more amenable to suggestions. Meanwhile, Horvath had asked for Allied and American aid through the consular representatives at Harbin.[72] He offered to guarantee a republican form of government for Russia and, in this case, even a military force that would restore the Eastern Front. But the Allies gave him no encouragement.

The support of Semenov, Kalmykov, and other ataman pretenders to power was by no means limited to the Japanese agents. Not only did the Allies support Semenov during the early months of 1918, but Horvath himself gave him encouragement and assistance.[73] As a part of his plan to form an anti-Bolshevik force, it was Horvath's policy at first to support every anti-Bolshevik effort. As he dictated his

[70] Horvath, *op. cit.*, Ch. xv.
[71] *Foreign Relations, 1918, Russia*, ii, p. 98; Kantorovich, *op. cit.*, p. 293; D. P. Barrows, "Japan as Our Ally in Siberia," *Asia*, xix, No. 9, September 1919, p. 929.
[72] *Foreign Relations, 1918, Russia*, ii, p. 99.
[73] C. H. Smith, "What Happened in Siberia," p. 378; Horvath, *op. cit.*, Ch. x.

memoirs in later years he remarked, apparently with some regret, "God forgive me, but I decided to support Semenov." As a matter of fact, his decision to withdraw support from him was apparently based upon the purely objective fact that Semenov seemed entirely incapable as a military leader. He therefore turned to Kolchak. But the Japanese continued to support Semenov. How much support they gave him is not known. In later years Kiyose Ichiro charged in the Diet that between December 1918 and February 1920 General Tanaka had used 21,110,000 yen in assisting White Russians. Semenov probably received the major portion of this.

There is reason to believe that even the early Soviet Government understood the position of the United States in the intervention. In any case, Kantorovich, a recent Soviet historian, has stated the case clearly.[74] "The international intervention in the Far East," he writes, "in which America chose to assume leadership, was directed against Soviet Russia, but the participation of the United States was, in effect, an important measure directed against Japan." Every step taken by responsible American leaders attests the truth of this analysis. President Wilson was firmly against the Siberian intervention on precisely these grounds—that intervention by way of Siberia was not only impractical but that it involved compensation for Japan in Asiatic Russia.[75] Colonel House objected to it on the grounds that in backing a Japanese intervention the Allies would place themselves in exactly the same position occupied by Germany toward European Russian, a position to which the Allies themselves were objecting so strongly.[76] Secretary of War Baker objected for very much the same reason.[77] In addition, the latter is credited with the only demand for American withdrawal as early as in November 1918, three months after the arrival of American forces. His reports from General Graves had kept him

[74] Kantorovich, op. cit., p. 294.
[75] R. S. Baker, op. cit., VIII, p. 175; Seymour, op. cit., III, p. 391; Janin, op. cit., p. 224.
[76] Seymour, op. cit., III, p. 391.
[77] F. Palmer, Newton D. Baker, America at War, New York, 1933 II, pp. 314–315, 394–395.

cognizant of Japanese activities. He knew to what extent the
Japanese had increased their forces and carried out the
occupation of the Chinese Eastern Railway zone. This had
all been accomplished with the apparent approval of the
United States, who had invited a joint intervention and
whose troops were present in Siberia along with those of
Japan. The moral he drew from this was that the longer
American troops remained, the more solidly entrenched the
Japanese would become. Therefore, let America withdraw before any further damage was done. But in Siberia General
Graves was not only sending in reports but was actively trying to make American policies effective in regard to the Japanese. Griswold, a recent writer on American Far Eastern policies, believes that the presence there of General Graves and
his small force was possibly the "only thing that prevented
some kind of Franco-British deal with Japan, paying her with
Russian territory for an anti-Bolshevik crusade."[78] Graves,
during his tour of duty in Siberia, succeeded in reminding
the world what the word "neutrality" meant. In return the
Japanese fostered publicity, terror, and obstructionist campaigns against Graves and the American forces, but without
any success.[79]

The first interventionist moves of Japan served notice that
she intended to do something soon if the Allies should refuse to
act. How soon after the November Revolution Japan began
to show signs of her intentions is uncertain. Kantorovich says
she had served notice by mid-November 1917, by informing
the Allies that she would send an intervention force with the
understanding that she be allowed to act solely and that
compensation be granted.[80] Maksakov and Turunov write
that an Allied conference of November 12, 1917 decided to
send forces to Siberia.[81] It is also known that rumors of the
imminent arrival of an Allied force in Harbin were rife there
during November. Down in Hong Kong "one morning in

[78] Griswold, op. cit., p. 237.
[79] Barrows, op. cit., p. 931; Foreign Relations, 1919, Russia, pp. 396–
397.
[80] Kantorovich, op. cit., p. 291.
[81] Maksakov and Turunov, op. cit., p. 49.

November" Colonel John Ward was ordered by Major General Ventris to hold himself and his detachment, the 25th Battalion of the Middlesex Regiment, in readiness "to proceed to a destination unknown" but one with a very cold climate.[82] Japanese plans for a Siberian intervention as disclosed in December are more definitely known. That they were frustrated may be due to a number of things. One, of course, was the American refusal to cooperate. But due weight must also be given to the arrest by the Soviets of the proposed Russian collaborators with the Japanese as well as to the effect of the publicity which the announcement of this disclosure involved. But on January 12, 1918, the Japanese cruiser *Iwami* arrived at Vladivostok without forewarning and also without sending in any shore parties. Within the next few days British and American ships followed, apparently to remind the Japanese that the agreements regarding intervention had not yet been completed and that, when they were, all would go ashore together. Taken together, these activities seem to bear out the assertion of Vilensky-Sibiriakov, the editor of the Pichon documents, that when all Allied activities in the Siberian intervention are considered, the Japanese were undoubtedly the initiators of the enterprise.[83] In the somewhat less committal words of his memoirs, David Lloyd George makes a similar statement when explaining why Vladivostok was chosen as the starting point for the intervention.[84] In concluding his remarks about the strategic location and apparent impatience of Japan, he writes, "It was difficult to refuse her proffered help."

On April 7, 1918 *Izvestiia* announced to its readers that, "Now the Japanese invasion is an accomplished fact." The imperialist enemies represented by Germany and Japan, it continued, were now engaged in a common effort to crush revolutionary Russia. This was the Soviet interpretation of the events which occurred at Vladivostok during April 4 and 5, 1918. According to the report of the American consul

[82] Ward, *op. cit.*, p. 1.
[83] Vilensky-Sibiriakov, *op. cit.*, p. 7.
[84] Lloyd George, *op. cit.*, vi, p. 162.

at Vladivostok, the beginning of this significant affair was the entry on the night of April 4 by some armed Russians into the premises of a Japanese business firm located in the central district of Vladivostok.[85] Upon being refused the money demanded, they shot three Japanese, killing one and wounding two. The shooting occurred at 11:00 P.M. At 5 o'clock the next morning, the Japanese landed forces from two cruisers and began patrolling the city. On the evening of the same day, the 5th, the British landed a party of sailors; on the morning of the 6th, the Japanese landed a still larger number. These events completed the second warning to the Allies of the seriousness of the Japanese demands for approval of an intervention. In his letter of February 14, 1931 to Harold Fisher, Charles Smith gave a somewhat different version of the allegedly provocative events of April 4, which served as an excuse for this act: "Neither the American nor the English authorities could find any proof of such acts being committed, also the Russians emphatically denied it." Even if the circumstances were as described, the murder at Vladivostok remains strangely reminiscent of that other convenient murder of two German missionaries in Shantung over twenty years before, a murder which resulted in a German occupation of Tsing Tao. If untrue it leaves the invasion unexplained by anything except the Japanese anxiety to get on with the development of a new sphere of "special interest." In any case, this act constituted the second open warning to the Allies of the seriousness of the Japanese intentions to achieve an intervention. It was also a warning that Japan might be ready to present the world with an accomplished fact if these open and obvious demands remained too long unheeded.

The reaction to the Japanese landing on the part of the various nations concerned amounted to a full and frank recognition that an event of great importance had occurred. It had, at the very least, taken out of the realm of secret dip-

[85] *Foreign Relations, 1918, Russia*, ii, pp. 99, 100, 105; also Tachi Sakutaro, "Teikoku Gunkanin no Vladivostok Joriku to Rokoku Seifu no Taido," *Gaiko Jiho* (Tokyo), No. 324, May 1, 1918, p. 1027.

lomatic channels and sporadic public rumor the course of events in the Far East. The protest from the Far Eastern Regional Committee of the Soviets at Vladivostok came on the day of the landing.[86] It charged the violation of Russian rights and intereference in her internal affairs. From Moscow, Robins reported one of the most serious effects of the events of April 4 and 5 so far as Americans were concerned: "Soviet government believes America can prevent hostile intervention, and if Japanese advance, it means America has consented."[87] This statement wâs doubtless somewhat of an exaggeration, but it represented the seriousness of the occasion as seen from Moscow. In Washington the State Department interpreted the momentous events as not constituting intervention, which in an official sense they were not.[88] In fact, Secretary Lansing characterized the landings as similar to many that the United States had made at Haiti, Nicaragua, and other places where the lives and property of Americans had been in danger. The British and Americans had, in fact, formally approved the Japanese landing by taking a part in it. A statement of French approval appeared in *Izvestiia* on April 28, 1918.[89] In Japan, of all places, a dissenting voice appeared in the *Gaiko Jiho* of May 1, 1918.[90] There existed no threat, wrote Tachi Sakutaro, and no strategic purpose was served by the landing. In fact, he concluded, "It is almost impossible to imagine a case of such urgency arising where it would become necessary to dispatch troops to Siberia."

This instance of Japanese dissent, however, far from representing the official views of the Japanese Government, was rather a protest against preparations for aggressive moves then taking place within Japan. The Japanese preparations for military action had, as a matter of fact, been evident for some months previous to April 4. The first were

[86] Maksakov and Turunov, *op. cit.*, p. 158.
[87] *R.A.R.*, pp. 134–135.
[88] *Foreign Relations, 1918, Russia*, ii, p. 178; "Japan and Siberia," *The Outlook* (New York), cxviii, No. 16, April 17, 1918, p. 610.
[89] *Foreign Relations, 1918, Russia*, i, p. 509.
[90] Tachi, *op. cit.*, pp. 1033–1034.

of course those which were observed in Korea and Manchuria during the latter part of 1917. But the early months of 1918 found Japan preparing in a far more direct way for what was obviously intended to be important military activity. In a report of February 19, 1918, Ambassador Morris told of the rumors of increasing activities in Japanese military circles and of the discussions of the question in the Diet.[91] On March 7 he wrote: "Japanese military preparations are being completed rapidly, reserves have been notified, troops are concentrating at west coast ports, two divisions already have been sent to Korea but the attitude of the Government as well as public opinion had undergone marked change during last week."[92] From January through March a violent newspaper campaign had been conducted to publicize and popularize the coming intervention.[93] The *Nichi Nichi* said that the reason the United States opposed intervention was that she herself had designs on Siberia. *Kokumin,* which had been against intervention before January, published a demand on January 22 that Japan defend herself against German encroachment through Siberia. The news of the Allied ambassador's departure from Petrograd, lurid reports of the release and arming of German prisoners, and the reports of the activities of German prisoners and of German spies all served to bring about a particularly violent outburst from the Japanese journals on February 25. By March 24 even Germany had become alarmed at the prospect of the Japanese action.[94] Robins wrote to Ambassador Francis on that date: "German war prisoner commission has asked officially that Siberian prisoners be given preference in exchange because of danger of their capture by allies in Siberian advance." These preparations in Japan were undoubtedly made in anticipation of a full-scale intervention. Failure to obtain Allied agreement and the realization that action without such agreement would be foolhardy resulted in the events

[91] *Foreign Relations, 1918, Russia,* II, p. 50.
[92] *Ibid.,* pp. 71–72.
[93] *Ibid.,* pp. 86–87.
[94] *R.A.R.,* p. 112.

of April 4 and 5, which were a warning that Japan did not intend to wait forever and let the end of the war find her objectives unrealized.

Meanwhile, Japan had been attempting in every way possible to prepare the way for a full-scale intervention. Semenov, the mercenary of all the Allies but particularly of Japan, had been attempting without any results to carry out an invasion into Transbaikal from northwestern Manchuria. He had made his first attempt in January. By the end of April it became apparent not only to Horvath but also to the Japanese that his expedition did not hold much immediate promise of success. With the failure of Allied support for a regular intervention, Japan turned to China for the official sanction necessary to go to the aid of Semenov. Early in the year negotiations, inspired by "steady penetration of hostile influence into Russian territory," had been initiated which culminated in the Sino-Japanese treaty of March 25, 1918.[95] The treaty contemplated cooperation between the two nations in North Manchuria and for this purpose, it should be added, Japan had already dispatched munitions to China. But the failure of Semenov as an independent intervention agent and the failure of the events of April at Vladivostok to bring about an Allied intervention, led to a Japanese reappraisal of the situation and to a renewed effort to achieve even closer cooperation with China. Hence, after some further negotiations, two secret agreements were signed by Japan and China on May 16 and 17, 1918.[96] The effect of these treaties was to permit the Japanese to send troops into northern Manchuria and to operate there with complete freedom so far as China was concerned. Japan was thus trying to create in Manchuria a base of operations against Russia. Now that her protégé, Semenov, appeared unsuccessful and, even worse, seemed in danger of drawing victorious Russian troops over into Manchuria to stamp out his force, Japan had found it necessary to strengthen herself for aggressive action against Russia under

[95] MacMurray, *op. cit.*, ii, *pp.* 1407–1408; Avarin, *op. cit.*, i, p. 183.
[96] *Foreign Relations, 1918, Russia,* pp. 106, 223–226.

the guise of protecting Chinese territory. Although these treaties were secret, Paul Reinsch, the American Minister to China, learned of them and reported their existence to the State Department. This fact cannot be overlooked when considering the formal consent of the United States to intervention a few weeks later.

In early July, after the Czech overturn in Vladivostok, President Wilson's consent to intervention was obtained and an Allied protectorate proclaimed over Vladivostok. Preparations were then made for the dispatch of troops to Siberia. On August 2 the Japanese Government issued a declaration stating the purposes of intervention.[97] According to this statement, the United States had decided to send a protective force to Siberia to guard against the eastward extension of German power and the attempt of the prisoners of the Central Powers to interfere with the Czech movement across Siberia. The present move of Japan, the statement continued, was intended to facilitate cooperation with this effort. No interference in the internal life of Russia was contemplated. Instead, the Japanese were coming with the friendliest of sentiments toward Russia, whose territorial integrity they pledged themselves to respect at all costs. These were the words which introduced one of the most gruesome and cruel episodes of the war, an episode which not only stimulated but which, in a very real sense, sustained the civil war in Eastern Siberia. Similar declarations, it should be noted, were made by the other Allies concerned during August and September 1918.[98] The real intent of the declarations was soon translated into action. The Japanese 12th Division landed at Vladivostok on August 3 and was soon followed by the 3rd Division.[99] Early in September Khabarovsk was occupied by the Japanese forces, and in October, Transbaikal. In the six weeks previous to October 25, Morris reported that about 40,000 troops had moved through northern Manchuria.[100]

[97] Shinobu, *op. cit.*, pp. 69–70.
[98] *Foreign Relations, 1918, Russia*, ii, p. 328; V. Vilensky-Sibiriakov, *op. cit.*, pp. 73–76.
[99] V. Vilensky-Sibiriakov, *op. cit.*, pp. 73–76; Shinobu, *op.cit*, p. 72.
[100] *Foreign Relations, 1918, Russia*, iii, pp. 278–280.

Of these about 20,000 were preparing to winter at Chita while some 12,000 were scattered throughout the Chinese. Eastern Railway zone. As they moved in they raised the Japanese flag over railway stations, evicted Russian railway employees to make room for the troops, and, in general, took the control of the railway entirely out of the hands of General Horvath. By early December there were between 70,000 and 100,000 Japanese troops in Manchuria and Eastern Siberia and the demands upon the Chinese for the surrender of the Chinese Eastern Railway had been renewed.[101] This was the expedition which the British were then urging as necessary to protect Russia against German invasion and economic exploitation.[102]

All the nations participating in the intervention tried with more or less success to base their penetration on a Russian force operating internally. The Japanese pursued the same policy with particularly bad results. The leaders they chose were mostly Cossacks, or operated as Cossacks. There was Semenov in Transbaikal; Gamov and Kuznetsov along the Amur; Kalmykov at Grodekovo and later at Khabarovsk; Ivanov-Rinov and Rozanov, officially representatives of Kolchak, at Vladivostok; and, finally, Orlov and Makovkin at or near Harbin. Of these the worst was Semenov, who was recently shot by the Soviet forces following the surrender in 1945 of Japan, the latter having sponsored his anti-Soviet activities during the years between the two world wars. After he succeeded in entering Transbaikal from Manchuria, Semenov made Chita his headquarters and dominated the intervening region as well as the railway both east and west from this point, his actual sphere varying from time to time.[103]

Semenov was born in 1890 in the Transbaikal and was himself part Mongolian or Buriat. He served as an officer in the Imperial Russian armies and saw some service in the

[101] *Peace Conference Papers*, II, p. 466.
[102] *Foreign Relations, 1918, Russia*, I, p. 391.
[103] United States Senate, Committee on Education and Labor, *Deportation of Gregorie Semenoff, Hearings April 12, 13, 17, 18, 1918*, pp. 9–10 (hereafter cited as *Semenov Hearings*).

First World War, reportedly on the Caucasus front. But in the spring or summer of 1917 the Provisional Government, in view of his origin and race, sent him to the Transbaikal to recruit a special detachment of Buriats to be used on the German front.[104] He established his headquarters at Harbin and began to enlist all who were opposed to the Bolsheviks. Upon the fall of the Provisional Government he began to employ the force thus far recruited to fight the Bolsheviks but apparently with little success. Estimates of the forces he had at hand vary widely, but it seems reasonable to assume that in January 1918, when he began his offensive into Transbaikal from Manchuli, he commanded about 600 men of various nationalities. It was at least a nucleus for any one who wanted to offer him support. Several did. He began with support from Horvath and the representatives of Japan, France, and Britain. After his incapability became evident his main support came from Japan, but Britain and France seem to have continued to send him some aid until about October.[105] He began to move from Manchuria into Transbaikal on the 1st or 2nd of January 1918.[106] The Soviet military efforts in this part of Siberia were largely occupied in driving him out of Transbaikal and by the middle of May they had given him the last of a number of defeats and forced him to retire again to Manchuria. Not until the Czechoslovak troops seized the railway and defeated the Soviet forces was he again able to move into Transbaikal.

Semenov's career of torture, murder, and robbery opened almost on the very day he began his drive into Transbaikal.[107] On January 3, 1918, the members of the Soviet, who had been arrested in Manchuria and sent westward, arrived at

[104] Varneck and Fisher, *op. cit.*, p. 231, n. 117; I. Osnos, "Semenov-Stavlennik Iaponskoi Interventsii," *Istoricheskii Zhurnal*, (Moscow), June 1937, p. 54.
[105] B. Bock, *The Origins of Inter-Allied Intervention in Eastern Asia, 1918–1920,* Unpublished Doctoral Dissertation, Stanford, 1940, p. 40, n. 48.
[106] Nilus, *op. cit.* Ch. xx; V. Maksakov, "K Istorii Interventsii v Sibiri," *op. cit.,* p. 135.
[107] Maksakov and Turunov, *op. cit.,* p. 54.

Chita in a sealed car—they had been tortured. From this time on Semenov carried out merciless and indiscriminate attacks on those who stood in his way or those who were merely unfortunate enough to be near him at the wrong time. He moved about in his famous armored railway cars. One of them, the *Destroyer,* had fifty-seven men and officers abroad, armour plate one-fourth to one-half inch thick with eighteen inches of reinforced concrete behind that.[108] It had ten machine guns, two three-inch guns, and two one-pounders. Wherever there was trouble one of these cars moved in and shooting and whipping with chains was applied to break up a disturbance. Cars often carried off large parties of unfortunates. In a single day, according to one report, 1,600 people were carried off and killed at Adrianovka station.[109] On another occasion ten cars full of prisoners were shot by one of Semenov's subordinates in order to show that, "shootings can be carried out on Sunday as well as any other day." In his more practical moments he robbed banks, stole from the customs station at Manchuli, and took what he wanted in goods or money from travelers or freight shipments passing through his territory.[110] He participated in the Japanese shipments of goods to Chita, where he had his own retail stores. Shipment of goods by others was possible only if he permitted it. His activities, moreover, had the complete support of the Japanese.

It had evidently been the British and French view that Semenov should perform the role later assigned to Kolchak.[111] He was expected to assemble his forces and eventually move westward where he would join the armies then operating in South Russia. Meanwhile, he would occupy the railway near Manchuli, where he would, they hoped, be able to stop any munitions moving eastward to supply the revolutionary forces in the Amur and Maritime areas. Later, when the British decided to support Kolchak at Omsk

---

[108] Stewart, *op. cit.,* pp. 268–269.
[109] Osnos, *loc. cit.,* p. 59.
[110] *Foreign Relations, 1919, Russia,* p. 486.
[111] *Foreign Relations, 1918, Russia,* II, pp. 38–40.

THE NEW INLAND SEA

with munitions and supplies, it became evident that Semenov could also stop ammunition from moving westward. In fact, this was one of the ways that the Japanese were able to frustrate the efforts of Kolchak to capture the Russian state from the Soviets. For his own part Semenov refused to recognize Kolchak and, with Japanese support, played a lone role with complete impunity.[112]

Pictures of the man who thus managed to carve out for himself such an unusually important niche among the perpetrators of cruelty are difficult to look at with impartiality. The only really distinguishing features of his face are a pair of beady eyes, a large black mustache, and the puffy, half-mocking expression around the mouth and chin. Colonel Ward has left a description that other observers seem to agree with.[113] He described him as "a man of medium height, with square, broad shoulders, an enormous head, the size of which is greatly enhanced by the flat, Mongol face, from which gleam two clear brilliant eyes that rather belong to an animal than a man. The whole pose of the man is at first suspicious, alert, determined, like a tiger ready to spring, to rend and tear, but in response the change is remarkable, and with a quiet smile upon the brown face the body relaxes. Colonel Semionoff is a very pleasant personality." This is the man in whose person the disruptive efforts of Japan were focused for so long and who, more than any other single individual, helped to make impossible a White victory in Siberia and thus, by one of those tricks of fortune, opened the way for the outcome which the Japanese feared most— a Soviet victory.

Another notorious participant in the civil war in Siberia was Ivan Kalmykov. Very little is known of his origin except that he had apparently served with Semenov on the Caucasus front in a Cossack unit.[114] It is also known that he was under thirty at the time of the events in Siberia. Having been sent into the Russian Far East at the same time as Semenov, he

[112] *Ibid.*, II, pp. 442, 444.
[113] Ward, *op. cit.*, p. 238.
[114] Kandidov, *op. cit.*, p. 19.

198

began his career there by securing a few hundred followers and obtaining the support, first of General Horvath, and then of the Japanese.[115] As the Japanese moved north from Valdivostok in August 1918, Kalmykov went with them and, finally, between September 4 and 7, he moved into Khabarovsk where he remained until driven out by the partisans in early 1920. His reign of terror there was second only to that of Semenov to the West. Characteristically, he began by having the legitimate candidate for ataman of the Ussuri Cossasks killed and himself elected in his place. His career will be more closely examined when considering the civil war. But his troubles with the American forces had significant international implications. As a part of the anti-American campaign of the Japanese, the latter are said to have made a special payment to Kalmykov to induce him to stir up trouble with the Americans.[116] Shortly after this payment was made Kalmykov arrested an officer and an enlisted man of the United States Army on the pretext that they were without Russian passports. The officer was given up on demand. But a detachment of troops was required to get the enlisted man, who was found to have been beaten almost to death with Cossack whips. The significant feature was that when the American detachment approached the place where the soldier was presumably confined by Kalmykov they were stopped by a Japanese force. When it became evident, however, that the Americans would open fire if hindered in their mission, the Japanese offered no further resistance. The soldier was released and the Japanese apologized—for protecting Kalmykov!

Since we know the Japanese objectives, the question inevitably arises as to the function these troublemakers were intended to fulfill in the total scheme of things. Undoubtedly one answer is that they were intended to create disorder, which would not only prevent the Russians from establishing a unified political regime in Siberia but would also make

[115] Varneck and Fisher, *op. cit.*, p. 233, n. 132; W. S. Graves, *op. cit.*, pp. 128–129.
[116] S. C. Graves, *op. cit.*, p. 241.

necessary the use of a Japanese force to "reestablish" order. An incident of early 1920 would seem to bear out this analysis as clearly as any single event could. At this time the Japanese were withdrawing their forces from the Far Eastern Region under Allied pressure.[117] Before leaving Khabarovsk they spread a rumor to the effect that it would be dangerous for residents to remain after the Japanese forces had left and that facilities were being made available for all who wished to leave under Japanese protection. The Chinese merchants in the town learned that the Japanese had already made arrangements with and supplied arms to a band of two thousand Chinese brigands who were to pillage the city as soon as the Japanese had left. The merchants passed this information on to the Chinese consul and then to the Chita Government, which was able to rush troops to the city and stop the destruction.

In the early months of 1919, another Japanese objective became clear through the reports of General Graves as well as via other sources. At the Paris Peace Conference, Mr. E. T. Williams, a Far Eastern authority of many years' experience, brought to the attention of the delegates the attempt the Japanese were then making to set up an independent buffer state in Eastern Siberia through Semenov, Ivanov-Rinov, Horvath, or whoever seemed most suitable.[118] By a newspaper campaign purporting to show that the American army was Bolshevik in sympathy, the Japanese hoped to gain the support of the propertied classes. In this they had considerable temporary success and some of this section of the population seemed ready to deal with the Japanese on the basis of the concession desired by the latter. A report of March 8 from Copenhagen alleged that Japan had gone so far as to demand from France the recognition of her "special interests in Siberia."

It was among the Mongol people, however, that the most significant Japanese efforts were made to form a buffer state.

[117] C. H. Smith, "What Happened in Siberia," *op. cit.*, p. 374.

[118] D. H. Miller, *My Diary at the Conference at Paris*, New York, 1924, xvii, pp. 245–248.

Here there were two factors that seemed to promise success to the Japanese. The first was the strategic location in which these people lived with respect to the Russian Far East. It will be recalled that the Buriats were a Mongol people who lived within the Russian Empire on the western, southern, and eastern sides of Lake Baikal. Immediately adjoining their territory on the South were the Barga Mongols of north-western Manchuria and the Khalkha Mongols of Northern or Outer Mongolia. Beyond these lived other Mongol people in western Manchuria, Inner Mongolia, and in the Kobdo area of western Outer Mongolia. If all these branches of the Mongol people could be assembled into a single political entity under a Japanese protectorate, it would mean not merely the addition of a vast territory but, due to the strategic location of the territory, it would have the effect of cutting Russia entirely off from the Pacific. A second factor was the breakdown of Russian authority, which seemed to promise success to such a Japanese venture. The Buriats were dissatisfied and active in trying to find a means of improving their status. Many of them had received an education in Russian schools and constituted an intelligentsia widely respected among Mongols of secular inclinations. Their efforts to achieve autonomy have already been noted. Furthermore, across the international boundary line the Outer Mongolians had enjoyed a kind of qualified independence or autonomy since 1911. Actually, they were increasingly dominated by Russia until the catastrophe of 1917 when Russian influence began to diminish. The other Mongol peoples had been subject to varying degrees of foreign pressure, particularly those of Inner Mongolia, whose resentments against Chinese colonization in their grazing grounds had for some years been receiving sympathetic attention from the secret expansionist societies of Japan. The power vacuum in Russia seemed to present an unequaled opportunity to build on the foundations so carefully laid by the Genyosha.

It was with this purpose in mind that the Japanese, during the summer of 1918, took the first steps in a renewed effort to create a Pan-Mongol movement, the object of which was the establishment of a Greater Mongolia under her own protection.[119] Grigorii Semenov, himself a Buriat from Transbaikal Province, was selected for the role of implementing the Japanese plan. Semenov had once been an officer in the Russian consular guard at Urga. He thus had both the necessary following among the influential Buriats as well as a knowledge of people and political developments at Urga. From his own point of view, Semenov looked upon the intended role of the Japanese in the Pan-Mongol movement as purely fortuitous.[120] He hoped to use the Buriat autonomy aspirations and the confused political status of the other Mongol peoples in a way that would be as distinctly to his own advantage as possible. In the course of his conversations with Klemm, Horvath, and other prominent members of the Russian community at Harbin he explained his ambitions and his hopes of thwarting, in the long run, the Japanese aims in the Mongol movement. For the time being, however, the common interest in the anti-Bolshevik struggle made the Japanese aid indispensable.

The Pan-Mongol program was opened with a propaganda campaign which had actually begun as early as 1917. The accumulated discontent of the Buriats, Khalkhas, Bargas, and other Mongol peoples received special attention. For the Barga area of northwestern Manchuria, Inner Mongolia, and Western Mongolia, a particular source of disgruntlement was the Tripartite Treaty of June 7, 1915 by which China and Russia had recognized the autonomy of Outer Mongolia. These three areas surrounding Outer Mongolia felt that they should have been united with that region and granted autonomy along with it. With the breakdown of the Russian power in the Far East, China began to aspire to its former predominance among the Mongols. Thus, in January 1919, there were rumors of the cancellation of the special

[119] A. F. Speransky, "Materialy k Istorii Interventsii," *Novyi Vostok* (Moscow), No. 2, 1922, p. 591.

[120] I. I. Korostovets, *Von Cinggis Khan zur Sowjetrepublik; Eine Kurze Geshichte der Mongolei unter Besonderer Berücksichtigung der Neuesten Zeit,* Berlin, 1926, p. 293.

status enjoyed by the Barga Mongols and of the imminent entry of Chinese troops into their territory. A Buriat committee headed by Tsokto Badmazhanov, a Buriat officer in the Transbaikal Cossacks, was organized to carry on propaganda in Outer Mongolia, calculated to foster internal dissension by every possible means. The *arats* (or common people) were incited against the relatively privileged *shabins* (or residents of special ecclesiastical estates). The secular-spiritual split among the Khalkhas was exploited to the full. In fact, it was estimated in 1919 that during the previous two years about 40,000 Buriats had entered Mongolia to carry on propaganda favorable to Japan.[121]

The Pan-Mongol movement fostered by Japan reached a climax in two conferences held in Transbaikal in February 1919.[122] The first of these assembled at Dauria under the sponsorship of Semenov. It was attended by representatives of the Mongol peoples already named, along with Tibetan and Kirgiz representatives. Appreciating both the extent to which the Wilsonian message concerning the self-determination of nations had influenced the aspirations of these various Asiatic groups as well as the potency of this idea as an incentive to unity among them, Semenov, through an American military officer who was present at the session, dispatched a telegram to President Wilson suggesting the sending of a Mongol delegation to the Peace Conference at Paris.

The prinicpal Pan-Mongol conference, however, was the one that assembled at Chita on February 25, 1919. The convocation of the conference was taken care of by Neice-Gegen of Inner Mongolia who issued invitations to princes of Outer and Inner Mongolia and Barga to send representatives. The conference was, in fact, attended by about fifteen or sixteen persons. There were six Buriats as well as several from Inner Mongolia and Barga. No representative came from Outer Mongolia. There was Semenov with his assistant, Volgin, and his interpreter, Shardrin. Japan was represented

[121] Speransky, *op. cit.*, p. 598.
[122] D. H. Miller, *op. cit.*, xvii, pp. 248–249; Speransky, *op. cit.*, pp. 592ff.; Korostovets, *op. cit.*, pp. 293–295.

by two "observers," Major Suzuki and Captain Kuroki. Semenov was the official sponsor of the session and all commitments were made in his name. In the long run he promised more than he was able to fulfill. The Mongols soon discovered that his influence with the foreign powers was limited and that, independent of the Japanese wishes, he could neither produce a foreign loan nor make possible the much-desired Mongol representation at the Peace Conference.

The plans formulated at the conference called for the establishment of an autonomous Greater Mongolia extending from Lake Baikal to Tibet and from Shanhaikuan on the Gulf of Chihli to Sinkiang. A provisional government was proposed which would have its capital at Hailar and in which Neice-Gegen would be the president of a council of ministers consisting of ministries for Foreign Affairs, Interior, Finance, and War. Each ministry would have a minister and an assistant minister representing a different Mongol section. The state over which this government presided would be a federation composed of the various related branches of the Mongols. But the provisional government would in time convoke a constitutent assembly which would decide whether the form of the new government would be a constitutional monarchy or a republic. In either case, it was understood that the new state would be a protectorate, probably of Japan. The state would, however, have its own military forces for defense purposes. In the absence of any representation from Outer Mongolia, provisional quotas for soliders from the remaining parts of the state were established: 20,000 from Inner Mongolia, 1,000 from Barga, and 3,000 from among the Buriats.[123]

There were a number of interesting features of this conference. One of these was the absence of any representatives of Outer Mongolia which formed both historically as well as geographically the logical center of any state that would gather around itself all the Mongol banners. The object of the

---

[123] Speransky, *op. cit.*, p. 594.

developments in Outer Mongolia since 1911 had been the attainment of independence rather than autonomy. All the new plan offered was autonomy backed by Japan instead of the autonomy as defined in the treaty of 1915. Thus the princes and lamas of Outer Mongolia avoided the Chita conference. But the sponsors of the new buffer state could not afford to let the matter pass off so easily. It was therefore planned to coerce Outer Mongolia by organizing a military invasion, one force to enter near Khulun Buir and the other from Kiakhta.[124] To carry out this project an effort was made both by Semenov and the Japanese to enlist the support of Chang Tso-lin in Manchuria. But other factors rendered these efforts meaningless.

Another interesting feature of the conference was the program it proposed for the movement of population.[125] Semenov had from the first objected strongly to the projection of any part of the new state into Russian territory. In the end this objection was partly overcome by a proposal to move populations toward the center of the state. In order that Transbaikal might be included in Greater Mongolia, all the Russians would be removed from this province while the Buriats from Irkutsk would all be shifted to Transbaikal. An alternative plan was to use Transbaikal as a Buriat area but to shift all the Russians to the north and the Buriats to the south. A similar situation presented itself in Inner Mongolia, where it was necessary to recognize the fact that the southern part of this region would have to remain Chinese and that only the northern part could be expected to be incorporated into Greater Mongolia.

Although both Semenov and the Japanese continued to desire the establishment of the new state, neither they nor the constituent members of the proposed federation seem to have been in agreement as to its status or objectives. Semenov, who was to have been the agent for securing the loan needed to finance the new government, never obtained any such funds in spite of his close relations with Tokyo.

[124] "Istoricheskie Uroki 15 Let Revoliutsii," *op. cit.*, p. 70.
[125] Speransky, *op. cit.*, p. 597.

What was equally disappointing to the Mongols, he was utterly unable to make it possible for a Mongol delegation to proceed to Paris, a project upon which great hopes were built. A delegation consisting of a Russian, Pavel Rashkovich, and two Mongols, Tusalakchi-Gunsu or Lebatakal-Chi and Tato-Dor, was chosen. But the Allied diplomatic representatives refused them a visa, and the Japanese also refused to encourage the project. Therefore, the delegation never went beyond Tokyo.

France, Great Britain, and the United States all abstained from any involvement in the new project and assured the Kolchak Government at Omsk that they had no part in the events taking place in Transbaikal. Japan, surprisingly enough, did the same in spite of the leading part she played as the real sponsor of the movement. In the end, the whole movement lost its internal cohesion because dissatisfaction arose, not only with Semenov for his inability to obtain any tangible support for the proposed government, but with the leading role being played by the Buriats.[126] Fusengge, a leader from Inner Mongolia, formed a plot to disarm the Buriats and murder the Russian officers who were part of a detachment that was to coerce Outer Mongolia into compliance. The plot was discovered and Fusengge was killed with some of his followers. From this point on the whole project began to fall apart. Neice-Gegen and Norimpil were shot and others escaped to the Aimak Tsetsen Khan in Outer Mongolia. There the episode ended.

These objectives of the Japanese Government, it should be noted, were apparent to many then present in Siberia and were by no means exclusively known to those in high places or to scholars concerned with investigations made after the events. Later studies, to be sure, have clarified these objectives and given them continuity with both previous and later developments in the Far East. But contemporaries on the scene had ample evidence of the turn of events. Before leaving San Franciso, General Graves was appraised of the situation and forewarned as to what he could expect from

[126] Korostovets, *op. cit.*, p. 295.

the Japanese in Siberia.[127] His own book is ample testimony that he was not in the dark as to Japanese intentions although he seems to have been somewhat puzzled as to exactly what he was supposed to do about it with his small force. It was perfectly obvious to all who observed daily events that Kolchak was intended to serve as the unifier of an anti-Bolshevik Russia and equally obvious that the Japanese, though also anti-Bolshevik, were against Kolchak and all he represented. Travelers found the Japanese almost literally everywhere in the area east of Lake Baikal.[128] Along the railway they guarded every village, city, railway bridge, and almost all public buildings. Their gunboats were in every navigable stream and river. In fact, concluded Mr. Ackerman, "by October, [1918] Japan had Siberia and Manchuria entirely under her power." The Japanese were, in fact, in a position to challenge the Allies.

Other Allied representatives in Siberia observed the Japanese propensity to act in complete disregard of Allied agreements regarding cooperation of military forces and noninterference in the internal affairs of the Russian people. Colonel John Ward, the commander of the British contingent, noted that the Japanese carried on as though eastern Siberia were their own "special preserve."[129] They seemed to him to look upon the other Allied forces as intruders, were continually suspicious of them, and at no time did they consult with Allied officials or commanders regarding military movements. Thus, without any previous consultation or word of warning, they sent an army detachment north in the spring of 1919 to reinforce their occupation of Nikolaevsk.[130] Since it was obvious that there was no railway to guard there, the Japanese explained that it was necessary to guard the fisheries, a task, it should be noted, which is usually performed by a naval force. Actually, they were securing for themselves the control of the Amur River. The massacre of the Japanese

[127] Graves, *op. cit.*, p. 55.
[128] Ackerman, *op. cit.*, pp. 233–234.
[129] Ward, *op. cit.*, p. 53.
[130] C. H. Smith, "What Happened in Siberia," p. 378.

THE NEW INLAND SEA

at Nilolaevsk a year later was in many respects a retaliation for these aggressive moves as well as for the offensive conduct of the troops while stationed there. Elsewhere in Siberia it had become apparent by early 1919 that the Japanese program of producing general chaos through interference in the internal affairs of Russian public institutions was by no means confined to military movements or to attempts to control the course of events through interference on the higher levels of administration. The Japanese were, Ambassador Morris observed, equally concerned with the suppression of all local representative institutions such as the zemstvos and city dumas.[131] Had they confined their persecutions to members of these institutions who were in any way radical in their political orientation, there would probably have been little reason for surprise. But men of the most moderate views were singled out for punishment if they showed any inclination to sponsor improvements in local affairs. It had become almost literally true that even the normal efforts of a public administrator to perform his duties for the welfare of his people had assumed the aspect of a major crime.

The tendency of the Japanese to conduct themselves not only as exclusive occupants of Russian territory but as a power intending to retain permanent possession there, was particularly evident in the economic aspects of their intervention. The appointment of a Japanese consular agent at Irkutsk in February 1918, for example, impressed the French commercial representative there as an unusual turn of events.[132] It must be said, however, that in view of other reports, it was not an unusual instance since other Japanese consular agents were also newly appointed during this period while even stronger methods were used to promote Japanese business. In August 1918 Ambassador Morris noted the appointment of an economic mission headed by Baron Megata, the purpose of which was to study conditions in Russia.[133] Furthermore, the Japanese monopoly of the railways

---

[131] *Foreign Relations, 1919, Russia*, p. 476.
[132] V. Maksakov, "K Istorii Interventsii v Sibiri," *op. cit.*, p. 147.
[133] *Foreign Relations, 1918, Russia*, III, pp. 138–139.

to further their own commercial plans was also known to Ambassador Morris.[134] The introduction of Japanese currency in both small and large denominations and the insistence upon its acceptance was viewed with alarm as an unmistakable sign of the intention of the Japanese to remain indefinitely in Siberia.[135] Finally, their free use of timber, fisheries, and other resources of Siberia was the act of a conqueror dealing with a subjugated land rather than that of a nation acting as a trustee for the property of an ally.

The Armistice found Japan in a position of dominance in Eastern Siberia. The original negotiations regarding the intervention had contemplated a limitation of the forces sent to about seven thousand. The fact that the total American force amounted to somewhat more than this seems to have been used as a pretext by the Japanese to explain the increase of their own force to at least 70,000.[136] But the rice riots and the political upset of September had already shaken the Japanese Government. The sudden end of the war brought into relief the inferiority of the Japanese troops in comparison with the first-rate armies of Europe and America, now released for other activity if necessary.[137] Thus the Japanese not only received the news with considerable misgiving but were forced to pay some attention to the protest which Secretary Lansing sent to the Japanese Government a few days after the armistice.[138] "The United States," he wrote, "has viewed with surprise the presence of the large number of Japanese troops now in north Manchuria and eastern Siberia. . . . Such monopoly is certainly opposed not only to the purpose of this Government to assist Russia but also to its views regarding China." It can be seen from this how closely the problems of Russia and China were associated at this time in the mind of Secretary Lansing.

The result of the protest was the removal of about 50,000

[134] *Ibid.*, II, p. 462.
[135] *Ibid.*, II, p. 372.
[136] David Lloyd George, *op. cit.*, VI, p. 179; Dennis, *op. cit.*, p. 288.
[137] A. M. Young, *op. cit.*, p. 149.
[138] *Foreign Relations, 1918, Russia*, II, p. 434.

Japanese troops from the area named by the Secretary. It was during the ensuing weeks that the railway agreement was forced through by the United States and some control of the situation instituted. The situation appeared more difficult for the Japanese after this change. But this was not necessarily true. By this time Kolchak was established in Western Siberia and the Allied hopes now rested on his success or failure. By support and control of Semenov in Transbaikal the Japanese could help to determine the outcome of this issue.

Throughout 1919 Japan, while maintaining the fiction of continued cooperation with her allies, never relaxed her drive to exert her own supremacy in Eastern Siberia. The defeat of Kolchak and the withdrawal of the Allies in early 1920 appeared to open for the first time the opportunity for the exclusive control which Japan had long been seeking. In fact, however, the situation both in Russia and in her own country had been altered to the disadvantage of those in Japan who wished to continue the intervention. In Russia the Soviet Government had survived all attempts to dislodge it, while in Japan there were complaints that the intervention was unprofitable. In other foreign quarters, it must be added, the Japanese monopoly of the wealth and commerce of the Far East was unfavorably regarded. The Washington Conference was the forum in which this view was brought to bear upon the activities of the Japanese expansionists.

CHAPTER 6

The New Eastern Front

THE desire of Britain and France for an intervention was officially based upon the claim that they would lose the war unless the Eastern Front against Germany could be reestablished. From the time the Russian withdrawal became certain until the establishment of Kolchak as Supreme Ruler, the question of finding an available and acceptable military force to replace the vanished Russian army remained in the forefront of Allied discussions. There were two general sources from which such a force could be drawn. The first was from Russia itself. Either the Allies could choose one of the anti-Bolshevik military or political leaders and give him financial and military support with the object of raising an army to reopen the war against Germany or they could try to persuade the Soviet Government itself to raise an army for the same purpose.

The second possibility was to find an available military force among one of the non-Russian Allied nations. The first choice among the Allies fell naturally on the Japanese. But this was objectionable to the United States because of the advantages such action would give Japan in Siberia. Furthermore, this choice was soon found objectionable to all the Allies when it became evident that the Japanese had no intention of sending troops to the proposed Eastern Front even if the desired intervention were sanctioned. Meanwhile, on the assumption that the Japanese would eventually move forces into Siberia anyway and that a sole Japanese intervention could not be controlled, every effort was exerted by France and Great Britain to obtain American consent to a joint intervention with the Japanese in the hope that the latter might be forced, under these circumstances, to conduct themselves as allies rather than as conquerors.

211

But before this was accomplished another Allied force appeared on the scene—the Czech army. The rise of the Czech forces to the status of an interventionary army was in a sense unexpected, being a by-product of the aggressive moves of Japan in the Far East, and was not, in any event, a final solution to the problem since it was assumed from the start that the Czechs would remain only until another Allied force could be sent. Their uprising and offensive against the Soviets was in due course followed by a general Allied intervention. Finally, upon the failure to find any other acceptable interventionary force, a leader was found in the person of Kolchak. By this time, however, the Armistice had changed the Allied objectives and needs. Kolchak, nevertheless, remained because he was not fighting in the Allied war with Germany and his cause was, therefore, little affected by the Armistice. With his eventual failure to overthrow the Soviet Government the Allied intervention ended. After this there remained only the Japanese, whose objectives predated not only the revolution but the war. Eventually the power reverted to the Soviet Government, whose military strength, unresponsive though it had been to a revival of an Eastern Front, grew rapidly under the menace of foreign intervention.

German dominance in Russia was more than a wartime threat to the Allies. It was easily seen that, should the resources of Russia become available to Germany, the whole balance of power in postwar Europe would be upset and sources formerly open for Allied investment and commercial enterprise would be in danger of being monopolized by Germany. Meanwhile, however, the war had yet to be won and the resources of Russia might annul the effect of the Allied blockade and give Germany strength to outlast the Allies. One item of critical importance to the Central Powers, for example, was food. In later years testimony was heard before the Reichstag to the effect that the food problem in Germany had reached such a critical stage by December 15, 1917 that there were a number of armies without a single day's advance ration of flour.[1] Another problem was that of petroleum supply. Before 1914 Germany

[1] David Lloyd George, *op. cit.*, VI, pp. 151–154.

212

had relied heavily upon American sources.[2] After the opening of hostilities the Germans looked to the resources of Galicia, Rumania, and the Russian Caucasus as possible future sources of supply. The failure of these areas to yield the anticipated supplies reduced the German army to a critical condition. After the Armistice it was found that only surrender had prevented the complete stoppage of large and essential parts of the military machine of Germany. Russia could, therefore, not be disregarded after she ceased to function as a military force. This was why reports of German activities there, whether exaggerated or not, were considered highly significant. There were in fact reports that German agents were active as far east as Lake Baikal.[3] Here representatives of German firms were allegedly making contracts to supply materials and goods while engineers and military experts were said to be preparing to build military installations.

Even after the abortive military effort of July 1917 the Russian Government had bravely announced its "inflexible decision to continue the war."[4] But by September suspicions were no longer confined to official circles. General Knox, the British representative at Russian Supreme Headquarters, reported that his gardener has asked him, "Why do those Russians not fight?"[5] After the November Revolution, however, it was no longer a question of preserving the Eastern Front but of reestablishing it.[6] On November 1 Kerensky gave an interview to the press in which he told of the vast share Russia had taken in the war while others had had time to prepare or even decide whether or not to enter. The time had now come, he added, for the Allies to bear the heaviest burden. In fact, by this time the conditions so well characterized later by Bruce Lockhart must already have been evident to many observers, i.e., that "the revolution was a revolution for land, bread and peace—

---

[2] B. H. Williams, op. cit., pp. 57–58.
[3] Vilensky-Sibiriakov, op. cit., p. 49.
[4] R.A.R., p. 33.
[5] Knox, op. cit., II, p. 678.
[6] Ibid., II, pp. 677–678; R.A.R., pp. 39, 49–50; Nabokov, op. cit., pp. 181, 182.

but, above all for peace.""[7] On November 25 General Berthelot, the French military attaché in Russia, announced to General Dukhonin, the Commander-in-Chief of the Russian armies, that France "will not recognize any government in Russia capable of entering into an agreement with the enemy."[8] This was the keynote of the demand for a new Eastern Front, and France was its most vigorous exponent.

The division which came about among the Russians regarding the question of intervention left an unfortunate and, for the most part, untrue impression on the Allied leaders. Intervention, some felt, was inevitable. The real question was whether it should be a German or an Allied intervention.[9] By July 1918 the idea had crystallized at Allied headquarters that the liberal and democratic elements within Russia wanted an Allied intervention while the reactionary and Bolshevik groups were prepared to try their luck with a German one. Yet it must be abundantly clear from what has already been said that, whatever the preferences of these two groups may have been in fact, they were not in a position to make a choice. Almost all except the most reactionary elements hoped that Britain or the United States would rescue them from their internal or external enemies. But neither Britain nor the United States ever offered to land an army in Russia capable of preventing the Japanese or Germans from having their way to a greater or lesser degree in the part of Russia adjacent to their own respective territories. Undoubtedly, neither the Bolsheviks nor the liberals wanted either the Germans or the Japanese, but they came anyway. One thing seems clear. The bourgeois elements were not strong enough to fight their way to power in Russia without external aid, and therefore they appealed to the Allies for aid. The answer to the appeal materialized in the shape of Japanese armies and a Kolchak dictatorship. The Bolsheviks, who were able to achieve greater unity of policy and action and who were therefore able to establish themselves in power in Siberia, wanted no external assistance. Their wishes were the

[7] Lockhart, *op. cit.*, p. 168.
[8] *R.A.R.*, p. 50.
[9] *Foreign Relations, 1918, Russia*, II, p. 243.

same in European and Asiatic Russia, where the Germans and Japanese respectively entered without an invitation.

In this way the Siberian intervention, in the sense that it attempted to restore a class that would not otherwise maintain itself, became particularly hateful to the Bolsheviks. An article in one of their official publications compared it with the support of the Tsarist regime by foreign governments during the period following the dissolution of the Second Duma and the Viborg Declaration of 1907.[10] Since that declaration, which asked the support of the Duma against the Imperial Regime, the Tsarist regime had been able to carry on for another ten years only because of the foreign support it received. This period was, continued the writer, a species of intervention in Russian history. Now these same foreign powers were attempting to establish spheres of influence and force their candidates into power against the will of the people.

There were some aspects of the intervention which, if considered in isolation, seemed to bear out this analysis of the Allied position. There was, for instance, an agreement signed on December 23, 1917, purporting to divide Russia into spheres of influence between the British and French according to their prevailing economic interest.[11] According to this agreement, Great Britain, who was interested in the oil fields as well as the approaches to India, would have as her sphere of interest the Cossack areas as well as the Caucasus, Armenia, Georgia, and Kurdistan, while France with her interests in the coal, iron, and railway investments would have a zone which would include Bessarabia, the Ukraine, and Crimea. In addition, the North Russia area was considered a sphere of special interest to Great Britain.[12] The latter was, in fact, asking for concessions there in exchange for support of the White Russian force led by General Miller. Among the concessions desired were a ninety-nine year lease for space to erect an office build-

[10] E. Adamov, "Rol Anglii v Interventsii," *Vestnik Narodnago Komissariata Inostrannykh Del,* Nos. 6–7, August 25, 1920, pp. 1–3.
[11] L. Fischer, *The Soviets in World Affairs,* New York 1930, II, p. 836; Potemkin, *op. cit.,* II, p. 318.
[12] *Krasnyi Arkhiv,* No. 19 (1926), pp. 49–52 as quoted in X. Eudin, *op. cit.*

ing in Murmansk, a lease for an equal period of time on a coastal area for the construction of docks and warehouses, a Russian agreement to the effect that if a commercial port were ever built British interests would receive the first chance to bid for its construction, and other valuable concessions. It was said that a company had been formed representing important English interests to exploit these various business possibilities. France, it must be added, objected to these arrangements—not because they compromised the independence of the Russian state but because some of the concessions included the right to natural resources. These she considered as security for her own huge credits to Russia. She therefore flatly refused to recognize any of these concessions in the North Russian area.

Moreover, it was evident to American observers that France and Great Britain looked upon the Russian Far East as an area over which Japan and the United States should come to a similar agreement, based upon their respective interests there.[13] This attitude had been evident since the fall of 1917 when various types of aid to Russia were assigned to the three major Allied powers. According to this arrangement the United States would have had charge of railway assistance, Great Britain of sea transport, and France of the army. Significantly, the arrangement was later revised so that Britain would oversee all communications leading to Murmansk in the North, while France would have general supervision over railways in Western and Southwestern Russia. The plan obviously left the Trans-Siberian Railway to the United States. Thus Russia was already thought of as an area where a "sphere of interest" on the Chinese pattern could be carved out.

Another fact that seemed to give credence to the Soviet view of the intervention was that the appeals for help from within Russia came from the bourgeois classes who were unable to maintain themselves unaided. A recommendation for an intervention from the American Consul, D. C. Poole, explained to Lansing that the well-to-do were being persecuted and that the disturbed business conditions and the threat of nationalizing business menaced their very existence as a class.[14] In East→

[13] *Peace Conference Papers*, ii, p. 474; Potemkin, *op. cit.*, ii, p. 302.
[14] *Foreign Relations, 1918, Russia*, ii, pp. 164–165.

ern Siberia many of this class were pinning their hopes on the drive toward Chita which Semenov initiated in January 1918.[15] The bourgeoisie were relatively weak as a class and dependent for their prosperity on political stability. Their interests corresponded neither with those of the Bolsheviks nor entirely with those of the numerous military leaders. But in the turmoil of the civil war and intervention they were forced to seek protection where at the moment it appeared available. If the Allies sympathized with them it was because as a class they were being squeezed between the armed extremists who were interested only in victory for themselves. Thus, the bourgeois predicament cannot be considered apart from the monopolistic objectives of Germany in the West, of the Japanese in the East, and of the antagonistic Bolshevik regime whose power grew as the anti-foreign struggle became more intense.

Among the three Western Allies the French were the most insistent upon an intervention, particularly after the signing of the Treaty of Brest-Litovsk.[16] They were also least ready to deal with the Bolsheviks—a fact which had rather notable consequences. In the first place, an intervention without the consent of the *de facto* government of Russia meant that a large army had to be found somewhere. The apparently greater willingness of the French to deal with the Japanese was based, therefore, on the fact that no other major force was available. But American objections were able to prevent the entrance of a Japanese force into Siberia for many months. Meanwhile, compromise proposals were made to the United States to try to gain her consent to a Japanese intervention. It was proposed, for example, that the Japanese should go in under Allied auspices, or with an Allied force, or with an Allied and American force. But none of these compromises was effective. It was not until the French were able to raise an army, the Czech Legion, on the Volga front and thereby present the American Government with an accomplished fact that America actually gave her consent to a general Allied intervention.

The intervention cannot be understood, however, in terms

[15] V. Maksakov, "K Istorii Interventsii v Sibiri," *op. cit.*, p. 137.
[16] Seymour, *op. cit.*, II, p. 401; "K Istorii Interventsii-Pravitelstvo Kolchaka i Soedinennye Shtaty," *op. cit.*, p. 54.

of such an accidental event as the rise of the Czechoslovak army against the Soviet Government in Siberia and the Volga region. The imminent threat of a seizure of Russian territory and wealth by Germany and Japan made Allied action imperative if the world balance of power was to be preserved. In the West the German armies were fully mobilized and in action while in the East the Japanese armies were impatiently awaiting an excuse to move northward into the Russian Far East. In these facts can be seen the reason for the impatience of European Allies to open an intervention and of the United States to avoid giving Japan any excuse to move troops into Siberia. If we look back to the summer of 1917, when Russian fighting power was already believed to be dwindling to a point of uselessness, it is easy to understand why the British, on the basis of the very same set of circumstances—the rapid decline of Russian political and military power, which had impelled the United States to propose railway regulation and abstinence from military intervention—found a more aggressive policy necessary. Writing of that period, David Lloyd George describes the breakdown in discipline and the collapse of the transport system which threatened Russia with famine even though ample grain was available in the Caucasus, Western Siberia, and other places.[17] "The Allies," he continues, "were attempting, with the aid of a technical Railway Mission from the United States, to reorganize the Russian railways, as the difficulties of transport seemed to be one of the chief causes of the trouble." Turning to the political and military aspects of the question, however, Lloyd George explains that there was little faith in Kerensky and his ability to carry on the war and that the only remedy for this weakness seemed to be the support of Kornilov as the one person capable of restoring discipline to the armies of Russia. After the November Revolution, he emphasized, the areas not immediately within the grasp of the new Communist Government were those richest in grain or oil, and it was therefore important that these in particular should not fall into German hands. The answer to the problem thus

[17] David Lloyd George, *op. cit.*, pp. 99ff.

presented, Lloyd George thought, was the support of Russian leaders who could control these areas in order to prevent their acquisition by either the Soviets or the Germans.[18]

This was the simplest statement of the intervention problem from the British viewpoint. It was not even intended originally that these intervention activities should be carried out in such a way as to offend the Soviet Government since, it was feared, they might then be driven into the arms of Germany. In December 1917 the War Cabinet studied ways and means of avoiding such a clash with the Soviet Government. But, in the long run, the two desires—war with Germany and peace with Soviet Russia—were incompatible. Intervention was believed too necessary to allow a possible break with the Bolsheviks to interfere.

The British position was based on the belief that victory in the war would be out of the question should Germany gain access to the raw materials of Russia. The blockade would be nullified. Even a military victory on the Western Front would be nullified by this new and unlimited source of supply.[19] The collapse of Russian resistance, writes Dugdale, was more than an alteration of the strategic balance of advantages. "The siege of Germany was over. The Central Powers were no longer hemmed in. The 'Eastern Front' had become hinterland that was almost a world in itself." The freedom to exploit Russia would give Germany such an advantage as to render the Allied effort useless. Also, the freedom to move troops from Russia to France was by no means the least of the advantages that accrued to Germany. It was also necessary, Balfour wrote to Lord Reading, to see the problem as one and to consider Europe and Asia as a single front.[20] Already German agents were starting trouble in Afghanistan, Persia, and Turkestan. It was necessary, the British Cabinet felt, to guard against any Pan-Turanian Movement which the Germans in cooperation with the Turks

[18] *Ibid.*, p. 110.
[19] Seymour, *op. cit.*, III, p. 103; Dugdale, *op. cit.*, II, p. 185.
[20] *Foreign Relations, 1918, Russia,* II, pp. 135ff.

might start and which might reach from Constantinople to China.[21] All this pointed to the immediate necessity of freeing Russia from hostile foreign control. The Soviet Government must be made to see the necessity of inviting an Allied force, mainly Japanese but including American troops, to enter Russia for this purpose. The force should be mainly Japanese, Balfour wrote in a later communication, so that no other Allied forces would be deflected from the Western Front for this purpose.[22] These terms left only the Japanese army, which was not otherwise available for use on the Western Front. Balfour, it should be added, was himself a member of the Russian Committee established in the British Government to coordinate the policy of the various ministries regarding Russia. This Committee was the one that decided in January 1918 to take a definite stand in favor of an intervention in Siberia.

Besides the proposal to utilize the Japanese army in the intervention, the support of Russian leaders was also carefully considered by Britain. The subsidization of these forces followed the pattern of the division of areas between Britain and France.[23] Thus France would finance any movements which centered mainly in the Ukraine or in the Crimea. Britain would finance those which centered in the Southeast and, in addition, would take the lead in any movements which should take place in northern Russia.[24] The financial support given to Semenov in Siberia by both these powers has already been noted. In the case of the spheres in the West, each nation would have agents and advisors with the forces supported by it. The British also sent their own forces into their allotted southeastern sphere. Generals Thompson, Dunsterville, and Malleson operated in the Baku-Caspian area and from there gave assistance to White movements at Tashkent.[25] In Siberia after the rise of Kolchak a somewhat similar territorial division was observed. While Kolchak was in commmand of all Russian

[21] David Lloyd George, op. cit., v, p. 119.
[22] Foreign Relations, 1918, Russia, ii, p. 316.
[23] David Lloyd George, op. cit., v, pp. 119–120.
[24] Peace Conference Papers, ii, p. 474.
[25] Adamov, loc. cit., p. 6; Chamberlin, op. cit., ii, p. 150.

forces, General Janin was sent by the French to assume command of all non-Russian forces operating west of Lake Baikal.[26] East of the lake, General Knox was in charge of supply, training, and other activities while actual command in that region was exercised by the Japanese General Otani. The exception to this division was the American detachment, which General Graves refused to allow anyone but himself to command.

As a part of the training duties over which General Knox had jurisdiction, an officers' school was established on an island off the shore of Vladivostok.[27] The school was authorized in the fall of 1918 and was under the actual headship of General Sakharov. The material backing for the school came from the British and the instructors were British officers. It was originally planned that three thousand commissioned and noncommissioned officers would be trained there for the new army which was to be built upon Russian soil. By February 15, 1919 the first group of five hundred officers and an equal number of noncommissioned officers were graduated. The training program was part of a plan which the British had considered as far back as the period of the Provisional Government.[28] The program contemplated the complete rebuilding of the Russian army, and was actually established only after the rise of Kolchak to power.

Some members of the British Government had expressed a desire for a Siberian intervention from the time when the full meaning of the Soviet-German negotiations at Brest-Litovsk became clear. In a meeting of January 1, 1918 the War Cabinet had expressed the fear that the Bolsheviks might obtain control of the military stores at Vladivostok and sell or give them to Germany.[29] A force, largely Japanese but including other detachments, was urged to prevent this. According to Graves, the British also wanted protection in order to secure these supplies for the use of anti-Bolshevik forces operating in

[26] *Foreign Relations, 1919, Russia,* p. 459.
[27] *Foreign Relations, 1918, Russia,* i, p. 386; W. P. Coates and Z. K. Coates, *Armed Intervention in Russia, 1918–1922,* pp. 201–202.
[28] *Foreign Relations, 1918, Russia,* ii, pp. 1–2.
[29] Baker, *op. cit.,* vii, p. 442.

South Russia.[30] The signing of the Treaty of Brest-Litovsk made the British more than ever fearful of the possible rise of German power which might follow the collapse of Russia represented by that treaty. In the Ukraine, Caucasus, and Siberia, for example, there were available the cereals, draught animals, leather, petroleum, copper, and iron which would renew the fighting power of Germany and leave it a postwar empire of terrible strength.[31] By the summer of 1918 the urgency of relieving the Western Front brought new demands for some action regarding an Eastern Front. Between March and August the German armies had staged a series of attacks which threatened a second time to place Paris itself in danger. It was feared then that the American forces would not arrive in time to stem the tide.[32] If an Allied force were sent immediately to Russia, it was urged, it could serve as a nucleus around which a Russian army could be built for an offensive in 1919. The Americans arrived, however, and the German offensive ended by August.

Meanwhile, the pressure on the United States had been so great that Wilson had given his consent during July to the intervention which followed in August. By October, when the German offensive had abated, a new approach was evident in the British demands for an Eastern Front. In a communication of October 2 Balfour urged that the armies in the South which had supported the Allies when the need was great must not be left in the lurch.[33] It was therefore urged that the Czechs, who were attempting to join forces with the southern armies, must be supported on the Volga Front. This was the view taken of the situation by the British at the time the Armistice was signed, and the military reasons for intervention ceased any longer to be valid. By this time also, wrote David Lloyd George in his Memoirs, "the situation was complicated by the fact that the anti-Bolshevik armies of Kolchak and Denikin had been called into existence by an Allied appeal and en-

---

[30] Graves, *op. cit.*, p. 64.
[31] David Lloyd George, *op. cit.*, VI, p. 150.
[32] Seymour, *op. cit.*, III, p. 410.
[33] *Foreign Relations, 1918, Russia*, II, p. 404.

deavor to organize an effective front against the Germans in Russia. We were in honor bound not to throw them over as soon as they had served their purpose."[34] Thus, disregarding for the moment the actualities of the struggle then taking place in Russia, it can be seen that the rational transition from a war against the German Empire to one against the Soviet Government was being made on a point of national honor.

Something has already been said regarding the role in the intervention played by class differences and special economic interests. Where the British were concerned, the importance of Russian good will was a significant factor, as would be expected from a nation so largely commercial in orientation. This courting of Russia influenced the British attitude toward both the Soviet Government and the candidates for anti-Soviet Governments, and made Britain's policy appear to fluctuate rather violently. Actually, though the immediate measures seemed contradictory, their general policy remained as consistent as could be expected when dealing with a civil war. The attitude which prevailed in business circles was probably most aptly expressed by a group of British business people whom Lockhart met in December 1917 as they were returning home from Russia. At all costs, they desired the restoration of order in Russia so that business might be carried on.[35] This might even mean, as members of this party pointed out, peace with Germany in order to cooperate with her in the pacification of the disturbed Russian scene. In August 1918 the British Government addressed a communication to the Russian people which expressed a similar objective.[36] The British desired, the declaration stated, "to restore the exchange of commodities, to stimulate agriculture, and to enable you to take your rightful place among the free nations of the world." This statement undoubtedly expresses the long-term and fundamental objectives of Britain in Russia. Yet in its realization the government was at a loss for a consistently reliable remedy.

[34] David Lloyd George, *Memoirs of the Peace Conference,* New Haven, 1939, I, p. 247.

[35] Lockhart, *op. cit.,* p. 210.

[36] *R.A.R.,* p. 244; also "American Intervention in Russia in 1918," *Current History* (New York), XXXII, No. 1, April 1930, p. 63.

The general objectives of the French were similar in most aspects to those of Britain. In General they were more insistent upon the intervention than Britain. One of the earliest public demands among the Allies for a Siberian intervention had appeared in the *Journal des Debats* on December 14, 1917.[37] There was also more urgency in the French demands for American consent to intervention.[38] There was also greater fear of the results of the internal breakdown of Russia and of the consequences of permitting Germany or Japan to enter unchecked into this disturbed and chaotic region.[39] The German and Austrian prisoners in Siberia troubled the French considerably. They might, the French feared, be used by the Germans as advance agents in Russia or by the Japanese as an excuse to declare that their interests were menaced and to find in the situation the necessity of a sole intervention in Russia. Behind the French feeling of urgency, of course, lay the fear of losing the war to a revived and greatly strengthened Germany. The war on the Western Front, it should be remembered, was being fought largely on French soil. Consequently, the urgency expressed by the British regarding the relieving of German pressure on the Western Front applied in even greater measure to France.

French efforts to gain support for an intervention took a number of forms. The first was a demand that Japan assume a share of the war burden.[40] It was urged that Japan should send a force of six and a half divisions. But, notwithstanding Clemenceau's personal insistence upon this to Colonel House, the negotiations were protracted and it was found that nothing was being realized. Meanwhile another favorite method was tried—the support of an anti-Bolshevik leader. This method offered many possibilities. It involved the search for a military leader and the granting of loans. The search for a leader began about December 1917 and ended with the establishment of

[37] Stewart, *op. cit.*, p. 126.
[38] David Lloyd George, *War Memoirs of David Lloyd George*, vi, pp. 166–167.
[39] *Foreign Relations, 1918, Russia*, i, p. 509; ii, p. 132; Maksakov, "K Istorii Interventsii v Sibiri, *op. cit.*, p. 127.
[40] Seymour, *op. cit.*, iii, p. 387; Kantorovich, *op. cit.*, p. 292.

Admiral Kolchak as Supreme Ruler in November 1918.[41] It was directed, insofar as the French were concerned, from three main centers—Peking, Moscow, and Jassy in Rumania until the defection of the latter power from the Allied camp in March 1918. Overtures were made by the French to General Dukhonin of the Russian Army, General Dovbor-Musnitsky of the Polish Corps fighting in Russia, the Czech Corps in Russia, the Ukranian Rada, and, finally, to General Kaledin at Rostov through whom Dutov, the Cossack leader, is said to have been influenced to initiate an anti-Bolshevik rising in the Ural region. The Dutov rising, incidentally, may be considered the beginning of what became eventually the Kolchak front. In Rumania the French General Berthelot was working toward a reconstituted Russian army under the Russian General Shcherbatev, then in Rumanian service. France is said to have favored this plan so strongly that even a Rumanian-German peace would not have been considered too great a price to pay in order to free the hand of Shcherbatev and to return the Russian armies to the active front. Rumania, of course, made peace with Germany, but Shcherbatev did not recover Russia for the Allies.

The chief political hope of the French in European Russia centered around an anti-Bolshevik organization known as the Committee for the Defense of the Country and of Freedom.[42] According to documents captured by the Cheka and published in *Izvestiia,* this organization eventually split into two parts on the question as to whether German or Allied support should be sought to carry out their plan of overthrowing the Soviet Government. The group which favored the Allies soon split off from the other and became known as the National Center. It was this organization, it will be recalled, which later proposed the establishment of Admiral Kolchak as Supreme Ruler.

The most interesting and systematic experiment in the promotion of an intervention was the result of an exploratory mission sent out in the latter part of 1917 by General Neissel, the head of the French Military Mission in Russia. Under his com-

[41] Potemkin, *op. cit.,* II, pp. 315–316.
[42] M. P. Price, *op. cit.,* pp. 288–290.

mand was a Major Jean Pichon, who had a fluent command of the Russian language.[43] Sometime after the November Revolution Major Pichon set out on a tour of Siberia, traveling with false passports, to investigate the prospects for a Russian anti-Bolshevik group which might form the basis for an intervention. On January 10, 1918 Pichon arrived at Tomsk.[44] Here he visited the members of the Siberian Government and was informed concerning the aims of the government and the general economic conditions of Siberia. It was soon obvious to him that this government could be used to good advantage in setting up an anti-Soviet political and economic front in Western Siberia where resources and stores were available which, if not utilized, would eventually pass into the hands of the Soviets. The results of his investigation were encouraging to the major as shown by his reports and his reaction to the arrest of the Siberian Government by the Soviets on February 8, 1918, which drew from him the comment, "Very annoying, just at the most critical moment."[45] The Siberian Government was dispersed after this, as already described. As Pichon went on through Siberia, he investigated the possibility of using Semenov as an interventionary leader.[46] But this proved undesirable since Semenov was not interested in the general program which Pichon had in mind. He finally moved on to Peking, where he submitted his report to the French Military Mission on April 4, 1918. Soon after this he was promoted to the rank of colonel.

Major Pichon's recommendations for an intervention show a strong preference for the political group to which most of the members of the Siberian Duma belonged—the Socialist Revolutionaries.[47] He recommended strongly a clear-cut statement regarding opposition to Bolshevism on the one hand and, on the other, an avoidance of any attempts at Imperial restoration which, he said, had no mass support and was in fact the

[43] V. Vilensky-Sibiriakov, op. cit., pp. 10–11.
[44] Maksakov and Turunov, op. cit., p. 55.
[45] Maksakov, "K Istorii Interventsii v Sibiri," op. cit., p. 130.
[46] V. Vilensky-Sibiriakov, op. cit., pp. 52–53.
[47] Ibid., pp. 52–53.

basis of the weak position of Alekseev, Dutov, and others. In the second place, the objective of establishing in Siberia a sound legal order based on the Siberian Duma should also be stated clearly as the purpose of the intervention. Finally, there must be a unified command for an army which could be organized in Manchuria for a war against the Bolsheviks. To achieve this end an effort should be made to rally all parties in a temporary coalition government until the objective should have been achieved. The report was submitted to Peking at a time when efforts were being made there to form this kind of a force to function under the general direction of Horvath. But Horvath was too closely linked with monarchistic leanings. In addition, support was denied him and thrown to Semenov by the Japanese, whose objectives varied significantly from those stated by Pichon. But in the meantime a third possibility was developing for the French—the Czechoslovak army. As a means of intervention this was in every sense unique and for this reason was probably not one of the means the French had originally considered as anything more than a mere possibility. Pichon makes no mention of it in his report or in his recommendations.

Since the attitude of the United States toward the Siberian intervention was conditioned by the knowledge of Japanese pretentions there, it must be noted that, before the question of a Far Eastern intervention arose definitely, the American view, insofar as it can be ascertained, seems to have been about the same as that of France and Britain. In a note to President Wilson on December 10, 1917, Secretary Lansing wrote that, after studying the Russian situation, he had come to the following conclusions: [48]

"That the Bolsheviki are determined to prevent Russia from taking further part in the war.

"That the longer they continue in power the more will authority in Russia be disorganized and the more will the armies disintegrate, and the harder it will become to restore order and military efficiency.

"That the elimination of Russia as a fighting force will pro-

[48] *The Lansing Papers,* II, p. 343.

long the war for two or three years, with a corresponding demand upon this country for men and money.

"That with Bolsheviks domination broken the Russian armies might be reorganized and become an important factor in the war by next spring or summer.

"That the hope of a stable Russian Government lies for the present in a military dictatorship backed by loyal disciplined troops.

"That the only apparent nucleus for an organized movement sufficiently strong to supplant the Bolsheviki and establish a government would seem to be the group of general officers with General Kaledin, the hetman of the Don Cossacks."

The attitude expressed here is the one that might be expected from the nation whose financial resources were being drawn upon so heavily in support of the war. That the United States took a diametrically opposite view regarding the Siberian intervention is equally comprehensible. In Siberia, intervention threatened the American economic interests; in Europe, according to Lansing, these interests were then seen as best served by an intervention.

Exactly when the possibility of a Siberian intervention began to color the views of President Wilson is uncertain. In a communication of January 20, 1918 to Secretary Lansing, however, he takes note of the Japanese threat there as if it were a relatively new idea to him.[49] In future months, the growing Japanese threat to the Russian Far East, developing simultaneously with the close cooperation of the United States with the Allies in Europe, were to have the unfortunate effect of making some of the President's utterances seem contradictory. But the two American policies were clear; it was the situation that was contradictory since it evoked the strange spectacle of one of the Allies trying to swallow the Far Eastern territory of a fellow ally.

Even while cooperating with the Allied intervention in North Russia, the President, thinking perhaps of the overwhelming significance to the United States of the Siberian intervention, expressed himself at all times in opposition to inter-

[49] *Ibid.*, II, p. 351.

vention in general. On his way to assume command of the Allied armies which were then fighting on the Volga front, General Janin stopped in Washington, where, in company with the French ambassador, he was received by President Wilson on September 18, 1918.[50] Here, much to the dismay of the French ambassador and himself, he was informed of the President's views regarding the Siberian front he was soon to command. The President said, "The French front is the principal front, the rest are a waste of forces," a statement representing the President's views as he expressed them on many occasions. Wilson was not only a strong exponent of Allied cooperation; he was also aware of the direct and immediate German danger impending in the far north. Therefore he supported the landings in North Russia which he would otherwise have considered useless. Out of this conflict of opinion grew the double and seemingly contradictory problem of intervention of which Lansing spoke in a letter to Wilson in May 1918.[51] In a conversation with Lord Reading, he said, he had pointed out that there were in fact two interventions. The intervention in North Russia had some conceivable military significance and did not involve the "racial difficulty" with which the Siberian intervention was fraught. Moreover, the favorable attitude of Trotsky toward the former, he thought, would surely not apply to the latter.

Here was a clear reference to the Japanese threat which had already been seen as the primary international problem in the Far East at that time. In early March, Wilson had already made a statement on the question of intervention in Siberia which remained the official position until intervention was forced on America in July 1918.[52] In a note to the Allied ambassadors he wrote that he had the utmost confidence in Japan and freely admitted that, if intervention were wise, Japan would be the logical one to carry it out. But intervention was itself an unwise step for the Allies to take since it meant doing

[50] M. Janin, "Fragments de Mon Journal Siberien," *Le Monde Slave* (Paris), No. 2, December 1924, p. 224.
[51] *Foreign Relations, 1918, Russia*, II, p. 160.
[52] Seymour, *op. cit.*, III, p. 419.

in the East exactly what Germany was doing in the West. While this statement was of course a cover for the Japanese problem, it was something more than that. Wilson was of the opinion that an Eastern Front by way of Siberia was impossible and that any intervention which might occur there would be merely a cover for anti-Russian activities. He had expressed this idea as early as the summer of 1917, and even the Treaty of Brest-Litovsk did not change his mind on the subject.[53] But eventually circumstances forced his hand on this principal issue and he consented to intervention.

In the course of his thinking over the problem and while still hoping to discover a solution that would avoid an attack on Siberia, President Wilson wrote to Colonel House on July 8, 1918: "I have been sweating blood over the question what is right and feasible to do in Russia. It goes to pieces like quicksilver under my touch. . . . "[54] But he finally evolved the desired formula and embodied it in a document which became known as the *Aide Memoire,* a document which was presented to General Graves before he departed for Siberia and later to the Allied governments. The *Aide Memoire* became, in fact, the basic American policy toward the Siberian intervention as well as the basic orders for General Graves and the blueprint for all of his activities in Siberia.

There were three parts of the *Aide Memoire* which are of special importance in understanding American policy in Siberia.[55] The first, which concerned the general purposes of American participation, states: "Military action is admissible in Russia, as the Government of the United States sees the circumstances, only to help the Czecho-Slovaks consolidate their forces and get into successful cooperation with their Slavic kinsmen and to steady any efforts at self-government or self-defense in which the Russians themselves may be willing to accept assistance . . . to guard military stores which may subsequently be needed by Russian forces in the organization of their own self-defense." The second part stated that nothing

[53] Baker, *op. cit.,* VII, p. 214; Seymour, *op. cit.,* III, p. 401.
[54] Seymour, *op. cit.,* III, p. 415.
[55] *Appendix* II.

in this document was intended as a criticism of the activities in which any other government might see fit to engage. Finally, the most solemn assurance was given to Russia that it was not contemplated that the intervention should involve "any interference of any kind with the political sovereignty of Russia, any intervention in her internal affairs, or any impairment of her territorial integrity . . . ."

Although no extended comment of this document will be attempted, certain salient features are worth noting. In the first place, the document is vague enough to lend itself to more than single interpretation. The document itself, it should be noted, not only calls for the steadying of "any efforts at self-government or self-defense," which the Russians may contemplate but also foreswears any interference in the internal affairs of Russia. Graves, on his part, understood that the *Aide Memoire* required absolute abstinence from any interference with the internal politics of Russia although he saw that this was, strictly speaking, impossible. Under these circumstances the best standard for determining the real intent of the document is to observe the experience of General Graves in applying his interpretation in the face of strong opposition from other governments and from other departments of the American government. About this it can only be said that, following several requests which Graves made to the War Department for confirmation of his policy, he was in every case sustained by the War Department and by the President himself. It must be concluded, therefore, that noninterference was intended.

Again, it should be noted that the part dealing with the Czechs stipulates only that they be helped to "consolidate their forces." This was later interpreted to mean "consolidate their forces at Vladivostok." Events transpiring in Russia at the time the *Memoire* was written would, on the other hand, seem to point to some such interpretation as "consolidate their forces on the Volga front." From these two instances it can be seen how the doctrine of noninterference was breathed into a document which might otherwise have been made the excuse of the most complete interference in Russian affairs. Meanwhile, compromises with the real situation were necessary which made it difficult for many observers to understand the nature of the American policy.

One of the confusing factors of American policy was the apparent difference of views on the part of the State and War Departments. General Graves was particularly conscious of this since his neutral position was the most unpopular of all attitudes in Siberia.[56] Speaking of the division of policy between himself and the representatives of the State Department, he writes, "There can be no difference of opinion as to the accuracy of this statement, and the results were bitter criticism of all United States agents." Consul General Harris at Irkutsk was a particularly troublesome person for Graves not only because of his opposition to the general's policy but also because of his location, where he could make his policy known to the Omsk Government first and thus leave the impression that Graves was willfully disregarding American wishes. In fact, Ambassador Francis was himself a strong exponent of intervention for various reasons. Even Frank Polk, who was Acting Secretary of State, on a number of occasions was bitterly opposed to the position Graves took regarding Siberian policy. It must certainly have appeared to many in Siberia that Graves was playing a lone hand. Nevertheless, the general was backed up completely by General March, the Chief of Staff, by Secretary of War Baker, and by President Wilson himself.

The position of China with respect to the intervention should not be forgotten. She was not only an ally but one with an extremely vital interest in the events in Siberia. In the first place, Horvath, Semenov, and other prospective rulers in Russia were using Chinese territory in Manchuria to assemble forces for unneutral activity regarding Russia. The fact that pressure from other sources prevented China from doing anything about it did not make it any less objectionable. Furthermore, an intervention would increase Japan's power on the mainland and, therefore, in the long run, give her greater control over the destiny of China. It is understandable that after an intervention had been decided upon by the Allies China requested a share in it. In an interview with Brecken-

[56] Graves, *op. cit.*, pp. 192–193.

ridge Long, Assistant Secretary of State, on July 26, 1918, Wellington Koo, the Chinese minister, requested that China be invited to participate both in the control of the Chinese Eastern Railway and in any military expedition which might be sent to Russia.[57] The use of Chinese troops abroad, he said, would have a good effect on the internal affairs of China and would enhance her standing among the powers. Enough has already been said about China and her relationship to aggressive forces in the Far East to convey the significance of this statement made during the World War.

In his book about his own Siberian adventure, Arthur Bullard mentions the legend about the danger of the German and Austrian prisoners of war which had been exploded by the time he arrived there in September 1918.[58] Almost with the proverbial "whiff of grapeshot" the Ussuri "front," presumably held by thousands of armed prisoners, was exposed as an invention of advocates of intervention, and the Japanese proceeded northward to Khabarovsk while the "armies" of prisoners melted away into the taiga. These were the prisoners who were supposed to be preventing the eastward passage of the Czechs or, according to another rumor, intended as the instrument of German control in Siberia. John Stevens was among those guilty of repeating this kind of exaggerated statement—a statement whose origin could have been nothing but rumor. According to one of his reports to Lansing, there were 18,000 organized prisoners fighting against Semenov for whom he was asking immediate aid.[59] The French, in building up their case for intervention, made much of the prisoner menace.[60] The French representative at Irkutsk, Henri Bourgeois, was concerned about their freedom of action around the Siberian towns of that area and considered them as potential reinforcements to the German army either on the Western Front or in Siberia. The official report made by American Consul Macgowan was particularly harmful in making these

[57] *Foreign Relations, 1918, Russia,* ii, p. 305.
[58] Bullard, *op. cit.,* pp. 148–149.
[59] *Foreign Relations, 1918, Russia,* ii, p. 181.
[60] V. Maksakov, "K Istorii Interventsii v Sibiri," *op. cit.,* pp. 145–146.

rumors and scares appear as an actual threat to those in Washington who read about them. Graves believed that Macgowan's report was highly colored by tales of the representatives of the nations which wanted to give the United States a reason for intervention.[61] In fact, Graves' observations convinced him that the whole prisoner scare was the result of false—perhaps purposely false—reports. It must be said that, regardless of the conflicting reports, the views of Graves and Bullard in this matter stand absolutely uncontradicted by any occurrence in Siberia during the intervention.

Fortunately two officers, one American and one British, have left a report of the situation which is a model of sanity in the midst of the confusion which characterized thinking about Siberia at that time. In March 1918, at the suggestion of Trotsky, Captain Webster of the United States Army and Captain Hicks of the British Army were selected to make a tour of inspection in Siberia and report on the prisoner situation.[62] Their report covered Siberia from European Russia up to Chita from which point eastward their investigation was supplemented by the report of Major Drysdale. The latter found that, as of March 30, 1918, there were no armed prisoners between Chita and Vladivostok.[63] Webster and Hicks found that there were in all about 1,200 armed prisoners in Siberia, mostly from the region on Omsk.[64] This count included the ones who were fighting Semenov. They also learned that, while the Soviets were anxious to have their military services, they were not, for reasons of their own safety, ready to arm just anyone. The prisoners who formed the armed detachment were, according to the report of the two officers, Socialists who had renounced their own national allegiances and had become Russian citizens. The report concluded: "There is no immediate danger of armed prisoners seizing the Siberian railway."[65]

[61] Graves, *op. cit.*, p. 31.
[62] *R.A.R.*, pp. 104–105; *Foreign Relations, 1918, Russia*, I, p. 483.
[63] *R.A.R.*, p. 121.
[64] *Ibid.*, p. 124.
[65] *Ibid.*, p. 167.

It was the findings of these officers which Graves found so difficult to understand in the light of official pronouncements on the subject. He believed the findings of Webster and Hicks substantially correct. "It is difficult," he concluded, "to understand why the United States sent representatives to get certain specific information about war prisoners, and then decided to send troops to Siberia to frustrate any action taken by organizations of German and Austrian war prisoners which United States representatives said did not exist."[66] The answer can only be that the troops were not sent because of the war prisoners, as Graves himself well knew.

The exaggerated reports of the number of armed prisoners undoubtedly grew out of the fear that they would be used by the Soviets either for their own purposes or in connection with German recruiting. In this regard, the miserable conditions among the prisoners should be considered. With the political confusion prevailing in Siberia there was no regular attention paid to their needs. Neglected in their miserable prison camps, they responded to offers of clothes and food extended to them by the Red army.[67] Many took advantage of an opportunity to work and earn some money. The Red Cross and Young Men's Christian Association worked with them in establishing recreation centers, schools, workshops, libraries as well as canteens where coffee, tobacco, tinned foods, and other articles could be bought. Theatricals and religious services were held and classes conducted by teachers and professors among the prisoners. Some of those with musical talent were furnished instruments and they played in places of entertainment. The desire to find occupation and somehow better their poor condition was, in fact, a strong force among them. They worked both for the Bolsheviks and the White armies after the latter were organized.[68] But in the reports which came out of Siberia, their presence assumed a sinister aspect which reportedly made them willing and natural tools of the Bolsheviks. One report told of a force of 35,000 to 40,000 including Red

[66] Graves, *op. cit.,* p. 26.
[67] Bullard, *op. cit.,* pp. 148–149; Stewart, *op. cit.,* p. 327.
[68] Bunyan, *op. cit.,* pp. 365–366.

army forces, operating somewhere east of Lake Baikal and preventing the passage of 13,000 Czechs through that area.[69] This was all the more remarkable since a few weeks later no troops at all could be found there. The scare, however, had served its purpose—the intervention had been accomplished.

While the number of armed prisoners of war was in reality negligible, there seems to be some evidence that the Central Powers not only made plans to utilize the prisoners for their own purposes but directed appeals to them to stir up their sense of loyalty to their homelands.[70] Ackerman, the correspondent of The New York Times, found communications addressed to them in the name of William II of Germany and Charles I of Austria-Hungary. These leaflets encouraged the prisoners to work for their country while in prison and suggested that rewards and punishments would eventually be meted out according to the zeal exhibited. Also, some demands seem to have been made by Germany upon the Soviet Government regarding the restoration of discipline among the prisoners and the cessation of anti-German propaganda.[71] This suggestion was probably preperatory to their return and use as a fighting force by the Central Powers, a possibility which was also contemplated. The return of some prisoners to Germany was actually carried out several months after the conclusion of the Treaty of Brest-Litovsk.[72]

The most important single activity among non-Russian people in Siberia was the rise of the Czechoslovaks to power in the spring and summer of 1918. According to Lloyd George, "It is not too much to say that the presence of the Czech Legion was the determining factor in our Siberian expedition."[73] In succeeding pages it will become clear that this statement is by no means an exaggeration. One Soviet official expressed the same idea to Colonel Emerson when he said,

[69] Foreign Relations, 1918, Russia, ii, p. 348.

[70] Ackerman, op. cit., p. 123; R. Medek, op. cit., pp. 24–25.

[71] V. I. Lebedev, " 'Chekhoslovatskii Front' i Moskovskii Protsess," Volia Rossii (Prague), Nos. 23–24, 1922, p. 9.

[72] Stewart, op. cit., pp. 328–329.

[73] David Lloyd George, War Memoirs of David Lloyd George, vi, p. 169.

"France, through concerted action with the Czech troops, has taken Siberia in twenty-four hours."[74] This statement contains a hint of the real controversial issue regarding the Czechs— was there, before the Czech uprising against the Soviets, an agreement between the Allies and the official Czech spokesmen to use the army of the latter against the Soviet Government, seize the railway, and establish a front against the Soviets along the Volga? All available evidence suggests that this was not the case. It is safe to conclude, therefore, that, while the Czechs actually touched off the intervention, in spite of the fact that the intervention was greatly desired by the French and other Allies, the actual rising did not result from any pre-arranged plan or "deal" between the Czechs and the Allied Governments.

The origin and reason for existence of the Czechoslovak Legion in Russia grew out of the desire of the Czech and Slovak people to dissolve their union with Austria-Hungary and establish themselves as an independent state. Even before 1914 there were Czechs living in Kiev and other Russian cities as well as in agricultural colonies in the Caucasus and elsewhere.[75] At Kiev, around which the wartime activities of the Czechs centered, they had their own school and newspaper. At the outbreak of the war the Czechs formed a separate detachment to fight in the Russian army. Moreover, during the course of the war about 300,000 Czechoslovaks in the armies of Austria-Hungary either deserted or were captured by the Russian army.[76] From these the Czech detachment serving in Russia was from time to time augmented until it eventually numbered in excess of 60,000. Since the Czechs were impelled by revolutionary purposes, their ranks included many who found congenial political companions among the Socialist Revolutionaries who played so large a part in the March Revolution in Russia. But this same propensity made them undesirable to the Imperial regime.[77] Since similar Czech detachments

[74] Stewart, *op. cit.*, p. 107.
[75] Stewart, *op. cit.*, pp. 96–97.
[76] Coates and Coates, *op. cit.*, pp. 103–104.
[77] V. I. Lebedev, " 'Chekhoslovatskii Front' i Moskovskii Protsess," *op. cit.*, p. 8.

THE NEW EASTERN FRONT

had begun to be formed simultaneously in Italy and France, negotiations were opened sometime previous to March 1917, the objective of which was to send the whole Czech Legion from Russia to France to join their fellow Czechs on the Western Front. Some actually went from Archangel to France under these arrangements. The first detachment reached France in October 1917 and a second arrived in February 1918.[78]

The March Revolution, however, found the Czech forces still in Russia. With a more congenial political atmosphere than was the case under the Empire and with a steady disintegration of the Russian armies, there now seemed to be a way of utilizing them in Russia, and their troops became in time one of the few dependable detachments in the Russian army. But the increase in Bolshevik strength, and particularly the November Revolution, again rendered their position difficult. The increasing disintegration of the Russian armies was fast leaving them the only reliable fighting force in Russia. In these circumstances, the advancing armies of the Central Powers, to whom they were deserters and traitors, made their position in the Ukraine exceedingly dangerous. In addition, the Bolsheviks were in time revealed as openly antagonistic to their plans and purposes. But the Communist propaganda, nevertheless, began to have an effect and in time caused divisions among them. The reasons were thus revived with greater emphasis for leaving Russia and going to the Western Front, where they could be of some service to their Allies. Decisions regarding such moves, as well as other administrative affairs of the Czechs, were then handled by the Czechoslovak National Council and its Russian branch at Moscow.[79] Eventually arrangements were made between this Council and the Soviet Government to the effect that the Czechs were to be transported to France by way of Siberia and Vladivostok.

That the Czech army was one of the Allied armies subject to the same general decisions as other national armies opposing the Central Powers is not a secret. Both Masaryk and Benes

[78] E. Benes, *My War Memoirs*, London, 1928, p. 352.
[79] Medek, *op. cit.*, p. 37; Bunyan, *op. cit.*, p. 100.

are perfectly clear on this point.[80] After support ceased from Russia, the Czechs, Masaryk explains, looked to France as well as the other Allies for financial support. The first contribution in fact came not from France but from Britain. Both these Czech leaders, it should be emphasized, worked for a single purpose—recognition of the Czechoslovaks as a separate nation—and understood perfectly well that in a war their army and its willingness to fight for their cause was one of the strongest supports they had. "In my opinion," wrote Edward Benes, "it is often forgotten that our Siberian army was our strongest political factor at the end of the war and during the Peace Conference. I made use of its retention in Siberia to win our peace terms." Therefore, they did not hesitate to place that army at the service of the Allies. By a French decree of December 16, 1917 and an official announcement by Masaryk on February 7, 1918 the Czech Legion in Russia became a part of the Czech force fighting in France. It became by these acts a unit of the French army subject to both Allied and French command. This was true, it must be added, with the important qualification, approved by the French Government on February 7, 1918, that the Czech army was not to be considered available to the Allies except by Czech consent.[81] The Czech Legion, therefore, had what might be termed an autonomous status within the framework of the French army.

Thus the French plans regarding the Czechs are of considerable significance. In a letter to the French Foreign Minister Pichon on April 26, 1918, Clemenceau stated the French policy regarding the Czech forces "All detachments of the Czech Corps should be transported with the swiftest means to the Western Front, where the presence of these excellent troops is very important . . . "[82] On July 12, 1918, Clemenceau wrote: "All our efforts must now be directed to diverting the action of the Czechs to the restoration of order in Siberia and to complete occupation of the Siberian Railway, in order to

[80] T. G. Masaryk, *The Making of a State: Memories and Observations, 1914–1918*, London, 1927, pp. 183, 188; E. Benes, "Chekhoslovatskaia Interventsiia v Rossii," *Volia Rossii* (Prague), Nos. 10–11, 1924, p. 55.
[81] Benes, *My War Memoirs, op. cit.*, p. 358.
[82] Chamberlin, *op. cit.*, II, p. 5.

prepare quick progress for Japanese intervention."[83] Two important facts are apparent from these two statements. In the first place, between the letter of April 26 and the one of July 12 a complete reversal had taken place in the French policy regarding the disposition of the Czech troops. In the second place, the Czech forces were considered by Clemenceau, even in his note of July, not as intervention troops in themselves but as a means of achieving a Japanese or general intervention. The latter conclusion conforms closely to the general Czech understanding of their role in Siberia.

According to Edward Benes, both he and Masaryk were at all times opposed to intervention both in principle and from purely practical considerations.[84] In a communication to Chicherin, the Soviet Foreign Commissar, on June 25, 1918, Masaryk expressed his position unequivocally.[85] He said, "I can prove by incontrovertible documents that I rejected every plan directed against your government submitted to me by your political adversaries; even of such adversaries who justly could not be called counter-revolutionary." The literature on the subject, it must be emphasized, offers no contradiction to these assertions regarding the general attitudes of the Czech leaders toward intervention. But the last statement is an interesting clue as to the pressure to which they were apparently being subjected. As a matter of fact, the representatives of all three major Allied powers at one time or another broached the subject of using the Czech force while it was so close to the scene of proposed action. Britain was interested in having them remain as a protection for India against Bolshevism at a time when France was still officially in favor of their transportation to the Western Front.[86] According to Charles Smith, both French and British representatives were advocating the use of the Czechs in April 1918.[87]

One of the most sinister aspects of this problem of Czech-Allied relationships was brought to light by papers allegedly

[83] *Ibid.*, II, p. 10.
[84] Benes, "Chekhoslovatskaia Interventsiia v Rossii," *op. cit.*, p. 46.
[85] *Foreign Relations, 1918, Russia*, II, p. 225.
[86] Masaryk, *op. cit.*, p. 183.
[87] C. H. Smith, to H. H. Fisher, February 14, 1931.

seized from the Czech headquarters after the rising in May 1918.[88] According to these documents there were negotiations in progress during 1917 regarding a separate peace between Austria-Hungary and the Allies. The Austrian objective was the preservation of the Dual Monarchy, recognition of which would have eliminated all possibility of Allied support for Czech independence. Since independence was the one great purpose of all political and military activitiy of the Czechs outside their homeland, these negotiations constituted, in effect, Allied pressure on the Czechs of no ordinary significance. These same documents purported to show that the Allies, particularly France, used alleged continuation of the negotiations with Austria as a type of blackmail to try to force the Czechs to consent to the use of their troops in Russia. These assertions may easily represent the kind of pressure to which both Benes and Masaryk allude when they emphasize their opposition to intervention as against the force which compelled them finally to place their stamp of approval upon an accomplished fact.

The close political kinship between the Czechs and the Socialist Revolutionaries and the close cooperation which came about between them during and after the Czech rising has been the basis for speculation as to the connection between these factors and the original cause of the rising. Horvath states that the relationship began with the Cooperatives which supplied the Czechs with their necessities as they moved eastward.[89] The close relationship which they are known to have had with the secret officers' organizations probably arose from an equally natural association. It should be remembered, for example, that the Czechs had been a part of the Russian army and had in their midst many Russian officers, including General Dietrichs, who led the first large body of Czechs to Vladivostok. It has also been seen how closely the Czechs were connected with the White Governments which overthrew the Bolsheviks in Siberia in the spring and summer of 1918. In addition, their part in building up the White armies must also

[88] M. P. Price, *op. cit.*, pp. 291–292.
[89] Horvath, *op. cit.*, Chs. xi, xv.

be mentioned.[90] Assertions are plentiful to the effect that the relationship of the Socialist Revolutionaries and the secret officers' organizations on the one hand and the Czechs on the other was one of the principal causes of the rising. Much of this aspect of the question is, however, shrouded in the darkness of contradictory evidence and accusations and counter-accusations. But about the cooperation between the two, once the misunderstanding between the Czechs and the Soviets developed into an open rupture, there is no doubt. However the relationship may have begun, from this point on until the rise of Kolchak the Czechs and White Russian leaders acted in close cooperation. On the Russian side the partnership was particularly weak from a military aspect. It was to fill this void that Admiral Kolchak was ultimately raised to the position of Supreme Ruler. This act, in turn, solidified the most reactionary trends among the White Russians and turned the Czechs completely against the whole Russian cause. By that time also the Armistice had eliminated the Czech reason for being in Russia. Many of the White Russians, however, have never since ceased to accuse the Czechs of desertion and to blame them for many of the disasters which followed the withdrawal of the Czechs from the Volga front.

In accounting for the ease with which the Czech uprising against the Bolsheviks was accomplished, the Czechs themselves are inclined to be somewhat sanguine about the enthusiastic welcome with which the people of Siberia received the assumption of power by the White governments, backed by their own and White Russian detachments.[91] More sober students of the question attribute this to the sheer military weakness of the Soviets.[92] At the very moment of the Czech attack most of the fighting forces available to the Soviets had been dispatched to the ends of Siberia to fight Dutov in the Ural region and Semenov in Transbaikal. As a result they had available only a few thousand poorly trained and equipped troops to match against the superb Czech Legion before which

[90] John Rickman, *An Eye-Witness from Russia,* London, 1919, p. 17.
[91] Medek, *op. cit.,* pp. 18–19.
[92] M. Klante, *Von der Wolga zum Amur. Die tschechische Legion und der russische Bürgerkrieg,* Berlin, 1931, pp. 146–157.

Japanese and Cossack armies hesitated. This is, of course, not to say that the Czechs and Whites were unwelcome. It has already been seen that the Soviets had instituted regulations, many of which were unpopular. Examples have been given of the requisitioning of grain and animals, which would in the normal course of things be highly undesirable to the more influential people as well as the large proportion of relatively prosperous farmers in Siberia. The large number of Socialist Revolutionaries elected to represent Siberia for various purposes and the program of propaganda which the Bolsheviks found necessary to gain voting strength will also come to mind when considering the relative strength of these two groups among the people of Siberia. It must also be remembered that, in the sense that the zemstvos were reestablished along with the White governments, the overturn must have appeared to many as a restoration of a government which, though enjoyed in the Far Eastern Region for only a very short time, had been urgently desired there for many years.

The close alliance which came about between the Czechs and the anti-Bolshevik elements must also be considered in the light of the keen competition, the purpose of which was to make their Legion a part of one of the factions in European Russia and Siberia.[93] Kornilov, Alekseev, and Miliukov made a strong bid for their services. The Ukrainians also desired to make use of the Legion. Trotsky wanted them as a nucleus for a new Russian army. As the Czechs fought rear-guard actions to cover their eastward retreat before the oncoming German army, they also covered the retreat of the Russian forces. It was thus perfectly obvious to all that they were the only militarily reliable fighting force to which the Soviet Government could look. An intensive propaganda campaign was therefore carried on by the Soviets to turn the Czechs in their direction. As the weeks passed, some Czechs did turn to the Communists. This had in itself a propaganda value which the Soviets were not slow to use. They began the publication of Communist newspapers for the Czechs.[94] In April, *Izvestiia*

[93] Masaryk, *op. cit.*, p. 181; Medek, *op. cit.*, p. 11.
[94] R. Khabas, "K Istorii Borby s Chekho-Slovatskim Miatezhom," *Proletarskaia Revoliutsiia* (Moscow) No. 5 (76), 1928, pp. 62–63, 65.

announced that a special commissariat for Czech affairs would be established. The Bolshevik gains were not great, but those who had reason to fear this development were impelled to begin their own propaganda campaign. In the course of this campaigns, the Czechs were told, for example, that the Bolsheviks were allies of the Germans and that they had a secret agreement with the Central Powers to send back to be shot any Czechs whom they might capture.[95] Neutrality in these circumstances was difficult and it is not too remarkable that the Czechs became the allies of the White factions. In fact, it might be asked, after quarreling with the Bolsheviks, with what other group could they have formed a political partnership?

The underlying and immediate causes of the friction which came about between the Czechs and the Soviets have been variously interpreted. Some have described them from a purposely partisan point of view, while others have attempted to explain them without sufficient evidence to support anything but a guess. Almost all who have essayed the problem have missed the world-wide—particularly Far Eastern—implications of the struggle and have thereby failed to see its most important aspects. It will, therefore, be of assistance in placing this problem in its proper perspective to trace the development of Czech-Soviet relations for the two months preceding the rising.

In referring once more to the retreat of the Czechs before the German armies as they moved into the Ukraine, it will be recalled that as they retreated the Czechs found it necessary to fight a number of engagements with the Germans to protect their rear. The first encounter with the German forces took place on February 24, soon after the beginning of the occupation of the Ukraine.[96] Between March 8 and 13 the Czech and Soviet troops fought together successfully against the advancing armies of the Central Powers at Bakhmach, an engagement in which the Czechs lost six hundred men. In gratitude for the protection which the Czechs had given the Bolshevik forces under Antonov-Ovseenko, the Soviet Government on

---

[95] *Ibid.*, p. 60.
[96] Benes, *My War Memoirs, op. cit.*, p. 354.

March 15, 1918 gave assurances to Prokop Maxa, a representative of the Czech army, that the Legion would be permitted to leave Russia by way of Siberia. On the following day, furthermore, a special message of thanks, signed by Antonov-Ovseenko, was given to the Czechs.[97] In it the Czechs are mentioned as "our Comrades" and the message informs them that, "The revolutionary armies will not forget the brotherly help which has been rendered by the Czechoslovak army corps." Ten days later, on March 26, 1918, the basic agreement was completed between the Czechs and the Soviets regarding the right of the former to move eastward over the Trans-Siberian Railway to Vladivostok, from which point, it was contemplated, they would be transported to Western Europe.[98] It was stipulated, moreover, that the Czechs were to move, not as military detachments, but as free citizens and were to surrender most of their arms at Penza. The order carrying this out was signed by Stalin. The disarming at Penza, it should be noted, was carried out without any unhappy incident by all Czechs who passed there before the rising. They surrendered 50,000 rifles, 5,000,000 rounds of ammunition, 1,200 machine guns, and other gear.[99] It may be added that the disarming of troops moving into Siberia from the front was a regular precautionary measure, and the Czechs were not in this respect subject to any unusual procedure. The Serbs had exactly the same experience some months later.

The first contingents of Czechs passed eastward as arranged, the very first detachment under General Dietrichs arriving at Vladivostok on April 4, 1918, just at the moment of the Japanese landing there. By the end of May, 12,000 Czechs had arrived there, but the Allies, who had agreed to furnish the Czechs transportation to the Western Front, had as yet not sent a single ship. It should be added that the first regular transport of Czechs did not begin for more than a year and a half after this date.

Meanwhile, throughout Siberia the local Soviets were be-

[97] V. I. Lebedev, " 'Chekhoslovatskii Front' i Moskovskii Protsess," *op. cit.*, p. 8; E. Varneck, "Siberian Materials and Documents."
[98] Maksakov and Turunov, *op. cit.*, pp. 61, 165–167.
[99] Khabas, *op. cit.*, p. 61.

coming alarmed at the passage of armed forces through their cities. In telegrams of March 22 and March 28 they expressed to the Council of Peoples Commissars their concern over these Czechs forces which might at any time, it was feared, be used by "counter-revolutionists and imperialists" to further their own purposes. [100] As he passed along the railway in 1918, Carl Ackerman saw Soviet notices posted in the railway stations concerning the Czechs.[101] One of them, in advocating the halt of the eastward passage of the Czechs, said significantly: "In view of the hostile attitude of international imperialism and threats of a foreign landing at Vladivostok, the Central Executive Committee of Soviets in Siberia considers the concentration there of these forces dangerous and inadmissible." They proposed that the Czechs be transported from Archangel instead of from Vladivostok. A similar suggestion had been made by the French through General Levergne, and the Soviets, entirely agreeable to the project since the Soviets of Siberia had advocated the same idea, issued the necessary order to stop all Czech trains west of Omsk and turn them toward Archangel.[102] But the Czechs, who had pledged neutrality and had cooperated both in the disarmament procedure at Penza and at other points to the east where Soviets had demanded additional surrender of arms, refused to go to Archangel. They suspected an unfriendly move on the part of the Bolsheviks and Germans. In a letter of May 12, 1918 Lieutenant (later General) Syrovy wrote that the Czechs would under no condition go to Archangel.[103]

The crucial order issued by Trotsky on May 25, 1918—which was aimed at disarming the Czechs but which, in fact, served as a challenge to them and set off their anti-Bolshevik uprising—was unquestionably motivated by the imminent threat of a Japanese landing at Vladivostok. The first warning of the direction things were taking came more than a month before the Trotsky order, thus leaving ample time for the

[100] Maksakov and Turunov, op. cit., p. 60; K. Zmrhal (trans. E. Varneck), *Armada Ducha Druhe Mile*, Prague, 1918, p. 24.
[101] Ackerman, op. cit., p. 123.
[102] Bunyan, op. cit., pp. 74–75.
[103] Varneck, op. cit.

Czechs to prepare a counterstroke. On April 21, 1918 during the course of this controversy as to which direction the Czechs should be sent, Chicherin sent the following telegram to the Soviets of Siberia: "Fearing Japanese attack in Siberia, Germany expressly demands that the evacuation of German prisoners from eastern Siberia into western Siberia or European Russia be started immediately and effected as quickly as possible. I request you to take all measures in your power. Czechoslovak echelons must not be sent eastward."[104] All single-tracked portions of the railway were to be kept open for this purpose. The unique position of the railway in Siberia made this order, incidentally, serve the purpose of others besides the Soviets. The Germans, for example, were anxious to prevent the transport of the Czechs to the Western Front. The next warning of danger to the Czechs came from Trotsky himself. On May 15 in conversation with three of their representatives, Cermak, Maxa, and Janik, Trotsky had already explained his position clearly.[105] It would be impossible, he said, to send any more Czech echelons eastward. "This," he added, "is in consequence of the Anglo-Japanese landing." The order which followed, on the 25th of May, ordered that all Czechs were to be immediately disarmed and that any found henceforth with arms were to be shot.[106] Any echelon containing even a single Czech was to be halted, disarmed, and placed in a prison camp. Failure of local Soviets to comply with the order would be regarded as treason.

The Czechs, it should be emphasized, had more than a mere oral warning to indicate to them the danger of their position. Two occurrences in particular had already brought them into conflict with Soviet authorities. The first was the Cheliabinsk incident of May 14.[107] At the Cheliabinsk railway station an altercation arose between some Czechs and several Hungarian prisoners, both in transit but in opposite directions.

[104] *Ibid; Foreign Relations, 1918, Russia,* ii, p. 260.
[105] Zmrhal, *op. cit.,* p. 28.
[106] Klante, *op. cit.,* p. 152: Vegman, *op. cit.,* p. 139; Maksakov and Turunov, *op. cit.,* pp. 66, 168.
[107] *Foreign Relations, 1918, Russia,* ii, p. 258; Zmrhal, *op. cit.,* pp. 31–32.

A Hungarian was killed and a group of Czechs who went into the town to testify in the resulting hearing was arrested by the local Soviet. Hearing of this, another detachment of Czechs went after them and secured their release. This action brought an order from the local Soviet to disarm all Czechs. An altercation resulted in which the Czechs were victorious and were able to leave. The second warning, an order issued on May 21 by Aralov, assistant to Trotsky, directed that all Soviets from Penza to Irkutsk either enroll the Czechs in a work group or enlist them in the Red army.[108] The order of May 25 must, therefore, have been received by the Czechs more as an enforcement order for the directive of May 21 than as something new and unexpected.

The events preceding May 25 had thus forewarned the Czechs and had indicated to them the wisdom of agreeing on some definite policy. Accordingly, on May 20, a Czech congress had assembled and arrived at a decision that they would move through to Vladivostok at any cost. The word was telegraphed all along the line and Gaida, Cecek, and Voitsekhovsky were assigned as commanders of various sections to carry out the decision of the congress.[109] Thus the Czech soldier and his commanders were determined to resist any effort to block the road to Vladivostok. Before the affair ended all Siberia was in Czech hands.

The direct responsibility for the conflict which began on May 25 between the Czechs and the Soviets has been variously attributed by writers, according to their respective prejudices, to the French, to the Czechs, or to the Soviets. The degree to which the Soviets were implicated in the rising has just been explained. As for the French, it should be remembered that the Czech troops were an integral part of the French army. It was thus natural that there should be among the Czechs a number of French officers, in particular, Major Guinet, Lieutenant Pascal, and Major Verge.[110] These officers were naturally in an ideal position to observe the growing disgruntlement be-

[108] Klante, *op. cit.*, p. 149.
[109] *Ibid.*, pp. 146–148.
[110] *Ibid.*, p. 151.

tween the Czechs and the Soviets and must surely have reported accordingly to Paris. Moreover, the month of April, it should be recalled, was a time of great activity in Allied interventionist plans. It was the month of the Allied landings at Murmansk. According to Lloyd George, the Allies were hoping that the Czechs could be persuaded to fight their way through from Western Siberia to meet an Allied force from Murmansk and form an anti-German front in North Russia.[111] It is clear, therefore, that there was on the part of the Allies both an understanding of the increasing difficulty of the Czech position in Russia and a definite desire for the services of the Czechs in the Allied intervention plans.

The French Military Missions at Jassy and at Moscow were accordingly busy with schemes the object of which was the use of the Czechs as an intervention force. One story is told, for example, of a Czech girl named Bozena Seidlova who, toward the end of April, was visited at Kishinev by a Czech officer formerly of the French Military Mission at Jassy.[112] He wanted her to undertake a mission to the Czech army in the Volga region to restore an Eastern Front with the aid of the White Russians. Not much more is known of the details or outcome of this venture except that Bozena eventually married one of the Czech officers in Siberia.

From other sources comes information to the effect that on April 14 a conference took place at the Moscow headquarters of the French Military Mission.[113] Military representatives of the British, French, Czechs, and Russians, including a special representative of the secret Russian officers' organizations, Captain Konshin, as well as Bruce Lockhart, a British representative, were in attendance. A plan for a concerted Czech attack was elaborated at this meeting. In return, the Allies were to offer the Czechs political support for independence from Austria and financial support for their army. After this

[111] David Lloyd George, *War Memoirs of David Lloyd George,* VI, p. 159.
[112] H. Baerlein, *The March of the Seventy Thousand,* London, 1926, p. 85.
[113] P. S. Parfenov, *Grazhdanskaia Voina v Sibiri 1918–1920,* Moscow, 1924, pp. 19–20.

conference Captain Konshin returned to Novonikolaevsk where, on May 3, another conference was held.[114] The plans as discussed at this second conference suggests the Gaida order, No. 38/1, dated Novonikolaevsk, May 3, 1918, the order under which the attack was carried out. These conferences thus become a connecting link between the French hopes for the Czech action in Russia and the attack as it developed along the railway line. One writer has concluded that the concerted action against the Soviets which characterized the Czech rising was inspired by the ambitious Gaida, who rose from captain to general in a very brief time.

The French Government—whether or not it played the active role in promoting the Czech rising which these facts might indicate—was nevertheless prepared to accept the rising after its occurrence. This may have been surprising to some who had taken their cue from the view expressed by Clemenceau in his note of April. Thus, after the rising which began on May 25, Major Guinet, French representative with the Czech Legion, informed the Czechs that he considered their actions disgraceful and feared that France would undoubtedly disavow any connection with it and that future relations with France would certainly be affected if their present course were not altered.[115] He reported the action to the French ambassador who, on June 22, gave a reply that must have shocked the Major: "The French Ambassador informs Major Guinet he can thank the Czecho-Slovaks for their action, this in the name of all the Allies, who have decided to intervene the end of June, and the Czech army and the French mission form the advance guard of the Allied Army."

As for the Czech position, the orders referred to above which Gaida issued, a well as the latter's supplementary plan, show conclusively that the official Czech reason for the seizure of the railway towns was to ensure their passage to Vladivostok.[116] According to this plan the Czech troops were ordered to move through to Vladivostok at. any cost. If the local

[114] P. S. Parfenov, *Uroki Proshlago. Grazhdanskaia Voina v Sibiri 1918, 1919, 1920 gg.* Harbin, 1921, pp. 29–32.
[115] *Foreign Relations, 1918, Russia,* II, pp. 250, 254.
[116] Varneck, *op. cit.;* Klante, *op. cit.,* p. 156.

Soviets refused to give their consent, they were to be removed and replaced by friendly governments. Gaida's orders were that the troops were not to go westward, except, ". . . . in the event that someone—whoever it might be—wanted to lead their echelons back to Russia, which would mean for us the beginning of a struggle with Soviet committees." It should be added that his own detachment was the most eastward of the Czech forces. The order to turn westward, if given, could thus mean that Gaida intended to give aid to the other Czech detachments. But the execution of the order would also have the effect of moving the troops back to the anti-Bolshevik battle lines. This vaguely worded order thus contains, whether purposely or not, the cue to the open hostilities against the Soviet troops which followed. Yet as it stands the general intent, and probably the official interpretation, was obviously to direct the forces to Vladivostok. Even this ambiguous document, therefore, leaves unchallenged the assertion that the French and the Czechs were officially uncommitted to any concerted anti-Soviet plan on May 25, 1918, however heavily involved any individuals may have been in contrary plans.

The question now arises as to when the Czech rising against the Soviets attained official Czech and Allied recognition. The answer is that this took place sometime between the middle of June and the first week in July. According to the available evidence a decision to make use of the Czechs was made in Paris sometime before June 20 and communicated to General Levergne in Russia on that date.[117] The directive to General Levergne stated that the Czechs were to act under the French command, to hold all positions presently occupied, and to proceed to occupy fully the Trans-Siberian Railway. Masaryk accepted this decision although it called for the eventual concentration of the Czech forces against the Bolsheviks in the Volga area. His acceptance was communicated to the Czechs and finally conveyed to them as a military order by General Cecek on July 7, 1918.[118] Thus, less than two months after Masaryk had openly advocated recognition of the Soviet

[117] Klante, *op. cit.*, pp. 179, 181; G. K. Gins, *Sibir, Soiuzniki i Kolchak*, Peking, 1921, I, p. 215.
[118] Bunyan, *op. cit.*, p. 109.

Government, his own order had made the Czech force the vanguard of a proposed Allied attack upon them. According to M. P. Price, the correspondent of the *Manchester Guardian,* a press campaign was begun during the latter half of June in all the Allied countries with a view to showing the Czechs as engaged in a war with the Central Powers who, through their prisoners in Siberia, had tried to prevent the Czechs from going to Vladivostok and to the Western Front.[119] Nothing was said about the 12,000 Czechs who were still waiting at Vladivostok for transportation to the Western Front. Finally, on July 20, Professor Masaryk said in an interview with President Wilson, "I am obliged to ask for the help of the United States and the other Allies for our army in Russia . . . "[120] By this time intervention had already been officially decided upon. But it included little direct aid to the Czechs in spite of the words of the *Aide Memoire.*

When the rising began on May 25, the Czechs were scattered along the railway from the Volga to Vladivostok. The figures showing their distribution differ, but the difference is relatively unimportant. According to Klante, the most westerly group at Penza consisted of about 8,000 troops under Cecek.[121] To the eastward at Cheliabinsk there were about an equal number under General Voitsekhovsky. In Central Siberia there were about 4,500 troops commanded by General Gaida. At Vladivostok by this time there were between 12,000 and 14,000 troops under the command of General Dietrichs. This distribution was basically the result of their slow eastward movement, but it was strategically well arranged for seizure of the entire railway if this proved desired. This is exactly what took place in the course of the next three months. On May 25 they won their first victory over the Bolsheviks, in the course of which they took Marianovka near Omsk.[122] On the 26th Novonikolaevsk and Cheliabinsk and on the 28th Penza were occupied. By July

[119] Price, *op. cit.,* p. 302.
[120] Baker, *op. cit.,* VIII, p. 288.
[121] Klante, *op. cit.,* p. 157.
[122] Chamberlin, *op. cit.,* II, p. 7.

6 the railway from the Volga to Irkutsk was largely in Czech hands. On August 31 the Czech detachments joined hands at Oloviannaia with those of Semenov. By this time the Allies had landed at Vladivostok and, in conjunction with the Czechs, they completed the capture of the railway to Vladivostok.

If there is any single outstanding and striking feature of these attacks, it is the weakness of the Soviet defense. At the first encounter at Marianovka, twenty-five miles west of Omsk, the struggle began with an ambush of the Czechs.[123] Relying on their opponents being poorly armed, the Soviet forces apparently tried to prevent their further eastward progress, particularly since they were nearing Omsk. But the Czechs in an amazingly short time disarmed their opponents and routed them. The fall of Irkutsk on July 11 showed a somewhat different development.[124] Here the city fell almost without a struggle and the local Red Guard retired as the Czechs entered the city. The cooperation between the Czechs from the outside and the White Guard forces which staged a rising within the city helped to produce this result. But during the period between the capture of these two cities, on May 25 and July 11, a transition had occurred in the whole Czech method. It was in fact the transition from the struggle for security of passage to intervention.[125] The Czechs had at first left the Soviets alone. But, starting with the fall of Omsk on June 7 and of Samara on June 8, they systematically helped to establish anti-Bolshevik governments in the towns of Siberia. Omsk and Samara, it will be remembered, were the seats of two of the new governments which merged in September. The new phase of the Czech activities received official Allied sanction in the communications of June 20 and 22 as already noted.

The capture of Vladivostok on June 29 is of special significance in the history of intervention. On the 28th the Czechs notified the French, British, Japanese, American, and

[123] *Foreign Relations, 1918, Russia,* II, p. 248.
[124] *Ibid.,* II, p. 309.
[125] Klante, *op. cit.,* pp. 176–177.

Chinese consuls of their intended action.[126] At 10.00 a.m. on June 29 they handed an ultimatum to the Soviet at Vladivostok which demanded complete disarmament and an answer in thirty minutes. Since no answer was received they began on schedule the occupation of Soviet headquarters and the disarmament of the Red Guard. Since the Czechs had given previous notice of their plans, the attack was characterized by general Allied participation.[127] Admiral Knight had sent a party of American Marines ashore to guard the American Consulate. The Japanese seized the powder magazine and the British the railway station. Among the participants was a small detachment of troops carrying green and white colors. These were the forces of the Siberian Government which supported the new administration in Vladivostok established under the presidency of Peter Derber. In the succeeding weeks the Czechs pushed the Red forces northward, taking Nikolsk-Ussuriisk on July 5 and Spassk on July 16. On August 24 they were joined by the Japanese forces who carried the invasion on to Khabarovsk in early September.

One of the things that must be emphasized regarding the Czech uprising is the fact that neither the Czechs nor the Allies considered it an intervention or even a substitute for intervention. The Czechs were promised that reinforcements would soon arrive to take over the positions they had seized. They themselves continued to regard the Western Front as their own real destination. In a conversation with Lansing in June, Lord Reading spoke of the Czechs and intervention as though the two were totally unrelated.[128] As late as July 2 Masaryk remained opposed in principle to fighting the Russians except in self-defense. Hence, the appeal for intervention which was received by President Wilson on July 2 from the Supreme War Council stressed the importance of supporting the Czechs while they were holding the railway

[126] *Foreign Relations, 1918, Russia,* II, pp. 234–235; Varneck, *op. cit.*
[127] A. R. Williams, *Through the Russian Revolution,* New York, 1921, p. 247.
[128] *Foreign Relations, 1918, Russia,* II, p. 200.

and the battlefront.[129] The appeal—or rather the events and forces which the appeal represented—brought a quick response. On July 5 President Wilson gave his consent to American participation in a limited intervention. On July 6 Admiral Knight of the United States Navy joined with the other Allied military commanders present in declaring a temporary Allied protectorate over Vladivostok.[130] This proclamation cited the danger to Russia from the activities of the war prisoners and the need of support of the zemstvo and municipal authorities in dealing with the threat and promised no interference in the internal affairs of Russia. On July 17 General Graves received his orders to assume command of an expeditionary force to Siberia. Intervention had been achieved.

[129] *Ibid.*, ii, pp. 241–242.
[130] *Ibid.*, ii, p. 271.

CHAPTER 7

The Civil War

THE beginning of the intervention was at the same time the opening of the civil war in Siberia. The movement of the Czechs from the west and the other Allied troops from the east had the effect of eliminating an established political order. In the course of crushing it the daily lives and very existence of the people were threatened by the military forces of the Allies and the Russian military leaders whom they supported. In their effort to strike back, the Bolshevik leaders were therefore able to enlist the active assistance of the large majority of the people. Out of the struggle the Bolsheviks not only regained their former political position in Eastern Siberia but, in addition, were able to enlist general popular support to an extent never before possible. The intervention had, therefore, the very opposite effect from that intended by most of the Allies. Only the American objectives were in part achieved. By observing the neutral attitude which President Wilson had requested of him from the beginning, General Graves made a major contribution to the preservation of Eastern Siberia as a part of the Russian state. Once again—this time by an intervention of which they were themselves the strongest supporters—the Japanese aims of 1905 were thwarted.

From the commencement of the rising on May 25 until the junction with the forces of Semenov at Oloviannaia on August 31, 1918, the Czechs were mainly engaged in the struggle to secure their occupation of the railway. With the Czechs thus engaged along the line, the decision in early July to establish a Volga front was ineffectively carried out. The Ural Cossacks had been fighting there for months, and they had been joined by about 3,000 Russian troops under

Kappel and Makhin.[1] In addition, there were about 3,000 to 4,000 Czech troops in the struggle there by August 1918. But the Czechs had not been hasty in moving forces into the Volga area because the only terms on which they had agreed to remain were that they would hold their positions temporarily until the Allies arrived or until a Russian army was mobilized to relieve them in all military positions. The latter they hoped would not be long delayed. A message from Girsa, Spacek, and Houska, members of the Czechoslovak National Council, to Professor Masaryk on July 31, 1918 in effect asked the question: "How much longer?"[2] On September 21, 1918 Masaryk himself, in a conversation with Secretary Lansing, urged the impossibility of an Eastern Front and the desirability of a Czech concentration at Vladivostok for shipment to Europe.[3] These were the months, it should be recalled, when the Czechs were urging a unification of Russian governments in Siberia in order to obtain greater political and military support for the struggle on the Volga. Finding all support, whether Russian or foreign, unpromising, the Czechs began by fall a general shift of their forces westward toward the Volga where the Soviet Red army was increasing its strength.

The failure of the promised or expected support from the Allies and Russians to materialize made the Czechs increasingly disgruntled with all their associates. On September 16 the Czech commander at Cheliabinsk addressed an urgent message to the American consul at Vladivostok.[4] The situation was critical, he said, and he demanded an immediate answer from the Allies as to whether or not they intended to do anything. Aid from the Russian army in the near future, he added, was doubtful. The message, in fact, reflected a situation that was beginning to take on the appearance of a retreat. The taking of Kazan on August 7 was not only a great step forward in the Allied strategy of joining

[1] Boldyrev, op. cit., p. 31; V. I. Lebedev, The Russian Democracy, p. 12.
[2] Foreign Relations, 1918, Russia, II, pp. 319–320.
[3] Baker, op. cit., VIII, p. 419.
[4] Foreign Relations, 1918, Russia, II, p. 384.

hands with the Czechs from bases in North Russia to form an anti-German front, but great stores of food and ammunition had been captured at Kazan. While the wealthier people of Kazan had given generously to the support of the military effort, the cooperation from the large number of former Russian officers there was disheartening.[5] But success had continued to encourage the Czech and other forces until the capture of Volsk on September 1. After this, the battle began to move in reverse in some sectors.[6] The westward movement of the Czech forces and the augmenting of their number through continued recruiting from Czech prisoners in Siberia swelled their own ranks. In addition, General Syrovy assumed the supreme command with a Russian officer, General Dietrichs, as his chief of staff. In early December 1918—after Kolchak had become Supreme Ruler but before the Czechs had withdrawn—there were said to be a total of 65,709 anti-Bolshevik troops actually engaged on the Volga front.[7] By January 20, 1919 all Czech forces had been withdrawn from the front lines and on February 1 the first trainload of Czechs moved eastward where they were to take up stations along the railway line.[8]

The Allied promises of active aid for the Czechs and the urgent demands of the latter for the fulfillment of these promises were the factors which forced President Wilson to consent to the limited form of intervention as defined in the *Aide Memoire*. The month of July was occupied in active preparations for the intervention. On August 3, 1918, the Japanese and British put the first troops ashore at Vladivostok.[9] The Japanese began the landing of their 12th Division which in time established its temporary headquarters at Nikolsk-Ussuriisk. The British sent a battalion of about eight hundred men of the Middlesex Regiment. Five hundred French colonial troops from Peking arrived soon after. The American troops came from the Philippine Islands as well as from

[5] Baerlein, *op. cit.*, p. 189.
[6] *Foreign Relations, 1918, Russia*, II, p. 364.
[7] *Ibid.*, II, p. 459.
[8] P. Janin, *Ma Mission en Siberie, 1918–1920*, Paris, 1933, p. 69.
[9] Stewart, *op. cit.*, p. 136.

the port of embarkation at San Francisco and were commanded by General William S. Graves. By September 4 the American forces in Siberia numbered more than 7,000 men.

None of these Allied troops or any that followed ever appeared on the fighting front to the west. The vast majority of them, those of Japan and the United States, remained to fight the battle for which they had come—the battle for Eastern Siberia. In this fact lies the key to an understanding of American neutrality toward the various Russian factions. The military action, as the United States Government saw it, was not against Russia or any part of it but against the Japanese who were seeking to divide Russia by factional strife as well as by political and economic confusion in order to impose a Japanese peace upon her. Under these circumstances the American interests, it was felt, would be best served by waiting until it was apparent whom the Russians wanted to rule them and then by seeing to it that Siberia was delivered in its entirety to the survivor. This had the effect of making the American policy at times appear pro-Bolshevik. But the long and careful consideration given by the American Government to the Allied proposal for extending recognition to Kolchak reduces any such view to a mere reflection of the thinking so characteristic of a confused and warring world which hated neutrals only a little less than enemies.

While American policy toward the Czechs was benevolent, actual military aid to them was obviously never contemplated. In a letter to Acting Secretary of State Polk on February 19, 1920, Secretary of War Baker effectively exploded the notion that the small American force could presume to "protect" the Czech Legion numbering more than 70,000 men.[10] But the United States did, along with the other major Allied powers, extend recognition to the Czechs and, shortly thereafter, a loan.[11] France was the first to extend recognition to the Czechs, allegedly in exchange for the Czech consent to remain temporarily in Russia. But

[10] *Foreign Relations, 1920,* III, p. 503.
[11] *Foreign Relations, 1918, Supplement I, The World War,* I, pp. 824–825; *Foreign Relations, 1919, Russia,* p. 279.

the other Allies soon followed, with Japan acting last on September 9, 1918. Also, the American Red Cross aided the Czechs with clothes other than uniforms as well as other supplies.[12] In addition, Vance McCormick of the War Trade Board, Bernard Baruch of the War Industries Board, and Edward Hurley of the United States Shipping Board all had a part in carrying out the official aid which the United States extended to the Czechs and, to a limited extent, the communities near which they operated.[13] It should be added that a continuing sense of obligation was felt toward the Czechs. In early 1919, when it appeared that a Congressional investigation of the whole Siberian question might be held, Acting Secretary of State Polk reminded Lansing, "Of course we have an absolute obligation to the Czechs . . . ."[14] The same attitude persisted until the Czechs had been transported back to Europe.

The number of Bolshevik forces operating in the Maritime Province and obstructing there the free movement along the railway of the Czechs has, like the problem of the war prisoners, been the subject of much disagreement, not to mention exaggeration. It will be recalled that after the Czechs had secured Vladivostok on June 29, 1918 and had established the Derber Government in power there, some of them turned northward in the direction of Nikolsk-Ussuriisk and Khabarovsk in order to clear away the Red Guard forces which were in control of the railway there. Immediately upon his arrival in August, Colonel Ward received orders to move his troops northward and to assume command of the "Ussuri front" against the Red force. As commander of this operation he had under his charge about one thousand troops.[15] At the same time he estimated the number of his opponents at 18,000 to 20,000 troops. Other guesses as to their number ran as high as 30,000 and even 50,000 Red troops; these exaggerated figures were used by the Czechs,

[12] *Foreign Relations, 1918, Russia,* II, p. 333.
[13] *Ibid.,* II, p. 385.
[14] *Foreign Relations, 1919, Russia,* pp. 324–325.
[15] Ward, *op. cit.,* pp. 5, 12, 18, 30.

THE CIVIL WAR

Japanese, and others who were anxious for one reason or another to accomplish a general intervention. There is no reliable evidence to support these large claims; on the contrary, there are many reasons for believing them entirely false. In the first place, the Czechs had more than 12,000 troops in the vicinity of Vladivostok which could have been used against the Reds had there been any necessity for it. Furthermore, when the Japanese arrived they established their division headquarters at Nikolsk-Ussuriisk and sent Colonel Inagaki to take command of the Ussuri operations there with only enough Japanese replacements to relieve the British who thereupon withdrew. With their own forces and a few followers of Kalmykov, the Japanese moved northward with no trouble at all. In fact, there is little reason to doubt that this weakly supported guerrilla fight was carried on by not more than a few hundred Red troops, all of whom shortly disappeared into the taiga along the Zeia River.

A student of the revolution and civil war in Russia has written, "One searches in vain in the records of the time not only for a consistent Allied policy, but even for a steadfast policy on the part of the individual Allies."[16] Enough has already been seen of the background of the intervention to know that this statement is only partly true. Each nation did have a policy, but it was in conflict with that of some of the others. The Japanese in particular had a very definite policy which had no relation to the real interests of anyone else in Siberia. Britain and France may have thought that the Japanese interest had an exchange value, for which they might be able to receive such gains as the protection for their Russian investments against the Bolsheviks or perhaps even troops for an Eastern Front. But it has been shown that when these two nations gave their approval to Kolchak as the commander of the new Russian front, the Japanese, directly as well as through their agents, made victory impossible, in order that continued confusion might leave open the possibility of a Japanese, rather than an Allied, intervention.

In retrospect, the conflict of policy between the United

[16] Chamberlin, *op. cit.*, ii, p. 151.

261

States and Japan seems very clear-cut: Japan wanted Eastern Siberia; the United States was determined to prevent her from acquiring it. Such objectives, however, are rarely broached in the circumspect language of diplomatic or other official correspondence. The openly announced objectives of the United States were aid to the Czechs and economic assistance to the Russians. Both these objectives were intimately related to the control of the railway and the maintenance of open communication throughout Siberia. In a reply of July 22, 1919 to a Senate inquiry, President Wilson stated very clearly this phase of American policy.[17] He stressed the work of Stevens and the railway experts and its relationship to the economic rehabilitation of Russia. This work, he said, could not be carried on without the presence there of American troops—a view of the situation by no means shared by the British, French, or the anti-Bolshevik Russians leaders, not to mention the Japanese. In a telegram of May 18, 1919 to Vologodsky, General Horvath expressed what so many were saying and thinking: "It is clear to me that the Americans do not intend to help us in our struggle against the Bolsheviks . . . ."[18] It appeared to him that all the other Allies had the proper attitude toward the Bolsheviks. The Americans came announcing that they would rescue the Czechs and give economic aid to the Russians. But, in the struggle with the Bolsheviks, he concluded, they refused to take part. Both General Knox and Colonel Ward expressed annoyance with the American attitude toward the struggle in Siberia. The Kolchak Government—which Britain and France were supporting in its increasingly hopeless fight with the growing strength of the Red army—expressed with galling frankness its resentment toward the unwanted neutral policy of the United States.[19]

It must be said in all fairness that American policy in Siberia was also misunderstood both in the State Department

[17] *Russian Series,* No. 4, pp. 5–6.
[18] "K Istorii Interventsii—Pravitelstvo Kolchaka i Soedinennye Shtaty," *op. cit.,* pp. 66–67.
[19] *Foreign Relations, 1919, Russia,* p. 502.

and in Congress. American representatives in Siberia were divided as to what the correct American policy was. Written close to the scene of action and based on information from strongly partisan sources, the reports of the diplomatic and consular agents showed the effects of having been written hastily in the midst of the titanic struggle. At home, as early as January 1919, the Siberian policy came under the threat of a closer scrutiny by the Republican leaders in Congress. Fiorello La Guardia and Senator Johnson and others became outspoken opponents of the administration policy of keeping troops in Siberia. The struggle for power in the Far East was a difficult thing to explain without using words that might arouse Japan to the point of an open rupture.

In Siberia the Japanese and all who accepted their support were engaged in a campaign of cruelty which must rarely have been exceeded. Even Colonel Ward, himself an opponent of the American policy, noted the overbearing attitude of the Japanese toward the Russian people. He discovered that they not only assumed that they were entitled to treat the Russians as they pleased but resented any presumption on the part of their Allies to interfere with their conduct.[20] On the station platform at Nikolsk-Ussuriisk Colonel Ward saw a Japanese sentry rush forward and jam the butt of his rifle into the center of the back of a Russian officer standing there. The sentry stood grinning while the officer rolled in pain on the station platform. When the sentry prepared to repeat the act, this time with a Russian woman, Ward drew his pistol and stopped him. Reporting this to Japanese headquarters, Ward was met by the greatest surprise that he should be interested in taking the part of a Russian, not to mention annoyance that he should presume to interfere in what was purely Japanese business.

The Japanese extended the same treatment to the people of the villages. Their treatment of the village of Ivanovka along the Amur is an example.[21] According to the official

[20] Ward, *op. cit.*, p. 54.
[21] The Special Delegation of the Far Eastern Republic to the United States of America, *A Short Outline of the History of the Far Eastern*

Japanese report, the cause of this incident was support of the Bolsheviks by the people of the village. The raid on the village was carried out on March 22, 1919. Two hundred and thirty-two of the inhabitants were killed, many of them when the Japanese set fire to the houses, shooting at those who tried to escape. About thirty were locked into a barn which was then set afire. In all, eighty-six houses and over two hundred other buildings were burned; large amounts of grain and agricultural machinery were destroyed. The machinery destroyed, alone, is said to have represented a loss of $100,000.

The attitude of complete disrespect for Russian persons and property was evident in all Japanese relationships with the cities and villages of Eastern Siberia. If there was any question of opposition to Japanese objectives or refusal to obey Japanese commands, it was the Russian who was denied the benefit of the doubt. Furthermore, persons of authority and trust among the people, instead of being respected and encouraged to serve the Japanese purpose, were alienated and embittered. An order issued by a Japanese captain to the elder of the village of Voznesensk in the Amur region shows this clearly.[22] The order read: "I order you, elder, to appear tomorrow the 24 of December, 1919 at 5.30 in the morning at my office at the Japanese staff headquarters in the village of Nikolaevsk: and if you, elder, do not appear with your assistant at the appointed time, then I shall have to go with my detachment and destroy all of your village and shoot the people both old and young along with your assistant." The purpose of the summons is not known, but the punishment for disobedience is a revelation of the local relationships under Japanese occupation.

In return, the partisans awaited every opportunity to isolate groups of Japanese small enough to handle and then wipe them out. An American officer who participated in the

Republic, Washington, 1922, p. 8; G. Reikhberg, "Partizany Dalnego Vostoka v Borbe s Iaponskoi Interventsiei (1918–1920)," *Istoricheskii Zhurnal* (Moscow), ix, 1938, p. 68.
[22] A. Shurygin and Z. Karpenko, *op. cit.,* p. 114.

Siberian campaign tells how thoroughly this was carried out on one occasion.[23] The partisans saw a detachment of Japanese approaching who, they well knew, were looking for just such a group as themselves. The partisans, therefore, awaited the enemy in the heavy underbrush of a riverbank near the village of Uspenskaia. Here the Japanese, if they continued in the direction they were going, would have to cross the river by ferry. One hundred and fifty or more Japanese boarded the ferry and started for the opposite shore where the partisans were awaiting them. When the party of Japanese reached about midsteam, the partisans opened fire on them. All but a very few were killed. As in these instances, the clash between the Japanese and their Russian opponents was an extremely bitter one and one in which neither side expected to give or receive any quarter. Knowledge of this struggle must have been in the minds of those Japanese writers who pleaded that this was not the way to promote the expansion of Japanese business on the continent.

Semenov, whose origin and exploits have already been described, was exclusively backed by the Japanese after October 1918, and was looked upon by the people of Siberia as nothing but a pensioner of the Japanese army and the executor of its desires. It seems the cruelest kind of irony that it was the Czechs who made possible his first real success at the end of August 1918. Under Czech pressure the Soviet forces retreated northward into the taiga, leaving Transbaikal at his mercy. It was against him that the Soviet Government had raised enough war prisoners to drive him back in the spring of 1918 and force him to take cover in Manchuria.[24] Aided by the arrival of the Czechs, however, he ventured out to wreak his vengeance on the civilians. He had regular places to which he transported carloads of victims for executions.[25] Makaveevo, Dauria, Andrian-

[23] G. G. F. Channing, *Siberia's Untouched Treasure. Its Future Role in the World,* New York, 1923, p. 203.
[24] D. Frid, "Cheshskie Voennoplennye v Borbe s Chekhoslovatskim Miatezhom," *Proletarskaia Revoliutsiia* (Moscow), No. 5 (76), 1928, pp. 159–160.
[25] Stewart, *op. cit.,* p. 287.

ovka, and Oloviannaia were some of these areas. Here his mass murders took place. There were three standard charges —being a Bolshevik, aiding the Bolsheviks, or hindering mobilization. The policy, as a matter of fact, was well calculated to produce Bolsheviks and swell the partisan ranks.

If it is possible to conceive of it, Kalmykov was reputed to have been even more cruel than Semenov. In May 1918, as Semenov was being beaten back in Transbaikal, Kalmykov and his original associate, Orlov, were suffering from the same treatment in the Maritime Province. It was under these conditions that they joined forces in June at Grodekovo. Until the summer of 1918, Kalmykov had remained a rather obscure participant in the struggle.[26] But by joining forces with the Japanese as they moved up the Ussuri Valley he was able to establish himself at Khabarovsk in September 1918 and became the ataman of the Ussuri Cossacks. Conditions in the ranks of his followers were brought to light by a mutiny which occurred among his forces on January 27, 1919.[27] About five hundred of the mutineers came to the nearby American headquarters where they were disarmed and taken under temporary protection. They claimed mistreatment as their reason for leaving Kalmykov. His own men, they said, were subjected to beatings and other brutality and, while Kalmykov and his officers spent freely and lived well, the men were so poorly paid that their families suffered. The men were eventually sent away under circumstances which would keep them from being sought out by Kalmykov. He continued his career of crime and by the end of the intervention was reported by sober estimates to have shot without trial at least 4,000 men and women. At the end of January 1920 the rise of the partisan strength along the Amur and Ussuri brought an end to his activities. He fled across the border into Manchuria, where he was taken into custody by the Chinese. He was then taken to Peking for trial, but on the way was shot by one of his guards "while trying to escape."

[26] A. N. Iaremenko (trans. E. Varneck), "Dnevnik Kommunista," *Revoliutsiia na Dalnem Vostoke,* p. 30.
[27] Stewart, *op. cit.,* pp. 258–259; *Semenov Hearings,* p. 10.

A. N. Iaremenko, a schoolteacher who became one of the partisans and left an unusually fine account of his experience, tells of his meeting with one of the Kalmykov men while both were in jail in Vladivostok.[28] He saw in him a striking example of the really criminal, sadistic type which seemed to him so characteristic of those who followed Kalmykov. In conversations with him he discovered that the man's name was Julinek, that he was a Czech, and that he had a consuming hatred for all Germans, Magyars, and Bolsheviks and would commit any foul deed for Kalmykov because he also hated them.

Julinek was a member of Kalmykov's "Military Legal Department" as the group was called which was in charge of carrying out murders. In this capacity he had carried out such notorious Kalmykov deeds as the robbing and murdering of the Red Cross agents, Hedblom (Swedish) and Opachang (Norwegian). But the deed of which he was particularly proud was the shooting of the sixteen Hungarian war-prisoner musicians who had played at various times at the Khabarovsk Public Assembly Hall, the People's Conservatory, and the Chashka Chaiu cabaret. He continued with fiendish excitement: "Some cossacks and I caught them all—sixteen men—like dogs; at 12 o'clock noon I led them into a garden by the Amur near the Muraviev memorial, where there is a chasm extending down the river. . . . I lined them up, the cossacks stood ready, I commanded, 'Fire'—and they rolled into the Amur to the devil's mother." With villians of this type turned loose on the community it is small wonder that even moderate men became Bolsheviks and partisans.

General Rozanov, the official representative of Admiral Kolchak in the Far East, has already been described as one of the willing assistants in the Japanese war against the people. That he was well qualified for this role is beyond question. Before coming to the Far East he was in charge of recruiting in the Krasnoiarsk district, which was particularly anti-Kolchak in sympathy even before he came there and, of course, more so after he left.[29] Under these conditions Roza-

[28] Iaremenko, *loc. cit.*, pp. 25–26.
[29] S. C. Graves, "The Truth about Kolchak," *The New York Times Current History* (New York), xiv, No. 4, July 1921, p. 671.

nov was at his best. Upon entering a village he demanded the name and residence of every partisan, the location of hostile bands, and "a guide to lead them in a surprise attack." If this was refused, he burned every house. If his demands were still not met, he shot every fifth male, regardless of age. One of his aides was Colonel Frank, who had acted as interpreter for Colonel Ward during the speaking tour which the latter made to try to enlist the cooperation of labor in the Kolchak effort. It must have made a great impression upon the Russian workingmen to find out that this same advocate of cooperation had a criminal career of his own. He conducted an expedition of his own in the vicinity of Omsk in which pillage, rape, murder, and burning were applied to all who showed a lack of enthusiasm for the Kolchak regime.

This was one of the ways by which Kolchak acquired a reputation closely connected in the popular mind with the Japanese. The peasants of Siberia were not able to meet Kolchak and note, as many did, that he was an honest and well-meaning man and a patriot who would not pay the Japanese price for assistance. But they did know that his agents curbed the zemstvos, censored both press and speech, and made constant arrests which were followed by secret military trials and the disappearance of prisoners. Kolchak justice, writes one competent observer, was worse than Tsarist Justice.[30] ". . . Here there was unrestrained cruelty —the settling of personal grudges under cover of the law and indiscriminate extermination." In July 1919 a Jewish pogrom was carried out in Ekaterinburg which must have been strongly reminiscent of Imperial days.[31] The victims were reported as amounting to at least 2,000 killed. It was difficult under these conditions to persuade the people that the Kolchak regime represented anything but the blackest reaction. Strikes, sabotage, and delays of all types played a large part in the final downfall of the Kolchak regime. In a popular ditty the people made a revealingly apt analysis of the role of their oppressors as they saw it. The song went:

[30] C. H. Smith, "What Happened in Siberia," *op. cit.,* pp. 375–376.
[31] S. C. Graves, *loc. cit.,* p. 671.

"English tunics,
Russian epaulettes,
Japanese tobacco,
And Omsk rulers."[32]

Later as the rumors grew that Kolchak was nearing the end of his anti-Bolshevik drive the words became:

"The tunic has worn out,
The epaulettes have dropped off,
The tobacco is smoked out, and
The Supreme Ruler is finished."

The reference made here to epaulettes concerns the popular and deeply felt opposition to one of the most hated aspects of the old regime—military discipline and everything pertaining to it. For centuries past the Russian peasant had hated his landlord and desired his land and had, on several notable occasions in Russian history, risen against him. Cruel punishments suffered at the hands of the landlords were by no means uncommon in a land where serfdom had so recently characterized the social position of the vast majority of the people. Upon being drafted into the army, the peasant once more looked into the face of a landlord or a landlord's son, this time attired in the uniform of a Russian officer and wearing epaulettes. Here also he found the same absolute subjection to authority, the same cruel punishments, and the same absence of any means of redressing the century-old grievances. Having during the long months and years of World War suffered particularly from military aspect of his social and economic bondage, it was natural that the peasant of 1917 and 1918 should be especially sensitive to anything which remotely suggested this hated service. Thus the wearing of epaulettes became closely associated in the peasant mind and in the earliest revolutionary activities with the same urge to revolt which resulted also in desertion from the front, seizure of land, and general destruction of the property of the landlords.

[32] Varneck and Fisher, *op. cit.*, pp. 277, 288.

269

Throughout the revolution and civil war, the wearing of epaulettes thus remained a symbol of all that was hateful to the peasant. To the White Russian leaders, on the other hand, the wearing of epaulettes came to symbolize the restoration of their military authority and of their traditional social and economic position in the state. When the White leaders, such as Horvath, Kolchak and others, promised their Allied supporters or well-wishers that they would restore a stable political order, they invariably mentioned the restoration of military discipline. Recognizing the feeling of the peasants in this matter, the Bolsheviks had, as one of their first measures, abolished military descipline of the traditional kind and instituted the making of fundamental military decisions by committees of soldiers. The restoration of authority and the wearing of epaulettes thus meant to the peasants a return to the old regime and a sacrifice of one of the important gains of the revolution. The story is told that, upon the capture of a particularly hated White Russian officer, the Red forces took a hot iron and burned epaulettes into his shoulders. The incident may be a fiction, but it is symbolic of many incidents which made the civil war a true gauge of all the pent-up hatreds of the past.

To Charles Smith, viewing the whole episode as a practical railway engineer, it represented a complete failure of leadership.[33] Instead of adherence to the views of men such as Admiral Knight and General Graves, the opinions of General Knox and General Janin, the "military diplomats," as he termed them, were allowed to prevail. These men thought in terms of "destinies" and counseled against a sound economic program which to them savored too strongly of the vulgarities of trade. The result was that the establishment of Kolchak was looked upon as a piece of constructive statesmanship. Kolchak, in turn, closed his eyes—perhaps because it would have done him little good to do otherwise—to the miseries around him and held up the victory over the Bolsheviks as the great goal. Unfortunately, the people all forgot

[33] C. H. Smith, "Four Years of Mistakes in Siberia," *Asia* (New York), XXII, No. 6, June 1922, p. 481.

why they were trying to attain this goal. As a result of this policy, Smith concludes, "We had mushroom governments and military movements in Siberia, and not harvesting-machines, binder-twine, locomotives, rakes and hoes."

The position of General Graves and the small American force in Siberia in the midst of this turmoil was extremely precarious. Graves, as the head of an armed force, carrying with him orders written by the President himself and representing in his person impartiality to factious and neutrality toward current issues, came to mean to the Japanese all the stubbornness of the American refusal to let them have their way. To the White Russian forces also, the American insistence on neutrality and upon leaving the Russians to settle their own problems, meant the disappointment of all their hopes which could be attained only by positive aid.

As the months went by, the views of the American State Department regarding intervention underwent a considerable change. Throughout the intervention, the neutral position taken by General Graves represented the views of the Chief of Staff, the Secretary of War, and the President himself. That it was at first also the view of the State Department can be seen from a letter which Secretary Lansing wrote to Ambassador Morris in September 1918[34] He wrote in part: "The ideas and purposes of the Allies with respect to military operations in Siberia and on the 'Volga Front' are ideas and purposes with which we have no sympathy. We do not believe them to be practical or based upon sound reason or good military judgment." But by the following May the War Department, which backed Graves unreservedly, and the State Department had grown somewhat apart. Consular reports and transactions with the Russian Embassy in Washington had helped to cast the whole affair in a different light. On May 9, 1919, Acting Secretary Polk wrote to Lansing complaining of the interpretation Graves was giving his orders which made it seem as though the orders required "a rigid and aloof neutrality on his part."[35] He continued, "The

[34] *Foreign Relations, 1918, Russia,* II, pp. 393–394.
[35] *Foreign Relations, 1919, Russia,* pp. 493–494.

American command in Siberia has always required a high degree of tact and large experience in affairs. I cannot help thinking that, in spite of the narrow limitations set by his instructions, General Graves has proved lacking in both these qualifications." In correspondence with John Stevens, the State Department was at times even more outspoken than this (as already noted in a previous chapter). The fact was that recognition for Kolchak was at that time being considered by the State Department as by the other Allies, and General Graves had shown little sympathy for Kolchak.

The aspect of Graves' neutrality to which so many parties took exception was his attempt to treat all factions with absolute fairness. At Paris, President Wilson was hearing the same complaints against Graves as those which the British Foreign Office had been handing in to the American State Department in Washington.[36] David Lloyd George told Wilson that, according to his information, Graves was responsible for the trouble between Russian and American troops while Ivanov-Rinov had tried his best to smooth the whole matter over. Wilson answered that Graves was "a man of most unprovocative character, and wherever the fault might lie, he felt sure it was not with him." Graves was at this very time making, against the most overwhelming odds, every effort to be fair to both sides in the Russian struggle. In March 1919 the Japanese demanded that he aid them in a case where all but three of a Japanese force of 250 had been wiped out by the partisans.[37] When he declined on the grounds that the people who attacked them were probably persons who had been mistreated by the Japanese, the Japanese opened up a newspaper campaign against him which purported to show that he was sympathetic to the Bolsheviks. But they were unable to maneuver him into doing or saying anything that would involve him in the struggle. On the other hand, Graves was not slow to take action where his neutrality was actually threatened. In October 1919 Semenov tried to stop a load of 50,000 rifles destined for Kolchak, demanding 15,000 for

[36] *Ibid.*, pp. 499–500; *Peace Conference Papers*, v, p. 608.
[37] D. H. Miller, *op. cit.*, xvii, p. 245.

himself as the price of letting them pass.[38] Lieutenant Ryan, who was in charge of the rifles, telegraphed Graves for instructions. Graves answered, "Do not give up." At this show of determination General Oi, the Japanese commander, instructed Semenov to let them pass.

Graves' impartial policy extended also to persons accused of being Bolsheviks. During an inspection, he discovered a case of a Russian who had been arrested because he was said to have been a Bolshevik.[39] To the officer who had made the arrest he said: "Because a man is a Bolshevik is no reason for his arrest. . . . The United States is only fighting the Bolsheviks when the American troops are attacked by an armed force." While the Americans were associated with the other Allies in the intervention, a great deal of this spirit exhibited by Graves seems to have been evident between them and the Russians. Before the overthrow of the Soviets in Siberia in 1918, it is said that the railway shop workers made a special effort to cooperate with the American railway men by speeding up their essential work.[40] In June 1919, when an American detachment under Lieutenant Channing captured the village of Uspenskaia, the Americans showed to the surprise of all the Russian people that it was possible to capture a village and confiscate all the firearms without murdering the people or destroying their houses or means of livelihood.[41] It is also recorded that on at least one occasion American troops, explicitly instructed to avoid hostilities with the Russians, held an entirely unofficial conference with partisan representatives.[42] The American officers told the partisan leaders that each had a duty to perform. Theirs (the Americans') was to guard the railway. If the partisans attacked the railway, the Americans would have to use force against them. Therefore, they proposed, "Do whatever else your duty demands but stay away from the railway." In that sector at least, the bargain was observed.

The social structure and recent internal disturbances in the

[38] *Foreign Relations, 1919, Russia*, p. 541.
[39] Ackerman, *op. cit.*, p. 188.
[40] A. R. Williams, *op. cit.*, p. 229.
[41] Channing, *op. cit.*, p. 197.
[42] C. H. Smith, "What Happened in Siberia," *op. cit.*, p. 375.

life of the people of Siberia were clearly reflected in the partisan movement which arose as a protest against the military, social, and economic upheavals resulting from changes of regimes and foreign intervention. In an earlier chapter where the social structure of Siberia was described, it was explained that the social cleavage in Siberia was not between landlord and peasant but between Cossack and peasant, old settlers and new settlers. Speaking of this situation, Chamberlin notes that, "As a general rule the partisan movement showed its greatest strength in regions where new settlers had come after the unsuccessful Revolution of 1905."[43] There was a considerable roving population which for one reason or another remained unsettled and a source of concern for the settled population, which had to protect itself against them. These unsettled and unsatisfied groups were some of the first recruits to the partisan movement. In addition, there were the soldiers returning from the front, the "frontoviks" as they are called in the Russian literature on the subject. The breakup of the Eastern Front and of the Russian army left these soldiers drifting back to their homes, in many cases with rifles and ammunition. It was only later that an effort was made to relieve the homecoming soldiers of their rifles as they moved eastward from the battlefront. These men were not only a restless element, but were equipped for fighting duty. From them came many partisans and much partisan military equipment. The American raids on villages suspected of partisan activity—such as the raid on Uspenskaia, already described—were mainly for the purpose of collecting these military supplies rather than for any punitive objectives.

As it progressed, the partisan movement came to include representatives of many elements of the Siberian population. The reason for this is not difficult to understand if the circumstances are considered. During the time he languished in jail at Vladivostok, Iaremenko, a Bolshevik former schoolteacher, was visited by a Japanese sentry who indicated his sympathy for Communism. Concerning this visit Iaremenko writes, "I enjoyed listening to him and realized that it was

[43] Chamberlin, *op. cit.*, II, p. 197.

THE CIVIL WAR

Labor, the Great Labor, which united people and created
a community of interest among them—labor and not any
idea of humanity. He is a worker and he feels and under-
stands our struggle—such is the power of the Communist
revolution . . . ."[44] As a statement of fact this observation
is open to serious question, but as a psychological clue to an
understanding of the partisan warfare it has considerable
value. An illiterate people have no taste for fine philosophical
distinctions. A comfortable peasantry has no desire to take up
arms and fight for theoretical objectives. But when calamity
strikes them, they all have something in common. The
prosperous farmer whose house and buildings have been
burned and whose family has been shot and who is himself
the object of a recruiting drive has thereby been drawn closer
to the vagabond who never owned a farm. This is essentially
what happened in the fall of 1918 when the Czechs from the
West and the Japanese from the South drove into the taiga
the last military protection of the existing order. The people
were suddenly left unprotected and, at the same time, at
the mercy of Semenov at Chita, Kalmykov at Khabarovsk,
and the Japanese everywhere. A common danger produced
in the long run a common effort to overcome it.

Against this background must be measured the later claim
that all partisan activity was organized directly by the Bolshevik Party.[45] The Bolsheviks conducted a strong campaign
of propaganda in late 1917 and early 1918, and by these
strenuous efforts they managed to maneuver themselves into
a strong voting position in the higher Soviet ranks. But the
people at large remained politically inert or voted largely
Socialist Revolutionary. Moreover, Soviet writers of the
partisan beginnings and the civil war complain about the
apathy and lack of class consciousness of the people at the
opening of the struggle. The tremendous popular forces soon
to be thrown into the battle cannot be explained entirely or
even largely in terms of the past activities of the Communists in Siberia. But it can be explained with reference to

[44] Iaremenko, loc. cit., p. 39.
[45] Karpenko, op. cit., p. 70.

275

the events just described. That no mere theoretical concepts lay behind the partisan organizations is also shown by the fact that many of them existed before the Bolsheviks assumed control. The Communist assertions that the partisan movement arose exclusively from Party efforts must, therefore, be qualified. It had its reason for being in the intervention. At this point the Communists assumed leadership and general direction of the movement. Finally, the partisan forces developed into the new Red army of the area. But this was the achievement of more than a year of planning and fighting.

While the mass response to the revolution came relatively late in Siberia, the intervention and the Kolchak regime roused the people to action the object of which was generally well understood. In an earlier chapter the relatively high level of prosperity among the peasants of Siberia was explained. This, in addition to the remoteness of Siberia from the early scenes of struggle, left the Siberian villages to a considerable extent passive to the storm mounting in their midst. But the needs of Kolchak for recruits and taxes would not long leave the villager impartial to the events outside his limited circle. The growing violence was fast leaving little room for those who wished to let someone else worry. In his testimony before the Senate hearing on the Semenov case in 1922, Ralph Baggs, a former American intelligence officer in Eastern Siberia, mentions this important phase of the struggle.[46] He said: "But a lot of people who did not necessarily coincide with the Bolshevik beliefs, and did not necessarily coincide with the other forces, were obliged to take one of those two sides because the only two military forces existing were of the two extremes."

This was the plight of Anton Zakharovich Ovchinnikov, a church sexton from the village of Kosteevo in Ufa Province.[47] In the summer of 1918 he found himself the victim of a Czech recruiting drive to build up Russian forces to fight against the Bolsheviks. When he finally realized that he was

[46] *Semenov Hearings,* p. 86.
[47] Varneck and Fisher, *op. cit.,* p. 269.

involved in a civil war and would be called upon to fight his fellow villagers in the interests of persons whose names were meaningless to him, his horrible predicament became clear to him. Why was he fighting his own people? Why were they talking about a war without mercy, a war in which no prisoners were being taken? He suddenly felt lost and isolated from his former life and home and friends. "Here," he concluded, "I was in some devil's circle, so that no matter which way I tried to escape, death would be waiting for me. It surely was so: should I run away from the ranks of the 'People's Army' and be caught, that would mean death as a deserter. Should I run away and be caught by the Red Army, also a People's Army, that would also be death, because I had been a 'volunteer' in the army against which they fought. Wasn't that a devil's circle?"

From the very days of the Czech rising and the assumption of power by the White Governments, the cruelties against the people became associated with these two elements. As the White Government replaced the Soviet at Irkutsk, the commissars found there were hanged.[48] The chairmen of the Soviets of the small nearby villages were given twenty-five to fifty lashes with an old-fashioned Russian whip. If recovery from such treatment came, it was at best a matter of several months. One of the early punitive expeditions into the Suchan Valley, a mining section north of Vladivostok, was made in September 1918 by the Czechs.[49] Iaremenko, the author of one of the best first-hand accounts of the Bolshevik side of the struggle, was himself captured in this raid and taken to jail in Vladivostok, where he learned, by what he saw daily, to associate the Czechs and Japanese with one another as the arch-oppressors of the people. The Suchan Valley was the scene of many succeeding raids, for recruits, for the punishment of strikers, or for other purposes. Raids were carried out at various times by Horvath, Ivanov-Rinov, as well as by the Japanese, the British, and the Americans. The coal of the area was vital for the continuance of railway

[48] *Foreign Relations, 1918, Russia,* II, p. 312.
[49] Iaremenko, *op. cit.,* pp. 12–14.

service in the Vladivostok area. Hence, the struggle there was particularly violent; the area was one of the first centers of partisan activity in the Maritime Province. It was also one of the places where American involvement with the people was at its worst since American troops guarded the railway to the Suchan Valley. While Ivanov-Rinov whipped women with ramrods and burned and pillaged generally, the partisans on their part showed no mercy where their opponents were concerned.

The real turning point in the struggle came in September 1918. In that month the Czechs were forced to give ground on the Volga front. It was also the month of the Japanese push north to Khabarovsk and Blagoveshchensk with the support to reaction and mass murder which this implied. Actual detachments of partisans were formed at Khabarovsk and in the Suchan Valley as a first reaction to the Czech offensive.[50] In August a Congress of Soviets in the Far East had already made a formal decision to carry on partisan warfare.[51] But it was with the retreat of the Bolshevik forces into the taiga in September, after their defeat by the Czechs and the Japanese, that the real beginnings of partisan warfare were made. From this time on the struggle became sharper and steadily more desperate. In his memoirs, General Graves notes a broadening of the meaning of the word "Bolshevik."[52] He found that the word meant, "a human being who did not, by act and word, give encouragement to the restoration to power of representatives of Autocracy in Russia." To judge by the oppressive measures taken against them, Bolshevik came to include the men of such prerevolutionary institutions as the zemstvos, city dumas, and the cooperatives. The Bolsheviks replied with such all-inclusive general terms as "Kolchakovshchina" to designate the whole regime of reaction and oppression which came to be associated with the name of Kolchak. A raid into the Suchan

[50] G. Reikhberg, "Dalnevostochnyi Proletariat v Borbe s Iaponskoi Interventsiei," *op. cit.*, pp. 156–157.
[51] A. Shurygin and Z. Karpenko, *op. cit.*, p. 113.
[52] W. S. Graves, *op. cit.*, pp. 101–103.

Valley by almost anyone might be spoken of or written about as a raid by Kolchak. Within the scope of these large generalities, the opponents in the civil war came to include all whom they hated for almost any reason.

The partisan movement not only followed carefully considered plans elaborated at periodical conferences but it was carried on from politically or militarily strategic centers out of which all activities radiated. At an All-Siberian conference of underground party organizations held at Omsk in March 1919, the goals of the partisan struggle in Siberia were discussed.[53] They included support of all spontaneous uprisings among the people, preparation for active warfare against the Whites, sabotage, agitation among all classes of the people as well as among the foreign military detachments. The carrying on of agitation among the proletariat of other nations of Eastern Asia was also proposed. In the Eastern Siberian region these objectives were carried out from such centers as the Suchan Valley, where the labor strike was a powerful weapon in the effort to sabotage the railway which, among other things, carried supplies to Kolchak. The middle Zeia Valley north of Blagoveshchensk was another center of partisan planning and activity. It was here that the Bolshevik forces driven north by the Japanese had taken refuge. It was to such a center as this that people could go when conditions drove them from their homes with the determination to fight their way back. Organizations were also mantained in cities such as Khabarovsk and Vladivostok, not only for agitation among the workers and promotion of strikes but also as information centers and centers of general strategic direction of the partisan and political activity. Control over the stevedores at Vladivostok as well as railway employees all along the line, especially at shops where they remained in large groups, was a particularly valuable weapon. General direction and coordination of all activities in Eastern Siberia were in the hands of the Dalburo or Far Eastern Bureau of the Communist Party at Khabarovsk.

In his testimony before the United States Senate committee

[53] Karpenko, *op. cit.*, p. 68.

investigating Semenov in 1922, Colonel Morrow, the commander of an American detachment guarding the railway in Transbaikal, explained how a center of partisan activity arose in the area of his command.[54] The Selenga Valley he describes as 150 miles wide and running 250 miles south to the Mongolian border. The people were peaceful, law-abiding, and hospitable. But in December 1919 Semenov sent into the valley General Levitsky and his famous "Wild Division" composed of 500 Cossacks and about 2,000 Mongols on Mongolian ponies and camels. There followed an orgy of murder, plunder, and robbery which ended in devastation and in the carrying off of 4,000 sleighloads of loot of all types including sewing machines, furs, and samovars. The ravaging of the village of Bobkina in this area was actually witnessed by American counsular officials. Against this the people arose against their oppressors in armed defense of their lives and property.

In general, the partisan bands, as distinguished from other Bolshevik Party activities, were organized with just such attention to local conditions as those just described. General party business was carried on in the cities. But the villages, well off the railway line and in the hidden valleys, were the centers of partisan activity. "The taiga became a fortress of defense," as one writer has characterized the situation.[55] Such localities as those around Verkhne-Udinsk and Chita in Transbaikal were organized particularly with the anti-Semenov struggle in mind. The center of the Zeia Valley was aimed at Kalmykov, but its position near the Japanese military centers at Blageveshchensk and Khabarovsk gave it other advantages. It should be added that the Amur became one of the largest and strongest centers of partisan activity. In January 1919 the Amur was divided into two parts, the area west of the Zeia River with headquarters at Serebriansk, that to the east at Krasnoiar.[56] By February

[54] *Semenov Hearings,* pp. 19–20.
[55] G. Reikhberg, "Partizany Dalnego Vostoka v Borbe s Iaponskoi Interventisiei," *op. cit.,* pp. 63ff.
[56] *Ibid.,* p. 65.

THE CIVIL WAR

1919 these groups together had forces numbering about 10,000. The Suchan development, already mentioned, was the chief partisan center for the Maritime Province as the Zeia organizations were for the Amur Province. These main headquarters as well as the many subsidiary centers of partisan activity were located back in the hills and the forests or in other places away from the railway lines.

In the course of 1919 the local partisan organizations were all coordinated in cantonal and regional groupings.[57] Each functional body was headed by a Revolutionary Staff which had general jurisdiction over all partisan activities in its area. It was through these staffs that the Bolshevik Party was able to guide the military activities of the local detachments. The staff maintained liaison between the various levels of command, issued orders, distributed information, and maintained a supply service for military and medical needs. In addition they carried on propaganda among the local people through lectures, supply of information, and the promotion of organizational work. A partisan newspaper, the *Partisan News,* published in the village of Frolovka in Suchan Valley, was edited by a partisan heroine, Klavdiia Ivanovna Zhuk.[58] In this way the Bolsheviks were given a unique opportunity to teach the class struggle in an area where it had previously meant little to the people.

As the struggle grew in violence, the popular support of the partisans increased in proportion. This, among other benefits, made the partisan supply problem easier. The people gave provisions, clothing, and shelter as well as pertinent information about the movements of the intervention armies and the various White forces. According to Reikhberg, the Japanese are supposed to have admitted that, "Every bush, every child, is a sleuth-hound for the partisans."[59] It was impossible to know who was a partisan or partisan

[57] *Ibid.,* p. 63; A. Iaremenko, "Partizanskoe Dvizhenie v Primorskoi Oblasti (1918–1920)," *Proletarskaia Revoliutsiia* (Moscow), No. 7, 1922, p. 73.
[58] Iaremenko, *loc. cit.,* p. 81.
[59] Reikhberg, *loc. cit.,* p. 63.

aide. The man who sauntered through a town as though on a shopping tour—meanwhile observing carefully all important developments—might be the one would lead a raid on an ammunition dump that night. All possessions of Whites or interventionists were potential supplies for the partisans. At the same time all movements of foreign or White Russian groups were of interest to the partisans. The child who played about the railway station might be gathering information about troop or supply movements. The torn-up track or the dynamite blast were the only evidence that the information thus gathered was accurate. How it was obtained was not known. Therefore, every Russian was a suspect to the anti-Bolshevik forces. To obtain the means of carrying out the widespread railway sabotage, for example, the support of the miners was important. The miners could smuggle their dynamite to the partisans with two results. In the first place, it would not be used for its intended purpose and would thus cut down the coal supply with which to run the railways. In the second place, it could be used to blow up bridges, railway beds, and water tanks and thus add in a direct way to the stoppage of railway service. It can be seen that working with the people was one of the central tasks of a partisan staff.

Another significant feature of the partisan warfare was the group cooperation which it both required and fostered. One observer has remarked about the group spirit and comradeship which made these guerrilla activities so successful.[60] It was his opinion that it grew out of the village life of the Russian people. Certainly the villages seemed always to act as a unit when engaged in any partisan activities, and they were likewise treated as a unit when there were any punishments to be meted out for these same activities. Punitive expeditions were sent into the villages in search of weapons, deserters from the White forces, members of the partisan bands, or information about them. It was usually found necessary to punish the whole village when these things were refused. All were implicated if any were. A treacher-

[60] J. Rickman, *op. cit.*, p. 15.

ous word from one member of the village meant punishment for all. This solidarity made it easy for partisan leaders to guide the mass activities toward specific goals. One such goal was the elimination of the Cossacks as a privileged class.[61] This goal was particularly popular since the Cossacks became so closely associated in the popular mind with the White Terror as carried out by Semenov, Kalmykov, and others and thus ultimately with the foreign interventionists who backed them. Such general goals were decided upon at the innumerable conferences and congresses held throughout the period. All partisan leaders and all major partisan activities had the sanction of a congress before they were accepted as official. Once given this sanction, they were accorded general support. In everything group consent and group cooperation were promoted.

In a general sense active resistance was carried on in the countryside while passive resistance was the rule in the city. It must always be borne in mind, however, that the direction of the movement and the general objectives were the same. In both cases, moreover, the centers of activity were well concealed. The widespread participation in the resistance movement which centered back in the hills or the villages off the railway line has already been noted. Fires in the fields might answer or precipitate a fire in the far hinterland.[62] That night a bridge or a railway bed might be found blown up. The underground in the cities was equally hard to locate or control.[63] This aspect of the partisan activity centered along the railway line and in such cities as Vladivostok and Harbin. Workers' houses were frequently searched for weapons just as the houses in the villages were and with the same cruel results if weapons were found to have been previously concealed. Labor unions were constantly watched and under suspicion. But sabotage in various forms occurred, nevertheless. Three major strikes, in May 1918, September 1918, and August 1919, were called

[61] Karpenko, op. cit., p. 25.
[62] Channing, op. cit., p. 175.
[63] Karpenko, op. cit., pp. 45, 62.

in the Chinese Eastern Railway zone. The inflation and consequent dislocation of wages and prices was of course an important factor in these strikes. But the political element was also prominent. In many cases of urban or railway troubles the workers simply fled to the hills and joined the active resistance.

One of the interesting features of the partisan struggle was the participation in it of non-Russian peoples. Many of the natives as well as the Chinese living in Eastern Siberia whose part in the Russian life of the area had been tenuous before this time joined the forces or aided them with food, clothing, and shelter. The Koreans in particular were strong supporters of the movement.[64] They had a partisan detachment of their own and fought in close cooperation with the Russian forces. Many prisoners of war joined the bands, especially those from Austria and Hungary, besides some of the Czech prisoners who had become Communists. The influence of the struggle was also reflected in the American and Japanese armies, where some of the soldiers showed noticeable sympathy for the Bolshevik cause. It was reported, for example, that a whole company of Japanese troops became infected with Bolshevism and were placed aboard the warship *Mikasa* and taken out to sea and shot.[65] Even beyond the borders of Siberia, in other parts of the Far East, the struggle in Siberia was reflected and there were marked signs of discontent with the colonialism which characterized the international position of so many of the people there. Revolutionary uprisings occurred, for example, in Korea in March 1919. In China the general dissatisfaction with the settlements at the Paris Peace Conference resulted in a boycott against Japan and other demonstrations of revolt. In spite of the separate origin of these activities Bolsheviks have seen in them expressions of sympathy for the struggle in Siberia.[66] Whether or not this was strictly true, it can at least be said that the circumstances which produced the various forms of revolt were very similar.

[64] Iaremenko, *loc. cit.*, p. 79.
[65] A. N. Iaremenko, "Dnevnik Kommunista," *op. cit.*, p. 41.
[66] Shurygin and Karpenko, *op. cit.*, p. 116.

As a prelude to these final stages of the conflict, the partisans had for some months before the final victory been gaining considerable ground and clearing large areas of enemy forces. By the summer of 1919, the Suchan Valley and Olga District (uezd) in which it was situated were almost entirely cleared of White military elements.[67] A Soviet wireless dispatch of September 24, 1919 claimed that on that date most of the railway between Irkutsk and Blagoveshchensk was in partisan hands.[68] This claim could be very close to the truth since it is known that by this time Semenov was suffering from considerable defection of his forces—some ordinary desertions and some going over to the Red side. It is also known that for long periods of time the railroad in this sector was almost impassable because of partisan activities. By the end of January things had reached a point where the partisan forces were able to march into Vladivostok with American, Japanese, and other troops standing by observing without raising a finger to stop them.

The partisan activities, which had from the start been concentrated on the sole objective of driving out all foreign or domestic forces opposed to the Soviet regime, culminated in a series of triumphs during the first two months of 1920. In those months the defeat of Kolchak and the decision of the Allies to withdraw also forced the Japanese to make at least a token withdrawal to the coast. As they left, the Bolsheviks assumed control and placed in power those whom they deemed it prudent to support. At Verkhne-Udinsk the government was formed by a compromise group known as the "Political Center" and was headed by Alexander Krasnoshchekov.[69] At Blagoveshchensk the most openly Bolshevik Government, that headed by Trelisser, was established for the Amur area. At Vladivostok most of the surviving zemstvo group were returned to their administrative positions under the former president, Medvedev. This in turn meant the elimination of the White military leaders such as

[67] Iaremenko, *loc. cit.*, p. 74.
[68] Coates and Coates, *op. cit.*, p. 226.
[69] M. Pavlovich, "Yaponskii Imperialism na Dalnem Vostoke," *op. cit.*, p. 23.

Rozanov at Vladivostok, Kalmykov at Khabarovsk, and Kuznetsov at Blagoveshchensk. These activities occurred during January and February 1920 under the protection of the partisans, who now boldly entered the cities to accomplish what was, for the most part, a series of bloodless overturns. In Transbaikal the struggle lasted somewhat longer. Semenov did not abandon that province until the fall of 1920.

One of the most unfortunate events of the closing period of this first phase of the civil war was the career of a partisan detachment which, toward the end of 1919, started down the Amur River from Khabarovsk under the command of Yakov Ivanovich Triapitsyn.[70] Formerly a metal worker in a Petrograd factory, Triapitsyn had been drafted into the army and served as a noncommissioned officer through the First World War. In 1918 he appeared in the Russian Far East and, although not a member of the Communist Party, he served with considerable distinction as a partisan leader in Eastern Siberia.

Having gained a reputation as an effective leader who could inspire considerbale sacrifice from those under his command, Triapitsyn was chosen in November 1919 to be the leader of an expedition which would advance down the Amur River toward Nikolaevsk. Starting with a nucleus of only ten men, he gathered others around him as he moved along the Amur until his force eventually numbered some 1,500 Russian, 200 Korean, and 300 Chinese partisans.[71] As he advanced toward Nikolaevsk, Triapitsyn defeated and drove before him the White Guard detachments sent out to prevent his approach to the city. As he drew near to the fortress of Chnyrrakh in the vicinity of Nikolaevsk, the partisan leaders decided to negotiate and sent a party into the fortress for this purpose. But, finding that the men sent to negotiate were murdered by the White Russians, the partisans proceeded to kill all the hostages in their hands and to surround and lay seige to the fortress and the city. In early February 1920 the Japanese and White Russian troops retired from

[70] Karpenko, *op. cit.*, p. 97; Varneck and Fisher, *op. cit.*, pp. 336ff.
[71] Miliukov, *op. cit.*, p. 330.

the fortress. Triapitsyn moved in and began to bombard the city from there. On February 24 negotiations were opened and four days later a peace was signed after which the partisans entered the city.

The city of Nikolaevsk, it should be noted, was strategically located near the mouth of the Amur River, where the fishing industry had long made it a flourishing center of considerable economic importance. Among its 15,000 people there was a prosperous Japanese group of about 350, including a certain Petr Nikolaevich Shimada, a millionaire known as the "King of Nikolaevsk." Since their acquisition of nearby southern Sakhalin in 1905, the Japanese had prosecuted their fishing interests in Nikolaevsk with such aggressive tactics as to bring themselves into general disrepute among the working classes and small business people. The larger Russian businessmen, on the other hand, were looked upon by most members of the community as close collaborators with the Japanese in the monopolistic conduct of the fishing business. Under these circumstances the revolution of November 1917 found the Russian and Japanese capitalists already separated from the rest of the community by a clear line of demarcation on one side of which was a considerable residue of hatred against the domestic and foreign monopolists. Furthemore, when Japanese troops arrived in the spring or summer of 1918 they functioned in close cooperation with the White Russian detachments which began to be formed for the protection of the upper business classes, thus preserving a social structure which was a natural target for Bolshevik agitators and organizers.

It can thus be seen that the economic life of Nikolaevsk had provided a good popular base for the Soviet Government established there in the spring of 1918. But the arrival of Japanese troops and the formation of White Guard detachments served not only to break up the new administration but also to institute the same reign of terror as was then being carried out in other parts of Siberia and thus fan the flames of popular hatred to an even higher degree than before. Under these circumstances it is easy to understand why a small Japanese garrison would have reason to be concerned about its safety and why the partisan forces under Triapitsyn were so well received by the people.

At about the time of the arrival of Triapitsyn, the Japanese had already decided upon a reoccupation of strategic points in Eastern Siberia, undoubtedly including Nikolaevsk, as soon as the Allies had withdrawn their troops from there. This fact may account for the complete disregard on the part of the Japanese Government of warnings and urgent requests for help sent by representatives in Nikolaevsk.[72] Such warnings, sent by the Japanese consul on January 7 and again on January 26, stressed the dangerous position of the small Japanese garrison in a rising tide of partisan and Bolshevik activity. Under the circumstances, it is difficult to avoid the conclusion that, in view of the previously determined program of the Japanese, an incident would not have been considered unwelcome in Tokyo.

On the other hand, the terrible destruction presently carried out by the partisans was strongly influenced by the aggressive activities of the Japanese forces operating elsewhere—activities about which the partisans became aware through wireless reception. They knew, for example, that following the departure of the Allied forces the Japanese had, by a series of closely coordinated moves during the night of April 4–5, 1920, reestablished their military authority at strategic points throughout the Maritime Province. From this time on it was considered by the partisans to be only a question of time until Japanese forces—whether by land or sea was uncertain—would arrive to settle once and for all the question of authority in Nikolaevsk.

Meanwhile, at Nikolaevsk the Japanese detachment, numbering some 300 men in addition to some Russian forces, had reconsidered their arrangements with the partisans and had decided to stage a counterattack against them, which took the form of a surprise attack carried out on the morning of March 12. The surprise gave the Japanese and White Russians an advantage in the early part of the fight. But in

[72] Varneck and Fisher, *op. cit.*, pp. 370–371.

time one after another of the four strongest points held by the Japanese were taken. The storming of the Japanese consulate by the partisans on March 15 was the last important military event of this struggle. On the following day the 136 surviving Japanese at the stone barracks in Nikolaevsk surrendered and the attack was over. Thereafter a Soviet Government was organized and an Executive Committee was chosen which, along with Triapitsyn in the role of Military Commissar, constituted the administrative authority in the city.

In addition to the already existing problem of obtaining from Vladivostok adequate food supplies for a region with a population of some 30,000 including the city, the month of April introduced for the inexperienced Soviet Government new problems and sources of irritation. There was the Japanese attack of April 4–5 in the Maritime Province. Then, on April 6, came the declaration of independence of the new Far Eastern Republic, a government which was outwardly liberal and which, therefore, in the absence of better understanding of its real role and purpose for existing, aroused on the part of the members of the Soviet Government at Nikolaevsk a profound sense of both disappointment and opposition.[73] In addition, news of the imminent arrival of a Japanese relief force was received from various sources. Furthermore, all available information about Japanese activities elsewhere indicated that their arrival would certainly mean a terrible revenge upon the partisans for the defeat they had inflicted upon the Japanese within the city.[74]

The hasty and panicky preparations for defense which the Soviet Government at Nikolaevsk proceeded to make resulted in an international incident of the greatest importance. Preliminary skirmishes between the partisan outposts and the Japanese approaching the city indicated the complete inadequacy of the former to cope with the incipient attack. The Soviet leaders thereupon began to prepare for the defense by evacuating noncombatants and organizing the rest

[73] Norton, *op. cit.*, pp. 278–279.
[74] *A Short Outline of the History of the Far Eastern Republic,* p. 14.

for action. According to some estimates, about 6,000 persons either were evacuated or left the city of their own accord. A reign of terror began under the direction of Triapitsyn in the course of which the city was destroyed and many were killed. Later reports fixed upon May 25 as the day when the Japanese civilians of Nikolaevsk were reputedly exterminated by the partisans. According to some reports, the dead numbered about 3,000 although more conservative estimates placed the number of those who lost their lives at about 350 civilians and 306 soldiers.[75]

For the future of Japanese-Soviet relations, the significance of these events lies in the fact that the massacres are, by all accounts, attributed directly to Triapitsyn, a partisan leader, and that among those murdered were all of the Japanese civilians as well as soldiers who had surrendered on March 16 and had been placed under arrest since then. With the massacre of their nationals by a Soviet leader, the Japanese proceeded to extract every possible ounce of propaganda value from the affair. In early June the Japanese forces arrived in Nikolaevsk and made a complete report to Tokyo. After this news had reached Japan, every means of arousing the Japanese public to a sense of hostility against the partisans was used by the Imperial Government.[76] The useful slogan, "Do not forget May 25" was said to have been found on a surviving wall in the city, presumably written by one of the murdered Japanese civilians. This was strongly and ominously reminiscent of such famous battle cries of the past as "Remember the Alamo" and "Remember the Maine." General Sato naïvely confirmed the suspicions already aroused in this respect when he declared: "The blood of only two men secured the lease of Kiaochau. . . . We do not mean to make the most of the blood of 600 people who came to a miserable end at Nikolaevsk, but something must be done that the spirits of those victims may go to rest." Liberal

---

[75] Miliukov, *op. cit.*, p. 332; *Foreign Relations, 1920*, II, p. 515.

[76] Stewart, *op. cit.*, p. 338; M. M. Sherower, "The Nikolaevsk 'Massacre,' " *The Nation* (New York), CXI, No. 2877, August 21, 1920, pp. 211–213.

THE CIVIL WAR

groups in Japan did nothing to quiet the spirits of either
living or dead when they declared that the whole episode
was a frame-up engineered by the Japanese expansionists.
The latter, meanwhile, carried on their war-mongering
propaganda with every resource at their disposal in the hope
of using the Nikolaevsk incident to recapture in the minds
of the Japanese public the excuse for intervention which the
alleged aid to Kolchak and the Czech Legion had once provided. Public meetings and parades were widely held. In a
single day, three million leaflets were distributed by the
school children of Tokyo. The newspaper *Kokumin* offered
prizes for the composition of war songs. On June 24 a cere-
mony was held in the Japanese capital in honor of those who
had died at Nikolaevsk with the apparent purpose of making
national heroes of them. In spite of the fact that the popular
response to all this was unenthusiastic, the Japanese Government announced on July 3 the price the Russian people
would be called upon to pay for the Nikolaevsk incident—
the occupation of northern Sakhalin and of Nikolaevsk along
with the whole Siberian coast from the Sea of Okhotsk to the
Korean border. Throughout the Washington Conference
as well as the conferences held almost simultaneously at
Dairen and later at Chang Chun between the representatives
of Japan and the Far Eastern Republic, the question of compensation for the Nikolaevsk massacre remained in the forefront of all Japanese claims.

Besides the loss suffered through renewed Japanese aggression, the Far Eastern Republic also suffered the loss of the
economically valuable city of Nikolaevsk and of prestige due
to the participation of a partisan leader in an outrage so
impossible to excuse. How complete was the destruction of
Nikolaevsk can be seen from the report of a Russian journal-
ist who went there in July 1920 to investigate.[77] He wrote:
"Everywhere, as far as eye could reach, there were only
ruins of houses; here and there lonely house chimneys, the
tall chimney of the blown-up electric plant, half sunken vessels. . . . Only on the outskirts of the town was smoke

[77] Varneck and Fisher, *op. cit.,* pp. 354–355.

coming from the chimneys of houses that had fortunately survived. . . . Almost no inhabitants were seen."

After his frenzied burning and blowing up of houses and other buildings of the city as well as the hurried massacre of the people, Triapitsyn tried to escape by fleeing westward. At the town of Kerbi, some miles southwest of Nikolaevsk, he was captured by other partisans and brought to trial by the Far Eastern Republic before a People's Court, the chairman of which was Anton Zakharovich Ovchinnikov, the village sexton whose forcible entrance into Kolchak's army two years before has already been described. Since Ovchinnikov had been a partisan commander with Triapitsyn at Nikolaevsk, he was well aware of the tragic events that had occurred there. Triapitsyn and twenty-five others were sentenced to death and were shot on July 25, 1920, three weeks too late to forestall the Japanese retaliation. Incidentally, it might be added that Ovchinnikov escaped from the turmoil of Siberia in January 1921 and made his way to the United States by way of Vladivostok and Shanghai.

The role of the railways of Siberia, so crucial in the maintenance of the economic life of the area during peacetime, was equally significant in undermining the economic structure during the harsh conditions of the civil war and intervention. The railways were of primary importance in the growth and development of Russia as a Far Eastern power, in the imperialistic penetration of the Far East by Japan and the Western European powers, and, finally, in the Japanese-American rivalry which bade fair to determine the future political and economic status of Siberia. It is therefore not surprising that during the civil war the major efforts of the partisans—and behind them the Bolsheviks—were concentrated on preventing the use of the railways by their enemies. It was their supreme strategic device for accomplishing the purpose for which they had been organized. By concentrating on it they hoped to disrupt the entire program of the interventionists and the anti-Bolshevik military and political groups. Fortunately, the chairman of the strike committee which carried out the strike on the Chinese Eastern

Railway in September 1918 has left his own version of the strike as well as his evaluation of it. The strike itself lasted less than two weeks and was broken up by the Japanese and Czechs. Yet he felt it had a number of important results.[78] In his opinion, it delayed activity on the railway for about twelve days, made the workers more class conscious, demonstrated that the workers would follow the Bolsheviks, eliminated the influence of the Mensheviks and Socialist Revolutionaries among the workers, and, finally, united the workers for future strikes whose ultimate goal would be the destruction of Kolchak. The long-range view and the clear-cut objective are obvious.

After the conclusion of the civil war, estimates were made of the damage done to the railways, one of the principal targets for partisan activity. Estimates of this damage vary greatly.[79] But the differences in such matters are unavoidable and leave the picture of the widespread destruction unmodified. Karpenko estimates that 826 bridges were blown up by one or another of the participants in the civil war. This includes the 420-foot bridge over the Amur at Khabarovsk which was not replaced until sometime after 1922. In addition, twenty railway stations and fourteen water supply stations were blown up. There is no estimate on another important item—the number of times tracks were removed or blown to bits. All railway delays, whether produced by the partisans or their opponents, in the end played a major role in bringing about the defeat of Kolchak and those who supported him.

While the partisan forces found the rationale for their activities in the theories and slogans of Communism, the Orthodox Church in a sense played the same role among the counter-revolutionary forces. Each successive step in the development of the revolution was reflected in the efforts of the clergy to counterbalance the losses of the established order.

[78] V. K. Iliushin, "Stachka na K.V. Zh.D. v 1918g," *Istoriia Proletariata S.S.S.R.* (Moscow), No. 2, 1934, p. 184.

[79] Karpenko, *op. cit.*, p. 61; The Special Delegation of the Far Eastern Republic to the United States of America, *Trade and Industries of the Far Eastern Republic*, Washington, 1922, pp. 16–17.

In the summer and fall of 1917 the bishop of Transbaikal launched a program for the organization of parochial societies to combat the growing political disorder.[80] Then in February 1918 a directive was issued by Patriarch Tikhon and a church assembly which called for a general program of anti-Bolshevik activity. The church took a strong stand against the recognition of the Treaty of Brest-Litovsk and the policy of separation of church and state. These views were fully implemented by the church in the Far East where priests refrained from cooperation with the Soviet regime both by the hostile sermons which they preached and by their refusal to disclose information regarding births, marriages, and deaths. Instructions were issued from diocesan centers for assisting the priests in combatting the Bolshevik advance while pamphlets were distributed among the people for the same purpose. The Old Believer sectarians, who were particularly hostile to the Soviet regime, published the anti-Bolshevik Far Eastern Old Believer as one of their contributions to the struggle.

This anti-Soviet orientation of the church was implemented by active cooperation in a number of ways with the White forces. The priests, while refusing to share the information at their disposal with the Soviets, shared it liberally with the Whites. The monastaries and churches were centers of counterrevolutionary activity. This policy, entirely normal for a church so closely associated with the old regime and so clearly threatened by the Bolshevik doctrines, had the unfortunate effect of bringing the activities of the priesthood into close relationship with the Cossack leaders as well as with the Japanese promoters of confusion. Thus, when Semenov took Chita in 1918, special public services of thankfulness were held to commemorate the event. A similar service was held for Kalmykov upon his arrival in Khabarovsk in September 1918. Matching their words with equally definite activities, the Old Believers supported the White cause by joining the armies and by helping to supply and support them. The Old Believer villages of Kamenka,

[80] Kandidov, *op. cit.*, pp. 22ff.

294

Iakovlevka, Petropavlovsk, and others gave strong support to the Whites not only by giving weapons, shoes, and clothing but also by helping to hunt partisans in their immediate vicinity. All this cooperation was, of course, bitterly resented by the Bolsheviks. On January 11, 1923 Bishop Safron of Chita and Anatolii Popov, the secretary of the Trans-Baikal diocesan council, were arrested on charges of having carried on espionage during 1919.

In the course of the struggle in Eastern Siberia a number of personalities acquired considerable prominence because they had supplied the partisan forces with leadership, inspiration, or just zeal for their work. One of the most outstanding leaders of the partisan movement was Sergei Georgievich Lazo.[81] He was born in 1894 and before the war had been a student in St. Petersburg Technological Institute. He served as an officer during the war and later served the Soviet Government in Siberia in a military capacity. As a partisan leader he functioned especially in the Suchan Valley and along the Suchan branch railway. He was, in fact, the president of the Revolutionary Staff of Olga District (uezd) in which Suchan was situated. After the partisan entry into Vladivostok on January 31, 1920 he became a member of the Provisional Government established there. During the Japanese attack of April 4 and 5, 1920 he and other members of the Military Soviet of Vladivostok, Sibirtsev, and Lutsky were arrested by the Japanese. Later he and his two companions were taken out by the Japanese and burned in a locomotive. His statue now stands in the Central Museum of the Red army.

There are many others whose names appear throughout the literature on the civil war. There was Umansky, whose murder near Harbin by the Orlov band precipitated the strike of 1918. There were Gubelman and Postyshev, both prewar party leaders who were prominent in the organizational and propagandistic work in the civil war. There were Iaremenko and Slinkin, school teachers from the Maritime

[81] *Trade and Industries of the Far Eastern Republic,* pp. 114, 117; Karpenko, *op. cit.,* p. 161.

295

Province who were active propagandists and organizers from the very start. Shumiatsky was a military commissar at Irkutsk when the Soviet first assumed power there in 1917; he acquired a reputation among his opponents as a braggart and generally undesirable character. Kryzhanovsky and Pika were two elderly peasants who were shot together but advocated resistance to the young people with their last breath and so lived on in the Bolshevik records as examples of undying loyalty to their cause. These people and many others were leaders or martyrs of the Bolshevik struggle to recapture their lost position in Eastern Siberia. In the official propaganda of the time, the Bolshevik cause was the rescue of Russian territory from traitorous Russian elements who were attempting, with the aid of international imperialism, to snatch away the country from the people and hand it back to a reactionary government which would be dependent upon foreign governments for support and therefore subservient to them. The Bolshevik cause was therefore identified in all propaganda with patriotism itself. This was the line, it will be recalled, which the Soviet Government in Moscow established at the first signs of the coming of intervention to Siberia.

CHAPTER 8

Eastern Siberia During the Civil War

THE clash of Allied interests in Siberia aggravated an already confused situation. The breakdown of governmental control rendered difficult the smooth functioning of an economy so largely dependent upon a single form of transportation and so closely tied to the economy of Eurpean Russia thousands of miles away. The American Government had taken the lead in attempting to preserve intact this important line of communications. But by this very act it aroused antagonisms among the Allies which in turn decreased the possibilities of using the railway to bring relief to Russia by satisfying her commercial needs. Proposals to apply economic remedies to economic ills were not wanting. American observers in Russia and some American leaders at home realized and sympathized with this approach. But the circumstances operated to place this relatively simple solution beyond reach. The result was that the confusion, which had been great enough initially, grew even worse as time went on. In Eastern Siberia the Japanese hoped to use the resulting chaos to promote their own economic if not political supremacy there. In the long run, the condition by which the Japanese had hoped to benefit—economic and political chaos—only made more certain the very thing they feared most—the triumph of the Soviet Government in the struggle for Eastern Siberia.

In an earlier chapter the historical developments of economic life in Siberia was described. The building of the railway across Siberia and North Manchuria was the most significant economic fact in the life of these regions. Before this event, life had been localized and had remained more or less on the level of a natural economy. The railway, however, made possible the settlement of additional population, the regional specialization of production, and the exchange

297

of goods over extensive areas. It was under these circumstances that Siberia as it was in 1918 had developed and had remained an economic appanage of European Russia. The output of wheat and dairy products in Western Siberia and of fish in Eastern Siberia grew up in response to the improved transportation which made available Siberian as well as Russian and other European markets. Moreover, the insufficient development of industrial enterprise was in part due to the availability of manufactured articles from non-Siberian sources by means of the railway and, to a lesser extent, the shipping lines.

The outstanding economic fact of the period of the civil war and intervention was the breakdown of this necessary link. An expert witness, comparing the period of the war with that of the civil war and intervention which followed, has described the conditions on the railway as follows: "Where production had only been impeded or halted, it was now totally disorganized. The railway was no longer a chain linking the whole continent. It was broken up into separate segments, each segment used as a military weapon by some upstart general or brigand."[1] The traditional tie with European Russia was broken and each of its parts was separated from the other. The port of Vladivostok and the shipping lanes to European Russia, Britain, and other traditional commercial outlets were closed.[2] Manufactured articles for the nonmilitary population were made and imported into Siberia in increasingly smaller quantities. Agricultural implements as well as machinery and machine parts—the two chief articles of import from the United States before the war—were at first brought to Vladivostok. But as time went on, priorities on the railroad favored military necessities to the almost total exclusion of these and other important but nonmilitary articles.

[1] C. H. Smith, "Four Years of Mistakes in Siberia," *Asia* (New York), XXII, No. 6, June 1922, p. 482.
[2] A. Bonch-Osmolovsky, "Vneshniaia Torgovlia Dalnego Vostoka za Vremia Voiny i Revoliutsii," *Novyi Vostok* (Moscow), No. 5, 1924, pp. 156ff.

In the wake of these developments followed the usual ills of economic collapse: dwindling commerce, speculation, inflation, rising cost of living, and the fall of general purchasing power. Shoes, watches, candles, and other basic necessities became unobtainable. Food became scarce and starvation appeared. The Cossack chiefs such as Semenov, Kalmykov, and others moved across this grim scene like the riders of the apocalypse. With the help of the Japanese they used their military strength to control the economic life of the area. The goods captured from others or those which came from favored producers in Japan were sold on terms suitable to the Whites and Japanese and, in many cases, in their own retail stores. They were thus able to benefit almost exclusively from the inflationary conditions that prevailed in such an area as Transbaikal, which depended wholly on the railway. The Maritime Province maintained a relatively higher standard of economic life than the other provinces.[3] It was nearer to the port of Vladivostok, suffered comparatively fewer atrocities during the civil war since it was more open to general Allied scrutiny, and, in addition, was able to keep its production and export at a higher level.

One of the significant results of the rapid economic deterioration of Siberia was the decline of commercial relations with North Manchuria and the tendency of the latter under the inducements offered by Japan to turn away from Siberia and seek markets, sources of supply, and financial support in South Manchuria or Japan. Manchuria had from the beginning of Russian settlement in the Far East been closely associated economically with Eastern Siberia. The latter had always made up its shortage of grain and cattle by shipments from North Manchuria and Mongolia. But the breakdown of transport and of purchasing power in Siberia cut down this traffic very severely.[4] As a result, the industrial enterprises of North Manchuria lost to a very large extent their northern markets. At the same time, disruption of the railways and the Vladivostok as a commercial port deprived

[3] *Ibid.*, p. 162.
[4] Chinese Eastern Railway Company, *op. cit.*, pp. 18–19.

the producers of North Manchuria of their outlet through the Maritime Province. This situation proved an open invitation to Japanese commercial and financial expansion into North Manchuria. The expansion of the economy of Japan during the war had resulted in an enlarged internal market capable of absorbing some of the Manchurian products formerly shipped into the Russian Far East. Furthermore, the economy of South Manchuria could be greatly enhanced by linking it with North Manchuria, an operation which would at the same time disrupt the economy of Eastern Siberia and prepare that region for rescue at the hands of the Japanese. It was with these objectives in mind that the Japanese opened a deliberate campaign calculated to orient the commerce of North Manchuria away from Siberia and toward Dairen. In time they did, in fact, succeed in establishing in North Manchuria trade relations, credit facilities, and commercial habits more suitable to the new situation. This action helped to produce the decline in the trade of Vladivostok which some feared would become permanent. Thus one observer noted that the goods awaiting export at Vladivostok had by February 1920 been reduced to something between one fourteenth to one twentieth of the prewar figure.[5]

The commercial decline of Vladivostok, to be sure, also reflects the developments in Eastern Siberia itself. It has been estimated that the industrial output of this area was reduced by about fifty percent between 1913 and 1923.[6] Fishing came largely into the hands of the Japanese. Lumbering was also carried on by the Japanese in an even more wasteful manner than under the Russians. The flour-milling center at Blagoveshchensk, which had depended to a large extent upon the grain of North Manchuria, was considerably reduced in output. Fortunately, the three remaining major industrial centers of Eastern Siberia—those at Vladivostok, Nikolsk-Ussuriisk, and Khabarovsk—were located in the Maritime Province,

[5] W. Irving, "Business Conditions in Siberia," *The New York Times Current History*, xiv, No. 3, June 1921, p. 475.
[6] Kireev, *op. cit.*, p. 10.

where the reduction of output was relatively less than elsewhere. Soap factories, breweries, sawmills, and other small industries managed to keep up some activity even during the worst of the fighting.

As for the agricultural output, the reduction in the area under cultivation was considerable but not by any means disastrous. An estimate of this change made for Amur Province places the area cultivated in 1918 at 1,655,919 acres as compared with 1,490,331 for 1919.[7] Also available stocks were found to be rather high in the wheat-producing areas. In the summer of 1918 it was estimated that in Western Siberia alone there was a surplus from the 1917 crop of 3,000,000 to 3,500,000 short tons.[8] This crop of course could not be moved at that time because of the Czech rising. The total grain production in Amur Province was reduced by about one fourth, and it is possible that this figure may represent the proportion in all but the areas where the most continual fighting took place. Moreover, surpluses of grain were produced in spite of the shortage of binder twine and the breakdown of agricultural machinery due to the impossibility of obtaining spare parts. In March 1919 information available at the Paris Peace Conference showed that in Western and Central Siberia and the Amur region there was an available surplus of 2,114,000 tons of grain.[9] In addition, there were the following items: 10,000 tons of fish at Vladivostok; 70,000,000 eggs and 1,800 tons of cheese at Irkutsk; 23,850 tons of butter and 13,860 tons of meat scattered at points between Irkutsk and Kurgan.

But the breakdown in transportation and in the currency system made these items unavailable to a population that was at this very moment suffering from starvation in a number of places. As Colonel Ward passed through the Maritime Province in 1918 he noted "hundreds of miles" of unharvested grain left standing in the fields to rot.[10] The un-

---

[7] *Trade and Industry of the Far Eastern Republic,* p. 44.
[8] *Foreign Relations, 1918, Russia,* III, p. 131.
[9] Miller, *op. cit.,* XVI, p. 232.
[10] Ward, *op. cit.,* pp. 66–67.

availability of farm labor and the general uncertainty of life at the time had, of course, much to do with this situation. But there was also another cause of this economic confusion, one which exemplifies so well the serious social breakdown which resulted from the civil war. In August 1919 General Graves notes that there were then some 27,000 tons of stored food which had spoiled because no one was interested enough in moving it to bribe the regional railway board.[11] It is not surprising that under these circumstances security from almost any source would seem welcome to the people with business interests. Speaking of these conditions as he saw them in early 1920, Walter Irving wrote: "The foreign business man, be he Japanese, British, American or French, feels that his business and capital are safe from nationalization and requisition only as long as the Japanese forces remain here . . . ."[12] It has already been seen, however, that the presence of the Japanese, far from being a cure for the economic chaos in Siberia, was in fact one of its basic causes. The Japanese had not come to Siberia to expend their accumulated wartime financial surplus for the benefit of foreign business interests or, for that matter, for the enhancement of Russian business.

The role of the currency depreciation in the deterioration of the Siberian economy can easily be surmised from the facts already discussed. The currency depreciation reduced the buying power of the people as the shortages of all types of trade goods increased. As the purchasing power of the ruble decreased the peasants became more and more reluctant to part with the farm surplus so badly needed to combat the growing shortages. Raids conducted on the villages to enforce requisitions of grain were always a source of political strength to the party not associated with their execution. The decline of purchasing power also resulted in demands for wage increases by the railway and other workers. These demands in turn could be organized and turned to political account by the Bolsheviks.

[11] W. S. Graves, *op. cit.*, p. 243.
[12] Irving, *loc. cit.*, p. 473.

The multitude of paper currencies was one of the many undesirable features of the successive governments which appeared and disappeared in Siberia. There were notes issued by the Imperial Government as well as by the Kerensky, Soviet, Horvath, Kolchak, and other governments which at one time or another aspired to supremacy in Siberia. Later came the currencies of the Verkhne-Udinsk, Blagoveshchensk, and Vladivostok governments. In addition, there were United States and Chinese dollars as well as Japanese yen. The hesitancy of the British and French to add their own currencies to the confusion was apparently based upon the expectation of effectuating the plan for a division of Russia into spheres of influence, leaving the United States and Japan to work out the division of spheres in Siberia.[13] The financial situation was even more confused by the fact that vouchers issued by such large firms as Kunst and Albers circulated as money.[14]

Another feature of the decline of the currency was the deliberate inflation which was practiced. Since there was a shortage of actual money, inflation was almost inevitable from the beginning. Moreover, the money printed by the Kolchak Government was printed on such cheap paper that it was easily duplicated and therefore resulted in the growth of counterfeiting. Bank notes printed in the United States were ordered by Kolchak but delivered too late to remedy the situation. In addition, it was charged that the Bolsheviks deliberately printed money in order to flood the markets. An American proposal in December 1918 to remedy this condition by establishing an international ruble guaranteed by the Associated Governments was not acted upon. Instead, the way was left open for the Japanese to try to force their special yen, the "headquarters note," upon Siberia.

The chaotic inflation which resulted made the position of the wage-earner deplorable and rendered the task of the railway management as well as other necessary business enterprises extremely difficult. In September 1918 the ruble, for-

[13] *Peace Conference Papers,* ii, p. 474.
[14] Horvath, *op. cit.,* Ch. xv.

merly worth fifty cents, had been reduced to ten cents.[15] By October 1920 it was quoted at 2,500 to the dollar.[16] Yamasaki and Ogawa, two Japanese economists, have estimated the decline in terms of the number of rubles exchangeable for one hundred yen.[17] The number of rubles exchangeable for one hundred yen was 535 in January 1919, 7,995 in December 1919, 5,795 in January 1920, and 39,250 in December 1920. This gives some idea of the fluctuation over about the same period covered by the above estimate in dollars. General Graves has translated this deterioration of money into terms which give a good idea of its meaning to the working people of Siberia. He has estimated that the average value of the salaries paid to railway conductors and engineers during the period of Kolchak was about $3.75 a month. This fact explains one of the chief problems faced by the American railway men and why, besides its economic implications, the depreciation of money values had such important political meaning. The same fact explains why payments in gold and concessions on natural resources are so frequently mentioned in proposed agreements between the Allies and the Russian governments.

The tendency of Japan to use to the full every opportunity to increase the value of her economic spheres of interest on the Asiatic continent was the most important of the many forces operating to produce a condition of absolute chaos in Siberia. The objective, insofar as relations with Russia were concerned, assumed two general forms: the effort to attract commercial activities away from North Manchuria and Siberia in order to enhance the economic strength of the city of Dairen in South Manchuria, and the drive to increase Japan's trade with Asiatic Russia. The first of these has already been described as one of the causes of the commercial decline of Vladivostok. This rivalry between Dairen and Vladivostok, it should be noted, was a part of the general pattern of Russo-Japanese rivalry in the Far East long be-

[15] Graves, *op. cit.*, p. 244.
[16] *Foreign Relations,* 1920, III, p. 525.
[17] Yamasaki and Ogawa, *op. cit.*, pp. 142–145.

fore the outbreak of the First World War. The coming of the war brought, not a break in this developmental pattern, but an increased tempo in the Japanese effort to achieve a trade monopoly. It was this pressure, exerted at a time of Russian decline, which would have led so logically to Japanese control, first of the Chinese Eastern Railway, and then of other Russian railways in the Far East. With the control of the railways, it was anticipated, there would in time follow all those things which fitted so naturally into the future structure of the Greater Japan of the New Inland Sea: the opportunity of tapping the trade of North Manchuria, Eastern, and even Western Siberia; the control of the natural resources of North Manchuria and Eastern Siberia; and the long-desired freedom of action in Mongolia.

The other and closely allied Japanese objective, the increase of her own trade with Asiatic Russia, was likewise an outgrowth of prewar conditions. It was, however, the business developments resulting directly from the outbreak of war which increased this trade to a point where it became a considerable item of Japanese foreign commerce. Between the years 1913 and 1916 Russo-Japanese trade increased thirteen times.[18] Even though this business was routed through Siberia, more than three quarters of it was with European Russia and most of it consisted of military supplies. But the idea of building a commercial outlet in Siberia or through Siberia had become an important factor in the minds of the Japanese business community. Hence, the withdrawal of Russia from the war, the breakdown of railway transportation, and the possible loss of an important market were developments of great importance to Japan. With the opening of the intervention, Japan prepared for an active campaign to increase her trade in Russia. Under the protection of her military forces she sent thousands of merchants and entrepreneurs into Siberia to secure the region as a sphere of economic control.[19] Under these circumstances, American

---

[18] Pavlovich, "Iaponskii Imperializm na Dalnem Vostoke," *op. cit.,* p. 44.
[19] C. H. Smith, "What Happened in Siberia," *op. cit.,* pp. 402–403.

efforts to control the railways or to conduct a form of relief by stimulating trade were only an added source of annoyance. Far from being prepared to cooperate in such undertakings, Japan made every effort to exclude the businessmen of all other nations.

By a liberal use of the strong-arm devices already indicated, Japan was able by 1922 to forge well ahead of her rival across the Pacific. By connivance with the military forces, customs duties were evaded, commercial consignments were passed through as Red Cross supplies, and the American orders were held up while cars loaded with Japanese shipments were expedited. When Semenov or one of the other military leaders confiscated something it was always of non-Japanese origin. In 1919, when trade in Siberia reached its highest point since before the revolution due to the sending of supplies to Kolchak, these methods had given Japan such an advantage that her export trade to Siberia was no less than five times that of the United States, while her imports from Siberia were sixteen times those of the United States.[20] In that same year the import, export, and transit trade of Manchuria with the surrounding Siberian provinces, while remaining below the standard of 1913, was between five and six times that of 1918.[21] But the destruction of this trade was beginning to show the effects of the Japanese efforts to secure control. Whereas in 1913 more than eighty percent of all goods leaving North Manchuria had gone to Vladivostok, by 1923 the trade had increased three times and over fifty-six percent of the total went to Dairen.[22]

The large increase of Japanese imports from Russia represents, at least to some extent, the natural resources which Japan needed so badly and took so liberally. The Japanese imports of Russian timber grew from one million cubic feet in 1916 to three million in 1919, five million in 1921, and twelve million in 1922. The rapid increase shown by the last figure is significant since it represents the wild grabbing for timber found necessary as the Japanese hold on Eastern

[20] Bonch-Osmolovsky, *op. cit.*, p. 159.
[21] *Ibid.*, p. 158.
[22] Conolly, *op. cit.*, pp. 83–84.

Siberia began to appear less secure.[23] Japan enormously increased her share in the fishing industry. Thus, in 1914 the Japanese production of crab was thirty percent of the Russian production. By 1924 it had grown to ninety-seven percent. In Sakhalin, Japan prepared to exploit the resources on an elaborate scale and, from all indications, on a permanent basis.[24] A company was organized to build a railway in the northern part of the island. A large syndicate of five firms was organized to participate in various industrial projects there. A Mitsubishi syndicate took over the exploitation of coal mines. Prospects of oil were investigated and exploitation was begun. Plans were made for the building of factories and railways on the mainland of Eastern Siberia. There is little doubt that the intervention, once carried out under American auspices, was intended to be permanent, without American participation if possible.

For a number of reasons the Far Eastern Republic, proclaimed officially on April 6, 1920, was scarcely able during its brief existence of hardly more than two and a half years to alter the prevailing economic conditions to any great extent. The retention of both Japanese and Semenov forces in the Transbaikal Province and the resultant fighting and turmoil during a large part of 1920 were major disruptive factors. So also were the Japanese occupation and control extended through the economically most important parts of the Maritime Province as well as along the Siberian coast up to the Sea of Okhotsk and the complete Japanese domination of the island of Sakhalin. Besides blocking off important commercial outlets, the occupation of these areas effectively cut off access to important sources of exchangeable food supplies such as meat in the Transbaikal Province, grain in the Maritime Province, and fish along the coast. As though the situation were not already difficult enough, a drought along the Amur River in 1921 reduced even further the already scanty food resources.[25] It was thus necessary to import such quantities of basic foods from Mongolia and Man-

[23] *Ibid.*, p. 45.
[24] Pavlovich, *op. cit.*, p. 21; A. M. Young, *op. cit.*, p. 261.
[25] Norton, *op. cit.*, p. 211.

churia as purchasing power and transportation facilities permitted.

Economic life under these circumstances was necessarily a struggle for bare existence. The maintenance of a standing army to protect the Republic was not only an item of great expense but it deprived the state of much-needed manpower. Great emphasis was placed upon the maintenance of such railway service as the importance of the railways would necessitate. But the chief problem in this case was the sheer inability of the state to pay the railway workers. The Minister of Transport, Vladimir Shatov, was a former labor organizer and, during his residence in the United States, had also been well known as an I.W.W. member and revolutionary agitator.[26] The workers could, therefore, hardly identify him with the "capitalists" against whom their slogans and strikes had so long been directed. The result was that he was able to ward off many incipient strikes by telling the prospective strikers that there was no money to pay them but that they could either continue to work for him or stop work and give the Japanese an excuse to reestablish themselves and then return to work for them at the point of a gun. Shatov also made a habit of posting slogans where the workers would see them constantly. There were such handy bits of advice as: "More miles more freight," or "You can't go far on rotten ties." His methods resulted in fairly good working conditions on very poor pay.

As a result of these methods, considerable progress was made in the restoration of the wrecked railway lines. Most of the bridges—with the notable exception of the large one over the Amur at Khabarovsk—were at least made usable on a temporary basis. Most of the freight cars were returned to use although this was by no means true of the passenger cars. The railway repair shops at Chita and Khabarovsk were restored to use.[27] There were even the beginnings of some necessary railway construction.[28] A short feeder line

[26] *Ibid.*, p. 184.
[27] O. Keith, "Re-birth of Industry and Commerce in Eastern Siberia," *The Far Eastern Review* (Shanghai), xviii, No. 2, February, 1922, pp. 127–129.
[28] Norton, *op. cit.*, p. 207.

was commenced between the smelter at Petrovsk-Zavod and the ore dumps, another to a lumber camp at Taltzinsk, and one to a coal mine at Hailiarta. There were also signs of recovery in the river transport service on both the Amur and the Sungari.

Unfortunately, however, even these brave beginnings were not duplicated in the fields of commerce and industry. Surpluses did not exist to support anything that could be called large-scale business. The fur catch was the most important available surplus. Had there been any capital as a means of exploiting them, gold and timber would have been two other easily available resources which could have stimulated trade. In April 1921 the Foreign Minister of the Far Eastern Republic addressed an urgent appeal to Secretary of State Hughes asking for capital with which to exploit these resources and thereby make the Republic able to withstand the Japanese pressure then being exerted with the object of forcing the Republic to make large concessions in exchange for economic assistance. This request constituted something of a dilemma for the American Government. For, while the preservation of the territorial integrity of Russia was the underlying reason for American interest in the Siberian intervention, the support of either the Japanese or the Soviets was equally objectionable. One salutary measure was instituted by the Republic which, had it been intended to continue as a separate political unit, would in the future have enhanced both the foreign and domestic commerce. This was the establishment by law of May 16, 1921 of a gold standard. This, it should be noted, was in contrast to the previous practice among Siberian governments of solving the monetary problems by the use of the printing press.[29] In the meantime, however, smaller commerce was the rule, mostly in the form of sales made by traveling Chinese merchants.

That there was, however, some improvement in economic conditions, not only in Eastern Siberia but also in North Manchuria, is shown by the reports of the railway Technical Board operating on the Chinese Eastern Railway. As early

[29] *Ibid.,* p. 215.

as the summer of 1920 it was evident that the decline in military traffic and the return to commercial business was having a salutary effect on the railway situation. Earnings began to exceed disbursements by 500,000 gold rubles during July 1920.[30] Both tonnage and earnings continued to rise in the succeeding months as the military situation cleared. Then in June 1922 came the blow that those close to the scene had perhaps anticipated. Japan engineered the signing of a tariff agreement between the management of the Chinese Eastern Railway and the South Manchurian Railway, the latter a Japanese firm, which gave Japanese interests the power to decide the tariff schedules between the two lines and, according to the interpretation given to the agreement by John Stevens, also gave these same Japanese interests the power over the control and marketing of the entire soya bean crop of North Manchuria.[31] This, Stevens explained, was a violation of the "open door" policy of the worst kind since it practically gave the Japanese the power to determine the world price of soya beans. Moreover, it threatened to negate all the efforts of the railway experts. Before 1914, 80 percent of the exports of North Manchuria had been shipped over the Chinese Eastern Railway to Vladivostok. During the war and civil war this figure had been reduced to 10 percent. During the past year or so this amount had been raised again to 70 percent. Now, at the stroke of a pen, all of these gains would be cancelled unless something were done.

The Cooperative Societies were one of the only truly constructive factors in the economic life of Siberia. Their great strength lay in the membership they enjoyed among the more prosperous farmers. They included also many urban and industrial workers, but their business amounted to only about thirty percent of the total business turnover of the Siberian cooperatives. Between 1911 and 1919 the cooperatives had grown from a membership of about 9,000 to about 16,000,-000, from an organization serving 46,000 to one serving 8,000,000 people, and from a yearly turnover of 695,000 to

[30] *Foreign Relations, 1920,* i, p. 705.
[31] *Foreign Relations, 1922,* i, pp. 900ff.

about 50,000,000 gold rubles.[32] The cooperatives were of course not unaffected by the surrounding confusion, finding it no less difficult than other persons or institutions to avoid siding with one or another of the various factions. Moreover, they did not all function as a unit, as might be expected from the existence of an organization known as the All-Russian Union of Cooperatives Societies. On the contrary, there was acute rivalry and competition between them.[33] This was true to such an extent that Mr. Heid, an American commercial representative in Siberia, found it difficult to carry on business with them without becoming involved in local political quarrels.

However, in spite of these understandable defects, the cooperatives were one of the most stable elements in a world of shifting and uncertain political and economic life. In the summer of 1918, when suggestions for economic aid to Russia were being made, it was proposed that the credit facilities of the cooperatives should be used since they had not been destroyed by the Bolsheviks.[34] In fact it was at this time that the all-Russian Union of Coopcrative Societies expressed its desire to strike a bargain with the Allies in order to bring some relief to the people.[35] To do this, it was reported, they were ready to deal even with the Germans. On the other hand, in exchange for support from the Allies, they were ready to take a stand against the Germans and even discuss compensations. In 1919 the United States War Department was authorized to sign contracts with the cooperatives for the sale of surplus war materials including shoes, clothing, and other items badly needed by the Russian people. In June of that year it was reported that three contracts had been signed with the Siberian Creameries, Union of Siberian Central Union of Consumers, and the All-Russian Central Union of Consumers, each to the amount of 5,000,000 dollars, and that additional contracts to make up a total of

[32] Varneck, *op. cit.*
[33] Bullard, *op. cit.*, p. 189.
[34] *Foreign Relations, 1918, Russia,* III, p. 132.
[35] *Ibid.,* II, p. 206.

25,000,000 dollars had been authorized.[36] When the Allies finally approved the opening of trade relations with Russia on January 16, 1920, twenty-four hours after the surrender of Kolchak, it was stipulated that trade was to be carried out through the cooperatives.[37] Alexander Berkenheim, Chief of the Foreign Directorate and Vice-President of the All-Russian Central Union of Consumers' Societies, was the agent for the agreement. It should be added that the agreement specifically stipulated that this move was not to be interpreted as recognition of the Soviet Government.

During the period of the Far Eastern Republic, the Co-operatives continued to form the core of continuity in the economic life of Eastern Siberia. The Ministry of Industry relied almost entirely upon them to carry on its program of reconstruction of home industry.[38] The Ministry, for example, took possession of all abandoned plants and factories and placed them in the hands of the Cooperatives for actual operation. In this way the Cooperatives became the managers of over 65 percent of the industry of Transbaikal Province and about the same proportion elsewhere. The smelter at Petrovsk-Zavod as well as gold mining, a glass works, three tanneries, a concrete plant, a fish cannery, a fur-curing establishment, two saw mills and other plants were either in process of restoration or were beginning their operations under Cooperative auspices by the end of the Far Eastern Republic in 1922.

The existence of these chaotic economic conditions brought forth, both from Soviet and Allied leaders, a number of significant proposals the object of which was both to provide direct economic assistance to the people and government of Russia and to avoid the destructive effects of an intervention and the civil war which it would inevitably invite. During the spring and summer of 1918, at the time the intervention was becoming an imminent possibility, the Soviet Government was urging that economic assistance be sent instead of a

[36] *Foreign Relations, 1918, Russia,* III, p. 132.
[37] *Peace Conference Papers,* IX, pp. 868–869.
[38] Norton, *op. cit.,* pp. 212–213.

interventionary force. As noted in a previous chapter, Raymond Robins, the American Red Cross representative in Moscow who was in close touch with the Soviet leaders as well as with current trends in Russia, found this suggestion a highly practical solution to the great problem of Russia. In a letter of July 1, 1918 to Lansing he summarized the situation.[39] "The Russian peasant," he said, "finds himself with a large quantity of grain and a large amount of depreciated paper currency. If he takes his grain to the local center of trade he finds none of the necessities of life for sale, and cannot exchange his grain except for more depreciated paper money. Consequently the grain is not brought to market." This passage is significant for a number of reasons. In the first place it represents a situation and a problem well known to many competent observers in Russia at the time. Secondly, it is important because it placed this problem before a responsible official of the American Government who was in a position to influence the course of events. Finally, the author of the statement had the confidence of the responsible heads of the Soviet Government and could have been instrumental in carrying out the proposed remedies had there been any means of gaining support for such remedies among the Allied Powers.

In the spring of 1918 members of the Soviet regime had thus stated their problems and needs to American representatives with complete frankness. During their visit to Siberia in April 1918, Captain Webster and Captain Hicks had heard and reported the situation they found there.[40] As elsewhere, the people of Siberia needed manufactured articles—especially agricultural machinery, spare parts, and binder twine to save the harvest. They wanted railway and industrial experts to help make the economic organism run smoothly. They were prepared to export wool, hides, furs, flax, lumber, sunflower seed oil, and minerals. In Moscow, Lenin was then saying very much the same thing to Robins. In a note of May 14, 1918 he invited the United States to assume as much of

[39] *R.A.R.*, p. 214.
[40] *Ibid.*, p. 183.

EASTERN SIBERIA IN THE CIVIL WAR

the Russian foreign market as she desired.[41] The bulk of the prewar Russian imports, he said, had come from the Central Powers. Under the present circumstances it could not be anticipated that much could be received from this source for some time to come. Thus the way was open for trade between the United States and Russia and for the permanent acquisition of the Russian market by the United States. Lenin indicated that by 1916 the home production and the importation of agricultural machinery had both been reduced to one-fifth of their prewar rate. The same great shortages existed with respect to the production of coal, pig-iron, and other branches of mining and manufacturing. By assistance from the United States both in imports and in expert advise he hoped to remedy this situation. In his letter to Lansing (already referred to), Robins explained what he considered the significant feature of this proposal: "There is now presented in the invitation coming from the responsible head of the Soviet Government for America's cooperation in economic reconstruction, the opportunity for taking a vitally important preliminary step toward complete economic and military cooperation in the creation of an effective Eastern front."[42]

In the spring of 1919, after the intervention in all its phases had begun and Kolchak had already been established as Supreme Ruler for four months, the Soviet requests were again renewed. This time the proposals came from the Soviet representative in the United States, L. C. A. K. Martens, who was later deported with considerable fanfare. To establish the Soviet credit, Martens indicated that he was prepared to deposit 200,000,000 dollars in gold.[43] As usual the list of requirements was headed by agricultural implements and machinery, the standard items of prewar American trade with Russia. The request continued by asking for railway supplies, tools, mining machinery, shoes, clothing, and other essential items. In exchange, the Soviet Government offered the raw materials already mentioned as possible Russian ex-

[41] *Ibid.,* p. 205.
[42] *Ibid.,* p. 212.
[43] *Ibid.,* p. 328.

314

ports then available. The readiness and desire to trade remained a feature of Soviet policy throughout this period. The door was particularly kept open to American business and even capital investment.

It was in response, not so much to these Soviet requests for aid as to the circumstances which prompted the requests, that a number of Allied leaders proposed economic rather than military remedies for what were essentially economic ills. One of the most comprehensive of plans for assistance to Russia was the one elaborated in the spring of 1918 by Raymond Robins himself. The objective of his plan was to rehabilitate the economy of Russia and thereby prepare the way for the reestablishment of the Eastern Front against Germany. The plan he proposed had therefore the same objective as the railway missions of the previous year. In the meantime, however, the Russian situation had changed materially, and it was in response to these altered conditions that he proposed a far more thoroughgoing effort to revive the Russian economy. No longer was it a mere matter of maintaining railway service; it had become a question of competing with Germany for the land and people of Russia.[44] The Germans, Robins reported, were making every effort to obtain Russian cooperation and full access to the human and natural resources of Russia. In the face of these German moves, Robins urged, an Allied intervention would inevitably be compared unfavorably with that of Germany. Unless it were invited by the Soviet Government, he felt that an intervention would not only result in completely ruining the entire basis of President Wilson's democratic war policy but that it would inevitably lead to civil war. Not even on military grounds could he see any justification for intervention since it could only provide Germany with an excuse to consumate more hurriedly her current Russian plans. Economic cooperation, on the other hand, would open the way for a friendly intervention after which the Eastern Front could be effectively rebuilt.

In addition to these immediate benefits, Robins was of the opinion that his plan would "lead inevitably to the modi-

[44] *The Lansing Papers*, II, p. 366.

fication, adjustment, and softening of the hard and impossible formulas of radical socialism."[45] This, it must be said, was a somewhat flattering view of the contemporary opinion held by the United States Government regarding the Bolsheviks. According to contemporary opinion, so "hard and impossible" were the theories which lay behind the Bolshevik Party that it was impossible to have any confidence in its ability to remain at the head of the Russian state. There were many, in fact, who held the Bolsheviks in even lower esteeem than this. As Harold Fisher has pointed out: "Bolshevism, it should be noted, in most minds did not represent a political or economic theory but the destruction of public order, the end of all security of person and property, the reign of bloody violence."[46] It is therefore entirely understandable that Washington at that time disregarded completely the Robins proposal. Yet it must be added that those closer to the scene —perhaps because they saw more clearly the strong differences of opinion existing within the regime—had greater confidence in the possibility of a different Soviet orientation toward the Western Powers and of the durability of the Soviet Government. To them the important question was more liable to be the one with which Robins and other competent observers were concerned: Would the future of Russia be in the hands of rulers who guided their activities by the "hard and impossible formulas of radical socialism"? Or would it be possible to temper these authoritarian principles by helping the less authoritarian elements to come to the fore and perhaps even by the full acceptance of the new state into the family of democratic nations? Since the intervention followed immediately, this second possibility was never tested in practice. However, the fluid situation characteristic of Russia, especially in the spring of 1918, would seem to indicate that this basic objective of Robins was by no means as great an impossibility as many then believed.

The Robins plan was so thoroughgoing as to involve

[45] *Ibid.,* II, pp. 366–372.
[46] H. H. Fisher; *The Famine in Soviet Russia, 1919–1923,* New York, 1927, p. 25.

almost a Russian-American economic and political partnership.[47] To carry it out he suggested the creation of a special commission the chief of which would be responsible only to the President of the United States. The work of this commission would be carried out in various parts of Russia through inspectors. In this part of its work he proposed making use of the organization, personnel, and experience of the Russian branches of such firms as J. M. Coates and Company, the New York Life Insurance Company, and the International Harvester Company. To ascertain the extent of local needs there were available the Soviets and Cooperatives. As to the activities of the commission, the program called for the complete management of railways, the reorganization of credit and finance, the commercial distribution of grain and manufactured articles, the supervision of industrial management, food administration, and a number of other important features. The plan was, in fact, so all-inclusive as to raise the question as to whether, even had she been willing, the United States would then have been intrusted by the Allies with the sole execution of it.

Raymond Robins was by no means the only one among the Allied representatives in Russia who considered an economic substitute for a forced military intervention a feasible project. In January 1918, even before the Robins plan was submitted to Washington, Charles Smith, the American member of the Inter-Allied Railway Commission, had worked out a somewhat less pretentious plan but one having similar objectives.[48] His frequent inspection tours over the railways had revealed to him the true state of affairs and had, at the same time, suggested the remedy. Smith's plan, it should be noted, had the approval of Admiral Knight and Captain Althouse of the United States Navy, the American Minister to China, Paul Reinsch, as well as of the British representatives, Commodore Paine, Colonel Robertson, Colonel Josiah Wedgewood, and Sir John Jordan, the British Minister to China.

[47] *The Lansing Papers,* II, pp. 366–372.
[48] C. H. Smith, "Four Years of Mistakes in Siberia," *op. cit.,* pp. 479–480.

Smith's point of departure was, "As with one voice, the country cried out for goods. The people were dissatisfied because they had nothing. Their unrest was caused, not by political ideas, but by lack of supplies." In these words are expressed both the objective of the plan and the method proposed to carry it out. As in the case of the Robins plan, the proposal was vetoed in Washington and with this act, Mr. Smith believed, began the career of Allied mistakes in Siberia.

In April 1918 Thomas Masaryk made a proposal which Ambassador Morris in Tokyo saw fit to pass on to Secretary Lansing with his approval.[49] Masaryk suggested the financing and organizing of a corporation by the Allies as a substitute for intervention. The corporation would sell manufactured articles to the Russians and buy and distribute grain. Along with this plan he urged the *de facto* recognition of the Soviet Government and the organization of a Russian army. He hoped the plan would accomplish the following: it would prevent the Central Powers from acquiring the wheat; it would provide an economic foundation for Allied propaganda; it would create a better understanding with the liberal movement in Russia without giving official recognition to the Bolshevik Government; finally, it would provide a constructive alternative to military intervention.

The most interesting feature of this plan is the fact that it corroborates the point made by Colonel Robins regarding the fluid political situation then prevailing in Russia. That such an authority on the life and institutions of Russia as Thomas Masaryk should have believed that the extending of economic and moral support to the new Soviet Government and to the Russian people might have resulted in bringing to the fore the advocates of a liberal rather than an authoritarian program, is a factor of the greatest importance. That future events should have substantiated that belief is perhaps of even greater importance. It is only necessary to recall the story of the intervention as related in the preceding chapters to see that the worst features of the revolution and

[49] *Foreign Relations, 1918, Russia,* III, p. 120.

civil war came only after the intervention had created an atmosphere in which moderation could no longer exist, in which there remained only two sides, each hoping only for the extinction of the other. The doctrinaire and authoritarian elements were considered to have won their right to direct the future course of the Russian state after their conduct of what was not only a class war of landlord against peasant but a patriotic war of Russian against foreigner. Out of that struggle, it should be recalled, grew not only an intensification of the mutual distrust which had even before the First World War been characteristic of the relations of imperial Russia with the other nations of the world, but a strong conviction on both sides of the Russian border that this situation could not possibly have developed otherwise.

A second important feature of the Masaryk plan is that which concerns the economic benefits the Central Powers might reap from their free access to Russian resources, a development which had been troubling the Allies for some time. On February 2, 1918 Ambassador Francis informed Secretary Lansing that the British and French Military Missions in Russia had already been authorized to purchase fats, oils, and other supplies in Russia to keep them from falling into German hands.[50] The Germans, he added, were at the moment buying these things. In his answer Lansing told Francis that a fund of 1,000,000 dollars had been made available to the American Military Mission for the same purpose. In March it was reported that 200,000 tons of Turkistan cotton were already loaded on cars destined for the Germans.[51] It was urged that this be purchased immediately. By June 13, 1918 the American purchasing fund had been increased to 6,000,000 dollars.[52] It will be seen from this that one of the objectives Masaryk hoped to achieve by his plan—keeping the grain surplus out of German hands—was not only one of the chief reasons France and Britain were demanding an intervention but it was at the same time one of

[50] *Foreign Relations, 1918, Russia,* III, pp. 107–108.
[51] *Ibid.,* III, p. 114.
[52] *Ibid.,* II, p. 126.

the policies then being carried out by these two nations as well as the United States.

In official Washington circles, thinking along these lines did not become serious until the intervention crisis became acute in the mid-summer of 1918. During the decisive summer weeks when an intervention was a factor which could no longer be disregared, both Colonel House and Bernard Baruch suggested that Herbert Hoover, already famous for his administration of Belgian relief, should undertake a program of Russian aid.[53] House, whose position made him especially aware of the tremendous pressure then being exerted upon President Wilson for an intervention, hoped this plan for economic assistance might, under favorable circumstances, be accepted as a substitute for intervention. But, failing this, it could be used as an accompaniment of intervention which would, he felt, make intervention easier for the Russian people to accept. By making the intervention subordinate to an economic relief mission headed by Hoover, the whole episode might be made to suggest to the people the Belgian relief. Baruch's reasons were somewhat less complex. He wished to send an economic mission for the simple reason that the greatest enemy of the Russian people was obviously going to be hunger and privation. Herbert Hoover, it must be added, consented to the scheme. But the President vetoed it at this time on the grounds that Hoover could not then be spared.

Although intervention of a military type was, as a matter of fact, forced upon the United States at this time, a genuine effort was made shortly after by the American Government to provide some kind of economic assistance to the people of Siberia. In October 1918 steps were taken to send necessary trade goods to Russia.[54] A Russian Bureau was established in the War Trade Board and 5,000,000 dollars allocated for its use. August Heid, former representative in Russia of the International Harvester Company, was ap-

[53] Seymour, *op. cit.*, III, p. 409; Baker, *op. cit.*, VIII, p. 281.
[54] *Foreign Relations, 1918, Russia*, III, pp. 148–154; *Peace Conference Papers*, II, pp. 472ff.

pointed as the representative of the Bureau in Vladivostok. Although officially denominated as relief, this was actually a commercial venture. Licenses were granted to private individuals to conduct business in Siberia. The National City Bank was invited to open a branch at Vladivostok. But the venture was not a success. The fact that the Armistice and the resulting lull in the anti-Russian and anti-American activities of Japan occurred soon after it was launched should have given the Bureau an opportunity to begin its work under favorable circumstances. Moreover, in January 1919, it will be recalled, the Allied railway agreement was forced through despite Japanese reluctance. But by the time this agreement was completed the monopolistic policy of Japan was once more in full swing. After this Japan consistently opposed all efforts of the United States to open trade with Russia. In previous pages it has been seen how Japan, under the slogan of preventing American imperialism, used her army as well as the forces of her henchmen, Semenov, Kalmykov, and others, to force her own goods into Siberia.

The extent to which the economy of Siberia deteriorated under the disruptive tactics of both the Japanese and the Kolchak Governments can be seen from the survey conducted by Ambassador Morris in the late summer of 1919.[55] During the time when recognition of the Kolchak Government was again under consideration by the Allies, President Wilson had requested Morris to undertake a special mission to Omsk with a view to finding an answer to the question: "Does Kolchak deserve recognition?" His report was discouraging, to say the least. Production and administration, he found, had broken down and clothes, shoes, paper, drugs, kerosene, sugar, and other basic necessities were urgently needed by the people everywhere. He proposed a minimum credit of 206,850,000 dollars to begin the process of bringing these things to the people. "The population," he wrote in his report, "is exhausted, local administration is corrupt and inefficient, pestilence threatens. I think that we should make

[55] *Foreign Relations, 1919, Russia*, pp. 403, 433–434.

321

every effort to revive economic life and render it possible for the population to work. Otherwise I fear that the country will fall into political chaos and become a field of international intrigue if not conflict." The rout and defeat of the Kolchak armies soon after the writing of this report is ample testimony as to accuracy of its findings.

Great Britain and France, it must be said, were no more cooperative in mitigating the internal economic decline of Russia than was Japan even though their disruptive tactics were largely of a negative rather than a positive nature. In Siberia this policy, unquestionably a part of the general blockade declared against Soviet Russia, took the form of an embargo lasting from January to June 1918 which closed the Manchurian border to all traffic with Siberia.[56] Although actually instituted by the Chinese Government, the blockade was carried out under pressure from the British and French Governments and it spite of the most urgent American objections. During the period of its operation the embargo prohibited exports of all types into Eastern Siberia. Among the results of such a policy were the large contributions it made toward the already existing shortages of essential goods and the encouragement it gave to smuggling.[57] The railways were filled with smugglers who carried into Siberia the tobacco, liquor, food, and clothing which were plentiful in Manchuria. Two items in the illegal trade which were of particularly great value were the American saccharine which was so welcome in sugarless Siberia and the opium from Turkistan which the smugglers brought back for sale in China. To what degree Japanese pressure contributed toward forcing this embargo is not known. It is certain, however, that the embargo could scarcely have been carried into effect if it had failed to meet the approval of Japan. It is also significant that the measure was rescinded in June 1918 when the Czech rising in Siberia had practically insured

[56] *Foreign Relations, 1918, Russia,* III, pp. 172ff.; *Foreign Relations, 1918,* p. 107; La Fargue, *op. cit.,* pp. 162–163.

[57] Ackerman, *op. cit.,* p. 67; R. Wilton, "The Rush for Siberia: Causes of the Present Crisis in the Pacific," *The Fortnightly Review* (London), cx, No. 659, November 1, 1921, p. 788.

American consent to the intervention so long desired by Japan. Were the Western Allies trading this economic pressure on Russia for some advantage they hoped to gain? Such a bargain was by no means unlikely as events already described must certainly have suggested.

That France and Britain were not unsympathetic to applying an effective form of economic strangulation to Russia is clearly exemplified by the blockade carried out against that country. Until the signing of peace with Germany a single blockade had served to prevent access to both Germany and Russia. After this event, however, it became a difficult problem to find a legitimate basis for a blockade against Russia alone. The Council of Four arrived at a temporary formula which, while not positively prohibiting trade with Soviet Russia, would at least provide a situation in which "there should be an absentation from any positive measures or public announcement indicating a resumption of such trade."[58]

Meanwhile, discussions of the question continued with a view to discovering what stronger measures could be applied which would at the same time be within the bounds of legality. One proposal was that the neutrals who had been carrying on trade with Soviet Russia should be informed that the Allies would consider the continuation of this practice an unfriendly act. Still another device suggested was that the Allies declare Bolshevik Russia at war with the Baltic states and therefore subject to a legitimate Allied blockade. The American representatives were sounded out as to their attitude toward one or another of these methods of applying pressure upon the Soviet Government. Both Henry White and John Foster Dulles were dubious of the possibility of establishing a blockade on any such grounds.[59] The latter replied with the obvious truth that the Allies had never been at war with Russia and therefore could not declare a blockade against her. However, the question was referred to President Wilson, who, in a note of August 8, 1919 to the Council of Five, gave the final answer to the question as far as the

[58] *Peace Conference Papers,* IV, pp. 17, 122.
[59] *Peace Conference Papers,* VII, pp. 133–134, 644, 645.

United States was concerned. A blockade, he wrote, was an act of war and he had no constitutional right to carry on war without an act of Congress.

The blockade, however, continued to be enforced in spite of its incomplete and highly unlegal character. British and French warships in the Gulf of Finland continued to "change the route" of ships bound for ports in Bolshevik Russia. Banks and commercial establishments were "encouraged" not to do business with Russia, and it was understood that no passports would be issued to Russia. In accordance with the accepted policy of cooperation with the Allies, the United States took part in the embargo by refusing to grant export licenses to those intending to do business in Russian territory under Bolshevik control and by refusing clearance papers to ships bound for Soviet ports.[60] One of the reasons given by the American Government was that trade might provide the Bolsheviks with the means of moving gold to the United States, there to be used for propaganda purposes. Furthermore, the official American statement continued, since the autumn of 1918 the Bolsheviks had discriminated against the middle class, and it was not desired that food or other necessities coming from the United States should be used as a means of "sustaining such a program of political oppression." A move which must have been somewhat confusing to many who had so recently left the battlefields of the Western Front was an Allied invitation to Germany to cooperate in this anti-Soviet blockade. On October 31, 1919 *The New York Times* noted that, "The German Government is asked to take measures similar to those indicated."[61] There was undoubtedly a sense of chagrin in some quarters when Germany announced her refusal to participate in the blockade on the grounds that this would in the long run be of assistance to the Bolsheviks. The blockade was carried on until January 16, 1920, when it was officially terminated by the Supreme Economic Council.

Against the background of these facts it is easy to under-

[60] *Russian Series,* No. 2.
[61] *R.A.R.,* pp. 349–350.

stand why the American economic assistance to Russia which eventually materialized in the program of the American Relief Administration was so long delayed. While the blockade was still an issue of importance to all the major Allied powers, Herbert Hoover had, during March 1919, sounded out President Wilson on the subject of a relief mission to Russia.[62] Receiving a favorable reaction, he proposed to Fridjof Nansen the undertaking of such a mission. The result of this was that on April 3, 1919 Nansen addressed a note to the Big Four expressing his willingness to undertake the mission if official approval and help could be obtained.[63] In it he informed the representatives at Paris that starvation and disease were rife in Russia and that a commission along the lines of the Belgian Relief Commission was needed to bring food and medical supplies to millions who were in dire need of them. The answer given by the Big Four was dated April 9, 1919. In principle there was complete agreement among the Allied spokesmen with Nansen's objectives. But they made one condition which in the end proved fatal to the whole scheme. They stipulated that the desired relief could only be approved by the Council if all hostilities were stopped. When Nansen sent his proposal to Chicherin, the Soviet Foreign Commissar, it was on this point that the whole plan met defeat.[64] Chicherin's reply of May 14, 1919 was highly respectful toward Nansen and his objectives but bitter toward the Allies, who had offered food and medical supplies to the needy and starving people of Russia only on the condition of a cessation of hostilities. They must have known, he said, that this suggestion came just at the time of Soviet military success. It was thus to be used, he concluded, as a means of permitting the defeated armies of Kolchak to recoup their strength and regroup for a renewed onslaught. The Foreign Commissar proposed a reconsideration of this condition in a direct conference between the Soviets and the Allies. But the French were absolutely opposed to any direct negotiations

[62] Fisher, op. cit., pp. 11ff.
[63] Ibid., pp. 15–16.
[64] Peace Conference Papers, v, pp. 744–747.

with the Bolsheviks and, in the end, the scheme was temporarily abandoned.

The final arrangements for bringing relief to Russia were largely the results of two factors: the continued and active interest of Herbert Hoover in the project and the increasingly acute conditions in Russia, which, in the end, forced the Soviet Government to take steps. The Soviets had continued to hope that relief might be arranged directly with the American State Department.[65] In this way, they hoped, diplomatic and commercial relations would result in the opening of trade which would be a more permanent form of relief and a means of achieving the much desired recognition. When the appeal from Russia came it was made through statements signed by Patriarch Tikhon and Maxim Gorky which were transmitted through Nansen to Secretary of State Hughes on July 15, 1921.[66] The necessary exchange of notes was rapidly completed and on August 1, 1921 Herbert Hoover directed Walter Lyman Brown, the European director for the American Relief Administration, to proceed at once to Riga where final arrangements were to be concluded.[67] One of the conditions for the opening of these negotiations had been the delivery of all American prisoners then being held by the Soviets. The prisoners arrived in Riga on the 9th of August and Brown arrived on the 10th. Ten days later the final agreements were signed at Riga by Brown and Maxim Litvinov and on August 27 the first contingent of the American Relief Administration arrived in Moscow.[68] In a note of September 2, 1921 Secretary Hughes informed the American ambassador in France that the efforts of France to participate in the activities of the relief mission would not be considered.[69] It was feared that factors would be introduced into the work of the mission which would obstruct the liberal and humanitarian purposes for which it had gone to Russia and would perhaps introduce another cycle

[65] Fisher, *op. cit.*, pp. 45–46.
[66] *Foreign Relations, 1921*, II, pp. 804–805.
[67] *Ibid.*, II, pp. 810–812.
[68] Fisher, *op. cit.*, pp. 61, 71.
[69] *Foreign Relations, 1921*, II, p. 821.

such as the one now happily brought to a close by the failure of the "military diplomats."

In Siberia the Soviet Government had from the very start placed great reliance upon the rivalry of Japan and the United States as a factor in preserving her territorial integrity. Just as the Provisional Government of March 1917 had looked to the American railway men for this purpose, the Soviet Government and the Far Eastern Republic gave frequent encouragement to prospective business investors. The Soviets were undoubtedly interested not only in enlisting American business in the struggle against the militaristic form of imperialism practiced on the mainland by Japan, but also in using American capital as a means of achieving recognition and of dislodging and holding off Japan until the Soviet Government had grown strong enough to carry on alone.[70] The nationalizations of property carried out during 1918 and 1919 did not then affect the International Harvester, Singer Sewing Machine, Westinghouse Air Brake, and other American companies having branches or properties in Russia. In fact, during the period of sole Japanese occupancy of key points in Siberia the Soviet Government granted large concessions there to Americans. In 1920 Washington B. Vanderlip, moving in an atmosphere of false impressions and general misconceptions, went to Russia and received oil, coal, fishing, and lumbering concessions, the total value of which was said to have been about 3,000,000,000 dollars.[71] If Lenin was uncertain as to the precise relationship between this man and Frank A. Vanderlip, the well-known New York financier and former president of the National City Bank, or between him and Warren Harding, the Republican candidate for president, he was in any case sure of the service he wished Vanderlip to perform for him. Lenin declared at the time that he was entirely willing to let America and Japan fight over Kamchatka and other areas where the concession rights

[70] Fischer, op. cit., I, p. 300.

[71] Ibid.; Albert Parry, "Washington B. Vanderlip, the 'Khan of Kamchatka,' " Pacific Historical Review (Berkeley), XVII, No. 3, August 1948, pp. 311–330.

had been granted. "Legally Kamchatka belongs to us," declared Lenin in a speech to the Council of People's Commissars, "but in fact has been grabbed by Japan. Should we offer Kamchatka to America, it is clear we will win."[72] The same objective lay behind the rights granted to the Sinclair oil interests in January 1922 for the exploitation of the oil of North Sakhalin and for the building of two ports on the eastern coast of the island. This grant also concerned an area then occupied by Japan and one which was therefore useless unless the Japanese were first dislodged. Yet, even this would not have made the grants valid since they were all contingent upon the granting of American recognition to the Soviet Government.

Eventually, however, all American firms lost their actual or potential Russian investments. In 1925 after a final settlement had been effected with Japan, the Soviet Government took over the properties of the International Harvester Company, leaving that company to write off losses amounting to some 31,000,000 dollars.[73] The Singer Sewing Machine Company lost over 84,000,000 dollars in the course of the liquidation. Parke, Davis and Company, Victor Talking Machine, Westinghouse Electric, New York Air Brake, and other companies lost substantial if lesser sums. This brought to an unfortunate conclusion the splendid beginnings independent American business had made in Russia during the early years of the century.

In the economic and political chaos which characterized Siberia during the civil war, the cost in human life and suffering is impossible to reckon with any degree of accuracy. The deliberate shooting, burning, looting, and torturing were only part of the suffering that took place. It has been estimated that—entirely apart from the foreign armies which marched into the area—the population of Siberia doubled during the civil war. Those returning from exile abroad were noisy and irritating to many observers. But the refugees from European Russia and then from Western Siberia during the

[72] Parry, op. cit., p. 315.
[73] C. Lewis, America's Stake in International Investments, pp. 295–296.

328

Kolchak retreat constituted most of the increase. Overcrowded conditions, housing shortages, displaced persons of all types living in tents or freight cars were characteristic results. To make matters worse, sanitary conditions were extremely primitive.[74] The natural outcome was that diseases became increasingly common. According to General Graves, the most frequently encountered diseases were plague, typhus, relapsing fever, typhoid fever, scarlet fever, and malignant sore throat. These conditions reached a climax during the height of the Kolchak retreat. In the press of humanity that jammed the railway and the roads beside the railway in a frantic effort to escape the oncoming Red Army, many fell by the wayside from exhaustion, disease, or starvation.[75] It has been estimated that between November 1919 and April 1920 in Novonikolaevsk alone more than sixty thousand persons died of typhus. Typhus, in fact, infested the whole retreat and the casualties must have been enormous. In Russia as a whole, it has been estimated that the loss of life through disease in 1920 was greater than that in 1922 through the famine.[76]

The only bright part of this extremely dark picture so far as Eastern Siberia is concerned is that the population of this area suffered less than Siberia as a whole or than European Russia.[77] There remained a larger percentage of persons in Eastern Siberia in the productive age group between the ages of sixteen and forty-nine. More of this age were apparently able to escape the Japanese and the military leaders who came to punish or recruit them. The forests and mountains of Siberia may be the factor which gave the people the means of escaping their tormentors and thus live to help in the reconstruction of their harried land.

[74] W. S. Graves, op. cit., p. 140.
[75] Stewart, op. cit., p. 300.
[76] Lorimer, op. cit., p. 29.
[77] Derber, op. cit., p. 105.

CHAPTER 9

The Allied Withdrawal

ALTHOUGH the Allied withdrawal from Siberia took place at the time of the collapse of the Kolchak Government, the reason for the withdrawal was the realization on the part of the Allies that a military force sufficiently strong to overthrow the Bolsheviks could not be raised or supported under postwar conditions. Since, however, the conflict in Russia was recognized by all as a danger to the peace of the world, before the withdrawal was agreed upon various schemes for settling the Russian problem were considered at the Paris Peace Conference. But the very scope of the plans that were considered necessary to achieve a satisfactory solution only served to emphasize the hopeless immensity of the problem and to point to withdrawal as the only solution possible under the circumstances.

Among the Allies, therefore, only Japan remained in Siberia after 1920, hoping to achieve alone what she had been unable to gain from the general Allied intervention. This fact, in turn, made impossible a complete and open occupation of all Siberia by the Soviet Government. Lacking the strength to challenge Japan in Eastern Siberia, the Soviet Government established there the Far Eastern Republic as a buffer state against Japan. In spite of the fact that the Republic was in all but a formal sense a part of Soviet Russia, it had a constitution which gave it the appearance of a liberal state. This was intended to meet the determined objection of Japan to the existence of a Communist government in Eastern Asia.

The liquidation of the Japanese intervention and of the Far Eastern Republic—whose existence was nothing more than a response to that intervention—was in large part a result of the Washington Conference or, more specifically,

330

of the new alignments resulting from that Conference. At the Washington Conference the national antagonisms among powers having interests in the Pacific and the Far East were the subject of discussion. Although receiving only the briefest mention in the conference itself, the Japanese intervention in Siberia achieved almost as much attention from the powers interested in the problem as though it had been listed as one of the major items on the agenda. The Japanese retreat before the decision of the conference was in many respects more formal than real. In the end, however, a Japanese withdrawal from some of the continental areas claimed by her, among them Eastern Siberia, was achieved in 1922 although not until 1925 was North Sakhalin returned to Soviet Russia.

As long as the World War was in progress Britain and France had acted as though no scheme was too vast, politically or financially, to receive their support. Minor differences were glossed over in their anxiety to form an "Eastern Front." But, after the Armistice had passed and the projects of the heated and anxious war years began to be examined in a more critical light, the prospects of the Siberian expedition appeared less promising. The expenditures of both British and French there had been very large.[1] In October 1919 it was estimated that France had poured over seven billion francs into the whole venture. What was even worse, there were no results to show for all this outlay. No anti-German front ever developed out of the Kolchak venture. Moreover, said Lloyd George to the Council of Ten at Paris on January 16, 1919, "It is impossible to know which party is gaining the upper hand, but our hopes that the Bolshevik Government would collapse had certainly been disappointed."[2] Bolshevism appeared to him to be growing stronger for the very reason that the peasants feared that all the other parties would restore the old regime.

[1] *Peace Conference Papers,* v, p. 903; *Foreign Relations, 1919, Russia,* p. 440: "Frantsiia v Borbe protiv Sovetskoi Vlasti," *Vestnik Narodnogo Komissariata Inostrannykh Del* (Moscow), No. 8, October 15, 1920, p. 22.
[2] *Peace Conference Papers,* II, p. 581.

At the Paris Peace Conference the Allied leaders were fully aware of the implications of the continuing struggle in Siberia. Winston Churchill expressed his view of the situation in words that recall the erstwhile British anxiety to promote an intervention.[3] He believed Russia to be the key to the whole peace settlement. He was not presuming that Germany would start another war immediately. But looking ten or fifteen years into the future, he saw the available conscripts to a new German army vastly exceeding those of France. Moreover, if the Allies were to abandon Russia without some settlement, would this not be an open invitation to Germany to become supreme there? With such a partnership the outcome of another war would not be difficult to predict. It should be the present object of the Allies to make Russia "a living partner in the League of Nations and a friend of the Allied powers," or, he added, "there would be neither peace nor victory."[4] Even Clemenceau, one of the strongest opponents of the Bolsheviks and all they represented, agreed with this analysis. He had previously expressed regret that it seemed necessary to treat the Bolsheviks as though they were equals.[5] But the Allies could stand no more war. In all the plans and schemes which had occupied the Allied leaders since the Russian armies began to withdraw from the front, nothing appeared to be settled. Many of the fears of two years before troubled the members of the Peace Conference.

The question thus arose as to what should be done about Russia. Lloyd George saw three possible solutions.[6] The first was to declare Russia as great a danger to civilization as German militarism and destroy it by military force. This, for reasons that will appear presently, he considered impossible. A second solution would be to erect a *cordon sanitaire* around Russia. This meant famine and death to the general population, all potential friends of the Allies. But even if this

[3] *Ibid.*, iv, pp. 15–16.
[4] *Ibid.*
[5] *Ibid.*, ii, p. 649.
[6] David Lloyd George, *Memoirs of the Peace Conference*, i, p. 219.

were done, who would overthrow the Bolsheviks? It was obvious that neither Denikin nor Kolchak could. A final possibility was a conference between the various Russian governments. President Wilson found this last suggestion agreeable.[7] It was his opinion that the only thing the intervention was accomplishing was to give the extremists an opportunity to resist compromise. The extremists at Moscow were able to say that the imperialists and capitalists were endeavoring to hand the country back to the landlords. There was, he said, a spirit of revolt against vested interest in the postwar world, a revolt not limited to Russia. Elimination of the grievances rather than force was the only antidote. In Russia the intervention was only aggravating the revolt. Therefore Wilson wanted a conference of all parties in order that reason might be tried where force had failed. This was not the reason Britain and France wanted a conference. But a conference at Prinkipo was proposed nevertheless.

The reasons for the elimination of Lloyd George's first two suggestions are an interesting commentary on the Allied position regarding the intervention. Thus, sending an army to coerce the Russians into accepting Kolchak was considered an impossibility. "The mere idea of crushing Bolshevism by force," said Lloyd George to the Council of Ten, "is pure madness."[8] The Germans could not do it with a million men.[9] The Allies could therefore not do it with less. This would mean conscription and the impossible task of persuading a citizen army that crushing the Bolsheviks was in the interests of liberty. Neither France, Britain, nor the United States was in a position to disregard this fact. Moreover, it was not overlooked that the intervention had greatly strengthened the Bolshevik hold on the Russian people and that more intervention could only be expected to increase this tendency. It had to be admitted, therefore, that the Allies had not the strength to crush the Bolsheviks into submission.

In the same manner that the idea of a large army to crush

[7] *Peace Conference Papers*, III, pp. 583–584, 645–648.
[8] *Ibid.*, III, p. 590.
[9] *Ibid.*, II, p. 582; Lloyd George, *op. cit.*, I, pp. 215–216.

Bolshevism grew out of the wartime plans to accomplish the same objective, the idea of encirclement also grew out of wartime plans to force Russia into returning to the Allied fold. The proposal was made by both British and French as a means of keeping such productive areas as Western Siberia, the Ukraine, and the Caucasus out of German hands. In a telegram of December 21, 1918 Clemenceau had given a somewhat different reason: "The plan of action of the Allies is to realize simultaneously the economic encirclement of the Bolsheviks and the organization of order by the Russian elements."[10] At the Peace Conference in 1919 Clemenceau was joined by Foch in advocating essentially the same policy.[11] The plan proposed at that time contemplated keeping Russia from falling a prey to Germany and upsetting the balance of power. In addition, the current plan was to the effect that all Eastern Europe, the Finns, Czechs, Rumanians, Poles, Greeks, and the pro-Ally elements in Russia would be mobilized for a vast onslaught against Russia. It would be less obtrusive, it was hoped, to send arms to these troops than to send the Allied forces themselves. Perhaps the greatest flaw in the plan was that Britain and France were financially incapable of implementing it.[12] They had therefore to look to the United States. But since the President had neither the will to do it nor the arbitrary and unlimited power of a military ruler, this plan also proved impossible.

On January 22, 1919 President Wilson, acting on the third possibility mentioned by David Lloyd George, invited all contending groups in Russia to send not more than three representatives to Prinkipo in the Sea of Marmora.[13] The conditions, were that there must be a true and a cessation of all aggressive military action between the parties invited. The Soviet acceptance was received on February 4, 1919.[14]

[10] L. Fischer, *op. cit.*, I, p. 152.
[11] *Peace Conference Papers*, IV, pp. 17, 122.
[12] *Ibid.*, XI, p. 83.
[13] *R.A.R.*, pp. 297–298.
[14] *Ibid.*, pp. 298–303; *Peace Conference Papers*, IV, pp. 13–14.

The Reds expressed their complete readiness to negotiate. They went further. They indicated their readiness to recognize all Russian financial obligations and to guarantee the payment of interest on loans with raw materials. They were ready to grant concessions on mines, forests, and other resources and even suggested territorial concessions. In addition, they offered to limit foreign propaganda and interference in other governments. Winston Churchill was moved to deny strongly that the concessions mentioned in the Soviet answer had any connection with the intervention.[15] A number of other non-Moscow governments accepted the proposal. Among these were the Latvian Government, the Soviet Ukrainian Government, the Government of Crimea, and others.

Among the White governments, that of Nikolai Chaikovsky accepted. Those of Siberia and South Russia, regarded as the chief contenders for power in a post-Soviet Russia, refused any negotiations with the Bolsheviks. It was their feeling that, "There is no conciliation possible between them [i.e., the Bolsheviks] and the national Russian groups. Any meeting would not only remain without effect, but might possibly cause to the Russian patriots as well as to the allied nations an irreparable moral prejudice." Kolchak protested violently that the invitation itself had undermined the prestige of the White cause in the eyes of his forces.[16] In fact, at the Peace Conference it was quite frankly recognized that both Allied and White Russian prestige had suffered by the refusal of the latter to accept the invitation when the Soviets had shown such readiness to attend the conference. Constantin Nabokov, Russian chargé d'affaires in London, felt after this episode that if Russia were to be saved she must save herself.[17] Outside interference would not help the situation. On March 1, 1919 George D. Herron and William Allen White, proposed American representatives to the Prinkipo Conference, were

[15] *R.A.R.*, pp. 305–306.
[16] *Peace Conference Papers*, IV, pp. 18–19.
[17] Nabokov, *op. cit.*, pp. 286–287.

directed not to proceed with the organization of their delegation.[18] The Prinkipo idea, for all practical purposes, was
dead.

The question of recognition for Kolchak had been thought
of in some quarters before May 1919. But starting in that
month it came before the major Allied powers for serious
consideration. Since recognition would involve a loan as
well as increased material support for the White armies, the
position taken by the United States, the only source of all
prospective aid, toward the question was of the greatest importance. As in all other phases of the intervention, there
was no doubt about the opinion held by Wilson regarding
the question of recognition. If it involved increased aid and
taking sides with Kolchak, as he knew it did, then he favored
clearing out and leaving the Russians to fight it out for themselves. But the question was not so simple. In this as in the
problem of opening an intervention, there was Allied pressure
to be considered. Therefore, Wilson sent Ambassador Morris
on a special mission to Omsk to find the answer to the question: Does Kolchak deserve recognition?[19]

The inquiry, as President Wilson outlined its objectives
for the guidance of Morris, was to be particularly concerned
with learning what Kolchak intended to do if he were successful in overthrowing the Bolsheviks. What assurances
could he give as to future reforms in land tenure or in the
extension and security of the suffrage? These questions
would depend, in turn, on learning something of the influences to which the Admiral was at present exposed. The
answer which Morris made to these questions has already
been commented on at some length. That Kolchak was subject to reactionary forces to such an extent that he could
hardly be said to be the determining factor in his government seems to be the general concensus among American

[18] L. I. Strakhovsky, *Intervention at Archangel; The Story of Allied
Intervention and Russian Counter-Revolution in North Russia, 1918–
1920,* Princeton, 1944, p. 151.
[19] *Foreign Relations, 1919, Russia,* p. 349.

observers.[20] As for future guarantees, Ambassador Morris expressed strong doubts of the ability of Kolchak to overthrow the Bolsheviks.[21] Drastic internal changes would be needed before the government could be strengthened to the point where it would be able to carry on a more successful war or gain the popular support necessary to carry out any civilian program at all. These reforms, Morris concluded, could be made only if immediate Allied help were extended to Kolchak.

The foreign intrigues then going on at Omsk, Morris indicated, were one of the reasons for the urgency.[22] A few days before the arrival of the American ambassador, a Japanese mission had reached Omsk. Taking advantage of the Kolchak retreat which had been in full progress since May, the Japanese had come to offer Kolchak a number of army divisions in exchange for the usual concessions in Eastern Siberia. But with the coming of the Americans, the expectations which had been aroused by the Japanese became centered upon the newer arrivals and the more honorable terms which might reasonably be hoped for from them. The reactionary group within the Omsk Government was not, however, favorable to undertaking any commitments or obligations involving the American Government. As evidence that neither the United States nor Great Britain could be looked upon as a dependable source of aid, they pointed to the labor troubles taking place in these countries and the unfavorable prospects this portended with respect to support for the anti Bolshevik government of Kolchak. So strong was this group at Omsk that, unless immediate Allied support were given to Kolchak, Morris warned, no guarantee could be made as to the future possibilities of the Kolchak Government.

The kind of aid which Morris found indispensable before

---

[20] *Ibid.*, p. 327, for report to Colonel House by Arthur Bullard, Director of the Russian Division of the Committee on Public Information.
[21] *Ibid.*, p. 407.
[22] *Ibid.*, pp. 418; Janin, *op. cit.*, pp. 149, 152.

recognition should be given was largely military and financial in character.[23] More troops must be sent. Credits must be established for military supplies as well as for commercial transactions. But these things could be done only with Congressional approval. The situation was well expressed by Lansing in a reply to Morris: "He [Kolchak] must realize that we are not as free as other governments are in respect to control of appropriations for expenditures abroad nor have we any long established machinery for effective assistance outside the United States such as has been available in the past to those governments whose colonies or other influences in foreign affairs have called for overseas effort."[24] The rescue of Kolchak, both from a military and a financial standpoint, was a risk which the Administration could not take without the consent of Congress and this consent, it has already been noted, was hardly to be expected.

Allied good will toward Kolchak was by no means unmixed with fears resulting from reports as to the reactionary nature of his regime, and particularly the fear that support of such a government by nations professing liberal political creeds would in the end be disastrous. Sir Charles Eliot and Eugene Regnault, respectively British and French representatives in Siberia, had long been in favor of recognition for Kolchak. But, by May 1919 the tardy reports reaching Paris indicated the possibility of an imminent Kolchak victory.[25] Considering the reactionary government of which, by all accounts, Kolchak was the recognized head, fears were aroused as to the results of such a political organization's becoming supreme in Russia. It would undoubtedly appear as though a reactionary or even an imperial government had been restored under Allied auspices and protection. Accordingly, it was proposed at the Peace Conference that recognition of Kolchak be considered but that the whole question should be made dependent upon certain definite political commitments on Kolchak's part. The very suggestion of

[23] *Foreign Relations, 1919, Russia*, p. 421.
[24] *Ibid.*, p. 422.
[25] *Peace Conference Papers*, v, pp. 497–498.

338

forcing Kolchak to make any promises in exchange for recognition or even continued support, it is interesting to note, aroused considerable protest in Western reactionary circles friendly to the Kolchak Government.[26] In Paris the *Action Francaise* openly advised Kolchak to promise whatever the Allies asked but not to be concerned about fulfilling any such promises. In London the *Morning Post* labeled the Allied demands as interference in the domestic affairs of Russia.

The message to Kolchak was dated May 23, 1919.[27] It stated that the Allied governments were "convinced by their experiences of the last year that it is not possible to secure self-government or peace for Russia by dealings with the Soviet Government of Moscow. They are therefore disposed to assist the Government of Admiral Kolchak and his associates with munitions, supplies, food and the help of such as may volunteer for their service, to establish themselves as the government of all Russia, provided they receive from them definite guarantees that their policy has the same end in view as that of the Allied and Associated Powers." There followed a list of items on which the Allies desired assurance. These points included: the summoning of a Constitutent Assembly upon reaching Moscow; the holding of free elections for the zemstvos, city dumas, and other institutions; abstaining from any effort to restore any class or regime overthrown by the Revolution; recognition of the national debt; a statement regarding the willingness of Russia to join the League of Nations and cooperate with the other members. On June 12, 1919 the Allies accepted Kolchak's answer in which he agreed substantially to all the points mentioned. On the question of the future land settlement, he replied that the Constituent Assembly was the body which must decide a matter of such basic importance. But his answer was accepted. In exchange the Allies offered continuing support but not recognition. The Allied troops remained in Russia as before.

[26] Coates and Coates, *op. cit.,* p. 214.
[27] *Peace Conference Papers,* vi, pp. 74–75.

The effect of the whole episode was very bad from the point of view of the Omsk Government. The presence of the neutral American forces there had long been a source of annoyance to Kolchak.[28] It was obvious that the United States was unsympathetic to a government which Britain and France were supporting. The United States was held among the Siberian peasants to be the very model of a government with free and democratic institutions. Therefore, the American troops, it was felt, would be supporting Kolchak if his government were acceptable to the United States. The neutral troops, therefore, implied at once a difference in Allied policy and an insinuation that the Kolchak Government was not in the highest favor in democratic circles. The Prinkipo proposal, associated with President Wilson, had itself been a bad blow to the morale of the fighting forces.[29] Furthermore, the negotiations over the question of recognition had raised false hopes, not to mention misunderstandings of Allied policy. In the long run, it was believed, this had also been a serious blow to the morale of the troops. The retreats of the summer of 1919 were considered by some to result from the upset caused by the poor relations between Kolchak and the Allies.

The question of recognition and increased support of Kolchak was not considered a closed issue even after the action of June 12. This merely left things as they had been. The Allies were in fact "riding the tiger" in a most undesirable sense. As the summer and autumn months passed, the Kolchak retreat grew in intensity. The question had to be faced: If Kolchak fails what shall be done? Consul General Harris at Irkutsk, a strong supporter of recognition for Kolchak, saw chaos as the only alternative.[30] The collapse of Kolchak, he thought, might provide the means for Bolshevism to achieve an easy triumph, or the political intrigues which follow would offer "opportunities and advantages that both Germany and Japan are looking for." By December the situation was so desperate that more concrete proposals

[28] *Ibid.,* v, p. 528.
[29] *Foreign Relations, 1919, Russia,* p. 391.
[30] *Ibid.,* p. 429.

were made with the hope of finding a remedy. In a statement to the International Council of Premiers, the British, still without a plan, asked that withdrawal of support for Kolchak, when it came, should not be carried out too precipitately. The result, as the British Government saw it, would be that the Bolsheviks would overrun Siberia and the Japanese would not be slow under such circumstances in sending in a powerful force and establishing themselves. This fear undoubtedly accounts in part for a British proposal made to the American Ambassador some days before, a proposal which recalls both the diplomacy of the prewar imperialism and the precaution taken by Britain and France after the November Revolution of dividing parts of European Russia into spheres of influence. The proposal of December 3, 1919 was to the effect that Britain would like to see Russia divided into a number of independent states, none of which would be large enough to threaten the peace.[31]

Meanwhile, the Omsk Government had done everything it could to obtain the support of the Allies. At the time recognition was being considered at Paris, statements of its financial position were placed before the Allied delegates.[32] In these they attempted to demonstrate that the financial status of the Omsk Government and its anti-Bolshevik predecessors had improved steadily. It showed an increase in the revenue and was careful to note the grants to zemstvos and cooperative societies among its outlays. Unfortunately, the picture of internal improvement was somewhat undermined, at least in American eyes, by the report of Ambassador Morris, already noted. His sober analysis had made it apparent that nothing less was required than a total assumption of economic and financial supervision by a future creditor in order to carry out a program of economic rehabilitation, a program which must necessarily start from the bottom and reach into the highest ranks of the overstaffed officialdom.

In a note to the French Government in October 1919 the

[31] *Foreign Relations, 1920*, III, p. 484.
[32] "Omsk, 30th May 1919"; "Liberated Siberia. Economic and Financial Progress" (mimeographed copies in Hoover War Library).

Russian Ambassador at Paris gave a good idea of the meager guarantees which the Kolchak Government could offer for any loan that might be made.[33] At the moment, he said, there were no raw materials available to Kolchak for export. Hence, purchases could be paid for only by export of gold. The shipment of gold, however, would undermine the monetary system and jeopardize the means of paying foreign debts. The ambassador therefore recommended recognition and foreign credits as the only sound way of adjusting the matter. This was a frank admission that the Kolchak regime lacked any other financial basis except the gold received from the Siberian Government and the Allied grants. The bankers of the United States and Britain never received the government guarantees necessary to grant a loan under these circumstances.

During the progress of these negotiations, Kolchak was in the process of being defeated by the Red Army. This fact is the key to an understanding of his willingness to make promises, of his urgent appeals for help, and of his impatience with American neutrality. As early as Februray 15, 1919 news reached the Peace Conference that the Bolsheviks were fighting with considerable success against Kolchak. But it was not actually until late spring that a complete breakdown became apparent in the Kolchak ranks. In July Ambassador Morris noted the complete demoralization of the army.[34] At that time, he reported, there were 35,000 cars filled with refugees moving eastward from the Ekaterinburg-Cheliabinsk area. By fall Kolchak was resorting to far more desperate measures. It has been noted that as conditions grew worse he attempted to make a desperate appeal for popular support by propaganda and by proposals to mitigate the severity of the military regime and create representative institutions. He also considered the use of religious sanctions to save the collapsing regime.[35] He planned to organize orders of the

[33] *Foreign Relations, 1919,* pp. 444–445.
[34] *Ibid.,* p. 394.
[35] V. Pepeliaev, "Razval Kolchakovshchiny," *Krasnyi Arkhiv* (Moscow), No. 31, 1928, p. 51; Pares, *op. cit.,* p. 541.

"Holy Cross" and of the "Yellow Banner" for the religious groups among the refugees and declare a holy war against the Bolsheviks. Bernard Pares relates that Dietrichs "organized a detachment of priests, who faced the enemy with crosses and church banners and made a remarkable impression."

Kolchak had staked everything on a military victory. His plans were said to call for popular support after the victory. The continuing retreat made him aware that he had, in this respect, somewhat reversed the proper order of things. In November the question of holding Omsk itself arose. The government had already been removed to Irkutsk in October. But the psychological value of holding Omsk was apparent to all. Since General Dietrichs claimed it could not be held and General Sakharov claimed it could, the latter was given a chance to prove his claim.[36] At the cost of 40,000 men and "complete trainloads of supplies" which fell into the hands of the Red Army, it was found that Dietrichs was right. Hereafter the demoralized refugees and troops moved westward without any hope except to escape as fast as possible. Of the more than 800,000 men who had once composed the Kolchak army, less than 20,000 reached Transbaikal as intact units and from here some of them crossed the border into Manchuria, where many were disarmed by the Chinese.[37] Some joined Semenov. On November 14 Omsk was abandoned. In an appeal to the United States on this occasion Kolchak called the retreat from Omsk a mere temporary thing.[38] The mass flights, he said, showed the popular fear of the Bolsheviks. The fight he was waging against the Bolsheviks, he added, was for Russia as well as for the rest of the world.

Kolchak arrived at Irkutsk on January 15, 1920.[39] The disintegration of his government had permitted its replacemen at Irkutsk on January 5, 1920 by the Political Center,

[36] S. C. Graves, "The Truth about Kolchak," *op. cit.,* p. 669.
[37] Filatieff, *loc. cit.,* p. 300.
[38] *Foreign Relations, 1919, Russia,* p. 448.
[39] Varneck and Fisher, *op. cit.,* pp. 215–216, n. 1; Miliukov, *op. cit.,* pp. 163–164; Janin, *op. cit.,* pp. 241–243.

a coalition government composed of various party and non-party people, some of them workers in the zemstvos and municipal dumas which had fared so poorly under Kolchak. The whole atmosphere of the Irkutsk area, under this new government representing the elements which had suffered so long from his regime, was extremely hostile to Kolchak. Demands for his surrender had been heard from partisan forces in Nizhne-Udinsk, where he had arrived on December 24, and were repeated as he moved eastward. But the climax of popular indignation against Kolchak came with the murder, in January 1920, of thirty-one hostages, all adherents of the Political Center group.[40] These were taken at the time Kolchak's forces had been compelled to leave Irkutsk. Among them were two former members of the Constituent Assembly, Pavel Milhailov and Boris Markov, who had taken part in the anti-Bolshevik movement in Siberia since 1918. The sentry posted by Kolchak's officers over these people was originally drawn from among his own troops. But Lieutenant-Colonel Sipailov, one of the most sadistic of the officers who later followed Baron von Ungern-Sternberg into Mongolia, arranged to have a sentry from the Semenov forces substituted for the original. With the ground thus cleared, Sipailov ordered the hostages, thirty men and one woman, placed aboard the ice-breaker *Angara* on the morning of January 6, 1920 and taken out onto Lake Baikal. Here they were severely beaten over the head with a heavy wooden stick used for knocking the ice crust from boards and thrown into the lake. The episode was investigated by a committee of Allied representatives, and the part played by Colonel Sipailov fully substantiated. But the gruesome mass murder had aroused feelings that were not easily appeased. Crowds gathered to demand the arrest of Kolchak. Moreover, his fate was in a sense decided by the fact that the government of the area through which he was then passing was controlled by the Political Center from whose number the thirty-one hostages had been taken.

[40] B. N. Volkov (trans. by E. Varneck), "About Ungern"; P. S. Parfenov, *Borba za Dalnii Vostok, 1920–1922*, pp. 47–48.

The surrender of Kolchak to the representatives of the Political Center which followed a few days after these events has remained one of the most controversial aspects of the intervention. Many of the Russian emigré feel to this day that Kolchak was betrayed by the Czechs and deliberately handed over to the Russian authorities. The question arises, therefore, as to the accuracy of this assertion. In the first place, the story of the intervention as already related has disclosed the fact that Kolchak was extremely unpopular among the people of Siberia. This relationship reached a climax in the popular gatherings, in which partisans appeared, after the murder of the hostages. In the second place, the Czechs also were out of sympathy with Kolchak and with the whole movement with which he was associated. This was true not only of the soldiers but also of the Czech high command, especially after the differences between Kolchak and the Czech General Gaida, as a result of which the latter had been deprived of his rank. Colonel B. O. Johnson of the Railway Corps, who was a close observer of all these events, is particularly emphatic about the feelings of the Czechs with respect to Kolchak.[41] He writes: "Even had Janin been personally anxious (and I think he was) to rescue Kolchak, any such command to the Czechs at Irkutsk would have provoked mutiny." Parfenov suggests that this undoubtedly helped to determine General Syrovy's answer when he was consulted by General Janin regarding the question as to whether or not to surrender Kolchak as the people and the Political Center were demanding.[42] Since both these commanders agreed on the question of the surrender, continues Parfenov, it remained only for Janin to stipulate that it should take place after his departure from Irkutsk. This would leave Janin unimplicated in the surrender in the eyes of the European public. If this latter is true it is obvious that Syrovy must have been more anxious to be rid of Kolchak than Janin since the arrangement was handled in such a way as to make the Czechs shoulder practically all of the guilt.

[41] Varneck and Fisher, *op. cit.,* p. 216, n. 1.
[42] Parfenov, *op. cit.,* p. 48.

Since the Czechs, therefore, had not only shown their complete disapproval of Kolchak many months before by withdrawing from the front lines and had, since then, exhibited nothing but impatience with the whole Kolchak regime as well as a strong desire to leave Siberia, it can scarcely be said that they had any reason to be loyal to the Supreme Ruler merely because he was in trouble. Moreover, since they were militarily under the command of the French General Janin, the Czechs were in no sense under any duty to support Kolchak either before or during his attempted flight from the Bolsheviks. The use of the word "betrayal" to describe their surrender of Kolchak to the Political Center cannot, therefore, have anything more than a moral significance. Even this last claim must be viewed in the light of the assurances given the Allies by the leaders of the Political Center that no harm would come to Kolchak. In the light of these facts, the point emphasized by Vice-Admiral Smirnov —that Kolchak and his staff boarded a coach attached to the train of the Sixth Czecho-Slovak Regiment after the guarantee of full Czech protection—seems to have little actual meaning.[43] The demands of the local people and the government would have required that the Czechs risk their lives for a man who, from their point of view, was not worth it.

It was under these circumstances that Admiral Kolchak, with Viktor Pepeliaev and forty-seven other members of his staff, entered Irkutsk in a car on the windows of which were the flags of the United States, Great Britain, France, Japan, and the Czechs, thus implying that his safe passage was guaranteed by these powers rather than by the Czechs alone. According to Admiral Smirnov: "On January fifteenth the train reached Irkutsk, where it was surrounded by armed workmen. A Czecho-Slovak officer entered the admiral's coach and announced that in accordance with the orders of General Janin the Czecho-Slovak guard would be withdrawn. The admiral listened to this decision quite calmly, only re-

---

[43] *Saturday Evening Post*, July 31, 1920 ás quoted in "The Betrayal of Kolchak," *The Far Eastern Review* (Shanghai), xvi, No. 10, October 1920, p. 528.

marking: 'This means that the Allies have betrayed me.' "
Kolchak was taken to Irkutsk prison after the Czech convoy
had passed on. Two writers on this period, it is interesting
to add, note that: "By a curious coincidence, in less than
24 hours after the surrender of Kolchak by the Czechs to the
Irkutsk revolutionaries, the Allied Supreme Council sitting
in Paris decided to open trade with the Soviet Government
through the Cooperatives."[44] The fall of Kolchak was indeed
the end of intervention.

On January 21 a series of hearings began which was intended to open up the whole story of Kolchak and the regime
he headed at Omsk. Unfortunately the story was never finished. On February 7, 1920, on the approach to Irkutsk of
General Kappel and his army, Kolchak's captors took him
and Viktor Pepeliaev, his last Prime Minister, out of their
prison cells and shot them. Meanwhile, the Political Center
had been replaced on January 21, 1920 by the Soviet Military Revolutionary Committee. It was this government which
actually decided on the execution of Kolchak. The Political
Center moved on to Verkhne-Udinsk, where it formed the
basis of the Far Eastern Republic whose organization and
role will presently be described. The end of Kolchak was the
end of civil war and intervention west of Lake Baikal. The
effort to bring the civil war and intervention to a conclusion
east of the lake is the history of the next two and half years
and of the development of the Far Eastern Republic, which
carried on the struggle in the Far East against Japan.

Why did Kolchak fail? To answer this question fully
would mean the repetition of most of the things explained
in previous chapters. It will be recalled that both Japan
and the Bolsheviks, who led the partisan movement, wanted
him to fail and that they were able to control to a considerable extent the railway supply line to the Volga front. At
the same time, it must not be forgotten that the railway was
the lifeline of Siberia. All the promises that Kolchak might
have given would not have brought either to his armies or
to the people of Siberia the munitions so much needed by the

[44] Coates and Coates, *op. cit.*, p. 240.

347

fighting forces or the manufactured articles required by the people to maintain anything but the most primitive life, or even the grain that was needed to prevent starvation and misery. Only the free functioning of the railway and the unrestricted access to the trade outlet at Vladivostok could do this. In assigning reasons for the failure of Kolchak, the civil war and intervention in the Russian Far East which throttled the supply line and maintained political disorder there must by all means be accorded first place.

A second reason for his signal failure was that a revolution was taking place in Russia and that Kolchak appeared to have disregarded all its implications. It has been shown that the Siberian Soviets were overthrown only by non-Russian agencies. The movement which produced Kolchak therefore grew because of foreign support. The democratic proclivities of this movement were overlooked more and more as centralization and compromise with supporters developed into the theoretically absolute rule of Kolchak. It has been seen that this rule led back to something in many ways worse than the Tsarist Government which had been overthrown in March 1917. One of the reasons Kolchak failed, therefore, was that he represented, not only a reversal of all the hopes of the people, but a government whose whole support lay in foreign nations.

Many other reasons have been assigned for his failure. But unfortunately most of them represent disappointed hopes, speculations, or amplifications of those already given. Some, for example, have felt that the timing of the whole Kolchak effort almost foredoomed it to failure. One writer feels that Kolchak would have had a better chance if Germany had held out for six more months.[45] Under these circumstances, he thinks, the Allies would have given more serious aid and the Czechs would not have left the front. It is, of course, impossible to deny this absolutely. But enough has already been said to indicate that these favorable circumstances would not have come about unless the minds of both the Czechs and the Japanese had, in the meantime,

[45] Filatieff, *loc. cit.,* p. 301.

undergone considerable change. Admiral Smirnov, a former chief-of-staff to Kolchak, has another suggestion: "But even now it is clear that the chief cause of the failure was the fact that the Civil War had to start too early, when destructive forces were stronger than creative ones, and it was impossible at that time to arrest the process of disintegration."[46] The Bolsheviks, he continues, wanted to destroy and build on the ruins, while the Whites, on the other hand, were asking for present sacrifices for the sake of the future. These thoughts were expressed thirteen years after the downfall of Kolchak and overlook the fact that, while sacrifices were certainly asked, it was by no means clear to the Siberian people why they were being asked to sacrifice or what these sacrifices would contribute to their future.

Smirnov is on firmer ground when he suggests that the condition of communications made the supplying of the fighting front difficult.[47] He adds that military discipline had degenerated earlier in the revolution and constituted a real problem for Kolchak. In a suggestion which takes a broader view of the situation, he names the lack of unity in Allied policy as one of the factors. This is a reason which is very close to the heart of the whole problem since it must certainly refer to the activities in the Russian Far East already discussed.

Finally, Kolchak's own reason must be considered. In an interview with Ambassador Morris, he attributed his failure to a miscalculation of Bolshevik strength.[48] According to Morris' report to the State Department: "He attributed the present collapse to a mistaken estimate of the Bolshevik strength: his government had made its plans on the assumption, which events proved to be false, that the Bolshevik Government would not survive an aggressive military campaign this spring; he had therefore concentrated his attention on the military situation to the exclusion of pressing

---

[46] M. I. Smirnov, "Admiral Kolchak," *Slavonic and East European Review* (London), XI, No. 32, January 1933, p. 373.

[47] *Ibid.*, p. 387.

[48] *Foreign Relations, 1919, Russia*, p. 415.

financial and economic problems." This statement reflects much of the character of Kolchak, a naval staff officer whose plans could be carried out by issuing orders, charting courses, and calculating the range of guns, who could be correctly considerate of those immediately around him but failed to see the significance of popular support for a war that, at best, was highly unpopular.

The Allied withdrawal, in a sense, began with the establishment of Kolchak as Supreme Ruler. This early beginning of withdrawal was made by the Czechoslovak army, which, it will be recalled, was one of the Allied armies and was subject to the command of the French army. The withdrawal of the Czechs from the Volga front which began in January 1919 was the result of a number of things. Among these were the long-standing desire of the Czechs to reach the Western Front and the promise of the Allies that their service in Russia was only a stop-gap until the arrival of replacements. Another reason was that, regardless of the desires of some individuals, the great bulk of the Czech army did not want to fight the Russians. Finally, there was the reason that perhaps accounts for their withdrawing at the particular time they did. According to the report of General Graves to the Secretary of War: "Many are not in sympathy with the type of government they believe Kolchak is trying to establish in Siberia and a feeling has developed in the ranks that by fighting against the Bolsheviks they are helping to maintain a government with ideas directly opposed to the Czechs' idea of a democratic form of government."[49] It should also be added that the Armistice had changed their plans so that, instead of aiming at transportation to France, all were now anxious to be transported to Czechoslovakia.

After their withdrawal from the front, the Czechs took up positions along the railway. But they remained impatient of all delay and of all demands made upon them. In June 1919 John Stevens of the Railway Committee noted that their morale was so low that discipline among them had

[49] *Ibid.*, pp. 277–278.

deteriorated and four regiments had already refused duty.[50] It was feared that they might defy their officers and make a bargain with the Bolsheviks to go home through European Russia. At Paris, Winston Churchill proposed a plan by which he hoped to make use of the Czech discontent.[51] This plan called for organizing 30,000 of the Czechs for a push through the Bolshevik lines to form a junction with the Allied troops in North Russia. If they could be organized for the push by mid-August, he thought, they could arrive in the north before the harbors were frozen. In exchange, the Allies were to guarantee the immediate transfer of these 30,000 Czechs back to Europe by way of Archangel. The remainder would be taken at the same time from Vladivostok. This would not only relieve the dangerous situation brought about by the Czechs' forced stay in Siberia but it would break up the Bolshevik front and put Kolchak in direct communication with General Ironside in the north. The plan was not tried, and the Czech danger remained as before.

The first actual evacuation of the Czechs was in December 1919.[52] The delay was caused by a shortage of Allied shipping space and by the difficulty of deciding how the expense of the repatriation should be divided among the Allies. Contrary to all expectations, the Soviets not only did not delay the evacuation of the Czechs to Vladivostok but actually expedited their movements.[53] The only deliberate attempt to delay them was on the part of the Japanese. It was agreed among the Allies that the Czechs should have priority of shipping space over the other Allied forces such as Poles, Serbs, and Italians as well as over the war prisoners of the Central Powers. But even with these delays all the Czechs had passed Irkutsk by February 25, 1920, and the rest of the Allied evacuees had passed there by March 3. By May 24 all Czechs had reached Vladivostok and some of the transports

[50] *Ibid.*, p. 281.
[51] *Peace Conference Papers*, vi, pp. 684–686.
[52] Klante, *op. cit.*, pp. 282–283.
[53] *Foreign Relations, 1920, Russia*, iii, pp. 565, 567.

for their repatriation were in the harbor. By September the last of them left Vladivostok harbor. The long Czech anabasis across Siberia had finally drawn to an end.

The downfall of Kolchak was the occasion of a general Allied withdrawal. The small British detachment of the Middlesex Regiment under Colonel Ward which had not been much more than a bodyguard for Kolchak left Vladivostok in September 1919.[54] The first major Allied body, the Czechs, began to depart in the following December. Seeing the trend in favor of a general withdrawal, the Japanese tried to delay the Czech evacuation because their departure would take away their own best excuse for remaining. The insistent demands in the Diet for withdrawal would make it difficult for the Japanese to remain if they were left alone. At Paris, therefore, Viscount Chinda on December 13, 1919 proposed that the Allies remain and that additional forces be sent immediately.[55] But the American decision had been made. On December 29, 1919 General Graves received a message from the War Department that orders for the departure of his entire command would shortly arrive.[56] On January 9, 1920 Secretary Lansing announced this decision officially to Ambassador Shidehara at Washington.[57] The message stated that the objectives of the intervention as outlined in the *Aide Memoire* of July 17, 1918 had been achieved insofar as this was believed possible. The United States had therefore decided to concentrate all its forces at Vladivostok preparatory to embarking for the United States.

The decision of the American Government to withdraw its forces from Siberia resulted partly from the general Allied determination to bring the intervention to a conclusion and partly from objections both from Congress and the press which made a continuance of American participation in the intervention impossible. As long as the war lasted, opposition to Germany remained the measuring stick for most editor-

[54] P. Hodges, *Britmis,* p. 97.
[55] *Peace Conference, Papers,* IX, p. 855.
[56] Graves, *op. cit.,* pp. 302–303.
[57] *Foreign Relations, 1920,* III, pp. 488–489.

ial and official thinking even about Russia. There was, for example, the fear that Germany would succeed in extending her control over Russia both during and after the war. Another fear that troubled many in America and elsewhere was the belief that the Bolsheviks were nothing more than accomplices of the Central Powers, partners in the German program of dominating Russia and the whole East. Still another source of alarm to the Allies was the danger that Germany might seize the military stores which they had sent to Russia and use them against the Allies. Finally, there was the concern lest the Germans, either directly or through the war prisoners of the Central Powers in Russia, might menace the friendly Czech Legion, reportedly trying to make its way to the war fronts in Western Europe. With respect to Japan, the fear of Germany assumed a double and indeed a somewhat contradictory aspect. There was, on the one hand, concern in some quarters about the possibility of an understanding between Germany and Japan with a view to a partition of Russia and, on the other hand, a strong feeling that Japan was after all a fellow Ally and that Allied solidarity must in any case be preserved. Opposition to Japan was, in this sense, not only considered unpatriotic but carried with it the danger of being considered pro-Bolshevik.

In spite of these strong incentives to give Japan a free hand in Siberia, there was, even during the war period, significant opposition to the direction events were taking in the Far East.[58] Through all the controversy over the merits of the Japanese demands for an intervention, one interesting fact stands out clearly—that the ambitions and objectives of Japan in the Russian Far East were, at least in their general outlines, known and pointed out by one or another member of the American press. It was the part that the American troops played in the intervention that was generally misunderstood. On one side of the controversy stood such

[58] "Japan's Proposed Entry into Siberia—An Invasion or a Rescue?" *Current Opinion* (New York), LXIV, No. 4, April 1918, pp. 233–235; "Russia and Japan in the Far East," *The New Republic* (New York), XIV, No. 174, March 2, 1918, pp. 130–132.

newspapers as the *Detroit Free Press* and the *San Francisco Chronicle*, both of which approved of the Japanese interventionist plans as a protective measure against the eastward extension of German power in Russia. The *Columbus Dispatch* agreed substantially with this view, but, in addition, noted that Siberia lay only a few miles from Alaska and ventured the opinion that Japan would make a more desirable neighbor than Germany. The *New York Evening Post* and *Springfield Republican*, on the other hand, warned of the dangers implicit in the Japanese demands. Both saw the moral issue involved in American association with such a venture, a point of view which, it will be recalled, President Wilson shared completely. *The New Republic*, after outlining the real objectives which Japan undoubtedly had in mind in demanding an intervention, concluded that such purposes were "incompatible with the political purposes for which the Western Allies are fighting."

With the conclusion of Allied hostilities against the Central Powers, information about events in Russia became more generally available and the mood, both of the press and of Congress, became increasingly hostile toward the continued presence of American troops in Siberia. Yet, even in this freer atmosphere for gathering and reporting facts, there seems to have been no general understanding, either in the press or in Congress, of the precise motives which had led President Wilson to accept participation in the Siberian intervention. The press, on its part, disclosed a growing awareness of the part played by Semenov and Kalmykov, of the excessively large numbers of Japanese troops in the Russian Far East, of the aggressive drive of the Japanese for commercial monopoly, of the apparent refusal of Japan to cooperate with the other Allies with respect to Kolchak, and of the fact that even the White Russians were displeased with the part the United States was playing in the intervention.[59]

[59] B. A. Roberts, *A Study of American Opinion Regarding Allied Intervention in Siberia*, Unpublished Master's Thesis, University of Hawaii, 1938; D. P. Barrows, *loc. cit.*, pp. 927–931; "Japan and Siberia," *The New Republic* (New York), XXI, No. 267, January 14, 1920, pp. 187–188.

One of the comments on the Siberian situation was to the effect that the very idea of trying to stop Bolshevism by sending troops to Eastern Siberia, meanwhile leaving the way open for its penetration into China through Mongolia or Sinkiang, was nothing more than a useless and futile gesture. Furthermore, the difficulty which President Wilson would have encountered had he tried to interpret his Siberian policy in the light of these facts increased as the war with its cluster of hopes and fears receded into the past. In time the Japanese and their Far Eastern activities came to be viewed in an increasingly unfavorable light. It was, therefore, impossible to defend the continued presence of American troops in Siberia on the grounds of a desire to cooperate there with Japan. On the other hand, to defend our participation on the ground that it was necessary to curb Japanese ambitions in Siberia might very well have endangered our meager fighting force in the Far Eastern Region and our outwardly peaceful relations with Japan, besides raising the possibility of the opposition's seeing in the policy of the administration a pro-Bolshevik motive. It should be added that the real outburst of editorial hostility toward Japan came after the Nikolaevsk incident of 1920.[60] In addition, moreover, to the Japanese aspect of the problem, the whole issue was complicated by the growing popular demand that the troops be brought home. The rescue of the Americans became as appealing an issue as the rescue of the Czech soldiers had once been.

The campaign in Congress against our wartime Siberian policy began soon after the Armistice. In December 1918 Hiram Johnson of California opened this campaign in the Senate by introducing a request for information regarding the policy itself and the need for the further maintenance of American forces in Siberia.[61] The senator, it is interesting to note, moved into the fight cautiously, fully aware that, due to the strong wartime feeling with respect to a too vigorous

[60] Sherower, *op. cit.*, pp. 211–213; N. Peffer, "Japan's Absorption of Siberia," *The Nation* (New York), cxiii, No. 2935, October 5, 1921, pp. 367–369.

[61] United States, *Congressional Record*, Sixty-fifth Congress, Third Session, Part i, p. 342.

opposition to the intervention, his remarks might bring against him the charge of expressing pro-Bolshevik sentiments. This had only recently been as meaningful a charge as pro-Germanism. He therefore stated plainly and positively at the outset that he was not a Bolshevik. As to the reason which actuated him in opening the inquiry, he stated that, "It is because no Senator with whom I have talked, no public official of whom I have inquired, knows, because, indeed, we do not know and our people do not know, what we do or what we seek in Russia or what our ultimate purpose is, that I present my resolution and these remarks."[62] His statement which followed shows that he was aware of many of the events that had clustered around the revolution and intervention in Russia and of some aspects of the American part in these events. But, if he understood the real motives which had impelled the President to accept a leading role in the Siberian intervention, he concealed it entirely.

It was the inquiry thus opened, without the benefit of a broad understanding and consideration of the crucial problem involved, that eventually made it impossible for the United States to continue its participation in the military aspects of the Siberian intervention and thus carry out successfully the only purpose the President had seen for entering Siberia in the first place. In June 1919, with the signing of the Treaty of Versailles, the ghost of the once lively German menace to Siberia was finally laid. In the following month the President found it necessary to make a report to Congress of his Siberian policy. In it he explained that the United States had made certain commitments with respect to Siberia and that their fulfillment required the presence of both Mr. Stevens and the railway men and of the military forces under General Graves to guarantee the success of the enterprise. But, unfortunately for the popularity of his remarks, it was necessary for the President to rest his entire case on the obligation to cooperate with Japan. In addition, the whole question became increasingly entangled with the party politics of the approaching national elections and with

[62] *Ibid.,* Sixty-Sixth Congress, First Session, Part III, pp. 3140–3141.

the bitter fight over the League of Nations. In the long run, therefore, the case for American participation in the Siberian intervention was never fought out on its merits, and withdrawal was eventually forced upon the President without his being able to offer any real objection or to explain what the actual results of American withdrawal were likely to be. If a moral were an appropriate epitaph for the Siberian episode, it could be said that, once more as in the first months and years of the century, it was demonstrated that the American people were not anxious to fight for the "open door" in the Far East.

One of the unfortunate results of the pressure for the withdrawal of the American forces from Siberia was that it left the Japanese in sole possession there. This fact, of course, was obnoxiously evident both to the critical Japanese public, who were paying the bill, as well as to the world at large, which looked with concern upon the sole Japanese occupation and the implications it might have with reference to the balance of power in the world. The Japanese expansionists, therefore, saw the necessity of finding some reasonably plausible excuse for continuing their intervention. This was found presently in the fact that General Graves had received word of his departure and issued a statement to this effect in Vladivostok before the official announcement of the American withdrawal was made to Japan. A pretended injury by reason of this "sudden" and unfortunately announced decision gave the Japanese Government the desired opportunity to announce later its decision to remain. In a book prepared for the Washington Conference, the propagandist K. K. Kawakami made as much as possible out of this alleged failure of the United States to consult Japan on her withdrawal plans.[63] Had Japan been consulted, he said, a simultaneous withdrawal might have been possible. It may be said in passing that the available correspondence on the subject shows the American "error" to be a Japanese misinterpretation without any real basis. In any case, the American withdrawal proceeded as planned and the last of the American

[63] K. K. Kawakami, *Japan's Pacific Policy,* p. 249.

357

forces, including General Graves, left Vladivostok on April 1, 1920. As the ships pulled away from the docks a Japanese band played "Hard Times Come Again No More"!

During the joint intervention the Japanese Government tried in every possible way to use the presence of American troops to her own advantage. At times she did this by a refusal to cooperate, at times by an apparent readiness to work in complete harmony. Japan's aggressive conduct, the full extent and effect of which has been described in previous chapters, was therefore at times but dimly visible in the diplomatic statements that were meanwhile being handed in to the State Department by the official Japanese representatives. Thus in April 1919 General Tanaka, Minister of War, proposed renewed efforts at cooperation in guarding the railway.[64] He also expressed regret at the newspaper campaigns in the United States and Japan against each other. Finally, he mentioned an entertainment he was proposing to give in honor of Ambassador Morris. But by August official relations had reached something like opposite extreme. In a note of August 30, 1919, the United States denounced the Japanese refusal to cooperate in guarding the railway and threatened to withdraw its forces from Siberia and announce to the world its reason for doing so.[65] By the end of October the Japanese were again proposing nothing less than complete harmony along the railway. This was only an introduction to the surprise which Lansing received on November 15.[66] In it the Japanese expressed regret that they had been so foolish as to believe that all those opposing them in Siberia were Bolsheviks. They saw now that those people were only the oppressed who in self-defense were fighting reactionaries. They expressed a complete lack of confidence in Kolchak and believed his fall imminent. They would like to see, they added, a government of the elements which made up the zemstvos and cooperatives and a policy of strict noninterference by the Allies. They were, in fact, anxious to furnish

[64] *Foreign Relations, 1919, Russia,* pp. 556–557.
[65] *Ibid.,* pp. 577–578.
[66] *Ibid.,* pp. 596–597; *Foreign Relations, 1920,* III, p. 481.

economic aid to Russia in exchange for raw materials. This strange message was interpreted by the State Department as an open bid to cooperate in ousting Kolchak. In the light of succeeding correspondence it must also be seen as a proposal for a joint Japanese-American agreement to share the markets and raw materials of Siberia. As though to corroborate the settlement of the whole Siberian episode by an affirmation of this new Japanese proposal, at an Allied conference in London on December 13, 1919, Lloyd George expressed the view that the Siberian affair was now a question to be decided between the United States and Japan.[67]

Since the United States not only found this proposal unacceptable but chose to emphasize her displeasure by a hasty withdrawal of her army from Siberia, Japan made full use of the alleged injury arising from the suddenness of the withdrawal and proceeded on February 27, 1920 to announce what appeared superficially to be a program of evacuation.[68] The plan then outlined called for complete withdrawal from all parts of Siberia except Vladivostok and Nikolsk-Ussuriisk. Transbaikal and the Amur would be evacuated as soon as the Czechs had passed these points. But no Bolshevik forces would be allowed along the Chinese Eastern Railway and Chinese and Japanese troops would be stationed in North Manchuria to prevent the Red Army from entering there. The occupation of Vladivostok would be deemed essential for the protection of Korea. It will be remembered that the Japanese used their occupancy of Vladivostok to carry out an economic strangulation of Siberia by preventing access to the port and blocking the use of the railway. It can therefore be seen that this "evacuation" order had the effect of entrenching Japan in North Manchuria and in Vladivostok where she could exercise the same kind of disruptive influence over Siberia as she had for the past year and a half.

As early as November 27, 1919 Japan had in a sense begun to lay the groundwork for the reoccupation of Eastern Siberia by announcing the claim under which she would

[67] Peace Conference Papers, IX, p. 853.
[68] Foreign Relations, 1920, III, pp. 504–505.

eventually seek to carry out that reoccupation. On that date a statement appeared in *Asahi* explaining that the chaotic conditions in Siberia might make it necessary to maintain at least a small garrison at Vladivostok, Chita, and other points.[69] This was indeed the basis on which Japan later built her elaborate excuse for remaining in Russia. After the false withdrawal decision of February 27, the Russian governments in the Far Eastern Region were becoming impatient of the Japanese delay. On March 2, 1920 the Maritime Provisional Government handed a note to the Japanese Diplomatic Mission requesting the Japanese to leave as soon as possible.[70] According to this note the Japanese were only committing atrocities and harboring criminals. The Provisional Government announced that it would assume full responsibility for the safety and protection of all. There was therefore every reason, the note concluded, why the Japanese should leave immediately. The Japanese answer came on March 31.[71] It repeated substantially the argument which had appeared in *Asahi* three months before. Japan, it explained, occupied a special position regarding the continent. Through her interests in Korea and Manchuria she would naturally be affected by the chaotic conditions prevailing in Siberia. When this danger was removed, the note concluded, and when the lives and property of Japanese nationals were deemed safe and railway communications were fully assured, the Japanese troops would be withdrawn "as early as possible."

As far as formal international agreements and understandings were concerned, this was indeed a new interpretation of the Japanese position in Siberia. Words were now being used which were reminiscent of those once used to define the Japanese relationship to Korea and then Manchuria. Territorial contiguity as a factor which creates special interests was, in fact, being invoked as a formula for exer-

[69] *Foreign Relations, 1919, Russia,* p. 602.
[70] The Special Delegation of the Far Eastern Republic to the United States of America, *Japanese Intervention in the Russian Far East,* Washington, 1922, pp. 103–106.
[71] *Ibid.,* pp. 36–37; Shinobu, *op. cit.,* pp. 75–76.

cising rights in Russia which international law denies to any but the territorial sovereign, but which previous experience in the Far East had taught her could be overlooked with impunity. An editorial in the periodical *Gaiko Jiho* for April 15, 1920 corrected the notion that this idea was new in its application to Siberia.[72] This article reiterated the reasons already given for remaining in Siberia, basing the whole argument upon the special position which Japan occupied by reason of the proximity of Manchuria and Korea to the chaotic regions to the north. From this it could be seen, concluded the writer, that Japan was remaining in Siberia for the very same reason she entered in the first place. The extension of this doctrine, formerly applied only to territories south of the Amur River, in a sense completed the rational background of the Japanese occupation of key points in Siberia. She had announced her intention and her right to remain.

While the events of April 4–5, 1920, when Japan reestablished her military control in the Maritime Province, were the logical results of this announcement, they were even more directly the results of developments then taking place in Eastern Siberia. Perhaps the most important reason that the reoccupation occurred when it did was the departure of the last American forces on April 1.[73] The departure of the Americans—and by that date of many of the Czechs as well —reduced the chances that the Japanese forces would run into serious difficulty when the attack should be carried out. At the same time, Japan increased her forces across the border in Manchuria to some 200,000 men. A second reason for staging the overturn in early April was the political development reflected in the conference which assembled at Nikolsk-Ussuriisk on April 1, 1920.[74] This conference was attended by delegates from all parts of Eastern Siberia who had assembled to discuss plans for the unification of the whole

[72] "Shibiri Mondai," *Gaiko Jiho* (Tokyo), xxxi, No. 8, April 15, 1920, pp. 701–702.
[73] S. C. Graves, "Japanese Aggression in Siberia," *op. cit.*, p. 243.
[74] Norton, *op. cit.*, pp. 111–112.

area east of Lake Baikal. The Japanese undoubtedly knew that the objectives of this meeting represented the firm intention of the Soviet Government. They also knew that should it result in success the people of the area would be united under a single government and would be more difficult to oppose in the future. Finally, the events which occurred at Nikolaevsk, as described in a previous chapter, provided an excuse which might not occur again.

In addition to acting at a time that was opportune, the Japanese had made careful preparations for the events of April 4–5. The reports of observers in Siberia indicate that a well-coordinated plan formed the basis for the attack. In Transbaikal, before their withdrawal into Manchuria, they had attempted unsuccessfully to delay the Czech movement eastward. Furthermore, the Japanese troops remaining in the Maritime Province had been augmented by those withdrawn from other parts of Eastern Siberia and left at strategic points throughout the province. Just before the attack these were alerted for simultaneous action. In Vladivostok itself the Japanese forces had, during the month of March, occupied important heights around the city.[75] By the end of March General Graves noted that Japanese troops were digging trenches and filling sandbags near Vladivostok as if preparing for a strong defense.[76] On March 31 the Japanese Government announced the postponement of her evacuation of Russian territory. Then, on April 1, the very day the last American departed, Japanese infantry took up positions commanding the railway stations and at the same time erected machine guns and field guns at Fort Number Six, one of the most important fortifications in Vladivostok. In the light of all this activity, most of it well known to General Graves, it seems something of an understatement that the General should report in such a matter-of-fact way the information given him by the Associated Press representative to the effect that it was definitely known that the Japanese were

[75] *Foreign Relations, 1920*, III, pp. 506–507:
[76] W. S. Graves, *op. cit.*, pp. 326–328.

planning something although it was uncertain exactly what it was.

With all preparations thus carefully made, the Japanese, on April 2, presented a set of demands to the Provisional Government at Vladivostok, compliance with which would have come close to making the Japanese supreme in the vicinity of that city.[77] Thus, without stipulating what agreements were meant, it demanded that the Provisional Government ratify all future Russian-Japanese agreements. It also demanded that barracks, food, and transportation should be provided for the Japanese forces and that immunity be guaranteed to all persons assisting them. All anti-Japanese press utterances and all movements that might threaten the Japanese forces or the peace of Korea and Manchuria were to be suppressed. To discuss these proposals a commission was appointed consisting of Japanese and Russians. By April 4 an agreement had been reached by this commission which substantially conceded all the demands. The conference was adjourned until 5.00 p.m. on the following day, when the final agreement was to have been signed.

While the Russian and Japanese sources are in substantial agreement regarding events immediately preceeding the outbreak of hostilities and on the fact that an armed clash did occur on the night of April 4, they are in complete disagreement about the cause and nature of the actual attack. Thus, according to the official Japanese statement: "At 10.15 p.m. of the 4th, however, our infantry patrol was suddenly attacked by the Russians and the latter took the offensive against us in many points of the town."[78] The only comment that can possibly be made on this statement is that nothing that happened on this occasion supports it. On the contrary, everything indicates a deliberate attempt on the part of the Japanese to reestablish their control in the Maritime Province. There were, first of all, the elaborate preparations preceding April 4 which have just been described. On the very

[77] *Foreign Relations, 1920,* III, pp. 506–507.
[78] *Ibid.,* III, p. 509.

day the Japanese-Russian commission seemed to be reaching an agreement, the Japanese posted notices in the railway stations along the Ussuri Line in the Maritime Province demanding that all Russian garrisons surrender their arms immediately.[79] This alone was an aggressive act. But on the night of the attack, before the action was opened, the watch officer aboard the *U.S.S. Albany* noted two red flashes, the signal to commence firing, from the direction of Vladivostok.[80]

Once these preparations had been made and the signal given, the attack was carried out rapidly and with complete coordination throughout the Maritime Province. Simultaneously, at Vladivostok, Shkotovo, Nikolsk-Ussuriisk, Iman, Spassk, Khabarovsk, and other railway towns the Japanese fell upon the Russian garrisons, disarmed them, and in a short time assumed control in most of these localities.[81] In many places the attacks were brutally carried out, a fact which is amply demonstrated by the estimated Russian casualties which numbered about 500 killed and 300 wounded. In Khabarovsk the bombardment went on for two days while people were machine-gunned at random in the streets. Important points in Vladivostok were occupied and the Russian troops were disarmed. All Koreans suspected of complicity in opposing the Japanese were taken and shot. It was on this occasion also that Lazo, Lutsky, and Sibirtsev of the Military Soviet were burned in a locomotive. P. S. Parfenov, also a member of the Military Soviet and the author of several books referred to in previous chapters, was able to escape this grim fate. Thus by the time the people of the Maritime Province awoke on Palm Sunday, April 5, they found that the intervention with all its accompanying horrors was not actually over as they had thought. The Japanese troops had swiftly assumed the occupancy which was to last another two and a half years.

[79] Stewart, *op. cit.*, p. 384.

[80] W. S. Graves, *op. cit.*, p. 328

[81] A. Iaremenko, "Partizanskoe Dvizhenie v Primorskoi Oblasti (1918–1920)," pp. 88–89; *A Short Outline of the History of the Far Eastern Republic*, p. 17.

In Tokyo the Minister of War, General Tanaka, was asked before the Imperial Diet why the troops had been ordered to resume the intervention.[82] The general explained—in words that are reminiscent of the reasons already given by the other Allies for remaining in Siberia after the Armistice—that it would have been against the principle of Bushido to abandon Semenov at a time when he was hard-pressed by the Bolsheviks. He failed to explain why Kolchak and Kalmykov, both allegedly faithful adherents of the Allied cause, had by this time not only been abandoned but allowed to be shot. Semenov, it is interesting to note in passing, waited nearly a quarter of a century before he met his end. At the close of the Second World War he was captured by the armies of the Soviet Union and shot.

The attack of April 4–5 reached its complete fulfillment only after the Nikolaevsk affair gave Japan the necessary excuse for the occupation of the important coastal areas. After this, by virtue of their troops in Manchuria, at Vladivostok and Nikolaevsk, the Japanese were in effective control of the outlets of Eastern Siberia. The region, so dependent upon outside sources for many aspects of its economic life, was effectively sealed from the outer world.

With the exception of the government organized at Chita by Ataman Semenov, the governments which took shape in Eastern Siberia after the defeat of Kolchak were under the general direction of the Dalburo, or Far Eastern Bureau of the Russian Communist Party at Khabarovsk. The Dalburo exercised a leadership in political affairs which made the real difference between the situation before and after the Kolchak regime. As in 1918, the fall of Kolchak in 1920 also saw the appearance of pretenders to political power. There was Nikolai Gondatti, former Imperial governor of the Russian Far East, who came forward with a proposal to establish a dictatorship in Eastern Siberia supported by Japanese troops. Semenov, claiming supreme authority by virtue of an appointment made by Kolchak on January 5, 1920, maintained a government at Chita as long as Japanese

[82] A. M. Young, *Japan under Taisho Tenno, 1912–1926,* p. 196.

troops supported 'him.[83] By October 1920 the forces of the Far Eastern Republic had driven him from Chita and back once more into Manchuria.

The Provisional Zemstvo Government of the Maritime Province which sprang into existence on January 31, 1920 was, from the standpoint of the Dalburo, a compromise government.[84] It succeeded the administration of General Rozanov, the Far Eastern representative of Kolchak, and was brought into existence after the overthrow of Rozanov by the partisan force under Shevchenko. Its existence was later approved by a Congress of Workers' Deputies of the Maritime Province held at Nikolsk-Ussuriisk in April 1920. The Provisional Government was a compromise government in an international sense because its existence as a separate entity was in response to the warnings issued by Japan against the establishment of a Communist regime near Japan or one of her territories. It was understood that failure to heed these warnings would furnish Japan with the excuse she eagerly desired to carry out a reoccupation of Eastern Siberia. Politically it was also a compromise body since it included non-Communist members while its president, Medvedev, was a Socialist Revolutionary. During the remaining two months of his tour of duty in Siberia, General Graves watched the Provisional Government with interest.[85] During this time, he reported, he "never saw anyone try harder to be fair and just to everyone than did these people." This observation was in contrast to the reports later circulated about this regime which tried to make it appear as an oppressive and irresponsible government.

On February 6, 1920 a partisan and openly Communistic regime was established at Blagoveshchensk.[86] The strength of the partisan forces in this region had long made it difficult

[83] P. S. Parfenov, *Borba za Dalnii Vostok, 1920, 1922*, Leningrad, 1928, pp. 41–42; *Foreign Relations, 1920*, III, pp. 555–556.

[84] A Iaremenko, "Partizanskoe Dvizhenie v Primorskoi Oblasti (1918–1920)," *Proletarskaia Revoliutsiia* (Moscow), pp. 82–83, 87.

[85] Graves, *op. cit.*, pp. 324–325.

[86] *A Short Outline of the History of the Far Eastern Republic*, p. 12; *Foreign Relations, 1920*, III, pp. 557–558.

for the Japanese troops to maintain their hold. Kolchak's defeat gave the Japanese less hope of survival here and furnished the partisans with renewed courage to assert their strength. The Japanese withdrew, some into Transbaikal, some in the direction of Khabarovsk, and some across the Amur into Manchuria. There followed the establishment of the openly Communist government headed by Trelisser. The regime never aspired to an independent existence but subordinated itself to the Far Eastern Republic on May 25, 1920 and was from this time controlled from Verkhne-Udinsk and later Chita. Trelisser, however, remained in charge of the local government.

The government which constituted, throughout the two and a half years after the Allied withdrawal, the major political unit east of Lake Baikal was the one known as the Far Eastern Republic. It had originally been intended that the Republic, sponsored by the coalition party known as the Political Center, should be established at Irkutsk.[87] However, the prospect of further trouble with interventionary forces still remaining in Transbaikal made the Bolshevik and partisan leaders unwilling to leave the strategic Baikal tunnels unguarded. This resulted in the establishment of a Soviet regime at Irkutsk and in the occupation of the tunnels by the Red Army. The government of the Political Center was therefore forced to move into Transbaikal, where it soon established itself at Verkhne-Udinsk. The western boundary of this government with the territory controlled directly by the Soviets was Lake Baikal and the Selenga River.

The nature of the Far Eastern Republic, while perfectly clear to its members, was the subject of some speculation at the time it was founded. A well-phrased if somewhat over-enthusiastic statement of its basic functions explains that: "The Far Eastern Republic represents a particularly outstanding example of Leninist, Bolshevist tactics: in the difficult international situation of the party, a state was established which would have the maximum of Soviet support

[87] F. B. Kirby, "Siberia's New Republic: Its Standing," *The New York Times Current History* (New York), xv, No. 3, June 1921, p. 476.

under the guise of a bourgeois democracy while at the same time preparing for the liquidation of the intervention."[88] The "difficult international situation" was of course the Allied effort of the previous two years to stamp out Bolshevism in Russia. Realizing that the establishment of a Communist regime near Japan or Japanese territory would bring a protest from Tokyo which might appeal strongly to the Allies and deprive Russia of any world sympathy to which Japanese aggression might otherwise entitle them, the Bolsheviks decided once more to compromise. They therefore established a liberal regime to which the democratic governments of the world would find it difficult to object. This gave the members of the government of the Republic the necessary political prestige to appeal to the Allied governments against the aggression of Japan.

The Far Eastern Republic was to a very large extent the result of the experience and planning of a single man—Aleksander Mikhailovich Krasnoshchekov. This man was born in 1880 of humble parentage near Kiev.[89] As a boy he had engaged in revolutionary activity for which he was in due course exiled to Nikolaevsk on the Amur River. In 1905 he was arrested again for the same reason, but this time he managed to escape and made his way to the United States. Eventually he was graduated from the University of Chicago and became a practicing attorney in the same city. Upon hearing the news of the revolution of 1917 he immediately made plans to return to Russia and landed at Vladivostok in August 1917. He soon became a member of the city government in Nikolsk-Ussuriisk. When the Soviets assumed power in Siberia he became president of the Far Eastern Council of People's Commissars. Upon the landing of the Allied troops at Vladivostok in the summer of 1918 he fled with his staff up the Zeia River, where the partisan center was located. His experience during the intervention convinced him that a democratic non-Communist buffer state in Eastern Siberia was the only answer to the problem posed by the presence

[88] A. Shurygin and Z. Karpenko, *op. cit.*, p. 117.
[89] Stewart, *op. cit.*, pp. 379ff.

of hostile Japanese forces there. He was able to come to an agreement with the Soviet Government in this matter and the eventual result was the establishment of the Far Eastern Republic. During the more than two years and a half of its existence, the Republic was under his actual control.

After an agreement on this basis with the Soviet officials at Omsk on January 18, 1920, Krasnoshchekov went eastward, finally arriving at Verkhne-Udinsk on the Selenga River on March 7.[90] This was also the day on which the partisans entered the city and drove out Semenov and his forces. Krasnoshchekov proceeded at once to the organization of a government which was then called the Provisional Local Self-Government of Pribaikal. The name Pribaikal here refers to the western part of the former Transbaikal Province. Because of Semenov's presence at Chita, the province was divided into two parts, Pribaikal being the part containing Verkhne-Udinsk and Transbaikal Province the remainder, with the city of Chita as its center. A Congress of Workers and Partisans on April 6, 1920 announced the declaration of independence of the Provisional Government of the Far Eastern Republic.[91] Recognition of the new state by the Soviet Government was sent from Moscow on May 14, 1920. The flag adopted was red with blue in the upper left-hand corner. On the blue section appeared the letters D.V.R., the abbreviation of the Russian words for Far Eastern Republic.

A Constituent Assembly which was in session between February 12 and April 26, 1921 formulated and approved the Constitution of the Republic which gave the government some of the outward semblances of a liberal state.[92] The executive power was vested in a group of seven persons known as the Government, the Chairman of which was the nominal head of the Republic. The Government was elected by the National Assembly for a period of two years, but once elected was independent of control by the Assembly. Under

[90] Norton, *op. cit.*, pp. 134ff.
[91] "Dalnevostochnaia Respublika," *Bolshaia Sovetskaia Entsiklopediia*, Moscow, 1920, xx, p. 218.
[92] The Constitution is given in Norton, *op. cit.*, pp. 282–307.

the Government and responsible both to it and the Assembly there was the Council of Ministers, a group of fifteen who carried on the actual administration. One interesting exception was the Minister of Nationalities, whose office was created independently under the Constitution. The legislative authority was exercised by the National Assembly, a unicameral body which served for two years. Its powers were such as to make it the highest organ of power in the Republic. It created not only the executive but also the judicial organs of the government. The latter consisted of a People's Court in which not only professional jurists but at least two citizens sat at a trial.

The provincial governments were nominally controlled by appointees of the central government known as Emissars, one for each of the five provinces. Actually the Provincial Assembly held the same place in the province as the National Assembly in the Republic. Its own executive creation was the Administrative Board which carried out all provincial laws while the Emissars were charged with the execution of Republic laws. The provinces were in turn subdivided into county, city, and village units, the last controlled by an Assembly consisting of all its citizens.

The rights of the citizen and the rights of land ownership were distributed in a way that made it difficult to determine how liberal or Communistic the state actually was. All the civil liberties and rights, including *habeas corpus,* freedom of speech and press, were fully guaranteed. All class distinctions and privileges and all civil and military titles were abolished. Minority national groups were guaranteed a measure of autonomy. This applied particularly to the large Buriat population of the Baikal area. Land, on the other hand, was not treated as in a democratic state of the western type. The ownership of land, forests, waterways, and resources was vested in the whole body of the people. The military forces of the Republic consisted of the People's Revolutionary Army, the members of which were drawn from volunteers over the age of eighteen or conscripts over the age of twenty-five. Universal, compulsory education was provided by the state.

This was the government which achieved a recognized status in all of the Far Eastern Region except the Pacific coastal areas and the southern part of the Maritime Province, areas which were under Japanese occupation. The location of the capital was at Verkhne-Udinsk until the seizure of Chita from Semenov by partisans on the night of October 20–21, 1920, after which it was moved to that city, where it remained until the Republic was dissolved and absorbed into the Soviet Russian state in 1922. There had at first been some rivalry between the governments of Verkhne-Udinsk and Vladivostok as to which should constitute the capital and center of the government of the Far East. But the note of recognition from Moscow on May 14, 1920, settled this question in favor of Verkne-Udinsk. The capital was to be where the Soviet Government rather than the Japanese could control it. This would obviate the dangers and temptations of asserting undue independence such as might have arisen from a compromise offer which came from Semenov before he was driven out of Transbaikal. He offered his services as commander-in-chief of the armies of the Republic and "protector" of the state.

The foreign relations of the Republic were dominated by its suspected relationship with Soviet Russia and its economic subordination to the whims of Japan due to the commanding position held by the latter with reference to the natural outlets of Siberia to the sea. The Republic had unofficial representation at Washington as well as at Peking during the Conference of 1921–22. Besides seeking recognition, these representatives tried earnestly to find assistance in getting rid of the Japanese armies and in obtaining economic assistance. When the removal of the Japanese armies was achieved, however, no further requests from foreign governments were necessary. On November 14, 1922 the Far Eastern Republic was absorbed in the Russian Soviet Republic.

CHAPTER 10

The End of Intervention

THE final phase of the Siberian intervention was the period
which began with the American withdrawal in April 1920
and ended with the Japanese evacuation in October 1922.
The transport carrying General Graves and the last American
contingent had scarcely cleared Russian Island in Peter the
Great Bay when the Japanese, ostensibly engaged in concentrating their own forces at Vladivostok preparatory to
evacuating, staged a military overturn and reasserted their
authority in the Maritime Province. On the very next day
the Far Eastern Republic, a non-Communist political creation of the Bolsheviks aimed at forestalling just such an overt
act by Japan, proclaimed its authority in all parts of the Far
Eastern Region. Finally, the tragic affair at Nikolaevsk on
the Amur provided the occasion for the Japanese occupation
of North Sakhalin and the coastal areas of the Maritime
Province. With the completion of these steps, the Allied
withdrawal, the occupation by Japan of all key strategic
positions from which both military and economic pressure
could be exerted and, finally, the organization of the Far
Eastern Republic as a buffer state, the essential features of
the Japanese period of the intervention were complete.

With certain important exceptions, the Japanese phase of
the intervention exhibited generally the same characteristics
as those already described with reference to the Allied phase.
There were the same White Russian leaders trying to find
external help and internal support for an anti-Soviet regime.
There was the same calculated disregard for the rights of the
people and the same propensity of both Japanese and White
Russian troops to punish the villagers on the slightest pretext. The contest for the railways, narrowed down finally to
the Chinese Eastern Railway and the Ussuri line in the Mari-

time Province, assumed if anything an even more far-reaching competitive aspect than formerly. Yet these various features of induced confusion were somewhat modified by the existence in the Region of the Far Eastern Republic, itself a product of Bolshevik political strategy and the growth of partisan military strength during the previous phase of the intervention. Finally, elements of potential stability were introduced by the greater independence with which China conducted her relations with Japan and by the presence near Lake Baikal of a Soviet Government and a detachment of the Red army.

It must be emphasized that this concluding chapter covers a period which is not only longer than that described in the foregoing seven chapters but one which is equally important. Therefore, only the main outlines of this two-and-a-half-year period can be included here. Local events, because of their similarity to those already discussed, will be mentioned only briefly. World events, constituting the significant difference between the two phases of the intervention, will receive relatively more attention. The first of these was the role the Soviets began to assume in China and other Far Eastern nations whose past or present bore the imprint of imperialistic aggression. The second was the new international position of Japan resulting from the desire of European and American businessmen to return to the markets, particularly in Asia and Latin America, which had fallen to Japan after the outbreak of the war in Europe. Finally, there was the Washington Conference where these Far Eastern problems were considered, as well as those other timely conferences which Japan held at Dairen and Changchun in order to keep her Siberian affairs out of the spotlight of the Washington Conference.

One of the most significant aspects of either domestic or international developments in the Far East after the Paris Peace Conference was the spirit of anti-imperialistic revolt which matured there and the leadership which the Bolsheviks attempted to assume in this movement. Instead of the appeal for a class war made by the Soviet Government in

373

Europe, the ideological campaign which the Bolsheviks opened in the Far East took the form of a crusade against agrarian backwardness in domestic affairs and imperialism in the international sphere. Before the war, Imperial Russia, though herself subject to imperialistic influences, had stood shoulder to shoulder with Japan and the Western Powers in the campaign against the sovereignty and territorial integrity of China. But throughout the war period the rapid and almost unopposed aggressions of Japan became the central fact of the international life of China. Moreover, the activities of the Peace Conference at Paris made it increasingly obvious that it was not intended that the principle of the self-determination of nations should be applied to the Far East. The strength of the Soviet appeal to the Eastern people was greatly enhanced by the fact that she herself had suffered from both these aspects of Allied policy. During and after the war the Soviets were forced to fight for their very existence against a Japanese and general Allied intervention. At the Peace Conference, furthermore, not only were the rights of Soviet Russia, as she saw them, completely ignored, but her presence at the Conference was neither requested nor desired. It was not without reason, therefore, that the Soviet Government decided to appeal to the Far Eastern peoples as a friend of all who suffered under the yoke of imperialism.

Almost at the very moment of the opening of the Siberian intervention the Bolsheviks had begun to lay the foundation for the appeal to the people of China, Korea, and other countries. In a letter dated August 1, 1918 the Soviet Government offered its moral support to Sun Yat-sen, hailing him as the leader of Chinese democracy against the government at Peking and against international imperialism.[1] "Our defeat," the Bolsheviks informed Dr. Sun, "is your defeat." During the following year, while Kolchak was experiencing the fleeting triumphs and the more permanent defeats at the hands of the growing Red army, the Soviets were carefully preparing to undermine the whole foundation of the im-

[1] Pollard, *op. cit.*, pp. 127–128.

perialists in Eastern Asia. Special schools and training courses were established for the study of Oriental peoples and for the training of agitators to carry the anti-imperialist message to all peoples of Asia. The Second Congress of the Communist International in the summer of 1920 was able to report great progress in their agitational work in China. They found excellent and promising material in the students, intellectuals, and workers of that nation. It was, in fact, at this congress that the policy of the Communist International with reference to Eastern peoples was established. In the words of a statement written by Lenin himself, "In backward countries it is especially important to support peasant movements against the landowners and all feudal survivals."[2] During 1919 and 1920 encouragement was given not only to Chinese anti-imperialist movements and to anti-Japanese activities in Korea but to the "incipient social disturbances in Japan," as well.[3] In the end these moves would, it anticipated, cut the very ground from under the Japanese Government both at home and abroad and render useless any temporary military successes that might be achieved in Siberia or elsewhere.

Not confining its efforts to groups with excellent causes but lacking as yet any political power, the Soviet Government also addressed itself to the regular governments of both Japan and China. On February 24, 1920 the Soviet Foreign Commissar, Chicherin, addressed a peace proposal to the Japanese Government.[4] In exchange for immediate evacuation of Russian territory, the Soviets offered various economic and commercial privileges. It was probably felt that, with the postwar maladjustments and disturbances in Japan and the imminent withdrawal of the American forces from Siberia, the time was opportune for a proposal which promised Japan some of the things she had so long struggled to attain. Events proved this hope to be ill founded.

[2] *Vtoroi Kongres Kommunisticheskogo Internatsionala, Iiul-Avgust 1920*, Moscow, 1934, p. 5.
[3] Dennis, *op. cit.*, p. 317.
[4] *Izvestiia*, March 31, 1920.

The Soviet approach to the government at Peking retained many of the features of the anti-imperialist program so widely proclaimed through propagandist channels. In a declaration of July 25, 1919 to the people and government of China, Karakhan, Deputy Foreign Commissar, proposed the opening of negotiations between China and Soviet Russia with the object of helping China to escape being transformed into a second Korea or a second India.[5] In this message it was explained that: "We are bringing to the people their liberation from foreign bayonets, from the yoke of the foreign gold which is strangling the enslaved peoples of the Orient, and first among them the Chinese Nation." It reviewed the events of the past two years, telling of the annulment by the new Soviet Government after its victory in 1917 of all the secret treaties concluded between the Russian Imperial Government on the one hand and Japan, China, and the Allies on the other. In particular, the Soviets had then expressed a readiness to open negotiations for the annulment of the Treaty of 1896 regarding the Chinese Eastern Railway as well as the treaties between Japan and Russia from 1907 to 1916. Negotiations along these lines, continued the declaration, were in progress in March 1918 when the Allies suddenly forced their discontinuance. "Without awaiting the return of the Manchurian Railroad to the Chinese people," the message concluded, "Japan and the Allies seized it themselves, invaded Siberia, and even forced the Chinese troops to assist them in that criminal and unprecedented theft." These were the months, it will be recalled, when Semenov made his unsuccessful attempt to invade Siberia, when the Soviet-Manchurian border was closed by orders from the Allies, and when the Sino-Japanese treaties for cooperation in North Manchuria and Siberia were being forced upon China. The declaration had in it, therefore, a significant element of truth which could hardly have avoided striking a responsive note

[5] Declaration given in V. A. Yakhontoff, *Russia and the Soviet Union in the Far East,* New York, 1931, pp. 381–384; see also N. Terentev, "Prodazha K. V. Zh. D. i Borba SSSR za Mir," *Tikhii Okean* (Moscow), No. 2 (4), April-June 1935, p. 100.

THE END OF INTERVENTION

in the hearts of all those in China who remembered these events.

Whether by design or otherwise, the declaration also contained a large element of deception. This concerned what appeared to be an offer to return the Chinese Eastern Railway to China. The Russian version of the declaration of July 1919 contains at least an implication that the railway might be returned or that at the time the negotiations of early 1918 were in progress such an outcome was contemplated. Furthermore, for reasons never explained, the official Chinese translation of the declaration contains the far more definite assertion that: "The Soviet Government returns to the Chinese people without demanding any kind of compensation, the Chinese Eastern Railway, as well as all the mining concessions, forestry, gold mines . . ." and anything else taken from China by the Imperial Russian regime. If these statements raised any expectations among Chinese that the Soviet Government was offering them a clear title to Manchuria, these hopes were soon dispelled by another note from Karakhan dated October 27, 1920.[6] Here, in the form of a proposed agreement to be considered by the two governments, the Deputy Foreign Commissar wrote: "The Russian and the Chinese Governments agree to conclude a special treaty as for the rules and regulations of exploitation of the Chinese Eastern Railway for the needs of the R.S.F.S.R." Two years later, during the Sino-Soviet negotiations on these and other problems, Adolph Ioffe, the Soviet representative, explained that " . . . even if Russia vests in the Chinese people her title to the Chinese Eastern Railway, this will not annul Russia's interests in this line which is a portion of the great Siberian Railway, and unites one part of the Russian territory with another."[7]

Clearly, the Soviet Government intended to claim for itself the benefits of the Chinese Eastern Railway even though these represented the imperialistic loot of the much maligned Tsarist aggressors. It seems obvious, therefore, that even the

[6] Yakhontoff, op. cit., p. 386.
[7] Pollard, op. cit., p. 174.

original Soviet intentions with respect to the Chinese Eastern Railway must be interpreted, not in the light of the Chinese translation of the declaration of July 1919, but rather in terms of the order from Lenin to the Soviets at Harbin in November 1917. This, it will be recalled, ordered the Soviets there to assume power in the railway zone. Once again, in October 1920 when the Karakhan statement was issued, the Soviet Government had assumed power in most of the Far East through the Far Eastern Republic. It was therefore in a position to turn back to the plans of 1917, which obviously called for receiving all the territories and rights of the Imperial Government. "Russia's interests" had recovered their old meaning. It should be noted, however, that this constituted the first obvious Soviet departure from the propaganda line then being used among the people as well as a contradiction of the appeal of July 1919 as the Chinese people understood it.

A second cause of Chinese disillusionment with the foreign policy of the Soviet Government arose from the activities of the latter in Outer Mongolia. The collapse of the Imperial Russian Government terminated the pressures heretofore exerted upon Mongolia from that direction and left open the possibility of the infiltration into the area of influences from other nations, especially Japan and China. The efforts of Japan to establish a great buffer state which would include Outer Mongolia, rising to a climax in early 1919 with the conference at Chita, have already been noted. Later in the year the Chinese reentered Mongolia with military forces and administrators and established a regime which had so many features of the old Chinese imperial regime in Mongolia that opposition became widespread. Then, in the fall of 1920, with the appearance on its borders of Baron von Ungern-Sternberg and his cavalry forces, the Chinese administration was eliminated and Mongolia became one of the theaters of operations of the Russian civil war.

The months during which Baron Fedor Romanovich von Ungern-Sternberg exercised military and political authority in Outer Mongolia—more than any other period in the sub-

378

jection of Mongolia to the interventionary struggle waged on its territory by the successive foreign powers—prepared the people of this unfortunate region for the eventual acceptance of the Soviet conquest which followed. The Baron had, during the civil war and intervention in Siberia, exercised military power at Dauria station in Transbaikal Province.[8] Here he had achieved a notorious record of arson, torture, and murder which, if somewhat less publicized than the activities of Semenov and Kalmykov, was nevertheless equally cruel and destructive. By June 1920, however, the menace of the nearby forces of the Soviet Government and of the Far Eastern Republic made it clear to the Baron that it would eventually be necessary to evacuate Transbaikal Province. He therefore made plans to move into Mongolia and establish there a base from which he could take the offensive against the Soviets at a number of points to the east of his present location. Accordingly, with about a thousand cavalry troops, he crossed the Mongol border on October 1, 1920 and set out along a route that would take him to Urga and later to Troitskosavsk. Beaten off in his first attack on Urga, he withdrew some distance from the city and made preparations for a renewed attack. During this interval, not only were his forces greatly augmented, but the Chinese, alarmed at his preparations and apparently at their own inability to withstand another attack, began to withdraw from Urga. His second attack was thus carried out under more favorable conditions than the first and resulted in the seizure of Urga by Ungern-Sternberg on February 2, 1921.

It was at Urga that Ungern-Sternberg intended to establish his base of operations against Soviet Siberia. His occupation there was begun with a period of looting, pillage, torture, and murder which all eyewitnesses describe with horror. Jews and suspected Communists were singled out for special attention, the second category being found especially useful when a person of means refused to make the required contributions. After the conquest, the Baron proceeded to

[8] B. N. Volkov, *op. cit.;* N. N. Kniazev (trans. E. Varneck), "The Legendary Baron"; Korostovets, *op. cit.,* pp. 300ff.

379

establish a friendly political regime by reinstating the Bogdo-Gegen, the spiritual primate in Mongolia and the former political ruler, as the titular head of the state. In May the Baron issued his notorious Order No. 15 which outlined his plans for the attack on Siberia.[9] According to this order, both China and Russia had overthrown their legitimate imperial rulers and had degenerated under the influence of revolutionary regimes. Mongolia, however, had now reinstated its legitimate ruler, the Bogdo-Gegen, and therefore formed a natural starting point for an attack against Soviet Siberia, the object of which would be the restoration of the imperial regime in Russia. This attack would be carried out against various points along the Trans-Siberian Railway. For this purpose three regional commanders were named: Colonel Kasagrandi for the Irkutsk area, Ataman Kasantsev of the Enisei Cossacks for the Uriankhai or Tannu-Tuva area, and the Cossack Captain Kaigorodov for the Irtysh area.

While this campaign was in preparation, the Soviets were in the final stages of planning their counteroffensive. In August 1919 the first step had been taken in preparation for the eventual entry into Mongolia by the issuance of a declaration to the Mongol people.[10] At that time, it will be recalled, the Red army was successfully driving back the forces of Admiral Kolchak. The victorious approach of the Soviet armies and the prospect of their coming to the rescue of the people of Mongolia in their struggle with the imperialist aggressors was, therefore, the theme of this declaration. The declaration announced that all imperial Russian treaties which in any way affected Mongolia were to be annulled, called upon the Mongol people to enter into friendly negotiations with Soviet Russia, and requested them to invite the Red army to cross the Mongol border as a liberator of the people. This appeal was implemented by the formation, on

[9] Lieutenant General Baron von Urgern-Sternberg, Chief of the Asiatic Cavalry Division (trans. E. Varneck), "Order to the Russian Detachments on the Territory of Soviet Russia, No. 15, May 21, 1921. The City of Urga," *Revoliutsiia na Dalnem Vostoke,* Moscow, 1923, i, p. 429.

[10] V. Vilensky-Sibiriakov, *Sovremennaia Mongoliia,* Moscow, 1925, pp. 52–53.

March 13, 1921, of a Provisional Mongol Peoples' Government at Altan-Bulak, formerly Maimachen, on the Mongol-Siberian border near Kiakhta.[11] It was this government which issued the actual invitation to the Red army, waiting nearby in Siberia, to enter Mongolia and join the people's revolutionary army of Mongolia in driving out the imperialist aggressors. Crossing the border under these circumstances, the Red army achieved a surprisingly easy victory over the forces of Ungern-Sternberg and on July 7, 1921 established the new Provisional Government at Urga. Ungern was soon completely defeated and captured. He was taken to Novonikolaevsk for trial by a special tribunal and shot on September 15, 1921.[12] According to the Soviet report of the trial, Ungern-Sternberg expressed no regret for anything he had done and to the very end felt himself entirely justified in his activities. His last words were: "No, I have nothing more to say." He was one of the worst scoundrels in Siberia, but he was never accused of any desire to enrich himself from his gains. Finally, about two weeks after this trial, on November 5, 1921, a Soviet-Mongol agreement was signed which granted mutual *de jure* recognition to the two revolutionary regimes and provided for mutual defense against any third party.[13] If the negotiations regarding the Chinese Eastern Railway had left any question in Chinese minds as to the meaning of the new slogans of the Soviet propaganda, this act of recognition extended to an area recognized as part of the Chinese Republic by the Russo-Mongol-Chinese Treaty of June 7, 1915 was a reassertion of old Russian imperialistic ambitions which for the Chinese was filled with implications for the future.[14]

Yet the roots which the Soviets had acquired in China struck deeper as the years passed. Introduced on their own initiative through propaganda and timely agitation, the

[11] Potemkin, *op. cit.*, III, p. 112.
[12] *Izvestiia,* September 23, 1921.
[13] E. D. Grimm, *Sbornik Dogovorov i Drugikh Dokumentov po Istorii Mezhdunarodnykh Otnoshenii na Dalnem Vostoke (1842–1925)*, Moscow, 1927, pp. 203–204.
[14] MacMurray, *op. cit.*, II, pp. 1239–1243.

influence of the Soviets acquired a firmer footing through the brief but important partnership with Sun Yat-sen. In January 1923 just three months after the Japanese withdrawal from Vladivostok, Dr. Sun came to an understanding with Adolph Ioffe, the Soviet representative, which led in time to the activities of Michael Borodin and Vasily Bliukher at Canton. This partnership arose in part because Dr. Sun had been unable to find in the West the support he felt his program warranted. But it was also due to the fact that, however different their solutions may have been, the Soviet and Chinese revolutionary leaders diagnosed their basic internal and international problems along similar lines.[15] Furthermore, the success of the Bolshevik Revolution in Russia was itself a factor of no little importance to a hitherto unsuccessful aspirant to revolutionary leadership such as Dr. Sun. Needless to say, the influence of these early Soviet beginnings is a fact of the greatest importance in the life of contemporary China.

These Far Eastern developments reflected the new stature which the Soviet Government had attained throughout her territories and in the world. During the course of the year 1920, all the main interventionary armies which threatened the Soviet regime had been forced to evacuate Russian soil. By March the armies of Miller in North Russia, Denikin in South Russia, and Kolchak in Siberia had all ended their careers. By October a truce with Poland brought an end to another struggle which must be counted among the wars of intervention. The Soviets were then able to concentrate their forces in the south where, in November, General Wrangel was finally driven out. Internationally the Soviet position was enhanced by the inauguration in London during May 1920 of conferences which led to the Anglo-Soviet trade agreement signed the following March. Treaties were signed with Latvia on April 16, 1920, with Lithuania on July 12,

[15] Tsui Shu-chin, "The Influence of the Canton-Moscow Entente upon Sun-Yat-sen's Political Philosophy," *The Chinese Social and Political Science Review* (Peking), xviii, No. 1 (April 1934), pp. 96–145; No. 2 (July 1934), pp. 177–209; No. 3 (October 1934), pp. 341–388.

1920, with Finland on October 14, 1920; the treaty with England was signed on March 16, 1921, and the peace treaty with Poland on May 6, 1921. There followed the provisional agreements with Germany on September 2, 1921, followed in December by treaties with Norway and Austria. In Asia the Soviet Government was likewise making progress in international acceptance by its neighbors. There were treaties with Afghanistan and Persia in February 1921 and another with Turkey in March of the same year. Even though her armies continued to occupy ·Soviet territory throughout these early stages of Soviet international adjustment, it must have become increasingly evident to Japan that the Soviet Government was beginning to feel firm ground under its feet and that it could no longer be considered a mere passing phase in the development of the Russian revolution. Even in the Far East the Soviet policy in China, Manchuria, and Mongolia must have made it evident that the Soviet Government was acting less and less like a political outcast and much more like the familiar old imperialistic rival whose Siberian possessions had once appeared not only as a challenge to aggression but as a threat to Japan's continental policy. Even the peace proposal sent to Japan by Chicherin in February 1920 had offered economic concessions only on condition of an immediate Japanese withdrawal. The succeeding months saw the rise of Soviet Russian power, not to the point where she dared invite an attack from Japan, but at least to a point of such strength as to make her a dangerous ally for any other power equally interested in seeing the Japanese forces removed from Eastern Siberia.

Foremost among these non-Asiatic opponents of Japan's aggressive policy was of course the United States. The strength of the new American navy and the example of rapid preparation for front-line warfare demonstrated by the American Expeditionary Force in Europe were factors that Japan could not afford to disregard, particularly in the light of her own industrial weaknesses and untested armies. In particular, the principle of territorial integrity, both in China and Russia, for which the United States stood was a troublesome point to Japan as well as to certain European powers which would have been equally willing to parcel out any areas of the Far East that might drop away as governments crumbled. Once again, in fact, the collapse of China was looked upon as a possibility. Should this happen, it would do no harm to have the Japanese armies in a position to seize the desired areas. In exchange for a clear title to these areas, France and England would of course be encouraged to help themselves to other parts of China. Standing staunchly in opposition to any such schemes, however, was the United States. In the long run the American position on this question was strong enough to bring together the Washington Conference and achieve a general agreement on the subject of territorial integrity and to have both the Anglo-Japanese Alliance and the Lansing-Ishii Agreement canceled.

The feeling of the Japanese toward the United States was in many respects reflected in the case of Lieutenant Langdon of the United States Navy. On January 8, 1921 the lieutenant was shot in the back and killed in Vladivostok by a Japanese sentry.[16] The subsequent investigations revealed that this was by no means an isolated case of molestation of American naval personnel by the Japanese troops. Captain Richardson of the *U.S.S. Albany* had during the previous four or five weeks been molested and threatened with bayonets on two different occasions. Furthermore, the same practices had been repeated several times after the Langdon incident. An officer and two marines sent to find Langdon's pistol were surrounded by ten Japanese soldiers and detained for eight minutes, all in the presence of a Japanese officer. Acting upon a demand from the United States which included a strong hint to the Japanese to clear out of Siberia, the Japanese command finally held a court martial. After the hearing, the sentry who shot Langdon was acquitted on the grounds that he acted under orders. Major General Nishihara, the commander at Vladivostok, was reduced in rank and placed on the inactive list for his responsibility in issuing the orders. Several other officers were punished by

[16] *Foreign Relations, 1921,* ii, pp. 354ff.

confinement to quarters. All in all, the results of the trial as reported were not much more than a gesture, but they were highly interesting from the standpoint of the frank revelation of the orders under which the sentry acted. Not until three years later was the case finally settled. In 1924 Japan finally brought the case to an end by the payment of $15,000.[17]

It was, in fact, the conduct of the Japanese armies in the Far Eastern Region which made the Soviet reassertion of the old Russian position in Manchuria and Mongolia seem somewhat less obvious at the time than it does in retrospect. Here the Japanese were repeating the familiar pattern of activity which had characterized their conduct during the Allied intervention. Once again they were searching for a Russian leader able and willing to establish a local regime friendly enough to Japan to grant her all the privileges she had so long desired in Eastern Siberia and for which she had by now expended an enormous amount of treasure. Not only might one such successful puppet regime have served, as it did in Manchukuo after 1931, both as a model and a basis for the extension of such aggressive activity to neighboring areas, but it might have helped to justify in the eyes of the critics in Japan all the efforts and prestige which the Japanese had already expended upon the Siberian venture. Meanwhile, there was not only the constant search for a more solid political foundation for the intervention, but there was also the equally difficult task, especially in the face of the existence of the Far Eastern Republic and its army, of preventing the achievement of unity in the Region under any but friendly auspices. All these activities called for the usual measures to prevent the people from aiding the wrong side: the raids by both Japanese and White Russian armies into the villages as well as the arrests and mistreatment resorted to on the slightest pretext.

To aid in carrying out this policy in Siberia, the Japanese were as usual in need of a Russian force which they hoped would disguise the foreign source of the intervention

[17] *Foreign Relations, 1924*, ii, p. 421.

and, to critical observers abroad, give it the appearance of a native movement. When the Japanese evacuated Trans-baikal Province in October 1920, they made railway trans-portation over the Chinese Eastern Railway to Vladivostok available not only to their own forces but also to as many White troops as possible.[18] All these troops were concentrated in the Vladivostok area for the future offensive in the Mari-time Province. Some of the best troops thus available to Japan in the Maritime Province were the so-called Kappel-ites. These were the last surviving intact body of troops that had fought under Kolchak. The reason they had survived so well as a group was that they constituted a unit which had fought under General Vladimir Oskarovich Kappel, by all accounts one of the most able and popular of all the White officers. In addition, these troops were drawn from a region near the Ural Mountains where there had been a strong opposition to the Reds on the one hand and to Kolchak on the other.[19] They had joined the latter as the lesser of two evils. Fighting the war from conviction and ably led by Kap-pel, this force had developed into one of the truly exemplary units of the White Armies. During their eastward retreat before the Red army, their leader, General Kappel, had been commander-in-chief during the last days of the Kolchak regime but had later died before reaching the Far East. It was, in fact, the approach of Kappel and his "sons of father Kappel" and the fear that this advance inspired in the mem-bers of the new Soviet at Irkutsk that prompted the hasty execution of Admiral Kolchak. This unit, meanwhile much changed in personnel, consisted of about 16,000 men who arrived at Chita in mid-February 1920.[20] Hoping to use them for obvious purposes, the Japanese agreed to transport them across Manchuria into the Maritime Province where they remained during the Japanese occupation.

It was with the aid of these troops, as well as the Semenov

---

[18] G. Reikhberg, *Iaponskaia Interventsiia na Dalnem Vostoke, 1918–1922,* Moscow, 1935, p. 95.
[19] Varneck and Fisher, *op. cit.,* p. 255, n. 224.
[20] Miliukov, *op. cit.,* pp. 336–337.

detachments still in Transbaikal Province and their own forces, that the Japanese were engaged, during the summer of 1920, in planning a large-scale offensive against the Far Eastern Republic.[21] The campaign was planned with great secrecy and therefore excluded the possibility of support from Manchuria since troop movements from there could have been easily observed. The general plan apparently called for the concentration of the main attack in the Amur region where the partisan strength had always been greatest. An intercepted order from General Oi to the commander of the Japanese forces at Khabarovsk stipulated that the entire action must be completed by the end of August. Then, two days later, the project was canceled. The reasons for this— as given by the representatives of the Far Eastern Republic who came to the Washington Conference—is a combination of two circumstances already described. The first was the necessity of solidifying the rapid gains that the Japanese were even then in the process of making by the attack at Vladivostok, the results of the Nikolaevsk incident, and particularly the occupation of the rich, easily accessible, and strategically located northern part of the island of Sakhalin. The other factor was the world situation, already hostile to the ambitions of Japan, which might find in a renewed outbreak of aggression of such great importance at that time a sufficient reason to organize a new intervention, this time not even formally in cooperation with Japan. Whatever the reason for canceling the proposed attack, this was an opportunity which the Japanese must have found it difficult to forego. Never again were the cooperating forces so well placed for a "pincers" movement against the difficult Amur region.

From this time on, Japan's prinicipal hopes centered around the concentration of both political and military forces at Vladivostok. Transbaikal Province was entirely evacuated by October 1920 and the emphasis was placed on holding the southern port of the Maritime Province as a base for future operations, meanwhile exercising an economic

[21] *Japanese Intervention in the Russian Far East,* pp. 59ff.

stranglehold on the Far Eastern Republic with a view to forcing it into compliance with Japanese wishes. The appeals which the representatives of the Republic made for economic assistance both to China and to the United States would seem to indicate that this latter part of the Japanese policy was not without effect.

The policy of concentrating all political and military forces at Vladivostok developed first of all into an effort to replace the indifferent to hostile Provisional Government headed by Medvedev with one that would be more adaptable to Japanese ambitions. Fortunately for these Japanese plans, the leadership for such an enterprise was already available at Vladivostok. In fact, the brothers Spiridon and Nikolai Merkulov, two merchants resident in the city, had long aspired to the establishment of a government that would be more conservative than the Provisional Government. They had, in fact, approached Semenov at Port Arthur with a view to instituting such a government with his support. The administration of which they became the leaders was planned in March 1921 at a conference of non-Socialist organizations which assembled at Vladivostok.[22] At this conference the brothers obtained general support for two basic objectives: that the Vladivostok region would maintain itself separately from the Far Eastern Republic, and that (in order to receive the necessary military support to accomplish this) the Japanese occupation must be prolonged. Having thus achieved a measure of consent for their projected government and found the military support to help them in the anticipated struggle with the Far Eastern Republic, the Merkulovs proceeded to plan the overturn by which they could replace the existing government with one more suitable to their own purpose. The first attempt was a failure, but the second uprising was more carefully planned and was completely successful. Troops under the command of General Lebedev were stationed at strategic points from Vladivostok northward. These troops, it is interesting to note, were furnished with supplies both from Japanese stores and

[22] "Dalnevostochnaia Respublika," *op. cit.,* p. 220.

from the great stockpile at Vladivostok which had once provided one of the main reasons for the intervention.[23] On May 26, 1921 the overturn was successfully carried out and Spiridon Merkulov became the head of the Priamur Provisional Government.

Preparations for an offensive against the Far Eastern Republic began in early June 1921. As in the case of the preparations for the Merkulov overturn, the troops were again furnished with arms by the Japanese.[24] The available evidence shows that the Japanese, in the course of this campaign, contributed: 500,000 yen, 12,000 rifles, 6 artillery guns, 50 machine guns, and over 350,000 cartridges. As before, some of these supplies came from the stockpile of stores at Vladivostok. Rifles from this stockpile could easily be identified by the label "Remington" which they bore.

However well-armed the troops may have been with these supplies, there is ample testimony to the fact that there was little enthusiasm among the White forces for the campaign they were about to undertake. There was, for example, a divided allegiance among the troops, some favoring the Merkulov administration, others preferring a regime in which Semenov could have played a leading role.[25] Furthermore, the preceding years of turmoil and strife had made the traditional notions of loyalties somewhat less significant than they had once seemed. To whom should one be loyal and to what end? In contrast to this diminished enthusiasm on the part of the White forces, there were many who observed that the Reds and all who fought on their side seemed to be inspired with a sense of enthusiasm for their cause. It should be added that within the Russian Soviet Republic the period of the New Economic policy had been inaugurated in the

[23] A. Efimov, "Deistviia Otriada Izhevtsev pri Zakhvate Vladivostoka v 1921 godu," *Vestnik Obshchestva Russkikh Veteranov Velikoi Voiny* (San Francisco), April–May, 1931, No. 59–60, pp. 18–20.

[24] Reikhberg, *op. cit.*, p. 102; *Foreign Relations*, 1922, II, p. 853.

[25] N. A. Andrushkevich (trans. E. Varneck), "The Last Russia"; R. A. Puchkov, "K Desiatiletiiu Khabarovskago Pokhoda," *Vestnik Obshchestva Russkikh Veteranov Velikoi Voiny* (San Franscisco), No. 65–66, October-November 1931, pp. 12ff.

spring of 1921. The question therefore arose as to whether it would not be possible after all to live with the new Soviet state. Even closer at hand was the Far Eastern Republic, which, in the absence of any accurate information as to its true role in Far Eastern affairs, must have led many to feel that perhaps they had judged the new regime in Russia too harshly. It is an interesting commentary on this somewhat less hostile atmosphere that General Boldyrev, who took part even in this final phase of the White struggle, did not leave Russia after the struggle ended. Also, N. A. Andrushkevich, who has left one of the best accounts of this final period, did not seem particularly troubled about the fact that almost to the very last it appeared that he himself would not be able to leave.

By November 1921 the forces operating under the Merkulov Government were ready to move northward against the Far Eastern Republic.[26] Under Generals Verzhbitsky, Sakharov, Malchanov, Puchkov, and others the troops opened the campaign on November 1 and by the end of the month had driven the partisan forces out of the Vladivostok region and back as far northward as Iman station. After this the campaign for Khabarovsk was begun and that city was taken by the White forces on December 21. Without waiting, the Whites pressed on toward In station to the west. Meanwhile the government at Chita had sent reinforcements and the anti-White forces fought their first successful battle against the Whites at In station on December 28. The real turning point in the struggle was the battle of Volochaev, planned and executed by General Bliukher of the Far Eastern Republic. The two-day battle ended on February 12, 1922 with the peoples' revolutionary army and the partisans in possession of the city. Bliukher moved on rapidly and by February 14 had captured Khabarovsk from the Whites. The movement southward was a White retreat and only the presence of Japanese forces at Spassk prevented the revolutionary army from driving the White forces entirely out of the Mari-

[26] I. Pokus, *Borba za Primorie,* Moscow, 1926, pp. 34ff; "Krasnaia Armiia," *Sibirskaia Sovetskaia Entsiklopediia,* Moscow, 1931, I, pp. 1003ff.

time Province. The military situation remained in this un-
easy stalemate until the evacuation of the Japanese in October 1922. One thing at least was clear after the conclusion of
this campaign: the Merkulov Government was a failure as
an instrument of Japanese penetration into the territory of
the Far Eastern Republic.

Of the many frauds that were perpetrated against the
Russian people in the course of the revolution and civil war,
the Priamur Government headed by Lieutenant General
Dietrichs which succeeded the Merkulov administration at
Vladivostok ranks among the worst. General Mikhail Kon-
stantinovich Dietrichs is already familiar as the leader of the
first Czech detachments which crossed Siberia to Vladivostok
in 1918. He later returned to Western Siberia and served as
chief-of-staff under Kolchak. At the time that various members of the Merkulov administration were looking around for
a candidate to assume the leadership of a stronger government, Dietrichs was in Harbin. In answer to an invitation
issued in the name of the Popular Assembly at Vladivostok
he arrived there on June 9, 1922 and reviewed the troops.
Andrushkevich observed him carefully and critically and
came to the conclusion that he was a poor choice. He noted
that Dietrichs was a small man with red hair, that he was
very nervous and had shifty eyes, and that his freckled hands
trembled. Andrushkevich obviously learned to look upon
Dietrichs with some contempt. Later, when the General
demanded the convocation of a Zemsky Sobor or Land
Assembly named and patterned after similar assemblies in
the sixteenth century, Andrushkevich wrote: "I tried to convince this puny little general who had now become the head
of the government on the last small strip of Russia, that we
needed to be cautious and not fall prey to outlived or chance
theories."

Dietrichs assumed power by a decree which he himself
issued on June 10, 1922. The Popular Assembly was dismissed and preparations made for the convocation of the
Zemsky Sobor or Land Assembly. This body opened its first
session on July 29. It consisted of 160 members, all chosen

391

from the most conservative circles. Twenty-five members were simply appointed outright from the army. The same procedure was followed in the case of government officials and persons representing the clergy. Others were chosen from such organizations in Vladivostok as the League of House Owners, the Improvement Association, the Parish League, the League of Defenders of the Orthodox Faith, and other similar groups. Even representatives chosen from rural districts were usually retired officers or officials. It was this body which confirmed the appointment of Dietrichs as Ruler of the Priamur Government as of August 8, 1922. But the days of the Priamur Government were numbered. The Japanese had already decided to withdraw, and a hasty inquiry made in international circles at Peking by General Boldyrev disclosed that there was no prospect of any other foreign support for the regime. A military draft ordered by Dietrichs in early October yielded 170 men. Meanwhile, the forces of the Far Eastern Republic were waiting only for the Japanese to withdraw before stamping out the whole empty show that was being carried on under Dietrichs' direction. The latter saw the futility of his own activities and fled to Japan on October 15. Spiridon Merkulov had already left. For a few days a Siberian regionalist administration tried to carry on. But on October 25 the Republic forces entered Vladivostok and assumed control. People fled in panic into Manchuria.

Impelled by the political, economic, and military pressure from Japan and fortified by the strong moral position in which these attacks placed it, the Far Eastern Republic protested vigorously and appealed for aid to the world at large, and in particular to China and the United States. In all their public utterances the officials of the Republic had one central theme: the urgent desire and necessity of getting the Japanese out of their territory. Beside this, other objectives were purely ancillary. Still, a number of interesting subsidiary approaches were made to their main problem. One of these appeared in their appeal to all nations announced in early December 1921.[27] After reviewing the developments up

---

[27] *Foreign Relations, 1921*, ii, p. 718.

to that time, the note announced: "the seizure of the Maritime Province . . . proved that Japan's aggressiveness in the Russian Far East is not objected to by other powers." Here was a taunt that must have been heard with interest both in Paris and London. But it must also be remembered that the note could have been issued only with Soviet approval and that, in view of the Soviet position regarding the Chinese Eastern Railway and Mongolia, the statement misrepresented the true intent and purpose of Soviet foreign policy. The Soviets were asking for the observance of the principle of territorial integrity with respect to their own country while refusing to recognize this principle with reference to a neighbor. The old imperialism had in fact returned to the Far East. But the Soviet Government chose to give its own aggression a different name and thus keep the imperialist label for the activities of Japan and certain other Allied Powers. By 1945, however, the cycle of Japanese preponderance which began in 1905 would be complete and the world would once more talk about the dreaded Russian aggression.

The appeal which the Far Eastern Republic addressed to China took the form of an earnest request for the establishment of commerce. But the negotiations conducted at Peking by the representative of the Republic had the misfortune of being carried on simultaneously with certain other events which affected them adversely and caused them all to end in failure. In late July 1920 Ignatius Iurin, the representative and future Foreign Minister of the Republic, arrived in Peking. Although he desired recognition for his government, his chief mission was the opening of trade relations so urgently needed by the economically hard-pressed Russian Far East. The negotiations were opened in November when the Far Eastern Republic had just won its first round against the Japanese-White Russian opponents and had moved its capital from Verhkne-Udinsk to Chita. In January 1921 the discussions ended because of a failure to reach any compromise regarding the payments of certain indemnities claimed by China. The Republic urged that it was financially unable to meet any such payments. Moreover, both

Chang Tso-lin and the French were opposed to any agreements between these two parties because of the implication this would have for introducing Soviet control into the Chinese Eastern Railway. In the spring of 1921 the discussions were resumed but then came the rumors of a growing friendliness between Moscow and Sun Yat-sen, the latter a possible rival of the Peking Government. This of course raised the question of the sincerity of the Russian representatives. Then in May came the Merkulov overturn which in turn raised the question of the stability of the Republic itself. This was soon followed by the Soviet invasion of Mongolia in pursuit of von Ungern-Sternberg. In the end the mission was not a success and a regular commercial treaty was not obtained.

The appeal of the Republic to the United States had two central themes: the responsibility of the United States for the presence of Japanese forces in Siberia, and the mutual interest of the United States and the Republic in getting them out.[28] In reality, of course, these appeals were both addressed to the same thing: the powerful political and economic position of the United States since the war and the implications this position might have with respect to the struggle of the Republic with Japan. The first of these—the assertion that the presence in Siberia of Japanese troops was an American responsibility—refers of course to the note of August 1918 in which the United States invited Japan to participate in a joint intervention. This point of view disregards completely the circumstances under which the invitation was issued, i.e., the threat of a sole Japanese intervention if joint action were not found possible. Furthermore, the Far Eastern Republic note of April 1921 which lodged this complaint with the American Government cited the continuing work of the Inter-Allied Technical Board in the Far East as proof that intervention was being carried on with American participation. In this way, each of the major steps taken

[28] *Japanese Intervention in the Far East*, pp. 148–151; *Foreign Relations, 1921*, ii, pp. 716, 747–748, 876–877.

by the United States to preserve the territorial integrity and property rights of Russia was now recast in the light of mere examples of American imperialistic tendencies and of America's willingness to cooperate with Japan for the purpose of attaining her own ends.

The appeal to the mutual interest of the United States and the Republic in the removal of the Japanese from Siberia was based on the American-Japanese rivalry in the Pacific upon which the Soviets had from the first placed so much reliance as a factor favorable to themselves. In this case the invitation to become a more active anti-Japanese partisan was urged on the grounds of the economic necessities of the Republic. A note of October 4, 1921 explained that it was absolutely necessary that the Republic establish commercial relations somewhere.[29] If this were not found possible in any other way, then the Republic would have to turn to Japan— even at the cost of accepting the harsh terms the latter was holding out as the price. In particular, these terms mentioned the possible cession to Japan of North Sakhalin, an area where concessions to Americans had recently been granted. The fact that these concessions turned out in the end to be useless to their recipients did not lessen their value at the time as a means of stimulating American interest in large future concessions of natural resources. Speaking of the possibility of having to give this prize to Japan, the note concluded: "Probably no such cession would be made if the United States could admit a commercial mission."

The American response to the Japanese aggressions which had given rise to these complaints took the form of the non-recognition doctrine which became more famous after the events of 1931. Back in the spring of 1920 the Japanese had sought to divide the responsibility for the aggressive policy they were then carrying out in Siberia by saying that they were acting in accordance with an established Allied policy. The United States hastily denied that this was true, adding that there had been no change in Allied policy since the

[29] *Foreign Relations, 1922,* ii, pp. 747–748.

railway agreement of January 1919. In February 1921 another American protest against Japanese action was made.[30] Finally, on May 31, 1921 a State Department Memorandum to the Japanese Government explained that: "the Government of the United States can neither now nor hereafter recognize as valid any claims or titles arising out of the present occupation and control, and that it cannot acquiesce in any action taken by the Government of Japan which might impair existing treaty rights, or the political or territorial integrity of Russia."[31]

The ground was thus fully prepared for the views expressed by Secretary of State Hughes eight months later at the Washington Conference. In December 1921 Hughes had received the members of the Far Eastern Republic delegation and had expressed his full sympathy with their objectives regarding Japan since they were identical with his own.[32] He refused, however, to give them the recognition they wanted, just as he had refused recognition to the Japanese conquests in the territory their government occupied. In both cases recognition would have constituted an infringement on what was then considered the rights of the legitimate Russian Government. But the secretary did see fit to force this issue during the Conference in spite of the strong objections of Japan. It was obvious that the latter was not using the conference then being held at Dairen between the representatives of Japan and the Far Eastern Republic for any purpose but to press for all the advantages she had been attempting to get since the beginning of the Allied intervention, meanwhile keeping the Siberian problem from becoming a subject of general consideration at the Washington Conference.

It was agreed between themselves that the representatives of Japan and the United States should make declarations of policy regarding Siberia before the Washington Conference. In his statement to the Conference on January 23, 1922, Baron Shidehara divided the Japanese relationship with

[30] Potemkin, op. cit., III, p. 128.
[31] Foreign Relations, 1921, II, p. 704.
[32] Potemkin, op. cit., III, pp. 136–137.

Siberia into two parts.[33] The troops stationed in the Maritime Province, he explained, were simply there to protect Japanese residents and Japanese capital investments and to guard against disturbances that might be reflected in Korea. They were not intended to constitute a military occupation. The situation in Sakhalin, however, was different. This was a temporary occupation based upon the Nikolaevsk incident, for which some stable government would have to furnish satisfaction before a withdrawal would be considered.

On the following day Secretary Hughes read a statement which took note of the assurances Shidehara had given regarding the promised withdrawal of the Japanese forces at the earliest possible moment.[34] He reiterated the American view that all the objectives of the intervention had been fulfilled when General Graves left in the spring of 1920. He expressed regret that the Japanese were continuing to occupy any part of Siberia, whatever the provocation might have been, and expressed the American hopes for an early withdrawal from all positions. Thus the case for nonintervention in the affairs of Russia was brought before the Conference in a way that had not been possible three years before at Paris. A few months after the close of the Conference, a degree of strategic balance was revived in the Far East with the withdrawal of the Japanese forces from continental Siberia. But that other great American objective—the maintenance of an open commercial and investment market—never received anything more than lip service and promises from either of the aspirants for power in Northeastern Asia.

The interests of the United States in the railways of the Far East suffered from the same propensity of Russo-Japanese expansionists to strive for exclusive rights in the political as well as in the financial and economic fields. The purpose of the American railway missions to Russia, so clearly stated by all previous Secretaries of State, was reiterated by Secre-

[33] United States Senate Document No. 125, Sixty-seventh Congress, Second Session, *Conference on the Limitations of Armaments,* pp. 76–78 (hereafter cited as *Washington Conference*).
[34] *Ibid.,* pp. 79–81.

tary Hughes as the "preservation of present and future opportunities for trade."[35] It was his conviction that the existing
disturbed conditions necessitated a continuation and even
strengthening of international control over the railway. He
urged in a number of notes on the subject that, should China
be given control both for herself and as a trustee for the
acknowledged Russian rights as she now desired, this would
undoubtedly mean little more than a transference of control of Japan since that nation was already urging upon
China the acceptance of much needed loans from her
bankers. To preserve intact all existing rights in the railway, Hughes expressed the view that only a loan made on
the consortium principle should be considered. Furthermore,
to insure against the use of undue force or pressure the object
of which would be to establish monopoly of financial control
of the railway, the Secretary urged a revision of the Allied
Railway Agreement of 1919 in order to increase the power
of the Technical Board over which John Stevens presided.[36]
The Board, it was proposed, should be given full control
over receipts and disbursements and over all personnel
connected with the railway, and should have power to fix
tariffs. In anticipation it must be said that such changes
were never made.

The desire to strengthen the management of the railway
arose from the experience of the previous two years and the
resulting realization that the powers of the Board were inadequate to deal with the forces that constantly rendered ineffective all efforts to administer the railway efficiently and
effectively. First among the causes of the difficulties in exercising railway control was of course the confused condition
existing in the North Manchurian and Eastern Siberian
regions before the defeat of Kolchak and the Allied withdrawal. Kolchak's officials had been as willing to flaunt the
authority of the Board as the Japanese.[37] Unable to subordinate the members of the Inter-Allied Committee and the

[35] *Foreign Relations, 1922,* I, p. 899.
[36] *Foreign Relations, 1921,* I, p. 565.
[37] *Foreign Relations, 1923,* I, pp. 763ff.

Technical Board, the Kolchak officials finally decided to disregard altogether these control bodies. Semenov, strategically located at Chita, seized cars, locomotives, shops, workers, and anything else that suited his fancy, thus creating endless confusion in railway traffic. Even the Czechs, Stevens reported, informed him that they had their own railway inspectors and would need no help from the Board along their sector of the railway. The confusion reached a climax during the evacuation, especially when the Czechs seized trains for their exclusive use. Once this episode was over, however, a marked improvement of conditions resulted. In June 1920 Stevens was able to report that conditions were better than they had been since 1914.[38] The railway was able once more to return to commercial business after the termination of the military movements, a move which brought receipts above expenditures for the first time in the experience of the Board.

Among the results of the Allied withdrawal was the fact that in the course of time the area under the control of the Board was restricted entirely to the Chinese Eastern Railway. With respect to the area which came under Soviet control after the Allied withdrawal—the Trans-Siberian Railway as far eastward as Khabarovsk—no attempt was made to secure any kind of cooperation there. But the Ussuri line had been administratively part of the Chinese Eastern, and this arrangement was continued for a while longer. The establishment of the Merkulov Government at Vladivostok in May 1921, however, had the effect of detaching the Ussuri line from Board control.[39]

The event which inaugurated the intense international phase of the struggle for the railway and gave the Chinese the incentive to attempt to guarantee their own rights in the railway at all costs, was the resignation in mid-March 1820 of General Horvath as Manager of the Chinese Eastern Railway.[40] While manager, Horvath had claimed and exercised

[38] *Foreign Relations, 1920,* I, p. 695.
[39] *Foreign Relations, 1923,* I, pp. 772–773.
[40] *Foreign Relations, 1920,* I, pp. 680–684.

political as well as business control in the railway zone. The Chinese, on their part, had denied his right to function in any capacity but that of a railway official. At the time of his resignation Chinese soldiers were in charge of policing the zone and were by all accounts doing an excellent job of keeping order there. The Chinese Government was able to use the strong position thus obtained for itself to arrive at a new and more favorable settlement of the problem of railway management between itself and the Russo-Asiatic Bank, the legal owner of the railway.[41] The agreement effecting this change was signed on October 2, 1920. According to its terms the Chinese Government would henceforth have the right to name to the Board of Directors of the railway, the President of the Board, and four directors out of a total of ten members. It would also have the right to name two out of a total membership of five of the Audit Committee, the president of which would be chosen from one of the Chinese members. The manager of the railway would still be a Russian, though there would be a Chinese assistant manager. The various departments would be staffed with Russians and Chinese in equal numbers.

This agreement gave the Chinese the opportunity they had so long been seeking to play an increasingly more prominent role in the affairs of the railway. Toward the end of September, about a week before the agreement was actually signed, the President of China had issued a mandate, according to which the Chinese assumed administrative control in the city of Harbin and the railway zone.[42] On February 15, 1921 the Chinese flag was raised over the municipal buildings in Harbin and other cities. In early 1920, when they assumed police control, the Chinese had disarmed all remaining Russian guards that they now considered their own troops the only ones legally in the zone. From this time on, after they had assumed military and political control in addition to predominance in railway administration, their relations with

[41] *Ibid.*, I, pp. 714–717; see also *Treaties and Agreement with and Concerning China, 1919–1929,* pp. 53–56.
[42] Pollard, *op. cit.,* pp. 156ff.

400

the Technical Board, the only legal instrument of control now impeding their assumption of complete jurisdiction, became steadily worse. In the end, the Chinese were anxious to abolish the Board itself. This anxiety to obtain control arose of course from the sovereign rights to which China was entitled in the area through which the railway ran. It stemmed also from the troubled political situation that followed the Allied withdrawal from Siberia. The period was rife with conflicting rumors about the seizure of the Chinese Eastern, at one time by Chang Tso-lin, at another by the Far Eastern Republic, and, especially after the invasion of Outer Mongolia, by the Soviets themselves. There was also the fear that if international dominance of the Chinese Eastern were carried on too long it might lead eventually to a proposal to control all Chinese railways by an international agency. Thus the Chinese had many reasons to try to obtain control of the railway at the earliest possible moment.

Japanese activities of this period, however, furnished ample reason for hope that the Chinese might not take over the railway management under conditions that would simply mean passing it on to the skillful operators of the South Manchurian Railway. Japan's ambitions in this direction were by no means new to Stevens or to anyone who had in the recent past had as extensive experience as he with the Far Eastern situation. In the summer of 1921 he noted, however, that the president of the South Manchuria Railway had come to Harbin to discuss the section of railway between Harbin and the station at Kuan Cheng-tze near Changchun. This was the strip, it will be recalled, which Japan claimed as her share of the Russo-Japanese agreement of 1916 and which Horvath had refused to surrender to her, thereby losing Japanese support for his projected anti-Bolshevik government. Now the president of the Japanese line was asking that the gauge of the Russian section of the line be changed, thus giving the Japanese a continuous run straight north to Harbin. Such a move was of course entirely unacceptable to Stevens. But he feared that the Japanese might make this a condition for opening negotiations with the Allies regarding the inter-

THE END OF INTERVENTION

national financing of the Chinese Eastern Railway and thus force acceptance of their proposal.

The problem of railway financing was the chief source of worry to all who were interested in keeping the line out of Japanese hands. A number of factors had reduced the financial condition of the line to the point where a loan had become absolutely necessary. The constant requisitioning of rolling stock for military transportation, for living quarters, and other purposes had seriously reduced the usefulness of the railway for commercial traffic. Then there was the evacuation of the Allied, especially the Czech, troops which have monopolized the service of the railway and run up large bills. The largest single bill, that for transporting the Czechs, amounted to nearly three and a half million dollars.[43] There was not even any agreement as to who was responsible for this large sum, although it was generally assumed the French, themselves owing nearly half a million dollars, would accept responsibility for all Czech liabilities. The settlement of these transportation bills, Stevens urged continually, would take care of all the needs of the railway. The refusal to pay these large bills, so important for the continuation of adequate railway service, was more than a simple disregard of a legitimate obligation. It was a frank testimony to the doubtful value of paying money over to an institution whose future usefulness as a communication service for commercial enterprise was so questionable. The necessity of finding somewhere a source of financial support, however, grew more pressing after the signing of the new railway agreement in October 1920.[44] The increase of earnings which had been noticeable soon after the Allied departure had changed again to a growing deficit in the finances of the railway. Stevens attributed the deficit to the arbitrary policy of lowering the tariff rates by the new Directors without reference of the Technical Board or to the needs of the railway. Lacking any real power, the Board was unable to stop these changes and was thus forced to stand by while the railway ran increasingly into

[43] *Foreign Relations, 1921,* I, p. 606.
[44] *Foreign Relations, 1920,* I, p. 762.

debt. It was thus fast becoming a question either of strengthening the powers of the Technical Board or of abandoning it altogether.

By its growing indebtedness the railway was also running constantly closer to the outstretched arms of the Japanese. For some time the Japanese had been offering large loans on the most liberal terms. Through the South Manchurian Railway they had advanced coal to the Chinese Eastern Railway until by the summer of 1921 the debt thus accumulated amounted to over 2,000,000 yen.[45] The Japanese of course urged that there was no hurry about paying, hoping meanwhile that necessity would eventually force the Chinese to turn to Tokyo for an outright loan. In the Maritime Province the Japanese were using their South Manchurian Railway Company and their Priamur Provisional Government at Vladivostok as go-betweens to carry on negotiations looking to the purchase of the Ussuri line. This project finally culminated in a decree of the Priamur Provisional Government dated February 27, 1922 which provided for the lease of the Ussuri line for a period of twenty-four years to a company organized for the purpose by the South Manchurian Railway.[46] Meanwhile Secretary Hughes had been exerting every effort to find among the Consortium group the $10,000,000 which Stevens had estimated was indispensable for the continuation of railway services. Since most of this money would necessarily come from the United States, the refusal of the American Group headed by J. P. Morgan and Company to participate in the loan practically brought the project to an end. In his answer to the note of refusal Mr. Hughes expressed his profound regret that the desired loan could not be made after all. He concluded: "The international importance of the Chinese Eastern Railway is quite obvious, and I had hoped that through adequate financial support it might be made an important instrumentality of our 'open door' policy."[47] Once again, as in the case of the failure of the

[45] *Foreign Relations, 1921,* i, p. 590.
[46] Reikhberg, *op. cit.,* p. 102.
[47] *Ibid.,* i, p. 598.

Allies to pay the transportation bills, the lack of confidence in the future of the railway for free competitive enterprise was amply demonstrated. Once again, also, the railway was shifted one step closer to the monopolistic control which was so much against the traditional American policy.

The Chinese on their part expressed confidence in their own ability to maintain the independent status of the Chinese Eastern Railway.[48] Japan's failure to reduce Siberia by force of arms raised China's hopes that this experience would constitute an expensive lesson for Japan. Moreover, neither the existing Chinese Government nor Chang Tso-lin was subservient to the Japanese. In addition, the growth of Soviet power offered China an ally against Japan in case of necessity. Finally, even if the Japanese should in some way gain control of the railway, they would in the end be forced to withdraw under international pressure, as they had in Shantung. It was with this cheerful outlook that the Chinese faced the year 1922, the year which ended with a Japanese withdrawal from the Siberian mainland and therefore with a promise that their confidence in the future was not in vain. Nine years later, however, the Japanese returned, not to Siberia but to Manchuria and to the railways concerning the safety of which the Chinese had expressed themselves so confidently.

Once the Japanese had announced their decision to withdraw from Siberia, they promptly notified the American Government that, in accordance with the railway agreement, the activities of the railway experts should terminate simultaneously with the military occupation.[49] By September 26, 1922 all their troops had been evacuated from the railway zone, well ahead of their evacuation schedule in Siberia. The railway agencies acted with corresponding promptness. The Russian Railway Service Corps had already withdrawn by May 1920, leaving only the American chief inspector and a few members of his staff. Chinese inspectors had replaced the members of the Corps on the Chinese Eastern, the only rail-

[48] *Foreign Relations, 1922,* I, pp. 890–891.
[49] *Foreign Relations, 1922,* I, p. 921.

THE END OF INTERVENTION

way left where they could have exercised any authority at all. On October 24, 1922, in view of the imminent Japanese withdrawal from Siberia, the Inter-Allied Railway Committee dissolved itself. On November 1 the Technical Board held its last meeting to vote itself out of existence. Finally, on November 23, John Stevens left for Peking on his way to the United States, leaving behind the secretary of the Technical Board to wind up a few remaining details. This brought to a conclusion the five-year service of Stevens in managing, in the interests of the "open-door," one of the most strategic railways in the Far East. With little actual power but with a leader and a staff of highly competent men, the Board weathered many a difficult storm to become one of the only centers of reasonably fair professional and business activity in the confused and confusing world of intervention and civil war.

The large financial interests of the French in the Russian railways had to a great extent been settled by the Soviet repudiation of all foreign debts of both the Imperial and Provisional Governments. This explains in part the great efforts expended by France in the planning and conduct of the intervention both in Siberia and Europe. The case of the Chinese Eastern Railway differed significantly from that of the other Russian railways since it was situated outside Russian territory. The railway was legally owned by the Russo-Asiatic Bank, the major portion of whose capital was ultimately French. Compensation for her great investments within Russia was of course almost impossible. There were some confiscations of railway and other materials belonging to Russia which were seized either in France or in South Russia where the major French interventionary efforts were concentrated.[50] The French also found it possible to compensate themselves for their part in the Kolchak adventure by releasing in Siberia limited quantities of paper money issued through the Bank of Indo-China. At best the compensation from these sources for the large French investment in Russia

[50] "Frantsiia v Borbe Protiv Sovetskoi Vlasti," *Vestnik Narodnogo Komissariata Inostrannyk Del* (Moscow), No. 8, October 15, 1920, p. 25.

405

was proportionately insignificant. In the case of the investment in the Chinese Eastern Railway, the Soviets eventually
compensated the French by the purchase of shares in the
Russo-Asiatic Bank. This deal was consummated in the
summer of 1924 by two Russian financiers acting as intermediaries.[51]

The Washington Conference played a role in bringing to a
conclusion the period of sole Japanese intervention which was
comparable in its importance to that of the Paris Peace Conference in bringing about the Allied withdrawal of 1920.
But, whereas the latter result was brought about by a purely
negative condition—the sheer inability of the Allies to carry
out their aims in Russia—the former was the result of positive
factors which demanded attention and action. The first of
these was the group of three strategic aims which the United
States had adopted in 1918 as a means of halting the enlarge-
ment of Japanese power on the Asiatic mainland. The Washington Conference represents the culmination of these three
objectives: the participation in the intervention in order to
thwart Japanese ambitions in Siberia and North Manchuria,
the formation of a second consortium to prevent the monop-
olization of the Chinese investment market, and the demand
for the retrocession of Shantung to China in order to give
active and positive expression to the principle of the territorial
integrity of China.[52]

Closely related to these objectives was the necessity of restoring and enlarging the world market both in commerce
and investment, a necessity shared by the United States,
Great Britain, and other nations. During the war the United
States had experienced a transformation from a debtor to a
creditor status. In order to retain this new position among the
financial leaders of the world and to prevent an internal
financial recession, it was important that the United States
exploit every economic outlet including the foreign market
in order to find a substitute for the vanishing wartime outlets

[51] Frederick Deane, "The Chinese Eastern Railway," *Foreign Affairs*
(New York) III, No. 1, September 15, 1924, p. 151.
[52] N. Terentev, *Ochag Voiny na Dalnem Vostoke,* Moscow, 1934, p. 22.

for production. This gave the United States a postwar aim which was at once parallel to and in competition with that of Great Britain, who was also seeking a restoration of her prewar commercial empire. To both these nations the commercial development of Japan during the war—not only in the Asiatic markets but also in those of Latin America—was a fact of overwhelming importance. In addition, the rise of Japanese power in Asia was becoming a threat to Britain even in the Yangtze River area where so much of her financial and commercial interest lay. Along with this it must of course not be forgotten that the war period saw a sharp rise in the economic position of the Far East, especially China and Japan, and this in itself held out prospects for even greater profits than had been available in 1914.[53] Thus, on both the economic and strategic fronts the United States and Great Britain were acquiring interests with respect to Japan that were increasingly similar.

The Japanese occupation, during the war, of the German islands in the Pacific had a similar unifying effect upon the Far Eastern policy of the United States and Great Britain. This wartime Pacific development constituted a threat to the United States not only from the standpoint of bringing Japanese bases closer to the American outposts in the Pacific but also because these bases were a potential obstruction to the free communications of the United States with the Asiatic mainland and with her Asiatic possessions in the Philippine Islands. This extension of Japanese power into the Pacific had a similar effect upon those members of the British Commonwealth which faced the Pacific Ocean or were situated entirely within it. Australia, for example, with her small population, located in relative proximity not only to the highly populated Asiatic countries but also particularly close to the islands over which Japan had assumed control, was bound to feel anxiety as a result of the southward extension of Japanese power. In fact, the view was expressed at the time that Australia would rather see the islands returned to Ger-

---

[53] B. Semenov, "Iapono-Sovetskoe Soglashenie," *Novyi Vostok* (Moscow), No. 7, 1925, p. 24.

407

many than left in Japanese hands.[54] Under these conditions, should a state of war arise between the United States and Japan—an eventuality not considered impossible at the time —the British Dominions in the Pacific area would undoubtedly find it difficult to avoid supporting the United States, or at least withholding support from the opponents of the United States. It was this fact which made continued adherence to the Anglo-Japanese Alliance increasingly impossible for the British. Japan was in a sense thrusting herself in between the members of the British Commonwealth. In these altered circumstances a return to the partnership of the Anglo-Japanese Alliance would seem less advantageous than a new partnership which, while not alienating Japan by excluding her, would include the United States.

At first wavering in her choice between supporting the Anglo-American or the Japanese side in the new Far Eastern alignment, France eventually joined the former and thus forced Japan herself to join the other powers if she wished to avoid isolation. At the time of the Washington Conference the representatives of the Far Eastern Republic published documents purporting to establish the existence of an agreement between Japan and France, signed in Paris in January 1921, the object of which was to transport the interventionary forces of General Wrangel, which had been driven out of South Russia by the Red army, to the Far East.[55] In exchange for permitting the use of this force to carry on the offensive against the Soviet Far East, the Japanese were purportedly guaranteed valuable and long-desired concessions in the Russian Far East. In the end, of course, no such scheme ever matured. Instead, the multi-power treaty was concluded at Washington which pledged the signatories to respect the principles of the open door and the territorial integrity of China. It was this very unanimity which Japan had feared would result from the Conference, knowing full well that it was a direct result not only of her own repeated attempts to grab territory and advantages while the Euro-

[54] *Ibid.*, p. 25.
[55] Potemkin, *op. cit.*, III, p. 137; Reikhberg, *op. cit.*, p. 97.

pean war was in progress but more particularly of her failure to secure these advantages before the return of her competitors. The treaties constituted, in fact, an international act comparable in both purpose and result to the Triple Intervention of 1895. The parallel is even more striking if it is recalled that nine years after the treaties of 1922 the Japanese returned to the attack in Manchuria just as they had opened the Russo-Japanese War nine years after the Triple Intervention of 1895 had forced the retrocession of the Liaotung Peninsula. The difference of course was that the attack of 1904 resulted from the provocations given by Russia, while that of 1914 resulted from the withdrawal of competing forces from the Far East.

In addition to a realization of the dangers inherent in such a significant alignment of powers against her interests, Japan came to Washington fully aware that the United States was in close touch with events in Siberia through a mission which had been at Chita for some months before the opening of the Conference. This mission not only constituted an available source of information but remained a constant threat to Japan. There was always the danger, for example, that too great a provocation from Japan might result in an understanding between the United States and Soviet Russia.

The publicity given to some of the instructions issued for guidance of the mission indicates that Japan had reason to interpret such a move as a warning. The first observers sent to Chita were Major W. J. Davis, assistant military attaché at Tokyo, and James F. Abbott, the commercial attaché in the same place.[56] They arrived at Chita on May 20, 1921, on a mission whose objective could be expressed in the words "general investigation of conditions." It was specified, for example, that there were to be no businessmen in the mission and that there was to be no promotion of business interests while it was at Chita. On November 2, 1921 John K. Caldwell, then a diplomatic official in Japan but long a consul in the Russian Far East, also arrived in Chita on a special as-

[56] *Foreign Relations, 1921,* ii, pp. 735, 741ff.

signment.[57] In spite of his long official standing in the Far East, it was specified that he was not now to act in an official capacity and that he was to give no impression of contemplating recognition. His attitude at Chita was to be confined to showing a friendly interest. Meanwhile the American consul at Dairen was given permission to say that, should the administrative or territorial integrity of Eastern Siberia be placed in danger or the status of Russian rights changed, it would be considered unfortunate, "especially in view of the coming Washington Conference." This message and its significance could hardly have avoided reaching the ears of the Japanese officials.

Under these circumstances of certain and general opposition to the retention of their wartime gains, the Japanese came to the conclusion that if they were to salvage anything at all from their costly Siberian venture they must at all costs prevent this item from being discussed at the Washington Conference. The solution they chose was to hold another conference at which only the Far Eastern Republic and Japan would be represented. By this device the members of the Washington Conference might be persuaded that Japan was making a genuine effort to solve the problem. Also, by holding this conference far from Washington and from the critical scrutiny of the representatives of other nations, the chances of getting what they wanted, it was hoped, would be infinitely better.

There were two conferences between the representatives of Japan and the Far Eastern Republic before the Japanese evacuation was carried out. The first of these convened on August 26, 1921 at the Yamato Hotel in Dairen and remained in session until April 6, 1922. Japan was represented by Matsushima and the Republic by its Foreign Minister Iurin. The Soviet Government was represented only by an unofficial observer because the Japanese had refused to accept an official Soviet representative. The conference, it should be noted, spanned not only the period of the Washington Conference, from November 12, 1921 to February 6, 1922, but

[57] *Ibid.*, II, pp. 745–748.

also the period of the Congress of the Toilers of the East, which met in Moscow from January 21 to February 1, 1922, with a closing session in Petrograd on February 2, and, finally, the period of the military operations in the Maritime Province between the forces of the Priamur Provisional Government and the Far Eastern Republic from November 1921 to March 1922.[58] The Congress held in Moscow was in part a protest against the failure of the Conference Powers to extend an invitation to Soviet Russia and in part an effort to turn the eyes of the people of Asia toward Moscow and away from the Western nations and Japan. With reference to the struggle in the Maritime Province, it will be recalled that it was this event which demonstrated the weakness of the Japanese support in Siberia.

The Conference at Dairen was divided into two periods.[59] The opening weeks of the conference were concerned with the issue upon which the representative of the Republic had insisted—the removal of the Japanese forces from Siberia before any agreement was concluded. Matsushima seemed willing enough to discuss the commercial and other parts of the proposed settlement. But, in spite of the fact that the Republic offered economic concessions as an incentive, the Japanese absolutely refused to remove the troops until the Nikolaevsk incident had been settled. Japan, it may be supposed, was confident that the army of the Priamur Provisional Government, then being prepared for the attack, would in time strengthen her position at the conference and may even have considered the possibility of a decisive military campaign in advance of the meeting of the Washington Conference. By October 1921 the Japanese were ready to present their own demands and thus open the second phase of the conference by placing the Republic on the defensive for the remainder of the long futile sessions.

[58] Reference to the Congress of the Toilers of the East in *Izvestiia,* January 21, 1922.

[59] M. Krichevsky, "Razryv Russko—Iaponskikh Peregovorov v Dairene," *Mezhdunarodnaia Zhizn* (Moscow), No. 124, May 10, 1922, pp. 4–7; Potemkin, *op. cit.,* III, pp. 129ff.

These demands consisted of seventeen public and three secret articles, all of which, however, were made known to the Washington Conference through the representatives of the Far Eastern Republic.[60] The demands included: the demolition of all coastal fortifications at Vladivostok as well as those along the Korean border and on the entire Pacific coast of Siberia; the undertaking to destroy all Russian naval forces in Pacific waters and never in the future to build any other; the promise of complete freedom for Japanese subjects to carry on trade and industrial occupations on a basis equal with that of citizens of the Republic; a guarantee to the Japanese of complete freedom to navigate the Amur River; the promise never to permit the establishment in the territory of the Far Eastern Republic of a Communistic regime; the transfer to Japan (as compensation for the Nikolaevsk incident) of all of North Sakhalin on the basis of an eighty-year lease. The secret articles provided that Japan should choose the date for the evacuation of the Maritime Province at a time convenient to herself and that the evacuation of North Sakhalin would take place only after the actual conclusion of a lease as provided in Article 15 of the demands. The debate on these demands went on intermittently and hopelessly for months. Neither Hughes' maneuver at the Conference in Washington in forcing Shidehara to commit Japan to a policy of withdrawal nor the skillful negotiations of Iurin at Dairen brought things nearer to an agreement. Finally, in April the whole weary process dragged to an exhausted conclusion.

A new conference was opened at Changchun on September 4, 1922. This time Japan was represented by Matsudaira Tsuneo, who had been the civilian representative in Siberia in all railway matters, who had then served as one of the representatives at the Washington Conference, and who was more recently the director of the European and American departments of the Japanese Foreign Office. Soviet Russia was officially represented by Adolph Ioffe and the Far Eastern Republic by its Foreign Minister Ianson. This conference

[60] Appendix III.

412

was concerned entirely with the problem of the terms of evacuation of North Sakhalin and the settlement of the Nikolaevsk incident. A Japanese note of July 19, 1922 to the Far Eastern Republic had communicated Japan's firm intention to withdraw her forces from the Maritime Province not later than November 1 and her willingness to discuss the Sakhalin issue with a view to settling all outstanding questions.[61] But the conference was as barren of results as the previous one at Dairen. It held its last session on September 27. While the business community in Japan was tired of the expensive and unprofitable intervention on the continent, it was still interested in the resources of North Sakhalin and determined to keep the memory of Nikolaevsk fresh until it received satisfaction in this respect.

On June 24, 1922 the Japanese Government issued the first announcement of its intention of withdrawing all its troops from the Maritime Province.[62] Evacuation from North Sakhalin, it was explained, would await the settlement of the Nikolaevsk affair. Meanwhile the Changchun Conference was held with the hope of getting as much as possible before leaving. But the Conference was a failure and so also was the new Dietrichs Government in the Maritime Province. A smashing defeat delivered by the forces of the Republic at Spassk on October 9, 1922 sent the White Russian forces flying southward and eventually into Manchuria. On October 25 the last Japanese forces left Vladivostok as the People's Army entered. It is not recorded that anyone played "Hard Times Come Again No More" for the Japanese as they had for General Graves two years and half before.

By November 14 the Far Eastern Republic had ended its existence and the Far Eastern Region had become a part of the Russian Soviet Federated Socialist Republic. Some days before, the Assembly had renounced its power, repealed the Constitution of the Republic, applied to Moscow to be united with the Soviet Government, and dissolved itself. These acts were formally noted and approved in Moscow and the Region

[61] M. Pavlovich, op. cit., p. 39.
[62] Foreign Relations, 1922, ii, pp. 853–854.

declared an integral part of Soviet Russia. Then the Far Eastern Revolutionary Committee was declared the authority in the territory of the former Republic.

The evacuation left unsettled the problem of the Japanese occupation of North Sakhalin, associated by the Japanese with the Nikolaevsk affair. It was with the hope of settling this question that a conference was opened in Tokyo on June 28, 1923.[63] This time of course the transactions were directly between the Japanese and Soviet governments. Each of the Japanese offers of settlement was turned down by the Soviet negotiator. The Japanese proposed buying the Russian part of the island for 150,000,000 yen, but the Soviets wanted ten times this figure. Then the Japanese suggested long-term leases for the exploitation of oil, coal, and lumber. But the Soviets refused this. Finally, the Japanese proposed that in settlement the Soviets recognize all Russo-Japanese agreements and all war loans. But the conference broke up on July 31 with nothing settled.

The actual settlement of the Sakhalin problem was effected by the Soviet-Japanese Treaty signed in Tokyo on January 20, 1925.[64] Among the provisions of this treaty and its attached protocols was that giving *de jure* recognition to the Soviet Government. Among past treaties, all but the Treaty of Portsmouth of 1905 were considered subject to revision. The Treaty of 1905, it was agreed, would remain in force. In particular, the Fisheries Convention of 1907 and the question of debts were among the problems reserved for future consideration. Japan agreed to withdraw all her troops from North Sakhalin by May 15. Valuable oil, coal, and timber concessions were to be given to Japan on the basis of leases ranging in duration up to 50 years. In due course the evacuation provision was carried out and all of the former Russian Far East was regained by the Soviets except the zone of the Chinese Eastern Railway. An agreement with Japan to

[63] R. H. Akagi, *Japan's Foreign Relations, 1542–1936; A Short History,* Tokyo, 1936, pp. 421–422.

[64] Treaty in Grimm, *op. cit.,* pp. 213–218; also in Yakhontoff, *op. cit.,* pp. 404–410.

carry out the oil and coal concessions was signed on December 14, 1925,[65] At the same time the Kita Karafuto Sekiyu Kabushiki Kaisha or North Sakhalin Petroleum Company was organized in Japan with a capital of 10,000,000 yen to exploit the oil leases. Similar companies for the exploitation of coal and timber were organized in 1926 and 1927. Finally, on January 23, 1928 a fisheries treaty was signed in Moscow. Relations were by this time taking on something of the appearance of regularity.

The end of the Siberian intervention and the reunification of Russia under the Soviet Government marked the end of a long and difficult era in Russian history. It was, in the first place, the conclusion of an eight-year period of war which had in effect been in progress since 1914. Instead of peace the Bolsheviks had, by their refusal to carry on the war against Germany, invited renewed attacks which had prolonged the war for Russia four years beyond duration of the war in Western Europe. The second important fact about this long military ordeal was the nature of this new phase of the struggle in Russia. The Bolsheviks interpreted the new phase as a transition from fighting beside the capitalists, imperialists, landlords, and others whom they designated as oppressors to the stage of fighting against these elements. The truth of this analysis is of minor importance when compared with the fact that it was the interpretation applied successfully by the Bolsheviks. Finally, the survival of the Bolsheviks as the legitimate rulers of Russia is the most important fact of all. The real significance of this is that they survived in spite of the efforts of the major powers to overthrow them and that they won their right to exist under slogans which identified all enemies of the regime as enemies of the people.

Contemporaries were apparently aware, if not of the entire significance of the presence of the interventionists in Russia, certainly of the possible effect of the destruction they were helping to carry on among the Russian people. Many examples of this awareness have been cited in previous chapters. Colonel John Ward, undoubtedly not looked upon in

[65] Akagi, *op. cit.*, p. 425.

415

those days as a seer, made a comment which in our own times appears to be sheer prophecy. He observed that: "The Allies had better be cautious how they proceed in the diagnosis and dismemberment of this great people or they may find themselves on the operating table with this giant holding the knife."[66] It must have been obvious to those on the scene that, even among a people as politically unschooled as the Russians then were, the cruelty inflicted upon the people by those who had always in their own conception stood between the peasantry and the land they wanted, was creating fertile ground for well-worded slogans which could promote lasting hatreds. Observers must also have noted that the same people who had refused to fight for the Imperial and Provisional Governments were taking up arms to fight for the Bolsheviks.

Through the civil war and intervention the Bolsheviks distinguished themselves by a unity of purposes which the other participants were unable to match. The well-developed organization and discipline of the Bolshevik Party was a force which stood in contrast to the universal confusion, uncertainty, and disintegration which accompanied the dissolution of the old political order. However, with their singleminded devotion to the achievement of the supreme power in Russia, the Bolsheviks—in a pattern which baffled and in the long run completely outmaneuvered the opposition—knew how to compromise on some issues while refusing to compromise on others. By contrast their enemies, whether domestic or foreign, found themselves drawn together by negative and, in many cases, by purely synthetic interests. The strongest domestic opposition was led by groups which, while refusing to compromise with the Russian people, were forced nevertheless to compromise in vital matters with a variety of foreign powers.

The foreign interventionary powers, on their part, lacked both agreement among themselves with respect to their objectives in the struggle they proposed to carry on and support at home for their Russian policy. In the Siberian intervention this disunity among the interventionary powers was best ex-

[66] Ward, *op. cit.*, p. 197.

emplified by the long-standing Japanese-American rivalry in the Far East. This relationship and the objectives out of which it grew seriously reduced any chances of success which Admiral Kolchak might otherwise have had. On the home front, moreover, the program of the Allied interventionists lacked any real support. This was clearly expressed to the Peace Conference at Paris by David Lloyd George when he said that the peoples of the Allied nations were unwilling to fight for the overthrow of the Bolsheviks. Not only had the people by this time had enough war, but they were unreceptive to the idea of interfering with the new government in Russia, the exact nature of which was poorly understood. In the United States, in particular, the issue of participation in the intervention, however different our motives for it may have been, was never actually decided on its merits. It was a millstone around the neck of an administration which had to sacrifice the intervention for other considerations. This left Japan as the sole foreign occupant in Siberia. But the altered circumstances in Russia, in addition to the growing opposition both at home and abroad to the aggressive tactics Japan was following, eventually forced a withdrawal and thereby a sacrifice of all the expenditure in prestige and treasure which the Japanese had made during the preceding four years.

Long before the close of the intervention, the Bolsheviks had elaborated the plans and techniques for a counterattack on three fronts. In the territorial aspect, they aimed, with the assistance of the Red army and of the available diplomatic channels, at extending their jurisdiction into all regions formerly under the Tsarist regime. In the ideological war which they projected against international capitalism, the Communist Party prepared for an offensive on two world fronts. In the economically advanced nations it was anticipated that the proletariat could be induced to see in the Bolsheviks their natural allies against the capitalists. In Asia, operating on the principles expressed at the Second Congress of the Communist International, the Baku Congress, and elsewhere, the program called for undermining international capitalism by depriving it of the eastern sources of wealth. Therefore, the program in Asia was twofold: opposition to imperialism as practiced by the Western Powers and Japan, and opposition to the landlords of Asia who, the Communists asserted, retained their hold on the peasantry only with the assistance of international capitalism. With this program Soviet Russia hoped to be able to parry the continental ambitions of Japan and, at the same time, prepare for the eventual collapse of all imperialist efforts in Asia. They hoped by this means not only to fill the old frontiers of Imperial Russia, but also to provide the solution to the problem which had baffled the Russian expansionists of 1903. With the treaty of 1945, it must be added, the territorial phase of the program at least seemed to have made excellent progress.

APPENDIX I

CHRONOLOGY

1583

October 25   Ermak captures Sibir

1689

September 6   Treaty of Nerchinsk

1891

May 31   Building of the Trans-Siberian Railway begins

1895

May 10   Japanese retrocession of the Liaotung Peninsula

1898

March 27   Russian lease to Port Arthur signed

1902

January 30   Anglo-Japanese Alliance

1905

July 29   Taft-Katsura Agreement
August 12   Anglo-Japanese Alliance renewed
September 5   Treaty of Portsmouth signed

1907

June 10   Franco-Japanese Treaty
July 30   Russo-Japanese Treaty

1908

November 30   Root-Takahira Agreement

1910

July 4   Russo-Japanese Treaty
August 22   Japanese Annexation of Korea

419

1911

| July 17 | Mongol princes request support from Russia |
| October 10 | Outbreak of the Chinese Revolution |

1912

| June 20 | First Consortium signed |
| July 8 | Russo-Japanese Treaty |

1914

August 1	Germany declares war on Russia
August 23	Japan declares war on Germany
November 4	Russia declares war on Turkey

1915

| June 7 | Russo-Mongol-Chinese Treaty |

1917

March 12	Establishment of the Petrograd Soviet of Workers' and Soldiers' Deputies
March 14	Soviets issue Order No. One
March 14	Establishment of the Russian Provisional Government
March 15	Abdication of the Tsar
March 22	United States recognizes the Provisional Government
April 2	President Wilson's war message to Congress
May 31	Stevens Mission reaches Vladivostok
June 15	Root Mission reaches Petrograd
October 16	Admiral Kolchak received by President
November 7	Petrograd Soviet assumes power in Russia
November 7	General Kaledin assumes leadership in Don region
November 18	Colonel Emerson leaves San Francisco for Siberia
November 20	Proclamation of the Central Rada at Kiev
November 23	Collective Allied note of warning to General Dukhonin
December 14	Public French demand for a Siberian intervention

December 15	Soviet-German armistice
December 23	Anglo-French treaty partitioning Russia
December 26	Chinese troops enter Harbin

1918

January 1–2	Semenov attack in Transbaikal
January 10	Major Pichon visit to Tomsk
January 12	Japanese cruiser arrives at Vladivostok
January 18	Convocation of the Russian Constituent Assembly
February 9	German treaty with Central Rada
February 18	Start of German advance into Russia
March 3	Soviets sign Treaty of Brest-Litovsk
March 5	Lenin and Trotsky request American aid
March 7	British land at Murmansk
March 25	Sino-Japanese Treaty
March 26	Soviet agreement to permit Czech return to Europe *via* Vladivostok
March 30	Report on war prisoners in Siberia by Webster and Hicks
April 4	First Czech forces arrive at Vladivostok
April 4	Report of Major Pichon at Peking
April 4–5	Japanese landing party at Vladivostok
April 13	The Thomas Masaryk plan for economic rehabilitation of Russia
May 3	Order of Gaida to the Czechs regarding movement to Vladivostok
May 14	First major Czech-Soviet incident
May 16–17	Sino-Japanese secret treaties
May 25	Trotsky order to disarm all Czechs
May 25	Beginning of the Czech uprising
June 7	First establishment of White governments under Czech auspices—at Omsk
June 20	Official Allied decision to use Czech Legion as a temporary interventionary force
June 29	Czech seizure of Vladivostok
June 29	Derber Government established at Vladivostok
July 1	The final Raymond Robins plan of economic rehabilitation of Russia
July 6	Establishment of a temporary Allied protectorate over Vladivostok

July 9	General Horvath declares himself Provisional Ruler
July 17	The Aide Memoire
July 26	Chinese request a part in the Siberian intervention
July 29	Lenin declares a state of war with Anglo-French capitalism
August 1	Soviet overtures to Sun Yat-sen
August 3	Japanese and British forces land at Vladivostok
August 7	Czech-White Russian forces take Kazan
August 16	First American Expeditionary Force lands in Siberia
August 31	Czech and Semenov forces meet at Oloviannaia station
September 1	Czech-White Russian forces take Volsk
September 8–23	The Ufa Congress
September 18	General Janin received by President Wilson
October 24	General Ivanov-Rinov assumes control at Vladivostok
November 5	American organization of the Russian Bureau to stimulate trade in Siberia
November 18	Admiral Kolchak becomes Supreme Ruler

1919

January 9	Inter-Allied Railway Agreement
January 20	All Czechs withdrawn from front battle lines
January 22	The Prinkipo Proposal
February 15	First graduation of Russians from British military school at Vladivostok
February 25	Pan-Mongol Congress at Chita
March 22	Japanese raid on village of Ivanovka
April 3	Fridjof Nansen proposal of a relief mission to Russia
May 14	Soviet refusal of proposed Nonsen relief mission
May 23	Allied message to Kolchak regarding possible recognition
June 12	Allies receive Kolchak reply to message of May 23, 1919

July 25	Soviet declaration to China
August 8	Official American refusal to participate in the Allied blockade of Soviet Russia
September	British withdrawal from Siberia
November 14	Kolchak abandons Omsk
December 3	British proposal to partition Russia
December 29	General Graves receives notice of American withdrawal from Siberia

1920

January 6	Murder of the thirty-one hostages on Lake Baikal
January 9	Official announcement to Japan of American intention to withdraw from Siberia
January 15	Kolchak arrives at Irkutsk
January 16	Allies declare opening of trade relations with Soviet Russia
January 31	Establishment of the Provisional Government at Vladivostok
February 6	Establishment of the Trelisser Government at Blagoveshchensk
February 7	Execution of Admiral Kolchak
February 24	Soviet peace proposal to Japan
February 27	Japanese official announcement of a qualified withdrawal from part of Siberia
February 28	Partisan-Japanese-White Russian peace at Nikolvaesk
March 12	Japanese-White Russian surprise attack on partisans at Nikolaevsk
April 1	Last American forces leave Vladivostok
April 1	End of Allied intervention
April 1–October 25, 1922	Japanese phase of intervention
April 2	Japanese present new demands to the Provisional Government at Vladivostok
April 4–5	Japanese reestablish military control in the Maritime Province
April 6	Declaration of independence of the Provisional Government of the Far Eastern Republic
April 6	General Horvath leaves Harbin

May 14	Recognition of the Provisional Government of the Far Eastern Republic by the Soviet Government
May 25	Partisan killing of Japanese at Nikolaevsk
July 3	Japanese announce occupation of North Sakhalin, Nikolaevsk, coast of the Maritime Province
July 25	Execution of Triapitsyn
September	Departure of last Czechs from Vladivostok
October 1	Baron von Ungern-Sternberg enters Outer Mongolia
October 2	Chinese-Russo-Asiatic Bank agreement regarding the Chinese Eastern Railway
October 15	Second Consortium signed
October 20–21	People's Revolutionary Army captures Chita from Semenov
October 27	Soviet proposal to open relations with China

1921

January 8	Japanese shooting of Lieutenant Langdon
February 2	Baron von Ungern-Sternberg captures Urga
February 15	China assumes political control in Harbin
March 13	Formation of Provisional Mongol People's Government
April 26	Adoption of a Constitution by the Far Eastern Republic
May 20	American mission to the Far Eastern Republic arrives in Chita
May 21	Baron von Ungern-Sternberg Order No. 15
May 26	Establishment of the Priamur Provisional Government
May 31	Nonrecognition policy of the United States regarding Japanese activities in Siberia
July 7	Provisional Mongol People's Government established at Urga.
July 25	Soviet appeal for an American relief mission

August 26– April 6, 1922	The Dairen Conference
August 27	First of American Relief Administration arrives in Russia
September 15	Baron von Ungern-Sternberg executed
November 1– December 28	White Russian offensive against the Far Eastern Republic
November 5	Soviet-Mongol agreement
November 12– February 6, 1922	Washington Conference

1922

January 21– February 1	Congress of the Toilers of the East at Moscow
January 23	Statement of Japanese policy in Siberia to the Washington Conference
February 10	Opening of Far Eastern Republic counter-offensive against White Russians
June 10	Establishment of the Priamur Government
June 24	Japanese announcement of intention to withdraw from Siberia
September 4–27	Changchun Conference
October 24	Dissolution of the Inter-Allied Railway Committee
October 25	Japanese departure from Vladivostok
November 14	Far Eastern Republic incorporated into the Russia Socialist Federated Soviet Republic

1925

| January 20 | Soviet-Japanese Treaty |

APPENDIX II
AIDE MEMOIRE

THE AMERICAN POLICY IN SIBERIA

THE whole heart of the people of the United States is in the winning of this war. The controlling purpose of the Government of the United States is to do everything that is necessary and effective to win it. It wishes to cooperate in every practicable way with the Allied Governments, and to cooperate ungrudgingly; for it has no ends of its own to serve and believes that the war can be won only by common counsel and intimate concert of action. It has sought to study every proposed policy or action in which its cooperation has been asked in this spirit, and states the following conclusions in the confidence that, if it finds itself obliged to decline participation in any undertaking or course of action, it will be understood that it does so only because it deems itself precluded from participating by imperative considerations either of policy or of fact.

In full agreement with the Allied Governments and upon the unanimous advice of the Supreme War Council, the Government of the United States adopted upon its entrance into the war, a plan for taking part in the fighting on the western front into which all its resources of men and material were to be put, and put as rapidly as possible, and it has carried out that plan with energy and success, pressing its execution more and more rapidly forward and literally putting into it the entire energy and executive force of the nation. This was its response, its very willing and hearty response, to what was the unhesitating judgment alike of its own military advisers and of the advisers of the Allied Governments. It is now considering, at the suggestion of the Supreme War Council, the possibility of making very considerable additions even to this immense program which, if they should prove feasible at all, will tax the industrial processes of the United States and the shipping facilities of the whole group of associated nations to the utmost. It has thus concentrated all its plans and all its resources upon this single absolutely necessary object.

In such circumstances it feels it to be its duty to say that it

426

cannot, so long as the military situation on the western front remains critical, consent to break or slacken the force of its present effort by diverting any part of its military force to other points or objectives. The United States is at a great distance from the field of action on the western front; it is at a much greater distance from any other field of action. The instrumentalities by which it is to handle its armies and its stores have at great cost and with great difficulty been created in France. They do not exist elsewhere. It is practicable for her to do a great deal in France; it is not practicable for her to do anything of importance or on a large scale upon any other field. The American Government, therefore, very respectfully requests its associates to accept its deliberate judgment that it should not dissipate its force by attempting important operations elsewhere.

It regards the Italian front as closely coordinated with the western front, however, and is willing to divert a portion of its military forces from France to Italy if it is the judgment and wish of the Supreme Command that it should do so. It wished to defer to the decision of the Commander-in-Chief in this matter, as it would wish to defer in all others, particularly because it considers these two fronts so closely related as to be practically but separate parts of a single line and because it would be necessary that any American troops sent to Italy should be subtracted from the number used in France and actually transported across French territory from the ports now used by the armies of the United States.

It is the clear and fixed judgment of the Government of the United States, arrived at after repeated and very searching reconsiderations of the whole situation in Russia, that military intervention there would add to the present sad confusion in Russia rather than cure it, injure her rather than help her, and that it would be of no advantage in the prosecution of our main design, to win the war against Germany. It cannot, therefore, take part in such intervention or sanction it in principle. Military intervention would, in its judgment, even supposing it to be efficacious in its immediate avowed object of delivering an attack upon Germany from the east, be merely a method of making use of Russia, not a method of serving her. Her people could not profit by it, if they profited by it at all, in time to save them from their present distresses, and their substance would be used to maintain foreign armies, not to reconstitute their own. Military

427

action is admissible in Russia, as the Government of the United States sees the circumstances, only to help the Czecho-Slovaks consolidate their forces and get into successful cooperation with their Slavic kinsmen and to steady any efforts at self-government or self-defense in which the Russians themselves may be willing to accept assistance. Whether from Vladivostok or from Murmansk and Archangel, the only legitimate object for which American or Allied troops can be employed, it submits, is to guard military stores which may subsequently be needed by the Russian forces and to render such aid as may be acceptable to the Russians in the organization of their own self-defense. For helping the Czecho-Slovaks there is immediate necessity and sufficient justification. Recent developments have made it evident that that is in the interest of what the Russian people themselves desire, and the Government of the United States is glad to contribute the small force at its disposal for that purpose. It yields, also, to the judgment of Supreme Command in the matter of establishing a small force at Murmansk, to guard the military stores at Kola, and to make it safe for Russian forces to come together in organized bodies in the north. But it owes it to frank counsel to say that it can go no further than these modest and experimental plans. It is not in a position, and has no expectation of being in a position, to take part in organized intervention in adequate force from either Vladivostok or Murmansk and Archangel. It feels that it ought to add, also, that it will feel at liberty to use the few troops it can spare only for the purposes here stated and shall feel obliged to withdraw those forces, in order to add them to the forces at the western front, if the plans in whose execution it is now intended that they should cooperate should develop into others inconsistent with the policy to which the Government of the United States feels constrained to restrict itself.

At the same time the Government of the United States wishes to say with the utmost cordiality and good will that none of the conclusions here stated is meant to wear the least color of criticism of what the other governments associated against Germany may think it wise to undertake. It wishes in no way to embarrass their choices of policy. All that is intended here is a perfectly frank and definite statement of the policy which the United States feels obliged to adopt for herself and in the use of her own military forces. The Government of the United States does not wish it to be understood that in so restricting its own activities it is seeking, even by implication, to set limits to the action or to define the policies of its associates.

It hopes to carry out the plans for safeguarding the rear of the Czechoslovaks operating from Vladivostok in a way that will place it and keep it in close cooperation with a small military force like its own from Japan, and if necessary from the other Allies, and that will assure it of the cordial accord of all the Allied powers; and it proposes to ask all associated in this course of action to unite in assuring the people of Russia in the most public and solemn manner that none of the governments uniting in action either in Siberia or in northern Russia contemplates any interference of any kind with the political sovereignty of Russia, any intervention in her internal affairs, or any impairment of her territorial integrity either now or hereafter, but that each of the associated powers has the single object of affording such aid as shall be acceptable, and only such aid as shall be acc ,ptable, to the Russian people in their endeavor to regain contr of their own affairs, their own territory, and their own desti j.

It is the hope and purpose of the Government of the United Sta'cs to take advantage of the earliest opportunity to send to Siberia a commission of merchants, agricultural experts, labor advisers, Red Cross representatives, and agents of the Young Men's Christian Association accustomed to organizing the best methods of spreading useful information and rendering educational help of a modest sort, in order in some systematic manner to relieve the immediate economic necessities of the people there in every way for which opportunity may open. The execution of this plan will follow and will not be permitted to embarrass the military assistance rendered in the rear of the westward-moving forces of the Czechoslovaks.—Washington, *July 17, 1918*. (From *Foreign Relations, 1918, Russia*, II, 287–290.)

APPENDIX III

THE JAPANESE DEMANDS
PRESENTED AT THE DAIREN CONFERENCE

(August 26, 1921 to April 6, 1922)

The Policy of Japan toward the Far Eastern Republic

Article 1. The government of the Far Eastern Republic shall make Vladivostok a purely commercial port, shall place it under foreign control and shall adopt no measures which would interfere with trade.

Article 2. The governments of the contracting parties shall, after the signing of this treaty, reexamine the Japanese-Russian fishing convention, shall increase the rights of the Japanese fishing enterprises, and shall extend to the Japanese wider rights with respect to coastwise trade along the Russian seacoast.

Article 3. The governments of the contracting parties shall, immediately after the signing of the present treaty, conclude an agreement regarding postal and telegraphic communications.

Article 4. The governments of the contracting parties shall observe freedom of commerce, communications, and navigation and shall not place the citizens or ships of either government in a less favorable position than a third power. The details of this problem shall be elaborated hereafter in a separate treaty of commerce and navigation.

Article 5. The governments of the contracting parties shall conclude an agreement concerning customs rules and customs tariff according to the principle stated in Article 4.

Article 6. Citizens of each of the contracting parties, residing in the territory of the other, shall enjoy the protection, the guarantee of personal safety, and the inviolability of property, and shall not be placed in a position less favorable than the citizens of their own government or of a third power.

Article 7. Citizens of each of the contracting parties may, in the territory of the other, engage in commerce, industry, manufacturing as well as handicraft, professional and other activities and shall not in this respect be placed in a position less favorable than in their own country or than citizens of a third power; conditions of industrial, professional or handicraft activities shall be comparable to those accorded a third power.

Article 8. Citizens of each of the contracting parties shall enjoy the right of entering the territory of the other and of unobstructed travel and residence according to the laws of the land. Upon entering the other country a citizen shall present his national passport.

Article 9. Both of the contracting parties shall refrain from carrying on activities inimical to the other, shall likewise abstain from any propaganda which would be dangerous to the other and shall take steps to prohibit the entrance and residence in their own territories as well as the activities of any organization which seeks to carry on activities inimical to the other power. The regulations for surrendering persons engaged in such activity to the other power shall be defined in a separate agreement.

Article 10. The government of the Far Eastern Republic assures the Japanese Government that at no future time will it introduce into its own territory a communist regime and that it will preserve the principle of private property not only with respect to Japanese subjects; but also among its own citizens.

Article 11. In recognition of the principle of the open door, the the government of the Far Eastern Republic shall abolish for Japanese subjects all restrictions pertaining within its territories and shall undertake not to introduce in the future any restrictions with respect to mining, agriculture, the lumbering industry or, in general, any of the extractive industries and shall, furthermore, permit Japanese subjects complete freedom with respect to commerce, handicrafts and industrial enterprise on an equal basis with citizens of its own state; furthermore, the government of the Far Eastern Republic shall grant to Japanese subjects the right to own land as well as complete freedom to conduct coastwise trade under the Japanese flag.

The government of the Far Eastern Republic shall grant to Japanese subjects freedom of navigation on the Amur River under the Japanese flag and shall notify the Chinese Government of its desire to extend to Japanese subjects the right of navigation on the Sungari River under the Japanese flag. The provisions of this article shall extend to Japanese subjects and shall not be extended to any other foreigners.

431

Article 12. The two contracting parties shall exchange representatives who shall have the rights of ambassadors, and shall establish the places of residence of consuls.

Article 13. The governments of the contracting parties shall recognize all treaties and conventions concluded between the government of Japan and the former government of Russia and shall likewise recognize all rights acquired by the citizens of both countries at the time of the signing of this treaty.

Article 14. The government of the Far Eastern Republic shall raze and, if necessary blow up, all fortifications and defense works along the entire seacoast in the vicinity of Vladivostok and near the borders of Korea and shall not, in the future, establish any such fortifications and shall, furthermore, refrain from conducting any military activities in regions adjoining Korea and Manchuria.

The government of the Far Eastern Republic shall permit the official residence and travel of special Japanese military missions as well as individual Japanese military officials throughout its entire territory. The government of the Far Eastern Republic shall at no time maintain any naval establishment in Pacific waters and shall destroy the existing ones. . . .

Article 15. In solution of the Nikolaevsk question, the government of the Far Eastern Republic shall lease to the Japanese Government the northern part of Sakhalin Island for a period of 80 years as compensation for the losses inflicted upon Japanese subjects at the time of the Nikolaevsk incident.

Article 16. This treaty shall come into force from the moment of its ratification by the governments of the contracting parties and shall remain in force until the conclusion of a permanent treaty in the future.

Article 17. This treaty shall be prepared in the Russian and Japanese languages, and both texts shall be considered authentic.

THE SECRET ARTICLES

Article 1. In case of an armed conflict between Japan and a third power, the government of the Far Eastern Republic shall maintain strict neutrality.

Article 2. The Japanese Government shall evacuate its troops from the Maritime Province at its own discretion, and at a time which it finds suitable and convenient to itself.

Article 3. The evacuation of Sakhalin Province shall be carried out after the actual conclusion of a lease on the northern part of Sakhalin Island in accordance with the terms stated in Article 15.

Dairen, October, 1921. (From M. Pavlovich, "Iaponskii Imperializm na Dalnem Vostoke," *Novyi Vostok* (Moscow), No. 2, 1922, pp. 32–34.)

BIBLIOGRAPHY

I. PRIMARY SOURCES

A. Published Books

Ackerman, Carl W. *Trailing the Bolsheviki; Twelve Thousand Miles with the Allies in Siberia.* New York, 1919.

Benes, Edward. *My War Memoirs.* London, 1928.

Boldyrev, V. G. *Direktoriia Kolchak, Interventy.* Novonikolaevsk, 1925.

Bullard, Arthur. *The Russian Pendulum. Autocracy—Democracy—Bolshevism.* New York, 1919.

Bunyan, James. *Intervention, Civil War, and Communism in Russia, April–December, 1918.* Baltimore, 1936.

Bunyan, James, and Fisher, H. H. *The Bolshevik Revolution 1917–1918. Documents and Materials.* Stanford University, 1934.

Carnegie Endowment for International Peace. *Treaties and Agreements with and Concerning China. 1919–1929.* Washington, 1929.

Channing, C. G. Fairfax. *Siberia's Untouched Treasure. Its Future Role in the World.* New York, 1923.

China. The Maritime Customs, *Treaties, Conventions, Etc. between China and Foreign States.* 2 Vols. Shanghai, 1917.

Churchill, Winston S. *The Aftermath.* New York, 1929.

Coleman, Frederic. *Japan Moves North; The Inside Story of the Struggle for Siberia.* London, 1918.

Cumming, C. K., and Petit, Walter W. *Russian-American Relations. March 1917–March 1920, Documents and Papers.* New York, 1920.

Denikin, General A. I. *Ocherki Russkoi Smuty.* 5 Vols. Paris, 1921–1925.

Francis, David Rowland. *Russia from the American Embassy. April, 1916–November, 1918.* New York, 1921.

Gins, G. K. *Sibir, Soiuzniki i Kolchak.* 2 Vols. Peking, 1921.

Golder, Frank Alfred. *Documents of Russian History, 1914–1917.* New York, 1927.

Graves, William S. *America's Siberian Adventure 1918–1920.* New York, 1931.

435

BIBLIOGRAPHY

Greiner, J. E. *The Russian Railway Situation and Some Personal Observations.* Baltimore, 1918.
Grimm, E. D. *Sbornik Dogovorov i Drugikh Dokumentov po Istorii Mezhdunarodnykh Otnoshenii na Dalnem Vostoke (1842–1925).* Moscow, 1927.
Harrison, E. J. *Peace or War East of Baikal?* Yokohama, 1910.
Hodges, Phelps. *Britmis; A Great Adventure of the War. Being an account of Allied intervention in Siberia and of an escape across the Gobi to Peking.* London, 1931.
Ishii, Kikujiro. *Gaiko Yoroku.* Tokyo, 1931.
Janin, Pierre. *Ma Mission en Siberie, 1918–1920.* Paris, 1933.
Knox, Alfred. *With the Russian Army 1914–1917.* 2 Vols. London, 1921.
Lockhart, R. H. Bruce. *British Agent.* New York, 1933.
Lloyd George, David. *Memoirs of the Peace Conference.* 2 Vols. New Haven, 1939.
Lloyd George, David. *War Memoirs of David Lloyd George.* 6 Vols., Boston, 1936.
MacMurray, J. V. A. *Treaties and Agreements with and Concerning China,* 1894–1919. 2 Vols. New York, 1921.
Maksakov, V., and Turunov, A. *Khronika Grazhdanskoi Voiny v Sibiri 1917–1918.* Moscow, 1926.
Masaryk, Thomas Garrigue. *The Making of a State: Memories and Observations 1914–1918.* London, 1927.
Miller, David Hunter. *My Diary at the Conference at Paris. With Documents.* 21 Vols. New York, 1924.
Mints, I. *Iaponskaia Interventsiia 1918–1922. V Dokumentakh.* Moscow, 1934.
Moore, Frederick F. *Siberia To-Day.* New York, 1919.
Nabokov, Constantin. *The Ordeal of a Diplomat.* London, 1921.
Pares, Bernard. *My Russian Memoirs.* London, 1931.
Pointkovsky, S. A. *Grazhdanskaia Voina v Rossii (1918–1921) Khrestomatiia.* Moscow, 1925.
Price, M. Philips. *My Reminiscences of the Russian Revolution.* London, 1921.
Repington, Charles à Court. *The First World War 1914–1918 Personal Experiences.* 2 Vols. Boston, 1921.
Rickman, John. *An Eye-Witness from Russia.* London, 1919.
Serebrennikov, I. I. *Moi Vospominaniia, Vol. I V Revoliutsii (1917–1919).* Tientsin, 1937.

436

Seymour, Charles. *The Intimate Papers of Colonel House.* 4 Vols. Boston and New York, 1928.

United States. *Congressional Record 1919–1922.* (Sixty-fifth, Sixty-sixth and Sixty-seventh Congresses.) Washington, 1919–1922.

United States. Department of Commerce, Bureau of Foreign and Domestic Commerce. *Commerce Reports.* Washington, 1920.

United States. Department of Commerce, Bureau of Foreign and Domestic Commerce. *Daily Consular and Trade Reports.* Washington, 1913–.

United States Senate. Committee on Education and Labor. *Deportation of Gregorie Semenoff.* Washington, 1922.

United States Senate Extracts from the Congressional Record, March 2, 1922. *Japanese Aggression in the Russian Far East.* Washington, 1922.

United States Senate Document No. 125, Sixty-seventh Congress, Second Session. *Conference on the Limitation of Armaments.* Washington, 1922.

United States Department of State. *Papers Relating to the Foreign Relations of the United States, 1918, Russia.* 3 Vols. Washington, 1931.

United States Department of State. *Papers Relating to the Foreign Relations of the United States, 1918 Supplement I., The World War.* 2 Vols. Washington, 1933.

United States Department of State. *Papers Relating to the Foreign Relations of the United States, 1919, Russia.* Washington, 1937.

United States Department of State. *Papers Relating to the Foreign Relations of the United States, 1920.* 3 Vols. Washington, 1936.

United States, Department of State. *Papers Relating to the Foreign Relations of the United States, 1921.* 2 Vols. Washington, 1936.

United States Department of State. *Papers Relating to the Foreign Relations of the United States, 1922.* 2 Vols. Washington, 1938.

United States Department of State, *Papers Relating to the Foreign Relations of the United States, 1923.* 2 Vols. Washington, 1938.

United States Department of State. *Papers Relating to the For-*

437

eign Relations of the United States, 1924. 2 Vols. Washington, 1938.

United States Department of State. *Papers Relating to the Foreign Relations of the United States. The Lansing Papers 1914–1920.* 2 Vols. Washington, 1940.

United States Department of State. *Papers Relating to the Foreign Relations of the United States, 1919. The Paris Peace Conference, I–IX, XI.* Washington, 1942.

United States Department of State. *Russian Series* Numbers 1–5. Washington, 1919.

Varneck E., and Fisher, H. H. *The Testimony of Kolchak and Other Materials.* Stanford University, 1935.

Vilensky-Sibiriakov, V. *Soiuznicheskaia Interventsiia na Dalnem Vostoke i v Sibiri.* Moscow, 1925.

Ward, John. *With the "Die-Hards" in Siberia.* London, 1920.

Williams, Albert Rhys. *Through the Russian Revolution.* New York, 1921.

Zmrhal, K. (trans. E. Varneck). *Armada Ducha Druhe Mile.* Prague, 1918.

B. ARTICLES, MANUSCRIPTS, LETTERS, AND MEMORANDA

Andrushkevich (trans. E. Varneck). "The Last Russia" (a manuscript in Hoover Library).

Benes, Edward. "Chekhoslovatskaia Interventsiia v Rossii," *Volia Rossii* (Prague), No. 10–11, 1924, pp. 45–56.

"The Betrayal of Kolchak," *The Far Eastern Review* (Shanghai), XVI, No. 10, October 1920, p. 528.

Chlen Zabaikalskoi Komissii. "Pravda ob Irkutskoi Boine," *Volia Rossii* (Prague), No. 23–24, 1922, pp. 10–13.

Efimov, A. "Deistviia Otriada Izhevtev pri Zakhvate Vladivostoka v 1921 godu," *Vestnik Obshchestva Russkikh Veteranov Velikoi Voiny* (San Francisco), No. 59–60. April–May, 1931, pp. 18–22.

Eudin, Xenia Joukoff. "Documents and Materials on Intervention" (a manuscript collection in Hoover Library).

Germanov, L. (M. Frumkin). "K Istorii Chekho-Slovatskogo Nastupleniia i Sverzheniia Sovetskoi Vlast v Sibiri," *Proletarskaia Revoliutsiia* (Moscow), No. 4, 1922, pp. 16–23.

Graves, Sidney C. "Japanese Aggression in Siberia," *The New York Times Current History* (New York), XIV, No. 2, May 1921, pp. 239–245.

Graves, Sidney C. "The Truth about Kolchak," *The New York Times Current History* (New York), xiv, No. 4, July 1921, pp. 668–671.

Greiner, Joseph E. "The American Railway Commission in Russia," *Railway Review* (Chicago), lxiii, No. 5, August 3, 1918, pp. 170–172.

Horvath, Dmitrii Leonidovich. "Memoirs" (a manuscript in Hoover Library).

Iaremenko, A. N. (trans. E. Varneck). "Dnevnik Kommunista," *Revoliutsiia na Dalnem Vostoke,* Moscow, 1923 (a manuscript in Hoover Library).

Iliushin, V. K. "Stachka na K. V. Zh. D. v. 1918 g.," *Istoriia Proletariata S.S.S.R.* (Moscow), No. 2, 1934, pp. 175–184.

"Istoricheskie Uroki 15 Let Revoliutsii. Doklad Predsedatelia Malogo Khurala Doksoma na Iubileinoi 21-i Sessii Malogo Khurala i Kratkoe Soderzhanie Doklada Amora," *Tikhii Okean* (Moscow), No. 3 (9), July–September, 1936, pp. 63–94.

"K Istorii Interventsii-Pravitelstvo Kolchaka i Soedinennye Shtaty," *Vestnik Narodnogo Komissariata Inostrannykh Del* (Moscow), No. 9–10, December 15, 1920, pp. 53–67.

Janin, Maurice. "Fragments de Mon Journal Siberien," *Le Monde Slave* (Paris), No. 2, Dec. 1924, pp. 221–240; No. 3, March 1925, pp. 339–355.

Japan—Delegation Propaganda. Paris Peace Conference, 1919, K. Horiuchi to the editor of the *Chicago Tribune,* 420 Rue St. Honoré, Paris, August 29, 1919.

Japan—Delegation Propaganda. Paris Peace Conference, 1919. K. K. Kawakami, *Japan and the World Peace.*

Japan—Delegation Propaganda. Paris Peace Conference, 1919. Y. Matsuoka (Chief of the Press Bureau), to editor of the *New York Herald,* 38 Rue du Louvre, Paris, July 22, 1919.

Japan—Delegation Propaganda. Paris Peace Conference, 1919. Vice-Admiral Tochinai, *Japan Guards the Western Oceans.*

Johnson, B. O. "Sidelights on the Russian Railway Situation," *The Railway Age* (Philadelphia) lxvi, April 25, 1919, pp. 1063–1064.

Khabas, R. "K Istorii Borby s Chekho-Slovatskim Miatezhom," *Proletarskaia Revoliutsiia* (Moscow), No. 5 (76), 1928, pp. 56–65.

Kniazev, N. N. (trans E. Varneck). "The Legendary Baron" (manuscript in Hoover Library).

Knox, Alfred W. "General Janin's Siberian Diary" (Review), *The Slavonic and East European Review* (London), III, No. 9, March 1925, p. 724.

Lebedev, V. I." 'Chekhoslovatskii Front' i Moskovskii Protsess," *Volia Rossii* (Prague), No. 23–24, 1922, pp. 7–10.

Maksakov, V. "K. Istorii Interventsii v Sibiri," *Krasnyi Arkhiv* (Moscow), No. 34, 1929, pp. 126–165.

Maksakov, V. "Vremennoe Pravitelstvo Avtonomnoi Sibiri," *Krasnyi Arkhiv* (Moscow), No. 29, 1927–1928, pp. 86–138; No. 35, 1929, pp. 37–106; No. 36, 1929, pp. 31–60.

"Materialy i Dokumenty," *Sibirskii Arkhiv* (Prague), No. 1, 1929, pp. 41–46.

Miroshnichenko, P. "Iz Istorii Kolchakovshchiny," *Krasnyi Arkhiv* (Moscow), No. 28, 1928, pp. 225–228.

Moore, Frederick F., Skvirsky, Boris E., Smith, C. H. *The Far Eastern Republic Siberia and Japan; Together with a Discussion of Their Relations to the United States,* New York, 1922.

Outline of the Activities of the Inter-Allied Railway Committee for the Supervision of the Siberian and Chinese Eastern Railways, 1919–1922 (a manuscript in Hoover Library).

Pares, Bernard. "Dopros Kolchaka," *The Slavonic and East European Review* (London), XIII, No. 39, April 1925, pp. 225–230.

Pares, Bernard. "John Ward," *The Slavonic and East European Review* (London), XIII, No. 39, April 1935, pp. 680–683.

Pepeliaev, V. "Razval Kolchakovshchiny," *Krasnyi Arkhiv* (Moscow), No. 31, 1928, pp. 51–80.

Pozdeev, P. "Sovetizatsiia Zabaikalia v Usloviiakh Interventsii (1918)," *Proletarskaia Revoliutsiia* (Moscow), No. 34, 1924, pp. 185–195.

Puchkov, F. A. "K Desiatiletiiu Khabarovskago Pokhoda," *Vestnik Obshchestva Russkikh Veteranov Velikoi Voiny* (San Francisco), No. 65–66, October–November, 1931, pp. 12–15.

Russia—Delegation Propaganda (anti-Bolshevik), Paris Peace Conference, 1919. *Liberated Siberia. Economic and Financial Progress* (mimeographed), 1919.

Russia—Delegation Propaganda (anti-Bolshevik). Paris Peace Conference, 1919. *Omsk, 30th May 1919* (mimeographed), 1919.

Serebrennikov, I. I. "K Istorii Sibirskogo Pravitelstva," *Sibirskii Arkhiv* (Prague), No. 1, 1929, pp. 5–22.

Smith, C. H., to Fisher, H. H., February 14, 1931, (a manuscript in Hoover Library).

Smith, Charles H. "Four Years of Mistakes in Siberia," *Asia* (New York), xxii, No. 6, June 1922, pp. 479–483.

Smith, Charles H. "The Smoke-Screen Between Siberia and Washington," *Asia* (New York), xxii, No. 8, August 1922, pp. 639–644.

Smith, Charles H. "What Happened in Siberia," *Asia* (New York), No. 5, May 1922, pp. 373–378, 402–403.

Stevens, John F. "Memorandum," January 28, 1931 (a manuscript in Hoover Library).

Ukhtomsky, Prince Esper. "A Russian View of American Sympathy," *Harper's Weekly* (New York), xlviii, No. 2475, May 28, 1904, p. 826.

Ungern-Sternberg, Baron von (trans. E. Varneck). "Order to the Russian Detachments on the Territory of Soviet Russia No. 15, May 21, 1921, The City of Urga," *Revoliutsiia na Dalnem Vostoke,* Moscow, 1923, pp. 429–430 (a manuscript in Hoover Library).

Varneck, E. "Siberian Materials and Documents," (a manuscript collection in Hoover Library).

Volkov, Boris Nikolaevich (trans. E. Varneck). "About Ungern," (a manuscript in Hoover Library).

II. SECONDARY MATERIALS

A. Published Books

Akagi, Roy Hidemichi. *Japan's Foreign Relations, 1542–1936. A Short History.* Tokyo, 1936.

Arsenev, Vladimir K. *Russen und Chinesen in Ostsibirien.* Berlin, 1926.

Avarin, V. *Imperializm v Manchzhurii.* 2 Vols. Moscow, 1934.

Baerlein, Henry. *The March of the Seventy Thousand.* London, 1926.

Bailey, Thomas A. *Woodrow Wilson and the Lost Peace.* New York, 1944.

Baker, Ray Stannard. *Woodrow Wilson, Life and Letters.* 8 Vols. New York, 1927–1939.

Barnes, Joseph, and Field, Frederick V. *Behind the Far Eastern Conflict.* New York, 1933.

Barthold, Vasilii Vladimirovich. *La Decouverte De L'Asie. His-*

441

toire de L'Orientalisme en Europe et en Russie. Paris, 1947.

Bau, Mingchien Joshua. *The Open Door Doctrine in Relation to China.* New York, 1923.

Baykov, Alexander. *The Development of the Soviet Economic System: An Essay on the Experience of Planning in the U.S.S.R.* New York, 1947.

Bienstock, Gregory. *The Struggle for the Pacific.* New York, 1937.

Bisson, T. A. *Japan's War Economy.* New York, 1945.

Borton, Hugh. *Japan Since 1931—Its Social and Political Development.* New York, 1940.

Bowman, Isaiah. *The New World: Problems in Political Geography.* Yonkers-on-the-Hudson, 1924.

Causton, E. E. N. *Militarism and Foreign Policy in Japan.* London, 1936.

Chamberlin, William H. *The Russian Revolution 1917–1921.* 2 Vols. New York, 1935.

Chinese Eastern Railway Company. *North Manchuria and the Chinese Eastern Railway.* Harbin, 1924.

Clark, Grover. *Economic Rivalries in China.* New Haven, 1932.

Cleinow, Georg. *Neu-Sibirien (Sib-Krai); Eine Studie zum Aufmarsch der Sowjetmacht in Asien.* Berlin, 1928.

Clyde, Paul Hibbert. *International Rivalries in Manchuria 1689–1922.* Columbus, 1926.

Coates, W. P., and Coates, Zelda K. *Armed Intervention in Russia, 1918–1922.* London, 1935.

Cocks, F. Seymour. *Russia and the Allies.* London, 1919.

Committee on Russian-American Relations; The American Foundation. *The United States and the Soviet Union.* New York, 1933.

Conolly, Violet. *Soviet Trade from the Pacific to the Levant; With an Economic Study of the Soviet Far Eastern Region.* London, 1935.

Cressey, George Babcock. *China's Geographic Foundations.* New York, 1934.

Darinsky, A. *Nature and Natural Resources of the Soviet Far East.* Moscow, 1936.

Dennis, Alfred L. P. *The Foreign Policies of Soviet Russia.* New York, 1924.

Derber, P. I., and Sher, M. L. *Ocherki Khoziaistvennoi Zhizni Dalnego Vostoka.* Moscow, 1927.

Dillon, E. J. *The Eclipse of Russia.* New York, 1918.

Dugdale, Blanche E. C. *Arthur James Balfour; First Earl of Balfour.* 2 Vols. New York, 1937.

Dulles, Foster Rhea. *Forty Years of American-Japanese Relations.* New York, 1937.

Field, F. V. *American Participation in the China Consortiums.* Chicago, 1931.

Field, F. V. *Economic Handbook of the Pacific Area.* New York, 1934.

Fischer, Louis. *The Soviets in World Affairs.* 2 Vols. New York, 1930.

Fisher, Harold Henry. *The Famine in Soviet Russia, 1919–1923.* New York, 1927.

Fisher, Raymond H. *The Russian Fur Trade, 1550–1700.* Berkeley, 1943.

Franke, Otto. *Die Grossmächte in Ostasien von 1894 bis 1914.* Braunschweig, 1923.

Golder, F. A. *Russian Expansion on the Pacific, 1641–1850.* Cleveland, 1914.

Grajdanzev, A. J. *Modern Korea.* New York, 1943.

Great Britain. Foreign Office. *Eastern Siberia* (handbooks prepared under the direction of the historical section of the Foreign Office, No. 55). London, 1920.

Gregory, J. S., and Shave, D. W. *The U.S.S.R. A Geographical Survey.* New York, 1944.

Griswold, A. W. *The Far Eastern Policy of the United States.* New York, 1938.

Gurko, Vladimir Iosifovich. *Features and Figures of the Past: Government and Opinion in the Reign of Nicholas II.* Stanford University, 1939.

Hard, William. *Raymond Robins' Own Story.* New York, 1920.

Hsü, Shuhsi. *China and Her Political Entity (A Study of China's Foreign Relations with Reference to Korea, Manchuria and Mongolia).* New York, 1926.

Jessup, Philip C. *Elihu Root.* 2 Vols. New York, 1938.

Jochelson, Waldemar. *Peoples of Asiatic Russia.* New York, 1928.

Kandidov, Boris. *Iaponskaia Interventsiia v Sibiri i Tserkov.* Moscow, 1932.

Kantorovich, Anatolii. *Amerika v Borbe za Kitai.* Moscow, 1935.

Karpenko, Z. *Grazhdanskaia Voina v Dalnevostochnom Krae (1918–1922).* Khabarovsk, 1934.

Kawai, Tatsuo. *The Goal of Japanese Expansion.* Tokyo, 1938.

Kawakami, K. K. *Japan and World Peace.* New York, 1919.

Kawakami, K. K. *Japan's Pacific Policy; Especially in Relation to China, the Far East and the Washington Conference.* New York, 1922.

Kerner, Robert J. *The Urge to the Sea. The Course of Russian History. The Role of Rivers, Portages, Ostrogs, Monastaries, and Furs.* Berkeley, 1942.

Kireev, B. *The Economic Development of the Soviet Far East.* Moscow, 1936.

Klante, Margarete. *Von der Wolga zum Amur. Die tschechische Legion und der russische Bürgerkrieg.* Berlin, 1931.

Kobayashi, Hiroshi. *Shosetsu Nippon Rekishi.* 3 Vols. Tokyo, 1929.

Kobayashi, Ushisaburo. *The Basic Industries and Social History of Japan, 1914–1918.* New Haven, 1930.

Kobayashi, Ushisaburo. *War and Armament Taxes of Japan.* New York, 1923.

Korostovets, Ivan Iakovlevich. *Von Cinggis Khan zur Sowjetrepublik; Eine Kurze Geschichte der Mongolei unter Besonderer Berücksichtigung der Neuesten Zeit.* Berlin and Leipzig, 1926.

Kuno, Yoshi S. *What Japan Wants.* New York, 1921.

Kuykendall, Ralph S. *Hawaii in the World War.* Honolulu, 1928.

LaFargue, Thomas Edward. *China and the World War.* Stanford University, 1937.

Langer, W. L. *The Diplomacy of Imperialism, 1890–1902.* 2 Vols. New York, 1925.

Lantzeff, George V. *Siberia in the Seventeenth Century. A Study of the Colonial Administration.* Berkeley, 1943.

Lebedev, Vladimir I. *The Russian Democracy in its Struggle against the Bolshevist Tyranny.* New York, 1919.

Lewis, Cleona. *America's Stake in International Investments.* Washington, 1938.

Lobanov-Rostovsky, A. *Russia and Asia.* New York, 1933.

Lorimer, Frank. *The Population of the Soviet Union: History and Prospects.* Geneva, 1946.

MacNair, Harley Farnsworth. *China in Revolution.* Chicago, 1931.

Maisky, I. *Sovremennaia Mongoliia (Otchet Mongolskoi Ekspeditsii Snariazhennoi Irkutskoi Kontoroi Vserossiiskogo Tsentralnogo Soiuza Potrebitelnykh Obshchestv "Tsentrosoiuz").* Irkutsk, 1921.

Marroitt, J. A. R. *Anglo-Russian Relations, 1689–1943.* London, 1944.

Mavor, James. *An Economic History of Russia.* 2 Vols. London, Toronto, New York, 1925.

Medek, Rudolf. *The Czechoslovak Anabasis Across Russia and Siberia.* London, 1929.

Miliukov, Paul N. *Russia To-Day and To-Morrow.* New York, 1922.

Miller, Margaret S. *The Economic Development of Russia 1905–1914.* London, 1926.

Motylev, V. *Zarozhdenie i Razvitie Tikhookeanskogo Uzla Protivorechii.* Moscow, 1939.

Nelson, M. Frederick. *Korea and the Old Orders in Eastern Asia.* Baton Rouge, 1946.

Norton, Henry Kittredge. *The Far Eastern Republic of Siberia.* London, 1923.

Palmer, Frederick. *Newton D. Baker, America at War.* 2 Vols. New York, 1931.

Parfenov, P. S. *Borba za Dalnii Vostok. 1920–1922.* Leningrad, 1928.

Parfenov, P. S. *Grazhdanskaia Voina v Sibiri 1918–1920.* Moscow, 1924.

Parfenov, P. S. *Uroki Proshlago. Grazhdanskaia Voina v Sibiri 1918, 1919, 1920 gg.* Harbin, 1921.

Pasvolsky, Leo. *Russia in the Far East.* New York, 1922.

Phillips. G. D. R. *Dawn in Siberia; The Mongols of Lake Baikal.* London, 1943.

Pokus, I. *Borba za Primorie.* Moscow, 1926.

Pollard, Robert T. *China's Foreign Relations 1917–1931.* New York, 1933.

Polner, Tikhon J. *Russian Local Government During the War and the Union of Zemstvos.* New Haven, 1930.

Potemkin, Vladimir Petrovich. *Istoriia Diplomatii.* Vols. II, III. Moscow, 1945.

Pozner, Vladimir. *Bloody Baron. The Story of Ungern-Sternberg.* New York, 1938.

Price, Earnest Batson. *The Russo-Japanese Treaties of 1907–1916 Concerning Manchuria and Mongolia.* Baltimore, 1933.

Price, M. Philips. *The Origin and Growth of the Russian Soviets.* London, 1919.

Price, M. Philips. *The Soviet, the Terror and Intervention.* New York, 1918 (?).

Reikhberg, G. *Iaponskaia Interventsiia na Dalnem Vostoke, 1918–1922.* Moscow, 1935.

Remer, Charles F. *Foreign Investments in China.* New York, 1933.

445

Russia. Pereselencheskoe Upravlenie Glavnago Upravleniia Zemleustroistva i Zemledeliia, *Aziatskaia Rossiia*. 3 Vols. St. Petersburg, 1914.

Sack, A. J. *America's Possible Share in the Economic Future of Russia*. New York, 1919.

Schuman, Frederick Lewis. *American Policy Toward Russia Since 1917*. New York, 1928.

Shinobu, Jumpei. *Taisho Gaiko Jugonen Shi*. Tokyo, 1929.

Shotwell, James T., and Deak, Francis. *Turkey at the Straits. A Short History*. New York, 1940.

Shub, David. *Lenin. A Biography*. New York, 1948.

Shumiatsky, B. Z. *Borba za Russkii Dalnii Vostok*. Irkutsk, 1922.

Sokolsky, George E. *The Story of the Chinese Eastern Railway*. Shanghai, 1929.

Spargo, John. *Russia as an American Problem*. New York, 1920.

Special Delegation of the Far Eastern Republic to the United States of America. *Fisheries of the Far Eastern Republic*. Washington, 1922.

Special Delegation of the Far Eastern Republic to the United States of America. *Japanese Intervention in the Russian Far East*. Washington, 1922.

Special Delegation of the Far Eastern Republic to the United States of America. *A Short Outline of the History of the Far Eastern Republic*. Washington, 1922.

Special Delegation of the Far Eastern Republic to the United States of America. *Trade and Industries of the Far Eastern Republic*. Washington, 1922.

Stewart, George. *The White Armies of Russia: A Chronicle of Counter-Revolution and Allied Intervention*. New York, 1933.

Strakhovsky, Leonid I. *Intervention at Archangel; The Story of Allied Intervention and Russian Counter-Revolution in North Russia 1918–1920*. Princeton, 1944.

Subbotovsky, I. *Soiuzniki, Russkie Reaktsionery i Interventsiia*. Leningrad, 1926.

Takeuchi, Tatsuji. *War and Diplomacy in the Japanese Empire*. New York, 1935.

Tanin, O., and Yohan, E. *Militarism and Fascism in Japan*. New York, 1934.

Terentev, N. *Ochag Voiny na Dalnem Vostoke*. Moscow, 1934.

Tokutomi, Iichiro. *Japanese-American Relations*. New York, 1922.

Tompkins, Stuart Ramsay. *Alaska. Promyshlennik and Sourdough.* Norman, Oklahoma, 1945.

Trewartha, Glenn Thomas. *Japan, A Physical, Cultural and Regional Geography.* Madison, Wisconsin, 1945.

Tsymek, A. *The Forest Wealth of the Soviet Far East and Its Exploitation.* Moscow, 1936.

Ulianitsky, V. A. *Snosheniia Rossii s Sredneiu Azieiu i Indieiu v XVI–XVII vv.* Moscow, 1889.

Viallate, Achille. *Economic Imperialism and International Relations During the Last Fifty Years.* New York, 1923.

Vilensky-Sibiriakov, V. *Sovremennaia Mongoliia.* Moscow, 1925.

Vtoroi Kongres Kommunisticheskogo Internatsionala. Iiul-Avgust, 1920. Moscow, 1934.

Williams, Benjamin H. *Economic Foreign Policy of the United States.* New York, 1929.

Yakhontoff, Victor A. *Russia and the Soviet Union in the Far East.* New York, 1931.

Yamasaki, Kakujiro, and Ogawa, Gotaro. *The Effect of the World War upon the Commerce and Industry of Japan.* New Haven, 1929.

Young, A. Morgan. *Imperial Japan 1926–1938.* New York, 1938.

Young, A. Morgan. *Japan Under Taisho Tenno, 1912–1926.* London, 1928.

Young, C. Walter. *Japan's Special Position in Manchuria; Its Assertion, Legal Interpretation and Present Meaning.* Baltimore, 1931.

Zabriskie, Edward H. *American-Russian Rivalry in the Far East; A Study in Diplomacy and Power Politics, 1895–1914.* Philadelphia, 1946.

B. ARTICLES AND MANUSCRIPTS

Abe, Hidesuke. "Shibiria ni tai suru Waga Keizaiteki Hatten," *Chuo Koron* (Tokyo), No. 356, May 1918, pp. 57–59.

Adachi, Kinnosuke. "Concerning Japan and Siberia," *Asia* (New York), xviii, No. 8, August 1918, pp. 637–639.

Adachi, Kinnosuke. "Why Japan's Army Will Not Fight in Europe," *Asia* (New York), xviii, No. 2, February 1918, pp. 117–120.

Adamov, E. "Rol Anglii v Interventsii," *Vestnik Narodnogo Komissariata Inostrannykh Del* (Moscow), No. 6–7, August 25, 1920, pp. 1–12.

BIBLIOGRAPHY

"Administrativnoe Delenie (xvii–xx vv.)," *Sibirskaia Sovetskaia Entsiklopediia*, Vol. 1 (Moscow), 1929.
"America and Japan; The Swing of the Pendulum," *The Far Eastern Review* (Shanghai), xvii, No. 5, May 1921, pp. 332–335.
"The American Commercial Invasion of Russia," *Harper's Weekly* (New York), xlvi, No. 2361, March 22, 1902, pp. 362–363.
"American Engineers in Siberia," *The Far Eastern Review* (Shanghai), xvii, No. 4, April 1921, pp. 245–247.
"American Intervention in Russia in 1918," *Current History* (New York), xxxii, No. 1, April 1930, pp. 59–70.
"An American Solution to Japan's Problem," *The Far Eastern Review* (Shanghai), xvii, No. 7, July 1921, pp. 419–420.
Baikalov, Anatole V. "The Conquest and Colonization of Siberia," *The Slavonic and East European Review* (London), x, No. 30, April 1932, pp. 537–571.
Baikalov, Anatole V. "Siberia Since 1894," *The Slavonic and East European Review* (London), Vol. xi, No. 32, January 1933, pp. 328–340.
Bakhmetev, Boris. "The Issue in Manchuria," *The Slavonic and East European Review* (London), viii, No. 23, December 1929, pp. 305–314.
"Bank of Chosen Enjoys Prosperous Year," *The Far Eastern Review* (Shanghai), xv, No. 4, April 1919, p. 338.
Barrows, David P. "Japan as Our Ally in Siberia," *Asia* (New York), xix, No. 9, September 1919, pp. 927–931.
Battle, Lyne O. "Japan's Policy of Expansion," *The New York Times Current History* (New York), xiv, No. 3, June 1921, pp. 459–463.
Bock, Benjamin. *The Origins of Inter-Allied Intervention in Eastern Asia 1918–1920*, unpublished doctoral dissertation. Stanford University, 1940.
Bonch-Osmolovsky, A. "Vneshniaia Torgovlia Dalnego Vostoka za Vremia Voiny i Revoliutsii," *Novyi Vostok* (Moscow), No. 5, 1924, pp. 156–164.
"China, Russia and Mongolia," *The Far Eastern Review* (Shanghai), No. 6, November 1913, p. 224.
"China's Effort to Recover Control Over the Chinese Eastern Railway," *The Far Eastern Review* (Shanghai), xvi, No. 11, September 1920, pp. 605–606.

448

"Concerning Japan and Siberia," *Asia* (New York), xviii, No. 8, August 1918, pp. 637–639.

"Dalnevostochnaia Respublika," *Bolshaia Sovetskaia Entsiklopediia* (Moscow), 1930, Vol. xx.

Deane, Frederick. "The Chinese Eastern Railway," *Foreign Affairs* (New York), iii, No. 1, September 15, 1924, pp. 147–152.

Debyser, F. "La Genese de l'Expedition de Siberie d'apres les Documents Americains," *Revue d' Histoire de la Guerre Mondiale* (Paris), xii, January 1934, pp. 40–60.

Derber, P. "Demografiia i Kolonizatsiia Sovetskogo Dalnego Vostoka," *Novyi Vostok* (Moscow), No. 7, 1925, pp. 103–114.

"Dobrovolnyi Flot," *Bolshaia Sovetskaia Entsiklopediia,* (Moscow), 1931, xxii.

Eidus, K. "Resultaty Chanchunskoi Konferentsii," *Mezhdunarodnaia Zhizn* (Moscow), No. 14 (132), October 31, 1922, pp. 33–36.

Eudin, Xenia Joukoff. "The German Occupation of the Ukraine in 1918," *The Russian Review* (New York), i, November 1941, pp. 90–105.

Filatieff, General. "L'Amiral Koltchak et les Evenements Militaires des Siberie (1918–1919)," *Revue d' Histoire de la Guerre Mondiale* (Paris), x, April and July 1932, pp. 165–200 and 271–303.

Fleming, Jackson. "A Counter-Thrust For Russia; World Democracy Must Strike Germany in Asia," *Asia* (New York), xviii, No. 7, July 1918, pp. 537–541.

Fong, H. D. "The Prospect for China's Industrialization," *Pacific Affairs* (New York), xv, No. 1, March 1942, pp. 44–60.

"Frantsiia v Borbe protiv Sovetskoi Vlasti (Po Bumagam Ministerstva Inostrannykh Del Omskogo Pravitelstva)," *Vestnik Narodnogo Komissariata Inostrannykh Del* (Moscow), No. 8, October 15, 1920, pp. 21–25.

Frid, D. "Cheshskie Voennoplennye v Borbe s Chekhoslovatskim Miatezhom," *Proletarskaia Revoliutsiia* (Moscow), No. 5 (76), 1928, pp. 158–165.

"Gaisei no Toitsu (Gaimu, Rikugun no Kyowa)," *Gaiko Jiho* (Tokyo), xxxi, No. 8, April 15, 1920, pp. 674–685.

Gilbreath, Olive. "The Sick Man of Siberia; The Story of the Trans-Siberian Railroad," *Asia* (New York), xix, No. 6, June 1919, pp. 546–552.

Goudkoff, P. P. "Economic Geography of the Coal Resources of

Asiatic Russia," *The Geographical Review* (New York), Vol. xiii, 1923, pp. 282–293.

Grimm, E. "Kitaiskii Vopros ot Simonosekskogo Mira do Mirovoi Voiny (1895–1914)," *Novyi Vostok* (Moscow), No. 6, 1924, pp. 43–62.

Gurevich, V. "Realnaia Politika v Revoliutsii. Rol i Znachenie Ufimskoi Direktorii. Taktika "Demokraticheskago Tsentra." Koalitsiia i Soiuz Vozrozhdeniia. Prichiny Neudachi," *Volia Rossii* (Prague), No. 14, 1923, p. 17–31.

Hall, Luella J. "The Abortive German-American-Chinese Entente of 1907–8," *The Journal of Modern History* (Chicago), i, No. 2, June 1929, pp. 219–235.

Hattori Bunshiro. "Waga Tai Shibirisaku no Kompon wo Keizaiteki Riken ni Oke," *Chuo Koron* (Tokyo) No. 356, May 1918, pp. 52–57.

Hirshfeld, A. "O Roli S Sh A v Organizatsii Antisovetskoi Interventsii v Sibiri i na Dalnem Vostoke," *Voprosy Istorii* (Moscow), August 1948, pp. 3–22.

Hodges, Charles. "Siberia—A First Lesson in International Politics," *The Outlook* (New York), cxxxiii, No. 2, January 10, 1923, pp. 69–71.

Horie, Kiichi. "Taishibiria Keisaisaku," *Chuo Koron* (Tokyo), ccclvi, May 1918, pp. 59–62.

Iaremenko, A. "Partizanskoe Dvizhenie v Primorskoi Oblasti (1918–1920)," *Proletarskaia Revoliutsiia* (Moscow), No. 7, 1922, pp. 72–96.

Iliukhov, N. "Dalnevostochnyi Krai," *Bolshaia Sovetskaia Entsiklopediia*, Moscow, 1931, iii.

"Interventsiia," *Bolshaia Sovetskaia Entsiklopediia*, Moscow, 1937, xxviii.

"Interventsiia," *Sibirskaia Sovetskaia Entsiklopediia*, Moscow, 1931. Vol. ii.

Irving, Walter. "Business Conditions in Siberia," *The New York Times Current History* (New York), xiv, No. 3, June 1921, pp. 471–475.

Iyenaga, T. "Why Japan Has Not Sent an Expeditionary Force to Europe," *The Outlook* (New York), cxviii, No. 2, January 9, 1918, pp. 52–53.

"Japan to Aid Her Allies Against Germany," *The Outlook* (New York), cxviii, No. 11, March 13, 1918, p. 401.

"Japan and Siberia," *The New Republic* (New York), xxi, No. 267, January 14, 1920, pp. 187–188.

"Japan and Siberia," *The Outlook* (New York), cxviii, No. 16, April 17, 1918, p. 610.

"Japanese Imperialism and the Peoples of Asia," *New Times* (Moscow), No. 10 (20), October 15, 1945, pp. 16–21.

"Japan's Proposed Entry into Siberia—An Invasion or a Rescue?" *Current Opinion* (New York), lxiv, No. 4, April 1918, pp. 233–235.

Kamido, Masao. "Beidoku no Shibiria Hatten ni tai suru Waga Keizaiteki Taikosaku," *Chuo Koron* (Tokyo), No. 356, May 1918, pp. 50–52.

Katayama, Sen. "Fevralskaia Revoliutsiia i ee Vlianie v Iaponii i na Dalnem Vostoke," *Proletarskaia Revoliutsiia* (Moscow), No. 2–3 (61–62), February–March 1927, pp. 112–125.

Keith, Orrin. "Re-birth of Industry and Commerce in Eastern Siberia," *The Far Eastern Review* (Shanghai), xviii, No. 2, February 1922, 127–129.

Kerner, Robert J. "Russia, the Straits, and Constantinople, 1914–15," *Journal of Modern History* (Chicago), i, No. 3, September 1929, pp. 400–415.

Khodorov, A. E. "Manchzhurskaia Problema," *Novyi Vostok* (Moscow), No. 2, 1922, pp. 560–567.

Kirby, Francis B., "Siberia's New Republic: Its Standing," *The New York Times Current History* (New York), xiv, No. 3, June 1921, pp. 476–478.

"Kolchakovshchina," *Sibirskaia Sovetskaia Entsiklopediia*, Moscow, 1931, ii.

Komarov, V. "Problemy Razvitiia Dalnevostochnogo Krai," *Planovoe Khoziaistvo* (Moscow), No. 2, 1936, pp. 168–181.

Kotliarevsky, S. "Pravovye Dostizheniia Rossii v Azii," *Novyi Vostok* (Moscow), No. 1, 1922, pp. 34–44.

Krainov, P. "Iaponskaia Agressia v Kitae vo Vremia Mirovoi Imperialisticheskoi Voiny," *Istoricheskii Zhurnal* (Moscow), ix, September 1938, pp. 72–81.

"Krashaia Armiia," *Sibirskaia Sovetskaia Entsiklopediia*, Vol. i, Moscow, 1931.

Krichevsky, M. "Razryv Russko-Iaponskikh Peregovorov v Dairene," *Mezhdunarodnaia Zhizn* (Moscow), No. 124, May 10, 1922, pp. 4–7.

Lattimore, Owen. "Land and Sea in the Destiny of Japan," *Pacific Affairs* (New York), ix, No. 4, December 1936, pp. 586–589.

451

Maisky, I. "Mongoliia," *Novyi Vostok* (Moscow), No. I, 1922, pp. 154–183.

"Mining Enterprises in Siberia," *The Far Eastern Review* (Shanghai), xv, No. 4, April 1919, pp. 334–338.

Mussey, Henry Raymond. "Our Armament Race with Japan," *The Nation* (New York), cxii, No. 2900, February 2, 1921, p. 179.

Neuberger, Richard L. "The Telegraph Trail," *Harper's Magazine* (New York), October 1946, pp. 363–370.

Nilus, E. K. *Istoricheskii Obzor Kitaiskoi Vostochnoi Zheleznoi Dorogi, 1896–1923.* 2 Vols. (Volume II a manuscript in Hoover Library.) Harbin, 1923.

Norman, E. Herbert. "The Genyosha: A Study in the Origins of Japanese Imperialism," *Pacific Affairs* (New York), xvii, No. 3, September 1944, pp. 261–284.

Osnos, I. "Semenov—Stavlennik Iaponskoi Interventsii," *Istoricheskii Zhurnal* (Moscow), June 1937, pp. 54–63.

Oyama, Ikuo. "Beikoku no Tairo Seisaku no Seiko," *Chuo Koron* (Tokyo), No. 356 (Pt. 2), May 1918, pp. 62–66.

Pares, Bernard. "New Trends in Eastern Policies," *The Slavonic and East European Review* (London), xiii, No. 39, April 1935, pp. 531–548.

Parry, Albert. "Washington B. Vanderlip the 'Khan of Kamchatka,'" *Pacific Historical Review* (Berkeley), xvii, No. 3, August 1948, pp. 311–330.

Pavlovich, Mikhail. "Iaponskii Imperialism na Dalnem Vostoke," *Novyi Vostok* (Moscow), No. 2, 1922, pp. 3–57.

Pavlovich Mikhail. "Tikho-Okeanskaia Problema," *Novyi Vostok* (Moscow), No. 1, 1922, pp. 16–33.

Peffer, Nathaniel. "Japan's Absorption of Siberia," *The Nation* (New York), cxiii, No. 2935, October 5, 1921, pp. 367–369.

Polevoi, P. "Mines and Mining in Siberia," *The Far Eastern Review* (Shanghai), xvi, No. 6, June 1920, pp. 277–286.

"The Rape of Mongolia," *The Far Eastern Review,* (Shanghai), ix, No. 4, September 1912, pp. 175–177.

Reikhberg, G. "Dalnevostochnyi Proletariat v Borbe s Iaponskoi Interventsiei," *Istoriia Proletariata S.S.S.R.* (Moscow), No. 2, 1934, pp. 153–174.

Reikhberg, G. "Partizany Dalnego Vostoka v Borbe s Iaponskoi Interventsiei (1918–1920)," *Istoricheskii Zhurnal* (Moscow), ix, Sepetmber 1938, pp. 63–71.

Reinsch, Paul S. "Japan's Lone Hand," *Asia* (New York), xx, No. 2, February–March, 1920, pp. 164–171.

Reinsch, Paul S. "Manchuria, Mongolia, and Siberia," *The Nation* (New York), cxiv, No. 2965, May 3, 1922, pp. 523–525.

Roberts, Beth Alene. "A Study of American Opinion Regarding Allied Intervention in Siberia," an unpublished master's thesis. University of Hawaii, 1938.

Rockhill, W. W. "The Question of Outer Mongolia," *The Far Eastern Review* (Shanghai), xii, No. 1, June 1915, pp. 1–11.

"Russia and Japan in the Far East," *The New Republic* (New York), xiv, No. 174, March 2, 1918, pp. 130–132.

Semenov, B. "Yapono-Sovetskoe Soglashenie," *Novyi Vostok* (Moscow), No. 7, 1925, pp. 20–48.

Serebrennikov, I. I. "The Siberian Autonomous Movement and Its Future," *Pacific Historical Review* (Glendale), iii, No. 4, December 1934, pp. 400–415.

Sherower, Miles M. "Japanese Imperialism," *The Nation* (New York), cxii, No. 2900, February 2, 1921, pp. 175–177.

Sherower, Miles M. "The Nikolaevsk 'Massacre,' " *The Nation* (New York), cxi, No. 2877, August 21, 1920, pp. 211–213.

"Shibiri Mondai," *Gaiko Jiho* (Tokyo), xxxi, No. 8, April 15, 1920, pp. 699–704.

Shoizhelov, Siren. "Avtonomistskoe Dvizhenie Mongolii i Tsarskaia Rossiia," *Novyi Vostok* (Moscow) No. 13–14, 1926, pp. 351–363.

Shurygin, A., Karpenko, Z. "Borba za Velikuiu Sotsialisticheskuiu Revoliutsiiu na Dalnem Vostoke," *Istoricheskii Zhurnal* (Moscow), October 1937, pp. 109–121.

"Sinister Happenings in Mongolia," *The Far Eastern Review* (Shanghai), xv, No. 8, August 1919, p. 537.

Smirnov, M. I. "Admiral Kolchak," *The Slavonic and East European Review* (London), xi, No. 32, January 1933, pp. 373–387.

Speransky, A. F. "Materialy k Istorii Interventsii," *Novyi Vostok* (Moscow), No. 2, 1922, pp. 591–603.

Tachi, Sakutaro. "Teikoku Gunkanin no Vladivostok Joriku to Rokoku Seifu no Taido," *Gaiko Jiho* (Tokyo), No. 324, May 1, 1918, pp. 1027–1036.

Terentev, N. "Prodazha K. V. Zh. D. i Borba SSSR za Mir," *Tikhii Okean* (Moscow), No. 2 (4), April–June 1935, pp. 96–108.

BIBLIOGRAPHY

Tsakni, I. "Zheleznye Dorogi," *Sibirskaia Sovetskaia Entsiklopediia*, Moscow, 1931, I.

Tsui, Shu-chin. "The Influence of the Canton-Moscow Entente Upon Sun Yat-sen's Political Philosophy," *The Chinese Social and Political Science Review* (Peking) XVIII, No. 1 (April 1934), pp. 96–145; No. 2, (July 1934), pp. 177–209; No. 3 (October 1934), pp. 341–388.

Vegman, V. "Kak i Pochemu pala v 1918g. Sovetskaia Vlast v Tomske," *Sibirskie Ogni* (Novonikolaevsk), No. 1–2. January–April 1923, pp. 127–147.

Vostrotin, S. V. "A Russian View of Manchuria," *The Slavonic and East European Review* (London), II, No. 31, July 1932, pp. 20–36.

"What Can They Do for Kolchak?" *The New Republic* (New York), XIX, No. 242, June 25, 1919, pp. 234–235.

Wilton, Robert, "The Rush for Siberia: Causes of the Present Crisis in the Pacific," *The Fortnightly Review* (London), CX, No. 659, November 1, 1921, pp. 782–805.

Yoshino, Sakuzo. "Iwayuru Shuppeiron ni Nan no Goriteki Konkyo ari ya," *Chuo Koron* (Tokyo), No. 355, April 1918, pp. 1–30.

Yoshino Sakuzo. "Tai Ro Seisaku ni tai suru Kokumin to shite no Kibo," *Chuo Koron* (Tokyo), No. 356, May 1918, pp. 42–49.

"Zemstvo," *Sibirskaia Sovetskaia Entsiklopediia*, Moscow, 1931, II.

Zippin, Max. "The Far East Gets a Respite," *The Nation* (New York), CXI, No. 2877, August 2, 1920, pp. 210–211.

Zolotarev, A. "Iz Istorii Narodov Amura," *Istoricheskii Zhurnal* (Moscow), July 1937, pp. 27–41.

III. MISCELLANEOUS

A. BOOKS OF REFERENCE

Bolshaia Sovetskaia Entsiklopediia, Moscow, 1931–

Kerner, Robert J. *Northeastern Asia: A Selected Bibliography. Contributions to the Bibliography of the Relations of China, Russia, and Japan, with Special Reference to Korea, Manchuria, Mongolia, and Eastern Siberia, in Oriental and European Languages*. 2 Vols. Berkeley, 1939.

Peacock, N. (comp. and ed.). *The Russian Year-Book, 1916*. London, 1916.

Russia. Glavnoe Upravlenie Zemleustroistva i Zemledeliia. Pereselencheskoe Upravlenie, *Atlas Aziatskoi Rossii*. St. Petersburg, 1914.
Sibirskaia Sovetskaia Entsiklopediia. Vols. I–III. Moscow, 1929–1932.
U.S.S.R. *Bolshoi Sovetskii Atlas Mira*. Moscow, 1937.

B. NEWSPAPERS AND PERIODICALS

Asia (New York).
The Chinese Social and Political Science Review (Peking). *Chuo Koron* (Tokyo). *Current History* (New York). *Current Opinion* (New York).
The Far Eastern Review (Shanghai). *Foreign Affairs* (New York). *The Fortnightly Review* (London).
Gaiko Jiho (Tokyo). *The Geographical Review* (New York).
Harper's Magazine (New York). *Harper's Weekly* (New York).
Istoricheskii Zhurnal (Moscow). *Istoriia Proletariata* (Moscow).
Izvestiia (Moscow).
The Japan Chronicle—Weekly Edition (Kobe). *Journal of Modern History* (Chicago).
Krasnyi Arkhiv (Moscow).
Mezhdunarodnaia Zhizn (Moscow). *Le Monde Slave* (Paris).
The Nation (New York). *The New Republic* (New York).
New Times (Moscow). *The New York Times* (New York).
The New York Times Current History (New York). *Novyi Vostok* (Moscow).
Oriental News and Comment (New York). *The Outlook* (New York).
Pacific Affairs (New York). *Pacific Historical Review* (Berkeley). *Planovoe Khoziaistvo* (Moscow). *Pravda* (Moscow).
Proletarskaia Revoliutsiia (Moscow).
The Railway Age (Philadelphia). *Railway Review* (Chicago).
Revue d'Histoire de la Guerre Mondiale (Paris). *The Russian Review* (New York).
Sibirskie Ogni (Novonikolaevsk). *Sibirskii Arkhiv* (Prague). *The Slavonic and East European Review* (London).
Tikhii Okean (Moscow).
Vestnik Narodnogo Komissariata Inostrannykh Del (Moscow).
Vestnik Obshchestva Russkikh Veteranov Velikoi Voiny (San Francisco). *Volia Rossii* (Prague). *Voprosy Istorii* (Moscow).

Index

Abbott, James F., United States representative in the Far Eastern Republic, 409

Ackerman, Carl, correspondent of *The New York Times*, 207, 236

agrarian nature of Russian Far East, 45–46

agricultural machinery, 31–32, 43, 298

agriculture in Russian Far East, 30 ff

Aide Memoire, American policy in Siberian intervention, 230–232, 352, 426–429, Appendix II

Aleksandrovsk, 33

Alekseev, Admiral Evgenii Ivanovich, Viceroy of the Far East, 32

Alekseev, General Mikhail Vasilevich, White Russian leader in South Russia, 94, 98, 100, 111

alliance systems of 1914, 5

Allied: agreement to partition Russia into spheres of influence, 215–216; attitude toward Kolchak, 338 ff.; blockade against Russia, 18, 323–324; consideration of recognition for Kolchak, 336 ff.; embargo against commercial traffic between Siberia and Manchuria, 322–323; expenditures in intervention, 331; fear of German activity in Russia, 212–213, 222; guard over Trans-Siberian Railway, 150–151; intervention, economic and strategic basis, 4–5; intervention in Russian peripheral areas, 2, 4; intervention note to General Dukhonin, November 23, 1917, 11; military at-

tack on Soviets, first phase, 16–17, second phase, 17, third phase, 17–18; military intervention starts at Vladivostok, 258–259; note to Kolchak of May 23, 1919, 339; objectives in Russia, 1918, 83–85, 86; policy toward intervention, 127, 261–262; pressure on Czechoslovaks to serve as interventionary force, 240–241; protectorate over Vladivostok declared, 194, 255; support of Semenov, 196; view of German penetration into Russia, 212–213; view of Greater Mongolia movement, 206; view of Japanese naval landing at Vladivostok, April 1918, 190–191; view of possible Kolchak victory, 338–339; view of Semenov, 197–198; withdrawal from North Russia and the Ukraine, 17; withdrawal from Siberia, 352 ff.

All-Russian Congress of Soviets at Petrograd, November 1917, 78

All-Russian Directorate, 99, 103, 110–111

American: business interests in Russia, 127–130; business losses in Russia, 328; commerce in Manchuria, 65–66; interest in Russian railways, 136; press opinion regarding continuance of intervention, 353 ff.; press opinion regarding Japanese in Siberia, 173–174; railway missions to Russia (*see also* Stevens mission and Emerson mission), 143 ff., 156; railway sup-

457

INDEX

business conditions under Soviets,
81–82
business decline in Russian Far
East during civil war, 299 ff.

Caldwell, John, American consul
at Vladivostok, 94, 409
Carter-Scott, C. J., British businessman, 113
Central Asia, prospects of German penetration, 13, 219, 319
Central Powers: effort to stimulate interest among prisoners
in Siberia, 236; in the
Ukraine, 2, 13; partition of
the Ukraine, 12
Chaikovsky, Nikolai Vasilevich,
head of White Russian government in North Russia, 335
Chang, General Tso-lin, 97, 394,
404
Changchun conference, September
1922, 412–413
Channing, Lieutenant C. G. F.,
273
Cheliabinsk, 49, 108
Cheliabinsk incident of May 14
involving Czechoslovak-Soviet
clash, 247–248
Chiang Kai-shek, 179
Chicherin, Georgii Vasilevich, Soviet Foreign Commissar, 247,
325, 375
China: a factor in the Far Eastern question, 19, 41, 51 ff.;
effort to gain control of the
Chinese Eastern Railway,
399 ff.; internal reforms, 69;
reentry into Mongolia, 1919,
202; troops in Chinese Eastern Railway zone, 14, 80, 97,
185; view of Siberian intervention, 232–233
Chinese Eastern Railway, 22, 24,
55, 56, 59, 82, 92, 96–99, 104,
127, 134, 137; building, 49;
Chinese effort to gain control, 399 ff.; Chinese treaty
of October 2, 1920, 400; contract for construction, 53;

economic conditions, 309–
310; financial needs, 402-403;
financial position, 397 ff.,
402–404; French interests,
405–406; indebtedness to
Japan, 403; labor strike, 283–
284, 293–294; Soviet claims,
377–378
Chinese people in Russian Far
East, 36, 38–39
Chinese Revolution: the proposed
Japanese intervention, 67; the
renewed Russian expansion,
67, 68 ff
Chinese-Russo-Asiatic Bank agreement of October 2, 1920, 400
Chinese version of Soviet proposal
of July 25, 1919, 377
Chita city, 25, 33, 34, 105, 158
Churchill, Winston S., 117, 121,
332, 351
Clemenceau, Georges, 239–240,
332, 334
Coates, J. M. & Co., 128, 317
commercial decline during civil
war, 299
Committee of Members of the
Constituent Assembly, see Samara Government
Communist International, Second
Congress, 1920, 375
concessions scramble in China,
1895–1898, 59
conference of April 1, 1920, at
Nikolsk-Ussuriisk for regional
unification, 361–362, 366
consortium as an American policy,
126–127, 130–133
consortium of 1920, 132–133
Constituent Assembly, 76, 100,
109, 344
Cooperative Societies, 36, 241,
310–312
Cordon Sanitaire, 332, 334
Cossack congresses in Far East, 77
Cossacks in Russian Far East, 33,
38, 44, 45–46, 195 ff.
Crimean War, 41
currencies circulating in Siberia
during civil war, 303

459

Hicks, *see* Webster and Hicks mission to Siberia
Hill, James J., 66
Hoover, Herbert, 320, 324–327
Horvath, General Dmitrii Leonidovich, Manager of Chinese Eastern Railway, 79, 95, 97–99, 118, 145, 185–187, 262; aid to Semenov, 186–187; as provisional ruler, 99; request for Allied aid, 186; support of Kalmykov, 199
hostages murdered on Lake Baikal, January 6, 1920, 344
Hu Kuang financial group, 66
Hughes, Charles Evans, United States Secretary of State, 326, 396, 397, 403–404
Hung Hu Tze, Chinese robber bands, 46, 180
Hungarian musicians murdered by Kalmykov, 267

Iaremenko, A. N., Russian school teacher and partisan fighter, 267, 277
inflation in Russian Far East during civil war, 302–304
Inter-Allied Railway Agreement, 148–150, 158; proposed revision, 398
Inter-Allied Railway Committee, 135, 148–150, 405; financial support, 151–152; relations with Russians, 152–153
International Harvester Company, 32, 36, 128, 155, 317, 320, 327, 328
intervention in popular verse, 269
intervention in Russia, internal basis, 3
intervention in Siberia, periods of development, 18–19
intervention of the Central Powers in the Ukraine, 3
intervention, relation of Allied and German, 14
Ioffe, Adolf Abramovich, Soviet negotiator in Far East, 377, 382, 412

Irkutsk city, 32, 37, 81, 95, 253
Irkutsk governor generalship, 32
Ishii, Viscount Kikujiro, Japanese statesman, 59, 175, 182
Iudenich, General Nikolai Nikolaevich, White Russian leader in Baltic area, 17
Iurin, Ignatius, member of Far Eastern Republic government, 393
Ivan IV, Tsar of Russia, 39, 40
Ivanov-Rinov, General Pavel Pavlovich, officer in Kolchak forces, 118
Ivanovka village, destruction by Japanese, 263–264

Janin, General Pierre, French representative in Siberia, 117, 151, 229, 345–346
Japan, 4, 5–6, 22, 24, 28, 29, 33, 41, 48, 51, 52, 53, 54, 55, 57, 59, 130–133; Japanese, activities in Mongolia, 70; aggressive relations to Asiatic mainland, 19; and Germany as primary aggressive factors in Russia, 1, 15, 57; attitude toward American effort to end intervention after 1920, 383 ff.; attitude toward Nikolaevsk massacre, 290–291; bargaining regarding sending of troops to Western Front, 170–171, 182–183; business in Russian Far East during civil war, 306–307; commerce with Asiatic Russia, 305–306; declaration of purpose of intervention, 194; defeat by partisans at Nikolaevsk, 286 ff.; demands at Dairen Conference, 412, 430–433; desire not to send forces to Western Front, 171; dominant position in Russian Far East, 20; economic strangulation of Far Eastern Republic, 387–388; efforts to create a buffer state in Eastern Si-

beria, 200 ff., 385 ff.; efforts
to form a Greater Mongol
state, 200 ff.; efforts to gain
control of the Chinese Eastern
Railway, 402 ff.; economic
aggression against Russia,
168–169; expansion of foreign trade, 166–168; eco-
nomic expansion during First
World War, 125 ff., 160 ff.,
300; expansionist societies,
178–180; expenditure on intervention, 187; first troop
movements into Korea and
Manchuria, 12; foreign trade
expansion, 166–168; import
of raw materials from Siberia,
306–307; inflation, 165; interest in Russian railways,
136; intrigues at Omsk, 337;
liberal opinion regarding intervention, 163–165; military
forces enter Siberia, 194–195;
military preparations against
Far Eastern Republic, 385
ff.; naval force at Vladivostok, January 1918, 14–15,
185, 189; naval force at
Vladivostok, April 1918, 14,
189–191; negotiations with
Allies for Russian concessions
in exchange for military cooperation in war, 182–183;
New Inland Sea policy, 176–
177

objectives in Siberia, 86,
167, 177, 261–262; objectives
in supporting Cossack leaders,
199–200; objectives known to
Allied representatives in Siberia, 206–209; official policy
regarding intervention, 194;
official reason for remaining
after Allied departure from
Siberia, 359–361; opposition
to American efforts in Siberia,
358 ff.; opposition to American railway activities in Siberia, 155–160; opposition to
expansion into Siberia, 163–

165; opposition to Kolchak,
20; opposition to withdrawal
of interventionary forces, 352;
plans for economic activity in
Siberia, 208–209; preparations for a military intervention, 191–193; preparation
for the military overturn of
April 4–5, 1920, 361 ff.;
pressure for an intervention
in Siberia, 188–190; proposal
for intervention in Chinese
revolution, 67; proposals for
an intervention in Siberia,
183–185, 188–189; reaction
to rice riots and Armistice,
209–210; reasons for withdrawal from Siberia, 166,
167–168, 382–383, 391, 406–
410; reassertion of power in
Maritime Province, April 4,
1920, 364; reestablishment of
military control at Vladivostok, April 5, 1920, 180, 361–
365; rice riots of 1918, 165–
166; role in Allied Intervention, 19–20; school for railway operatives, 157–158;
share in Allied diplomatic
bargains, 169–170, 177–178;
social development before
1922, 162 ff.; "special interest" doctrine, 64; strangulation of Far Eastern Republic, 307–308; use of Russian
Orthodox Church in inter-
vention, 180–181; view of
American economic interests
in Russia, 155–157, 172–175;
view of Armistice of 1918,
170, 209; view of German
threat to Russia, 164, 169;
withdrawal from Siberia, 19,
404–405

Japanese, and American methods
of economic penetration compared, 174; communists, 162–
163, 284; demands to Pro-
visional Government at Vladivostok, April 2, 1920, 363;

people in Russian Far East, 36, 39; phase of the intervention, 18–19; question at Washington Conference, 406 ff.; surrender to partisans at Nikolaevsk, 289; treatment of Russian people, 263 ff.
Japanese-American rivalry, 63 ff., 88, 154 ff., 157 ff., 292
Japanese Far Eastern Republic conference at Changchun, September 1922, 412–413
Japanese Far Eastern Republic conference at Dairen, 1921–1922, 410–412
Japanese-French bargaining after end of Allied Intervention, 408–409
Japanese-Russian business competition in Manchuria, 136–137, 299 ff., 304–306, 310
Jewish pogrom, 61, 120, 268
Johnson, Colonel B. O., American railway expert in Russia, 152, 345
Johnson, Hiram, California senator, 263, 355–356
Julinek, Czechoslovak terrorist, 267

Kaledin, General Alexei Maximovich, White Russian leader in Don region, 15
Kalmykov, Ivan, Cossack ataman, 198–199, 266–267, 294; arrest of American soldiers, 199
Kamchatka, 21, 25, 28, 32, 327–328
Kappel, General Vladimir Oskarovich, White Russian commander in Siberia, 386
Karakhan, Lev Mikhailovich, Soviet Deputy Foreign Commissar, 376–377
Kawakami, K. K., 357
Kazan, 101, 110, 258
Khabarov, Erofei Pavlovich, 38, 41–42
Khabarovsk city, 22, 25, 26, 29, 32, 34, 50, 79, 200

Khanka lake, 25, 26
Kiachow, 53
Knight, Admiral, United States Navy, 254, 255, 317
Knox, General Alfred, British representative in Russia, 74, 84, 117, 213, 221
Kolchak, Admiral Aleksander Vasilevich, Supreme Ruler of Russia, 17, 18, 98, 107, 111, 112–121, 141–142, 145, 184; abandons Omsk, 343; aims thwarted by Japanese actions, 20; answer to Allied note, 339; as seen by the people, 268 ff.; attitude toward neutral policy of United States, 262; atrocities, 268; execution, February 7, 1920, 347; defeat and retreat, 18, 342 ff.; efforts to gain Allied aid and recognition, 341–342; government, 115–117, 118–119, 336–337; overturn, November 17–18, 1918, 115–117; reasons for failure, 347–350; recognition considered by Allies, 336 ff.; surrender at Irkutsk, January 15, 1920, to the Political Center, 343 ff.; surrender, Czechoslovak responsibility, 345–347; trial, 347
Kolchakovshchina, 278
Korea, 51, 52, 55, 60; Japanese annexation, August, 1910, 67
Korean partisans, 284
Koreans in Russian Far East, 36, 39
Kornilov, General Lavr Georgievich, White Russian leader in South Russia, 11, 15
Krasnoshchekov, Aleksander Mikhailovich, member of government of Far Eastern Republic, 80, 185, 285, 368–369
Kuan Cheng-tze station, 56, 137, 401
Kuchum Khan, 40

INDEX

Nabokov, Konstantin Dimitrievich, Russian diplomatic representative in Britain, 182, 335
Nakashima, General, proposals to General Horvath for concessions for Japan, 186
Nansen, Fridjof, 325
National Center, 107, 225
natives in Russian Far East, 36 ff.
Nerchinsk treaty, September 6, 1689, between China and Russia, 40, 41
New Economic Policy in Soviet Russia, 389–390
New Inland Sea policy of Japan, 176–177
New York Life Insurance Company, 317
Nikolaevsk city, 25, 26, 41, 287; massacre, May 1920, 290; partisan attack, 286 ff.
Nikolsk-Ussuriisk, 29, 34, 254, 261, 263
Nishihara, Kamezo, Japanese representative in China, 126, 168
Nizhne-Udinsk, Kolchak arrival on December 24, 1919, 344
Novgorod, 39

Officers' Union, 94–95
oil in Sakhalin, 29
Old Believer sectarians, 294
Omsk, 47, 49, 50, 108, 337; abandoned by Kolchak, 343; government effected by failure of Allied recognition, 340 ff.
Open Door notes of 1899–1900, 64
Open Door Policy of the United States, 130, 131, 133, 134; in Russia, 133 ff., 357; not achieved in intervention, 397
Order Number One issued by Soviets, 10, 87
Orenburg Cossacks, start of anti-Soviet struggle in Orenburg region, 11–12
Oriental Institute of Vladivostok, 35

Orthodox Church in the Russian Far East, 33–34
Otani, General, 151, 221
Ovchinnikov, Anton Zakharovich, partisan fighter, 276–277, 292

Pacific problem at Washington Conference, 407 ff.
Panama Canal, significance in American Far Eastern Policy, 65–66, 133
Pan-Mongol movement, 200 ff.
Pan-Turanian movement, 219–220
Pares, Bernard, British representative to Russia, 115, 120
Parfenov, P. S., 345, 364
Paris Peace Conference, the Russian question, 331 ff.; role in liquidating Allied intervention, 406
Park, Davis and Company, 328
partisan, attitude toward Japanese, 264 ff.; destruction of railways, 292–293; leaders, 295–296; movement in Siberia, 273 ff.; non-Russian, 284; organization, 278 ff.; sources of recruitment, 273 ff.
Partisan News, 281
People's Army, 101, 277
Pepeliaev, Viktor Nikolaevich, Kolchak official, 107, 109, 111, 121, 346
Petrograd Soviet of Workers' and Soldiers' Deputies, 77
Petropavlovsk, 41
Petrovsk-Zavod, 309, 312
Pichon, Major Jean, French agent in Siberia, 105, 137, 226–227
Polish-Soviet War, 1920, 18
political center, mixed political group, 285, 343–344, 345, 347, 367
Port Arthur, 53–54, 60, 61
Portsmouth treaty of September 5, 1905, 62; Japanese reaction, 62–63
Poset Bay, 22, 25

466

INDEX

Priamur Government, June 10,
1922 to October 25, 1922,
391–392, 403
Priamur governor-generalship, 32,
56
Priamur Provisional Government,
May 26, 1921, to June 10,
1922, 389 ff.
Priamur Provisional Government,
campaign against Far Eastern
Republic, 390–391
Price, M. Phillips, correspondent
of the *Manchester Guardian*
in Russia, 252
Prinkipo Conference proposed,
333, 334–336
prisoners of war in Siberia, 93,
164, 192, 233–236, 247
Proposals for economic rehabilitation in Russia, 312 ff.
Provisional Government, *see* Russian Provisional Government
Provisional Zemstvo Government
of the Maritime Province,
January 31, 1920, to May 26,
1921, 366, 389
punitive expedition against Siberian villages, 263–264, 267–
268, 277–278

Rada-German treaty of February
9, 1918, 12
Rada, Ukrainian Government, 3
railway, breakdown during civil
war, 298; damage during civil
war, 293; economic improve-
ment in 1920, 309–310
railway rivalry in China, 59
Red Army, 17 ff., 82, 87, 95, 121,
123, 257, 329
Red Banner, organ of Vladivostok
Committee, 78
Red Guard, 80, 253
Repington, Lieutenant Colonel
Charles C., British General
Staff representative, 182–183
rice riots in Japan, 165–166
Robins, Colonel Raymond, head of
American Red Cross Mission
in Russia, 1917–1918, 84–85,

90–91, 136, 155, proposal for
economic rehabilitation in
Russia, 312 ff.
Roosevelt, Theodore, President of
the United States, 55, 61
Root, Elihu, head of American
Mission to Russia, 1917, 74,
114, 141–143, 155
Root-Takahira notes, 1908, 6
Rozanov, General Sergei Nikolaevich, White Russian officer in
Far East, 118–119, 267–268,
366
Rusanov, N. A., Commissar of
Provisional Government in
the Far East, 74–75
Russia: advance against China,
1895–1903, 41, 52, 53–55,
60, 68 ff.; Black Sea Fleet, 7,
86, 142; confronted with an
intervention, 214–215; debts,
83, 92; expansion into Mongolia, 68 ff.; expansion into
Siberia, 39–40; fear of Japan,
55–56; military collapse, 10,
213–214
Russian, business classes in the
civil war, 216–217; question
at the Paris Peace Conference, 331 ff.; view of military
collapse, 214–215
Russian-American plan for international telegraph, 156
Russian Bureau of the United
States War Trade Board,
320–321
Russian Empire, as a Eurasian
power, 1; as a Far Eastern
power, 51; between Germany
and Japan, 1
Russian Far East: administration,
32–33; agricultural decline
during civil war, 301–302;
agriculture, 30–32; animal
husbandry, 31; annexed by
Russia, 41; climate, 27–28;
commerce, 28, 35–36; economy, 35–36; food shortages,
31; frontiers, 22–23; geography, 25–28; industry, 22, 29,

467

over, 150–151; breakdown
during civil war, 298 ff.; construction, 47–50; in economy
of Russian Far East, 50; partisan damage, 292–293; physical condition, 138–139; used
by Japan to defeat Kolchak,
20
Triapitsyn, Iakov Ivanovich, partisan leader, 286 ff.
Triple Alliance, 1882, 5
Triple Entente, 1894, 1904, 1907,
5
Triple Intervention of Germany,
France and Russia against
Japan, 1895, 51, 53, 57–59,
62
Trotsky, Lev Davidovich, 85, 90,
183–184, 243, 246, 247; proposal for Allied assistance to
Soviets, 85–86
Tsentro-Sibir, Soviet government
at Irkutsk, 81, 93
Turkey, 7–8
Twenty-One Demands, 1915, 6,
170

Ufa Conference, 101, 108–110
Ugria, 39
Ukraine, 3, 13, 14, 17, 42
Ungern-Sternberg, Baron Fedor
Romanovich von; captures
Urga, February 2, 1921, 379;
Order No. 15, 380; role in
Mongolia, 378–381
Union for the Regeneration of
Russia, 16
Union to Defend the Country and
Liberty, 16
United States: attitude toward
continued Japanese interven-
tion after 1920, 383 ff.; atti-
tude toward Czechoslovaks,
259–260; attitude toward
recognition of Admiral Kol-
chak, 321–322, 336–338;
blamed for initiating Siberian
intervention, 172, 394–395;
Congressional attitude to-
ward Siberian intervention,

263, 355–357; consent to intervention, July 5, 1918, 255;
contracts with Russian Cooperatives, 311; credit to
Russian Provisional Government, 144; loan to Czechoslovaks, 259; Department of
State opposition to General
Graves, 271–272; efforts to
carry out economic rehabilitation in Russia, 320; entry into
First World War, 139 ff.;
forces land in Siberia, 258–
259; military forces in Siberia, 137; military forces
leave Siberia, 357–358; mission to Far Eastern Republic,
409–410; mission to Russia
(see Elihu Root); naval officer shot by Japanese, 384–
385; non-recognition doctrine
regarding Japanese aggression in Siberia, 395 ff.; objective in Siberian intervention, 261–262; policy re-
garding Siberian intervention,
187–188, 230–232, 261–263;
protest against Japanese activity in Siberia, 209; recognition of the Russian Provisional Government, 73,
140; rise to a creditor nation,
125; State Department attitude toward intervention in
Siberia, 145, 262–263, 271–
272; view of general intervention, 127–128, 227–230;
view of importance of the
Eastern Front, 135–136; withdrawal from Siberia, 352 ff.,
358
United States Railway Advisory
Commission to Russia, 145–
147
Ural-Volga theater of the civil
war, 17, 18, 100, 113, 256
ff., 342
Urga, 34, 69
Urquhart, Leslie, British businessman, 112